THE
INDESTRUCTIBLE
BOOK

Examining the History of Our English Bible

Erasmus' Desk

Dr. David L. Brown

Disclaimer

The author of this work has quoted the writers of many articles and books. This does not mean that the author endorses or recommends the works of others. If the author quotes someone, it does not mean that he agrees with all of the author's tenets, statements, concepts, or words, whether in the work quoted or any other work of the author. There has been no attempt to alter the meaning of the quotes; and therefore, some of the quotes are long in order to give the entire sense of the passage.

Printed in the United States of America
Library of Congress Control Number: 2014955520
REL006201: Religion: Biblical Studies - Topical

ISBN 978-0-9987778-9-4

All Scripture quotes are from the King James Bible except those verses compared and then the source is identified.

Address All Inquiries To:
THE OLD PATHS PUBLICATIONS, Inc.
142 Gold Flume Way
Cleveland, Georgia, 30528
U.S.A.
Web: www.theoldpathspublications.com
E-mail: TOP@theoldpathspublications.com

Cover and Title page picture is Erasmus' Desk taken by Dr. David Brown at the Erasmus Museum in Brussels, Belgium. Erasmus worked on his 1516 Greek/Latin New Testament there. It is copyrighted ©.

1.0

DEDICATION

This work is dedicated to my dear wife, Linda, who is my helper, companion, friend, and lover. For more than 45 years, she has unselfishly and joyfully set aside her own desires and done all in her power to help me be successful in everything I do. She has spent countless hours editing and proofing this work.

David L. Brown

"O taste and see that the LORD is good: blessed is the man that trusteth in him." **(Psalms 34:8)**

PREFACE

The Indestructible Book by Dr. David Brown is a very valuable tool for anyone interested in the modern debates over preservation, the Traditional Text, and the King James Bible. There are many, many issues that influence this debate. When a person first starts studying these issues he is often surprised how many many different points come up during the discussion. Over the last several decades many books have been written to address these issues. *The Indestructible Book* does more to gather all these subjects into one volume than any other work I am acquainted with.

Church history, doctrine, controversies, debates and practical application are all here in one volume. This book is well documented, thorough and readable. That is not surprising to anyone who has heard Dr. Brown speak in public or who has engaged in private conversation with him over these issues. He has a gift in addressing this discussion.

These areas are the hot bed of debate among evangelicals and fundamentalists today. Independent Baptists have spent an amazing amount of time focused on these debates in recent years. It is easy to be loud and controversial. It is not so easy to be well informed. It takes a lot of diligent study to "get up to speed" on the many points of controversy that are part of this discussion. *The Indestructible Book* is a great head start on understanding these issues.

The greatest thing about this book is that it demonstrates clearly that we have an Indestructible Bible. It has survived campaigns to literally destroy it, it has survived conspiracies to corrupt it and it rises above all the foolish debates over it. In a time of great controversy, the Bible provides us with both answers and strength. The preserved Word of God convicts of sin, has the power to save and provides us with everything we need to know in the middle of a pagan world.

The Indestructible Book by Dr. David Brown reinforces, educates and strengthens our faith. It is worthy of your time and attention.

Pastor Phil Stringer
Ravenswood Baptist Church
Chicago, IL

TABLE OF CONTENTS

FOREWORD

I went through Bible College and Seminary and never heard of John Wycliffe, William Tyndale, Myles Coverdale, John Rogers, or any of the historic English Bibles that lead up to our King James Bible. When I signed up for my Romans class, my professor told us we would have to go out and buy an American Standard Bible of 1901 because it was a far better translation than our King James Bible. He gave no further explanation! I was puzzled, but passed it off, figuring he was the professor and knew more about these things than I did. It was not until I got into the ministry that I discovered a missing verse in the NIV. To my surprise, I discovered a total of seventeen missing verses and hundreds of partial verses and words missing. So I began my quest to find out why. Since the Bible is the foundation of literally everything in New Testament Christianity, it is imperative that we have an uncorrupted Bible. If something does not have a biblical base, it should be rejected. We read in 1 **Thessalonians 5:21 "Prove all things; hold fast that which is good."** The English word **prove** is a translation of the Greek work dokimazete (dok-im-ad'zate). The word carries the idea of **proving a thing whether it is worthy or not**. So, the question is, "How are we to go about proving something"? I believe **Isaiah 8:20** gives us insight into the answer to this question—"To the law and to the testimony: if they speak not according to this word, it is because there is no light in them." In other words, **examine everything by the words of the Bible** and if it does not line up, reject it!

I am especially thankful for three men God brought into my life that helped me to get a hold on the History of Our English Bible and the underlying textual issue: Dr. David Otis Fuller who gave me a copy of his book, *Which Bible,* Dr. Jewel Smith, and Dr. Ken Connolly who first took me on the fascinating journey of the history of our English Bible.

Friends, our King James Bible is the "GOLD STANDARD" for EVERYTHING in Christian life for English speaking people!

The purpose of *The Indestructible Book* is to explain the wonderful history of the English Bible and the underlying textual issue in the hopes you will see how God has preserved His Words for us as He promised, and to show why you should use the King James Bible.

May God bless and enlighten the reader,

Dr. David L. Brown

Pastor David L. Brown,
First Baptist Church of Oak Creek, WI
December, 2014

CHAPTER #1

IT ALL BEGAN ON MOUNT SINAI

IT ALL BEGAN ON MT. SINAI: GOD'S WRITTEN WORD REVEALED TO MAN

A close personal friend of mine, the late Dr. Kenneth Connolly, wrote this – "The Bible is the most remarkable piece of literature this world has ever seen." There is absolutely no doubt that that is true. "Probably more has been written about the Bible, over a longer period, than any other subject." (*The Book: A History of The Bible; Christopher De Hamel; Introduction; Phaidon Press Limited*). I want to take you back to where the Bible began - Mt. Sinai.

In 2008 I took a group of people on a trip to see the important biblical places in the Middle East. We arrived at St. Catherine's Monastery guesthouse in Sinai, Egypt for a late supper. It was already dark. The monastery is a Greek Orthodox monastery located at the foot of Mt. Sinai. It is said to be the oldest, continuously inhabited Christian Monastery in the world. It was founded in 527 A.D. by the Roman Byzantine Emperor Justinian. It replaced a chapel that was built by Constantine's mother, the Empress Helena in 337 A.D.

1

In about 1280 B.C. the first written communication from God came on Mount Sinai, etched in stone tablets by the finger of God. "These sacred words from the Ten Commandments have shaped the world and its ethical system for 3,500 years." (*A Visual History of the English Bible* by Donald L. Brake; Baker Books; p. 25).

Although Moses destroyed the tablets God had written on when he descended from the mountain and saw the idolatry of the people (Exodus 32:19), God instructed Moses to, *"Hew thee two tables of stone like unto the first: and I will write upon these tables the words that were in the first tables, which thou brakest."* (Exodus 34:1). But, in spite of a bad start, it is on Mount Sinai that God began to communicate with human beings in written form using the language that the people knew. He continued His progressive revelation for the next 1500 years.

To give you an overview of how God revealed His word to us, I will share with you what William Smith wrote in the 19th century. "There are 31 to 36 different authors, who wrote in three continents, in 13 different countries, in three languages (Hebrew, Aramaic and Greek), and from every possible human standpoint. Among these authors were kings, farmers, mechanics, scientific men, lawyers, generals, fishermen, ministers and priests, a tax collector, some poor, some city bred, some country born, thus touching all experiences of men, extending over 1500 years." (Adapted from *Smith's Bible Dictionary;* by William Smith; published 1884; p.91).

Smith goes on to say, "Yet the Bible is but one book, **because God was the real author**, and therefore, though He added new revelations as men could receive them, He never had to change what was once revealed. The Bible is a unit because: **1)** It has but one purpose, the salvation of men. **2)** The character of God is the same **3)** The moral law is the same **4)** It contains the development of one great scheme of salvation." (*Smith's Bible Dictionary;* by William Smith; published 1884; p.91).

The most important book that has ever been written or ever will be written is the Bible. It towers above all other books because **God uniquely inspired it. God is the real author**. John Wycliffe put it this way; "The authority of the Holy Scriptures infinitely surpasses any writing, how authentic soever it may appear, because the authority of Jesus Christ is infinitely above that of all mankind. The authority of the Scripture is independent of any other authority, and is preferable to every other writing..." (Wycliffe quote from - *Rome and The Bible;* by David W. Cloud; Way of Life Literature; p.52).

As I take you back to where many believe it all began, you could climb to the 7,498 foot summit of Jabal Musa, the traditional site of Mount Sinai (others believe Mt. Sinai is Jabal al Lawz, in Saudi Arabia). Many tourists get up very early to see the sunrise from the top of Mt. Sinai. It takes about 3 hours to climb the 3,750 "*Steps of Penitence*" that wind along the Sikket Saydna Musa or "*The Path of Moses*." Once at the top there is a small mosque and a Greek Orthodox Chapel that is said to enclose the rock from which God made the **Tablets of the Law**.

From that lofty perch, when the climactic conditions are right, the sunrise is an awe-inspiring sight to see. As I thought about Mt. Sinai, my mind shifted to **Exodus 19**, which gives the account of Moses being on Mt. Sinai early one morning. There God visited him accompanied by thunder, lightning, loud trumpets, fire, and smoke. The whole mountain shook. As I looked at Mt. Sinai I thought, this may have been the place where Moses received the stone tablets of the Ten Commandments written by the finger of God three and one half millenniums earlier. **It was on Mt. Sinai that Moses received the very first written communication from the Lord God Almighty**. It was on Mt. Sinai that the written progressive revelatory journey of God speaking to man began.

CHAPTER #2

THE HEBREW-ARAMAIC
OLD TESTAMENT

In order to trace the history of the Bible's translation into English, you need to understand something of the origin of the Bible and its preservation. Let's begin with the Old Testament. The Old Testament was written primarily in Hebrew, but portions of the books of Daniel and Ezra are written in the language of Babylon, which was Aramaic. The Hebrew language did not distinguish between capital and small letters and it had no vowels or punctuation marks. Unlike English, Spanish, French, German, etc. the writing was from **right to left**.

בראשית ברא אלהים את השמים ואת הארץ:

In the beginning created God — the heaven and the earth.

THE HEBREW-ARAMAIC OLD TESTAMENT CANON

- **There are 24 books in the Jewish Bible (Old Testament).** But, these 24 books cover the same material that we have in our 39 book English, non-Catholic Bible, Old Testament. Below is the Hebrew Arrangement. (Note: Catholic Bibles contain 12 additional Apocryphal books not found in the Hebrew Canon).

- **The Law or Torah** (5 Books) - Genesis, Exodus, Leviticus, Numbers, Deuteronomy

- **The Prophets or Nebhiim** (8 Books)
  The former prophets - Joshua, Judges, Samuel, and Kings
  The latter prophets - Isaiah, Jeremiah, Ezekiel, and the twelve prophets we call the Minor Prophets. Let me explain: The Hebrew Bible subdivides the prophets into two divisions - **Major Prophets** (Isaiah, Jeremiah and Ezekiel) and the **Minor Prophets** which they count as one book (Hosea, Joel,

Amos, Obadiah, Jonah, Micah, Nahum, Habakkuk, Zephaniah, Haggai, Zachariah and Malachi).

- **The Writings** Kethubhim or Hagiographa (11 books)

- **Poetical books** (3 books) - Psalms, Job, Proverbs

- **Five rolls or Megilloth** (5 books)- Ruth, Song of Songs (Solomon), Ecclesiastes, Lamentations, Esther

- **Historical books** (3 books) - Daniel, Ezra-Nehemiah, Chronicles

As you can see, the difference is accounted for by the fact that **1 & 2 Samuel, 1 & 2 Kings, Ezra and Nehemiah** and **1 & 2 Chronicles** and the **12 Minor Prophets** were treated as one book by the Jews.

I must point out that the oldest known recorded witness to the number of books in the Old Testament is quite recent, found in 4th Esdras, which was written between 85-96 A.D. This apocryphal book says – "Make public the twenty-four books that you wrote first, and let the worthy and the unworthy read them; but keep the seventy that were written last, in order to give them to the wise among your people." (14:45-46).

Note: **In the Latin Bible** 1 Esdras is Ezra and 2 Esdras is Nehemiah, which are part of the Hebrew Canon. However 3 Esdras and 4 Esdras are Apocryphal.

Josephus, a first century Hebrew historian says, in his testimony *Against Apion* 1:8: "For we have not an innumerable multitude of books among us, disagreeing from and contradicting one another (as the Greeks have) but only **twenty-two books**, which contain the records of all the past times; which are justly believed to be divine, and of them, *five belong to Moses*, which contain his laws, and the traditions of the origin of mankind till his death. This interval of time was a little short of three thousand years; but as to the time from the death of Moses till the reign of Artaxerxes king of Persia, who reigned after Xerxes, **the prophets**, who were after Moses, wrote down what was done in their times in thirteen books. The remaining **four books contain hymns to God**, and precepts for the conduct of human life. It is true, our history has been written since Artaxerxes, very particularly, but has not been esteemed of the like authority with the former by our forefathers, because there has not been an exact succession of prophets since that time; and how firmly we have given credit to those books of our own nation is evident by what we do; for during so many ages as have already passed, no one has been so bold as either to add anything to them or take anything from them, or to make any change in them; but it becomes natural to all Jews, immediately and from their very birth, to esteem those books to contain divine doctrines, and to persist in them, and, if occasion be, willingly to die for them."

He is two books short of what is written in 4 Esdras. That may be **accounted for in one of two ways**. First, some Jews did not recognize the book of Esther, and doubted the inspiration of Ecclesiastes. He might have been one from that school. Or, perhaps his count combined some of the books together. My point is simply this. The same material that we find in the Old Testament of our English Bible finds its source in the Hebrew Bible.

Since we are studying the History of our English Bible, I think it is important to point out that **ancient English Bibles identified some of the 39 books of the Old Testament by different names than we have today**. Here is a listing of the ancient name differences –1 Samuel is called **1 Kings,** 2 Samuel is called **2 Kings,** 1 Kings is called **3 Kings,** 2 Kings is called **4 Kings,** 1 Chronicles is called **1 Parlipomen,** 2 Chronicles is called **2 Parlipomen,** Ezra is called **1 Esdras,** Nehemiah is called **2 Esdras,** Song of Solomon is called **Song of Songs.**

HOW THE OLD TESTAMENT CAME TOGETHER

The Pentateuch - Genesis, Exodus, Leviticus, Numbers and Deuteronomy are sometimes referred to as: the "*Five Books of Moses*," because the writings themselves identify the author as Moses, or the "*Pentateuch*," a Greek term meaning "*pente (5) teuchos (volumes)*," or the "*Books of the Law*," or the "*Torah*" (a Hebrew word meaning "*instruction*").

7

These books were originally written as a single unbroken scroll. Sometime before the 2nd Century B.C. it was divided into the 5 books that we see today.

There are about two dozen verses in the Hebrew (Old Testament) Scriptures and about half that many in the New Testament Scriptures which state or strongly imply that Moses was the author of the first five books of the Bible.

"Ancient Jewish and Christian writers, such as Ecclesiasticus, Josephus, Philo, and Origen were essentially in full agreement that the Pentateuch was written solely by Moses. The Mishnah and the Talmud also confirm this. Tradition during the first millennium of Christian history agrees with this belief." (R.K. Harrison, "*Introduction to the Old Testament*," Page 497 [cited in R.B. Dillard & T. Longman III, "*An Introduction to the Old Testament*," Zondervan, Grand Rapids, MI, (1994) Page 39]).

Before the rise of the so-called Higher Criticism (18th Century) it was held almost universally that **Moses wrote the Pentateuch** substantially as it exists today. That is what I believe and I base that on the internal evidence found in the Bible itself.

The Pentateuch itself claims Mosaic authorship. "In **Exodus 24:4** we read: '*And Moses wrote all the words of the Lord.*' These were placed 'inside of the Ark of the Covenant,' according to **Deuteronomy 31:26**." (*The Indestructible Book* by W. Ken Connolly; Baker Books 1996; p.14)

Exodus 17:14 "*And the LORD said unto Moses, Write this for a memorial in a book, and rehearse it in the ears of Joshua: for I will utterly put out the remembrance of Amalek from under heaven.*"

Exodus 34:27 "*And the LORD said unto Moses, Write thou these words: for after the tenor of these words I have made a covenant with thee and with Israel.*"

Leviticus 1:1 "*And the LORD called unto Moses, and spake unto him out of the tabernacle of the congregation...*"

Leviticus 6:8 "*And the LORD spake unto Moses...*"

Deuteronomy 31:24-26 *"And it came to pass, <u>when Moses had made an end of writing the words of this law in a book, until they were finished</u>, 25 That Moses commanded the Levites, which bare the ark of the covenant of the LORD, saying, 26 Take this book of the law, and put it in the side of the ark of the covenant of the LORD your God, that it may be there for a witness against thee."*

OTHER PASSAGES IN THE OLD TESTAMENT AFFIRM MOSES AS THE AUTHOR

Joshua 1:7-8 *"Only be thou strong and very courageous, that thou mayest <u>observe to do according to all the law, which Moses my servant commanded thee</u>: turn not from it to the right hand or to the left, that thou mayest prosper whithersoever thou goest. 8 This book of the law shall not depart out of thy mouth; but thou shalt meditate therein day and night, that thou mayest observe to do according to all that is written therein: for then thou shalt make thy way prosperous, and then thou shalt have good success."*

Joshua 8:31-34 *"As Moses the servant of the LORD commanded the children of Israel, <u>as it is written in the book of the law of Moses</u>, an altar of whole stones, over which no man hath lift up any iron: and they offered thereon burnt offerings unto the LORD, and sacrificed peace offerings. 32 And he wrote there upon the stones a copy of the law of Moses, which he wrote in the presence of the children of Israel. 33 And all Israel, and their elders, and officers, and their judges, stood on this side the ark and on that side before the priests the Levites, which bare the ark of the covenant of the LORD, as well the stranger, as he that was born among them; half of them over against mount Gerizim, and half of them over against mount Ebal; as Moses the servant of the LORD had commanded before, that they should bless the people of Israel. 34 And afterward he read all the words of the law, the blessings and cursings, according to all that is written in the book of the law.*

Joshua 22:5 *"But <u>take diligent heed to do the commandment and the law, which Moses the servant of the LORD charged you</u>, to love the LORD your God, and to walk in all his ways, and to keep his commandments, and to cleave unto him, and to serve him with all your heart and with all your soul."*

9

2 Chronicles 34:14 *"And when they brought out the money that was brought into the house of the LORD, <u>Hilkiah the priest found a book of the law of the LORD given by Moses.</u>"*

THE LORD JESUS CHRIST TELLS US THAT MOSES WROTE THE LAW

Luke 24:44 *"And he said unto them, These are the words which I spake unto you, while I was yet with you, that all things must be fulfilled, <u>which were written in the law of Moses,</u> and in the prophets, and in the psalms, concerning me."*

Mark 12:26 *"And as touching the dead, that they rise: <u>have ye not read in the book of Moses,</u> how in the bush God spake unto him, saying, I am the God of Abraham, and the God of Isaac, and the God of Jacob?"*

Luke 16:29 & 31 *"Abraham saith unto him, They have Moses and the prophets; let them hear them. 31 And he said unto him, <u>If they hear not Moses</u> and the prophets, neither will they be persuaded, though one rose from the dead."*

John 5:46-47 *"For <u>had ye believed Moses</u>, ye would have believed me: for <u>he wrote of me.</u> 47 But if ye believe not his writings, how shall ye believe my words?"*

John 7:19 *"<u>Did not Moses give you the law</u>, and yet none of you keepeth the law? Why go ye about to kill me?"*

OTHER NEW TESTAMENT VERIFICATION

Acts 26:22 *"Having therefore obtained help of God, I continue unto this day, witnessing both to small and great, saying none other things than those which the prophets <u>and Moses did say</u> should come:"*

Romans 10:5 *"<u>For Moses describeth</u> the righteousness which is of the law, That the man which doeth those things shall live by them."*

10

Dr. Alvin Sylvester Zerbe, Ph.D., D.D. explains, "It was allowed that he (Moses) may have used documents and employed amanuenses (a person whose employment is to write what another dictates); but his approval of what the latter wrote, would render the work practically his own." (*The Antiquity of Hebrew Writing and Literature* by Dr. Alvin Sylvester Zerbe, Ph.D., D.D.; published in 1911 by Central Publishing House of Cleveland Ohio; p.9).

A plethora of Bible scholars, before the German Higher Critical movement, believed that "**Moses had access to genealogical tables, ancient records and even tablets in the cuneiform script brought by Abraham from Ur of the Chaldees and containing the essential data of the first eleven chapters of Genesis.**" (*The Antiquity of Hebrew Writing and Literature* by Zerbe; p.9).

While that may seem plausible, I believe God revealed to Moses what He wanted him to know and what he was supposed to write down. But, with the spread of German Higher Criticism, the liberal critics alleged that the Hebrews were not in a position to cultivate literature in the Exodus period and that Moses did not write or compose the Pentateuch. Several books in my library state that *nobody was supposed to have known anything about writing until a much later period.* The foolishness of these scholars was exposed in 1887. In that year "an Egyptian peasant woman was walking among the ruins of Tel el-Amarna looking for something to sell when her foot hit a hard object in the sand: it was a piece of hardened clay, covered with unusual markings. She invited a friend to help her dig, and they did not give up until they had a bag full of these baked clay tablets." (*The Indestructible Book* by Connolly; p.14). What she stumbled upon was the Egyptian Foreign Office archives from about 1380 B.C. Oriental scholars found that these tablets were official correspondence of Egyptian governors or vassal-princes, stationed in Palestine with their master, King Amenophis IV of Egypt, and his ministers in Egypt.

Here is why that discovery is so important. These tablets are from the same time that Joshua and the Hebrews were overrunning southern Palestine. These cuneiform tablets are contemporary with the events described in the Book of Joshua, and, in part, relating to those very events! Remember, Joshua was a contemporary (lived at the same time) of Moses (Basic information from - *Our Bible and the Ancient*

PROOF OF WRITING DURING TIME OF MOSES AND JOSHUA

Manuscripts by Dr. Frederic G. Kenyon; published in 1895 by Eyre and Spottiswoode, Edinburgh; p.17).

Indeed, Moses was literate and the first five books of the Bible were written by Moses just as we read in **Exodus 24:4** and just as Christ says in several places in the Gospels.

The Pentateuch was added to. Later Joshua added to what Moses had written (the book of Joshua). Still later *Samuel "told the people the manner of the kingdom, and wrote it in a book, and laid it up before the Lord"* (**1 Samuel 10:25**). Much later *"Hilkiah the high priest said unto Shaphan the scribe, I have found the book of the law in the house of the Lord..."* (**2 Kings 22:8**).

These passages from the Old Testament show that the records gradually grew and were safely protected. There is also historical material outside the Bible that indicates the process of the development of the Old Testament Canon. **Jewish tradition** teaches that Ezra, a priest and scribe, collected and arranged the order of the books in the Hebrew Bible in about 450 B.C. Kenyon writes, "Taking the latest dates assigned by good authorities, the Law was fully recognized as inspired Scripture by about B.C. 450, the Prophets (including the earlier historical books) about B.C. 300, and the Hagiographa about B.C. 100." (*Our Bible and the Ancient Manuscripts* by Kenyon; p.28).

THE PRESERVATION AND CONVEYANCE OF THE HEBREW SCRIPTURES

That brings me to my last point in dealing with the canonicity of the Hebrew-Aramaic Old Testament.

Who preserved and copied the Old Testament and how was that done?

God saw that special care was taken for the preservation of the Old Testament text, but historical details are sketchy at best. But, there is more solid information available to us from about the beginning of the Christian era. The famous schools of Hillel and Shammai trained rabbis and scribes who carefully copied and preserved the Hebrew text. "The fall of Jerusalem (A.D. 70) and the destruction of Judaea as a nation only intensified the zeal of the Jews for their

Bible; and the first centuries of the Christian era witnessed a great outburst of activity in the multiplication, the transmission, and the recording of the traditional learning with respect to the Scriptures. Two great centers of Jewish scholarship were Palestine and Babylonia, the former having its headquarters at Jamnia and Tiberias, and the latter in Babylon, where the Jewish colony had remained since the days of Exile. It is from the records of these schools...that we derive our earliest direct knowledge of the Hebrew text as it existed among the Jews themselves." (*Our Bible and the Ancient Manuscripts* by Kenyon; p.29).

What makes the Old Testament uniquely more reliable than any other ancient literature passed down through time?

Let us take a closer look at the multiplication, transmission and recording of the Scriptures and tell you what makes the Old Testament uniquely more reliable than any other ancient literature passed down through time.

First, God promised to preserve His Word(s)! We read in **Psalms 119:160** *"Thy word is true from the beginning: and every one of thy righteous judgments endureth for ever."* Another verse reads, **Isaiah 40:8** *"The grass withereth, the flower fadeth: but the word of our God shall stand for ever."* Jesus Christ said, **Matthew 24:35** *"Heaven and earth shall pass away, but my words shall not pass away."* We will take a closer look at the preservation of the Bible later in the book. Suffice it to say that God HAS promised to preserve His Word(s).

Second, we will examine the extreme care with which the copyists transcribed the Old Testament manuscripts.

THE TALMUDISTS (100-500 A.D.)

During the period of 100 to 500 A.D. a great deal of time was spent in cataloging Hebrew civil and canonical law. The Talmudists had quite an intricate system for transcribing synagogue scrolls. (*Samuel Davidson* in *the Hebrew Text of the Old Testament*, 2nd ed., p. 89, cited in James Hastings (ed.) *A Dictionary of the Bible*, IV, 949.)

Samuel Davidson describes some of the disciplines of the Talmudists in regard to the Scriptures. These minute regulations are as follows:

1. A synagogue roll must be written on the skins of clean animals.
2. Prepared for the particular use of the synagogue by a Jew.
3. These must be fastened together with strings taken from clean animals.
4. Every skin must contain a certain number of columns, equal throughout the entire codex.
5. The length of each column must not extend over less than 48 or more than 60 lines; and the breadth must consist of thirty letters.
6. The whole copy must be first-lined; and if three words be written without a line, it is worthless.
7. The ink should be black, neither red, green, nor any other color, and be prepared according to a definite recipe.
8. An authentic copy must be the exemplar (the original), from which the transcriber ought not in the least deviate.
9. No word or letter, not even a yod, must be written from memory, the scribe not having looked at the codex before him ...
10. Between every consonant the space of a hair or thread must intervene;
11. Between every new parashah, or section, the breadth of nine consonants;
12. Between every book, three lines.
13. The fifth book of Moses must terminate exactly with a line; but the rest need not do so.
14. Besides this, the copyist must sit in full Jewish dress,
15. Wash his whole body (before writing the word "Jehovah" & repeat this every time they write it),
16. (Wipe the pen and) begin to write the name of God with a pen newly dipped in ink,
17. And should a king address him while writing that name he must take no notice of him.

There was to be a review of the new scroll within thirty days, and if as many as three pages required correction, the entire document had to be redone. The letters, words and paragraphs had to be counted, and the document became invalid if two letters touched each other. The middle paragraph, word and letter must correspond to those of the original document. (Basic information from - *The Indestructible Book* by W. Ken Connolly; Baker Books 1996; p.16). Davidson adds – "The rolls in which these regulations are not observed are condemned to be buried in the ground or burned; or they are banished to the schools, to be used as reading books." Now, let us move on to the Masoretes.

THE MASORETIC PERIOD (500-900 A.D.)

Until the recent discovery of the Dead Sea Scrolls, the oldest extant Old Testament Hebrew manuscript was around 900 A.D. It was a product of the Masoretes. These Jews took up where the Talmudists left off. They were likewise meticulous in their copying, following the strict rules that had been established previously and adding some of their own.

The Masoretes comes from the Hebrew word *"masora"* or *"masorah"* which simply means "**tradition.**" They accepted the laborious job of editing the text and standardizing it. Remember, the Old Testament Hebrew text was all in capital letters with no vowels, and there was no punctuation or paragraphs. The Masoretes added vowel points in order to insure proper punctuation. The Masoretic text is the standard Hebrew text of our day. However, it should be noted that it is the Masoretic text edited by **Ben Chayyim** that underlies our King James Bible. We will explain in coming pages the textual differences in the text.

The Masoretes were well disciplined and treated the text "with the greatest imaginable reverence," and devised a complicated system of safeguards against scribal slips. For example, they counted the number of times each letter of the alphabet occurs in each book; they pointed out the middle letter of Pentateuch and the middle letter of the whole Hebrew Bible, and made even more detailed calculations than these. "Everything countable seems to be counted," says Wheeler Robinson (*Ancient and English Versions of the Bible* (1940), pg. 29) and they made up mnemonics (formulas) by which the various totals might be readily remembered. In case you are wondering, the Torah (Pentateuch) has 304,805 letters and 79,976 words. (*The Story of The Bible* by Larry Stone; Thomas Nelson; p.21).

H. S. Miller, writing in his book *"General Biblical Introduction,"* says: "Some of these rules may appear extreme and absurd, yet they show how sacred the Holy Word of the Old Testament was to its custodians, the Jews, and they give us strong encouragement to believe that we have the real Old Testament, the same one that our Lord had and which was given by inspiration of God."

Sir Frederic Kenyon concurs writing, "the Massoretes undertook a number of calculations which do not enter into the ordinary sphere of textual criticism. They numbered the verses, words, and letters of every book. They calculated the middle word and middle letter of each. They enumerated verses, which contained all the letters of the alphabet, or a certain number of them; and so on. These trivialities, as we may rightly consider them, had yet the effect of securing minute attention to the precise transmission of the text; and they are but an excessive manifestation of a respect for the sacred Scriptures which in itself deserves nothing but praise. The Massoretes were indeed anxious that not one jot nor tittle, not one smallest letter nor one tiny part of a letter, of the Law should pass away or be lost." (*Our Bible and The Ancient Manuscripts;* Kenyon; p.33).

"The importance of the Masoretic edition to us lies in the fact that it is still the standard text of the Hebrew Bible. All the extant manuscripts of the Hebrew Old Testament contain substantially the Massoretic text." (Ibid. p.33)

Perhaps you are wondering if there is any support for the accuracy of the Masoretic text of the Old Testament, since the oldest manuscripts we had were from 900 A.D. forward. Thanks to the discovery of the Dead Sea Scrolls we now have proof of the accuracy of the Masoretic text.

The Dead Sea Scrolls (primarily fragments of scrolls) were discovered in eleven caves (5 caves discovered by Bedouins and 6 by archaeologists) between the years 1947 and 1956. About 100,000 inscribed fragments were found in the caves around the Dead Sea. From these fragments more than 900 manuscripts have been reconstructed thus far. Many extra-biblical manuscripts and fragments were discovered that shed light on the religious community of Qumran. One of the scrolls found was a complete manuscript of the Hebrew text of Isaiah called The Great Isaiah

<u>Scroll</u>. It is dated by paleographers around 125 B.C. This scroll is more than 1000 years older than any other Old Testament manuscript we previously possessed. The liberal skeptics expected that when this scroll of Isaiah was compared with the Masoretic text of Isaiah, it would show that there had been major changes, making it obvious that God had not preserved his Word. But, just the opposite happened. The scroll of Isaiah from the Dead Sea find was virtually the same as the Masoretic text of Isaiah from which all English Bibles are translated. "Of the 166 words in Isaiah 53, there are only seventeen letters in question. Ten of these letters are simply a matter of spelling, which does not affect the sense. Four more letters are minor stylistic changes, such as conjunctions. The remaining three letters comprise the word 'light,' which is added in verse 11, and does not affect the meaning greatly. Thus, in one chapter of 166 words, there is only one word (three letters) in question after a thousand years of transmission-and this word does not significantly change the meaning of the passage." (*A General Introduction to the Bible, Chicago, Moody Press, 1968* by Norman L. Geisler and William E. Nix).

Therefore, "the impact of this discovery is in the exactness of the Isaiah scroll (125 B.C.) with the Massoretic text of Isaiah (916 A.D.) 1000 years later. This demonstrates the unusual accuracy of the copyists of the Scripture over a thousand year period." (*Evidence that Demands a Verdict*, by Josh McDowell, 1972).

I have laid this foundation in order to make this point: It is the Hebrew Masoretic text that forms the basis of the Old Testament of our English Bible.

THE TEXTUAL CRITICISM OF THE OLD TESTAMENT

"There are two basic texts in existence in Hebrew, the false one, edited by Ben Asher, and the true one, edited by Ben Chayyim. Both texts are still referred to as "Masoretic" so care must be taken as to which text is being referred to.

The Ben Asher text was based on a text called the **Leningrad Manuscript** (B19a; also called simply L), which was dated around 1008 A.D., and <u>differs widely from the Traditional Hebrew</u>

Masoretic Old Testament. The Ben Asher is exhibited in Rudolf Kittel's Biblia Hebraica (BHK, 1937) with all of his suggested footnote changes, as well as in the Stuttgart edition of Biblia Hebraica (BHS, 1967-77) with all of their suggested footnote changes. It had apparently not dawned on Kittel (and others) that **the Ben Asher version was based on a small handful of corrupt manuscripts**. Both of these false Biblia Hebraica (BHK & BHS) Hebrew texts offer in their footnotes about fifteen to twenty suggested changes per page (changes from the authentic Ben Chayyim Masoretic text). This adds up to about 20,000 to 30,000 changes in the entire Hebrew Old Testament text. **One or the other of these false Hebrew texts, either BHK or BHS, are used as the basis for the Old Testament in all modern bible versions, as can be shown by reading their introductory pages**.

The true text of Ben Chayyim on which the KJV is based is the authentic Hebrew Masoretic text. It is called the **Daniel Bomberg edition** or the **Second Great Rabbinic Bible** (1524-25). **This is the traditional Hebrew Masoretic Text represented by the vast majority of existing Old Testament manuscripts. The Ben Chayyim Masoretic text was the uncontested text of the Old Testament for over four hundred years**. In fact, Rudolf Kittel, in his first two editions of 1906 and 1912, used that text in his Biblia Hebraica. It was not until 1937, that he changed his Hebrew text from the Ben Chayyim to the Ben Asher text. Kittel found a large and receptive market in the rapidly growing modernist camp that had grown to hate the traditional texts of both the Old and New Testaments.

In 1516, Daniel Bomberg published a text of the Old Testament under the name "First Rabbinic Bible." This text was followed in 1524 by a second edition that had been compiled from ancient manuscripts by a Hebrew scholar and converted Jewish Rabbi named Abraham Ben Chayyim. Today this work is called the Ben Chayyim Masoretic Text, and is the text that underlies the Old Testament of the King James Bible. The word "masoretic" comes from the Hebrew word "mesor" meaning traditional.

God's appointed guardians of the Old Testament Text were the Jews. *"What advantage then hath the Jew? or what profit is there in circumcision? Much in every way: chiefly, because that unto them were committed the oracles of God."* (**Romans 3:1-2**). The methods used by the Jews in fulfilling their responsibilities as the guardians of these sacred texts is an interesting study.

So then, our only choice is between the traditional Hebrew Masoretic Text that has been the standard text of the Old Testament for well over two thousand years, and is represented by the vast majority of the existing Old Testament manuscripts, or the new, modern text that has only a little minor manuscript support, and introduces errors into the text. **The choice is obvious, only the Traditional (Ben Chayyim) Text can lay claim to uninterrupted use for all the generations from the time of David (Psalm 12) until now."** (This section was taken from - www.angelfire.com/la2/prophet1/ott.html; The bolding and underlining I have added).

THE SEPTUAGINT – LXX

This section is used by permission of Dr. Phil Stringer, Pastor of Ravenswood Baptist Church in Chicago.

Was the Septuagint the Bible of Christ and the Apostles?

CONVENTIONAL WISDOM

Conventional wisdom (politically correct theology and church history) states that Christ and the apostles routinely used the Septuagint (a Greek translation of the Old Testament done about 200 B.C.) as their daily Bible and quoted from it often in the New Testament.

What is this statement based? Does Christ or the apostles ever say that they are quoting the Septuagint? The answer is clearly NO! Yet it is not hard to see that the "conventional wisdom" is dogmatic—that Christ and the apostles were using the Greek translation.

For example "Christ frequently quoted from the Septuagint. The Septuagint, with dates ranging from 250 to 160 B.C., is a Greek translation of the Old Testament. Christ used the Septuagint frequently in His quotations and references to the Old Testament. The use of the Septuagint was widespread in Christ's day!" (Robert Lightner, *The Savior and the Scriptures*, p. 13).

"The Septuagint was the Bible of Christ and the apostles, they most usually quoted from it." (Ira Price, *Ancestry of Our English Bible*, p. 182).
"But as the Septuagint is the oldest translation of the Hebrew Bible, as it is constantly quoted by the writers of the New Testament. . . ." *Smith's Bible Dictionary*, p. 432).

"It was the Bible of most writers of the New Testament. . ." (*International Standard Bible Encyclopedia*, p. 2724).

Dozens (and probably hundreds) of other such examples could be cited. But how do they know? Neither Christ nor the apostles ever said they were quoting from the Septuagint! The New Testament never mentions the Septuagint. Why is the idea that Christ and the apostles used the Septuagint the conventional wisdom of our day?

Why are so many "scholars" so devoted to the Septuagint?

THE APOCRYPHA

Why are so many scholars determined to believe that Christ and the apostles used the Septuagint?

Roman Catholics use the idea that Christ quoted the Septuagint to justly include the Apocrypha in their Bibles. Their reasoning goes like this: "Christ used and honored the Septuagint, the Septuagint includes the Apocrypha, so Christ honored and authorized the Apocrypha." Since no Hebrew Old Testament ever included the books of the Apocrypha, the Septuagint is the only source the Catholics have for justifying their canon. Many Reformers and Lutherans wrote at great length refuting the validity of the Septuagint.

One Catholic lesson posted on the Internet states: "Me, I will trust the version of the Old Testament that was loved by Peter and Paul." This is in a lesson entitled "The Canon of the Bible and the Septuagint." The only reason given for accepting the Apocrypha is that Christ and the apostles quoted the Septuagint. One quote reads,

"Let me reiterate: the then 300+ year old Septuagint version of Scripture was good enough for Matthew, Mark, Luke, John and Paul, etc., which is evident in their referencing it over 300 times (out of 360 Old Testament references) in their New Testament writings - and the Septuagint includes seven books and parts of Esther and Daniel that were removed from Protestant Bibles some 1,600 years after the birth of Christ." Almost every "fact" given in the statement is incorrect but it illustrates why Roman Catholicism is so devoted to the Septuagint.

THE BIBLE IN MY OWN WORDS!

The Septuagint is a very loose translation of the Old Testament. It has much more in common with the "Revised Standard Version" or even "The Living Bible" than the King James Bible. It is used to teach against the doctrine of verbal inspiration. It is used to justify "dynamic equivalence" in translation rather than the formal literal equivalence method (which is based upon the concept of verbal inspiration).

After all, if Christ did not care about the specific words of Scripture, why should we? (For example, see *The Nature and Authority of the Bible,* by Raymond Abba, p. 106).

If Christ used the Septuagint then you can put the Bible in your own words in either a paraphrase or your own translation. You are now God and private interpretation is your method of rule and your source of authority.

WHY EVANGELICALS?

It is easy to see why Roman Catholics and modernists are so devoted to the idea that Christ used the Septuagint! But why are so many evangelicals devoted to an idea for which they cannot offer any proof? The answer is simple! Many proud evangelicals value the idea of being accepted as "scholarly" and "educated" by the world (the Catholics and the modernists). It is a fact that the Catholics and modernists will mock you and call you uneducated and unscholarly if you don't believe that Christ used the Septuagint. If you asked them how they know that Christ used the Septuagint they will attack you, often hysterically, (but they won't answer your question).

Far too many evangelicals value acceptance by the world. They substitute conventional wisdom for doing their own research and getting solid answers. They declare themselves as scholars, they repeat conventional wisdom and they never do any thorough study. They react condescendingly when they are asked questions they cannot answer!

The evidence clearly refutes the idea that the Greek translation of the Old Testament, currently called the Septuagint, was used by Christ and the apostles.

WHAT IS THE SEPTUAGINT?

According to *General Biblical Introduction: From God to Us* (by H.S. Miller, p. 220): "The Septuagint Version is a translation of the Hebrew Old Testament into the Greek language for the Greek speaking Jews of Alexandria. The abbreviation is LXX. It is sometimes called the Alexandrian Version."

But why would Christ, when preaching to the Jews of Palestine, use a Greek version designed for the Greek speaking Jews of Alexandria Egypt?

The existence of this translation is based upon a letter called the "Letter of Aristeas." This letter is referred to by Aristobulus (in a letter to Pharoah Ptolemy Philometer—(182-146 B.C.), Philo (40 A.D.), and Josephus (70 A.D.). It is also referred to by several of the early Christian writers.

Aristeas claims to be a high official in the court of the Egyptian King Ptolemy Philadelphius. According to this letter, the royal librarian, Demetrius Phalarius, suggests that it would be good to have a Greek Translation of the Old Testament in the Egyptian royal library. The king sent Jews living in Egypt (including Aristeas) to Jerusalem to ask for help.

They asked the high priest to send six scribes from each tribe of Israel to Alexandria in Egypt to make this Greek translation of the Old Testament. According to "The Letter of Aristeas," scribes were sent. They were sent to the island of Pharos. There is no suggestion that any Greek scholars were included in this group. They each did their own translation of the first five books of the Old Testament. All 72 translations were identical (after 72 days of translation work). This supposedly proved that the translators were inspired by God!

Of course, no one today believes that this story is factually true but still many base their doctrine of Scripture upon it. *One Bible Only?* (Roy Beacham and Kevin Bauder) calls it "a mixture of fact and fable" (p.29). Geisler and Nix, A *General Introduction to the Bible* says, "The details of this story are undoubtedly fictitious but the letter does relate the authentic fact that the LXX was translated for the use of Greek speaking Jews of Alexandria (p. 308).

But if this story is "fictitious": then there is no "factual" information about the origin of the Septuagint. There are no other historical references to the translation of the Old Testament into Greek in Alexandria. Every other historical reference is a retelling of the story of "The Letter of Aristeas."

The Introduction to the Septuagint (p-ii)(a modern printing of Origen's Septuagint) states that the "Letter of Aristeas" is "...not worthy of notice except for the myth being connected with the authority which this version (LXX) was once supposed to have possessed."

It also says (p-i), "No information, whatever, as to the time and place of their execution (ancient versions), or by whom they were made exists, we simply find such versions in use at particular times..."

The New Schaff - Herzog Religious Encyclopedia admits: "Of the pre-Christian period of its history (referring to the Septuagint) next to nothing is known." (Volume II, p.117) There are no historical references to the Septuagint before the time of Christ except for the "Letter of Aristeas." Aristobulus, Philo, Josephus and all of the early Christian writers refer to the same story. A story that no one today believes!

For some reason the work of the Seventy-two began to be commonly referred to as the LXX or the Seventy. There is no clear explanation for why it is called "the Seventy" instead of "the Seventy-two." The lack of a clear explanation is not unusual in this story.

EARLY CHRISTIAN WRITERS

Supporters of the "Christ used the Septuagint" theory often refer to early Christian writers (such as Justin Martyr, Irenaeus, Tertullian, Cyril of Jerusalem and Augustine) as proof that Christ and the apostles used the Septuagint. The writers quoted can all be found in either the Ante-Nicene or Post-Nicene Fathers.

Every one of these men based their acceptance of the LXX on the bogus "Letter of Aristeas." They all accepted it as a fact. They all believed that God had inspired a Greek translation of the Old Testament or at least the Pentateuch. Does anyone that quotes these men believe the legend of the "Letter to Aristeas?" The early Christian writers do not add any other information about Christ using the Septuagint. If you do not believe the legendary story of "The Letter of Aristeas" then these writers do not add anything to the discussion.

Jerome was a contemporary of Augustine. Jerome wanted to see a new translation of the Old Testament into Latin from the Hebrew. He and Augustine exchanged letters about this idea. Augustine opposed the use of the Hebrew because he thought the Greek Septuagint was "inspired."

Jerome understood that the Septuagint of his day was developed by Origen. He believed that Origen used several different Greek manuscripts and that all of them had been corrupted! He disputed Augustine's assertion that the apostles usually quoted from the Septuagint! He pointed out that their quotations often don't match any version of the Septuagint or any other Greek Old Testament.

H. S. Miller's classic book, (General Biblical Introduction: from God to Us, p. 222) states that Jerome was the first to challenge the conventional wisdom of his day about "The Letter to Aristeas." But Miller goes on to say that "The Letter to Aristeas" has been doubted, then denied and that "now it has few, if any, defenders."

It is clear that what is called the Septuagint today has nothing to do with the story of "The Letter to Aristeas." What is called the Septuagint today is the work of Origen (almost 200 years after the time of Christ).

Advocates of the "Christ used the Septuagint" view are quick to pass off statements like the one above as "King James propaganda." One writer said: "So, why is the King James only advocate so desperate to put the completion of the Septuagint after the writing of the New Testament Scriptures? It is because the Septuagint is not identical to the Hebrew Scriptures from which the King James was translated, yet Christ and the apostles often quoted it." This attack on the advocates of the King James Bible ignored the testimony of Jerome from the fourth century. The recognition of the history of the Septuagint is not new.

In 1588 (23 years before the release of the King James Bible) William Whitaker wrote: "Learned men question, whether the Greek version of the Scriptures now extant be or be not the version of the seventy elders. The sounder opinion seems to be that of those who determine that the true Septuagint is wholly lost, and that the Greek text as we have it, is a mixed and miserably corrupted document. Aristeas says that the Septuagint version was exactly conformable to the Hebrew originals, so that when read and diligently examined by skillful judges, it was highly approved by the general suffrage of them all. But this of ours differs amazingly from the Hebrew copies, as well in other places and books, as specially in the Psalms of David." (William Whitaker, *Disputations on Holy Scripture,* 1588, p. 121; Soli Deo Gloria edition 2000).

Whitaker was the foremost defender of the Protestant doctrine of Scripture against Catholicism in his day. He also wrote: "From these and innumerable examples of the like sort we may concede either this Greek version which has come down to our times is not the same as that published by the seventy Jewish elders, or that it has suffered such infinite and shameful corruptions as to be now of very slight authority. Even Jerome had not the Greek translation of the seventy interpreters in its purity; since he often complains in his commentary that what he had was faulty and corrupt." *(Disputations on Holy Scripture, p.* 122).

This is not "King James Only" propaganda. It is a sound review of history.

In Ira Price's, *The Ancestry of Our English Bible,* he mentions several important manuscripts of the Septuagint, p. 52-80. Every one (except the John Rylands' fragment) is the Origen version of the Septuagint, produced long after the New Testament. Every manuscript was produced at least two hundred years after the New Testament that "scholars" claim that it quotes. "But the earliest extent manuscript of this version (the Septuagint) is dated around 350 A.D..." (H. S. Miller, *General Biblical Introduction, p.* 120).

THE DEAD SEA SCROLLS

"Scholars" are fond of saying that the Dead Sea Scrolls prove the Septuagint. In fact the phrase "the Dead Sea Scrolls proves" is used to justify any number of ideas that have nothing to do with the Dead Sea Scrolls.

In fact, there is not one single verse of the Old Testament in Greek in any manuscript found in the Dead Sea Scrolls. There is nothing about the Septuagint in these scrolls. There are no quotes from the Septuagint or references to it. None of the Dead Sea Scrolls mention anything about the Septuagint. All of the Dead Sea Scrolls are in Hebrew or Aramaic.

Some of the Old Testament books found among the Dead Sea Scrolls don't match the Hebrew of the traditional text. Some scholars call these Hebrew manuscripts "the Qumran Septuagint." They suggest that these manuscripts were the Septuagint translated back into Hebrew. There is no reference to this in any of the scrolls or anywhere else in history. So why do they believe this? Because they really wish it was true. There is no Qumran Septuagint!

The Dead Sea Scrolls do prove that the "sacred language" (the language used in sermons, rituals and commentaries) of the Jews in Palestine around the time of Christ was Hebrew—not Greek.

GREEK SCRAPS

One of the most commonly suggested evidences for a Septuagint translation before the time of Christ is the existence of four manuscript scraps which contain verses from Deuteronomy. These manuscript scraps actually date from before the time of Christ and they are the only manuscripts in Greek of any part of the Old Testament ever found that date before the time of Christ.

The first three manuscript scraps (Rylands Papyrus 458) were found together and contain Deut. 23, 25:13, 26:12, 17, 19 and 28:31-33. A fourth scrap found in Fouad, Egypt repeats some of these verses and adds Deut. 32:7.

No New Testament writer quotes any of these verses and they prove nothing about what Bible Christ and the apostles used.

These are the only manuscripts of a Greek Old Testament from before the time of Christ. All they prove is that someone had translated part of Deuteronomy into Greek before 150 B.C. Since they are never quoted they don't prove who used this translation or how widespread it was.

THE WORK OF PROFESSOR KAHLE

Professor Paul Kahle (1875-1964) challenged the conventional wisdom of the Septuagint theory. He was not a King James Only advocate. He was a German professor of Oriental Studies. He was a recognized scholar of Mideastern languages.

Professor Kahle simply refused to accept the legend of "The Letter of Aristeas." He called it "propaganda." He refused to follow the conventional wisdom that treats "The Letter of Aristeas" as fictional but authoritative history at the same time.

Kahle's theory states that what we call the Septuagint today is actually the result of an attempt to standardize a Greek translation of the Old Testament. This took place over 150 years after the time of Christ and the apostles. He believed that various scraps of manuscripts and attempts at translations may have been consulted. He found some evidence for a Greek translation of the first five books of the Old Testament before the time of Christ but he did not believe that this translation had anything to do with the legend of "The Letter to Aristeas." (See *The Romance of Bible Scripts and Scholars,* Prentice Hall, 1965, p. 16).

He clearly did not believe that there was any one prototype for the Septuagint of Origen. He saw no reason to believe that Christ or the apostles quoted the Septuagint (which was not produced until at least 150 years later).

Most "Septuagint scholars" reject the Kahle theory. It does not fit with their pre-conceived notions about the Septuagint or with their theological needs. They simply "dismiss it" but they can't refute it.

Fredrick Kenyon writes, "It must be admitted that Kahle makes a strong case." Dr. Kahle's theory fits with the record of Jerome.

THE OLD TESTAMENT IN GREEK -WHAT REALLY HAPPENED

Jewish people spread throughout the Greek kingdoms of the Mideast. As the Roman Empire spread through the Mideast, the Jewish dispersion increased.

Some Jews, known as Grecians or Hellenists, adopted the Greek lifestyle as did much of the Roman Empire. Some of these Jews began to use Greek as their main language. They were represented in religious circles by the Sadducees.

Some entire Jewish communities began to adopt the Greek language, including the large Jewish community in Alexandria, Egypt. Some historians have estimated that one third of Alexandria was Jewish.

Many supporters of the "Christ used the Septuagint theory" teach that all the Jews used Greek as their main language and as their sacred language. This, they say, is why Christ and the apostles used a Greek Old Testament. This statement is absolutely against all the historical evidences. Outside Alexandria and a few other distant cities, the number of Jews who used Greek as their main language was very small.

The main language of the Jewish people was Aramaic. This language is related to Old Testament Hebrew. According to the unanimous testimony of the Jewish Mishnah and the Jewish Targums, the language of the synagogues and the rabbis of Palestine was Aramaic. No Greek Old Testament could ever have gained any acceptance among the Jews of Palestine.

There was an Aramaic translation of the Old Testament in common use among the Jewish people. It was called the *Targum of Onkelos*. It was printed in 1517 by Cardinal Ximenes (who was also responsible for *The Complutensian Polyglot*).

Only in the far regions of the dispersion was there a demand for a Greek Old Testament. There were probably several attempts to translate parts of the Old Testament in Greek.

According to "The Letter of Aristeas," Philo, Josephus, and a writer named Aristobulous, a Greek version of the first five books of the Old Testament was translated in Alexandria. Alexandria was one of the few places where a demand for a Greek Old Testament might have taken place. These authors clearly maintain that this version closely matched the Hebrew of the first five books of the Bible. The translation currently known as the Septuagint does not match the Hebrew closely at all.

The scraps of the John Rylands' manuscript apparently come from a pre-Christian era translation of Deuteronomy.

Someone invented the legend of the 72 elders in order to give credibility to a Greek translation, possibly one from Alexandria. Philo (who some believe invented the legend) and Josephus promoted this legend. Eventually someone expanded the story to refer to the whole Old Testament. Whenever someone used a Greek translation of part of the Old Testament, they called it the Septuagint to try and connect it to the legend of the "inspired" Alexandrian translation.

Some early Christian leaders fell for this myth. Greek translations of the whole Old Testament began to appear in the Mideast. Around 140 A.D., a Greek translation was produced by Aquila. According to Jerome, he studied under the famed Rabbi Akiba from A.D. 95 until A.D. 135. This translation, made after the New Testament, purposely obscures the Old Testament prophecies about Christ that are fulfilled in the New Testament. Because of this, it found some acceptance among the Jews. Of course, it did not contain the Apocrypha - if it had it would never have been accepted by the Jews. Some writers have called Aquila's translation "the Septuagint" or "a Septuagint." There are no existing copies of this text.

Theodotian (around 180 A.D.) presented a Greek translation of the Old Testament. He was an "Ebionite" Christian—a heretical sect that denied the deity of Christ. Mohammed's wife was an "Ebionite" Christian. She persuaded him that the "spirits" who were speaking to him were not really demons but angels.

Theodotian claimed to be correcting the original Septuagint. (How do you correct an inspired translation?) He also obscures many Old Testament prophecies about Christ. Since he was writing for a heretical Christian audience and not a Jewish one, he included some of the Apocrypha. His work was also called "a Septuagint" or "the Septuagint."

A third translator, Symmachus, was also an Ebionite. He produced a Greek translation around 211 A.D. He did not include any of the Apochrypha. His work was also called "a Septuagint" or "the Septuagint."

Origen worked on "restoring" the Septuagint between 220-240 A.D. He claimed that there were as many different Greek translations as there were manuscripts. As he worked on his restoration, he had the translations of Aquila, Theodotian and Symmachus in front of him. He also claimed to have two other Greek manuscripts that he found in a jar and at least two "corrupted" copies of the true Septuagint.

Of course, Origen had the New Testament. He wrote commentaries on every book of the New Testament. He collated these Greek manuscripts and created his own version of the Septuagint. As the *International Standard Bible Encyclopedia* declares. "It was Origen who claimed to be able to give the church the true text of the Old Testament and its true meaning." (ISBE, p. 2276).

Origen clearly believed that the Old Testament prophecies referred to Christ. He worked hard at making the Old Testament match the New Testament - even when it didn't.

His Septuagint is what people call the Septuagint today. There is no copy of a Septuagint from Alexandria to compare with his copy. There is no way to know how much of Origen's Septuagint he simply invented.

Some writers have said that to declare Origen's Septuagint to be the document called the Septuagint today is simply "King James propaganda." "Scholars" like Ira Price, H.S. Miller, Frederick Kenyon and Gleason Archer are clearly not "King James fanatics." They all recognize that the current document called the Septuagint is the work of Origen. This is simply history. The *New Schaff - Herzog Encyclopedia* refers to Origen's Septuagint as "the so called Septuagint." (vol. II, p. 116).

The Encyclopedia Britannica, (vol. 5, p. 63) states that the text of the Septuagint is, "contained in a few early, <u>but not necessarily reliable,</u> manuscripts. The best known of these are the Codex Vaticanus and the Codex Sinaiticus both dating from the 4th century and the Codex Alexandrinus from the 5th century." All of these early texts are Origen's Septuagint.

Smith's Bible Dictionary (p. 432) states about the Septuagint, "moreover it has come down to us in a state of great corruption, which renders it difficult to ascertain what the first translators wrote."

Francis Turretin writes: "Finally, who can assure us that the seventy faithfully followed their Hebrew text and that the Greek text (which we now read) is the very same with that which the seventy wrote." (*Institutes of Elenctic Theology*, p. 119, 1696).

He also wrote: "We have only its ruins and wreck, so that it can hardly be called the version of the Septuagint. . ." (p. 128)

In the fourth century, Jerome complained that the only editions of the Septuagint available were those of Origen's redaction of the Septuagint. <u>He also claimed that Origen "borrowed" things to place in his Old Testament.</u>

When writers like Irenaeus and Justin Martyr (who wrote before Origen) refer to the Septuagint, we have no idea what Greek version they were referring to. It doesn't exist today.

Origen's Septuagint was made popular by Eusebius. As a result... "evidence of Septuagint readings prior to the time of Origen have been confused or lost." (Ira Price, *The Ancestry of Our English Bible*, p. 79).

When "scholars" discuss the Septuagint today they discuss a translation produced after the New Testament by a famous commentator on the New Testament.

THE EVIDENCE THAT CHRIST DID NOT USE ANY VERSION OF THE SEPTUAGINT

LAW, PROPHETS AND PSALMS

Christ continually refers to the Hebrew division of the Old Testament—The Law, Prophets and Psalms (see Matt. 7:12, 11:13, 22:40; and Luke 24:27, 44 for example). No known version of the Septuagint has any such division. Origen's Septuagint has the Old Testament in an entirely different order with the books of the Apocrypha interspersed among them. Christ took it for granted that His hearers used an Old Testament with the historic three-fold division (Law, Prophets, and Psalms) found in the Hebrew Bible.

PROVERBS 30:5-6

The testimony of Proverbs 30:56 is clear. *Every word of God is pure; he is a shield unto them that put their trust in him. Add thou not unto his words, lest he reprove thee, and thou be found a liar.* Proverbs 30:5-6 clearly condemns adding or subtracting from the words of the Hebrew Scriptures. Even the strongest defenders of the Septuagint admit that many words are added that are not found in the Hebrew Scriptures (thus their claims against verbal inspiration). Origen may have been comfortable violating Proverbs 30:5-6 but Christ wouldn't have been.

If he had violated Proverbs 30:56, the Pharisees would have been very quick to condemn him for this.

READING IN THE SYNAGOGUE

Jesus frequently read the Scriptures and preached from them in the Jewish Synagogues (see Luke 4 for example). Hebrew was the language of the Synagogue and Christ was clearly using a Hebrew Bible when preaching there. No copy of any Greek Old Testament has ever been found in a Jewish Synagogue.

THE COMMON PEOPLE HEARD HIM GLADLY

Jesus' public preaching and teaching drew great crowds of the common people. If he had preached in Greek he could never have drawn such an audience. Many Jewish people learned Greek for use in trade and dealing with the Roman Empire but they never accepted it for communication among themselves or in sacred matters.

The Hellenists (Grecians) who favored Greek were a small group often distant from the majority of the people. If Jesus had preached in Greek both the Pharisees and the Zealots would have used that against Him and the crowds would never have flocked to Him. He undoubtedly preached in Aramaic (the daily language of the Jews - closely related to Hebrew) and read the Scriptures from Hebrew. The Synagogues of Palestine refused to use the Greek and considered the Hebrew sacred (see H.S. Miller, *General Biblical Introduction*, p. 224).

The Hebrew Mishnah makes it clear that this was expected from all Jewish teachers.

IS DISOBEDIENCE THE WAY TO GET AN HONORABLE TRANSLATION OF THE SCRIPTURE?

If the story told in "The Letter of Aristeas" had any truth in it at all, it would involve activities in disobedience to Scripture. The Scripture was clear that the holy writings were to be handled only by Levites-Deut. *17:18, 31:25-26*. The scribes involved in the Aristeas story would be acting in disobedience to Scripture.

Furthermore, God had told the Israelites to stay out of Egypt - see Jeremiah 42:13-22 and 44:25-26. He condemned all those who returned to Egypt and promised to judge them.

Would Christ have put His stamp of approval on such disobedience?

THE SEPTUAGINT AND THE APOCRYPHA

The Greek translation of the Old Testament currently known as the Septuagint (Origen's Septuagint) contains the books of the Apocrypha.

No Hebrew Bible ever contained the books of the Apocrypha. No Jewish council ever endorsed these books and at least one Jewish council specifically rejected them (Council of Jamnia A.D. 90).

No Jewish teacher or rabbi ever endorsed any book of the Apocrypha. One of the main reasons for rejecting them is because they were written in Greek. They did not believe that any sacred writings could ever be in Greek. Jewish leaders would also use this same argument against the books of the New Testament.

It is unthinkable to believe that the Jews in Palestine used a Greek Old Testament containing the rejected books of the Apocrypha. It is against all the evidence of history to think that they used a Greek Old Testament at all.

WHY DON'T NEW TESTAMENT REFERENCES MATCH THE OLD TESTAMENT WORD FOR WORD?

"Well they had to be quoting something—it must be the Septuagint." This is the argument of advocates of the "Christ used the Septuagint theory." So what were the New Testament writers and Christ quoting?

There are 268 references to *"as it is written"* in the New Testament. Few match the exact wording of the Hebrew Old Testament passages they refer to. Eighty-eight match (or are matched by) Origen's Septuagint. Most of the other 180 don't match any ancient document word for word.

Some have suggested that perhaps an Aramaic translation of the Old Testament or a Chaldean paraphrase is being quoted but this is unlikely.

Actually the explanation is simple and has been known for a long time. The Greek phrase "as it is written" is a common one in ancient Greek writings. It is never an indication of an exact quote—in the New Testament or anywhere else. Frederick Spitta wrote a century ago, "According to the unvarying practice in the New Testament, the citation formula 'as it is written' is never the introductory clause but rather always follows a report of something seen as the fulfillment of a prophetic word." The phrase implies not a quotation but a reference to a fulfillment of a prediction or a prophecy. For example, see the way the phrase, "as it is written," is used in the writings of Justin Martyr.

These passages are simply not quotes at all—they are allusions to Old Testament prophecies. These are Holy Spirit inspired allusions—they are not quotations at all. This was clear to the Reformed theologians and many of the old Church of England writers. A little bit of research gives a clear explanation. The critics of the King James position would be well served to read more widely.

ORIGEN'S SEPTUAGINT COPIES THE NEW TESTAMENT

Many more examples could be shown. Origen's Septuagint adds nine names to Genesis 46:20 to make it add up to the 75 mentioned in Acts 7:14. Origen's Septuagint often changes the Old Testament to match the New Testament. For instance the Old Testament Hebrew is ignored and the Greek Old Testament is made to match the Greek New Testament.

Philo, Aristeas and Josephus refer to a Greek Old Testament that matches the Hebrew Old Testament. Origen provides a Greek Old Testament "coordinated" in many places with the New Testament.

This should not come as a surprise. Origen produced his Greek Old Testament 150 years after the last book of the New Testament was given. As a noted commentator on all of the books of the New Testament, he was very familiar with the New Testament.

It is not a surprise that 88 Old Testament allusions in the New Testament match Origen's Septuagint. The New Testament came first.

WHAT ABOUT THE KING JAMES TRANSLATORS?

Advocates of the 'Christ used the Septuagint' point to the fact that some of the King James Bible translators believed this theory. This is true.

However, no one suggests that the King James translators were infallible in their understanding of church history. If they had been, they would have left the Church of England and joined the Baptist churches of their time.

It is interesting that many who believe that the King James translators can be corrected by every college student with two years of Greek, suddenly find them authoritative when they speak about church history. Their expertise was in the Greek, Hebrew and Latin languages, not in church history.

Rev. Prabhudas Koshy, of the Far Eastern Bible College sums this issue up well: "The claim that Jesus and the New Testament writers always used the Septuagint to quote from the Old Testament is without biblical evidence. It has been said that in the New Testament there are about 263 direct quotations from the Old. However, many of these Old Testament quotations in the New are significantly different from the Septuagint. If Jesus and the apostles relied on the Septuagint for all their Old Testament quotations, such a difference would not have resulted.

There was no need for Jesus and the New Testament writers to rely on the Septuagint to quote the Old Testament, Jesus Himself was the Author of the Holy Scriptures. He could quote Hebrew Scriptures and translate them infallibly into Greek. As far as the apostles were concerned, the Holy Spirit was their Chief Aide who supervised their writing of the Scriptures. There is nothing against them citing the Old Testament and translating the words into Greek themselves. Let us be mindful that both Testaments were inspired of the Holy Spirit; and that the Spirit was their infallible Author.

The New Testament's translations and interpretations of the Old Testament are not taken from any corrupt human work. Whatever the New Testament says about the Old Testament, whether it is a translation into Greek or an interpretation, it must be viewed as the infallible and inerrant work of the Holy Spirit. Every word of the New Testament, including quotations, interpretations and applications of the Old Testament, is not from any corrupt human translation but from the Holy Spirit Himself. As such it is highly unlikely that Jesus and the New Testament writers quoted from the corrupt Septuagint as some allege.

Moreover, Jesus made no mention of the Greek Septuagint. Neither did He assert that His quotations were taken from the Septuagint, nor mention the Septuagint. However, He did speak about the Hebrew text of the Old Testament. In Matthew 5:18, He referred to the Hebrew text of the Old Testament when He said, *"For verily I say unto you, Till heaven and earth pass, one jot or one tittle shall in no wise pass from the law, till all be fulfilled."* The *jot* (or *yodh*) is the smallest letter in the Hebrew alphabet, and the *tittle* is a portion of a letter that distinguishes two similarly written letters. Here Jesus spoke authoritatively about the accuracy of the Hebrew text of the Old Testament. Jesus also declared His commitment to every letter of the Hebrew text of the Old Testament (**Matt. 5:17-18**). It is impossible to think that Jesus who affirmed His absolute commitment to every letter of the Hebrew Text of the Old Testament would quote or endorse its corrupt translation. If Jesus used the Greek Septuagint, His scriptures would have not contained the jots and the tittles. He obviously used the Hebrew Scriptures and not the corrupt Greek version!"

CONCLUSION

According to Dewey Beagle, only in recent years (he was writing in 1960) have "scholars" begun to value the Septuagint again. *(God's Word Into English,* p. 44). Could it be that the Biblical and textual "scholars" from the 1500s to the 1900s were right after all?

The Scripture offers many warnings about being careful what we believe.

Beware lest any man spoil you through philosophy and vain deceit, after the tradition of men, after the rudiments of the world, and not after Christ. **Colossians 2:8**

(This is the end of Dr. Stringer's article.)

THE APOCRYPHA OR DEUTEROCANONICAL BOOKS

An increasing number of the Bibles being published today include the Apocrypha. I am convinced that we will see this alarming trend continue.

WHAT IS THE APOCRYPHA?

The word ***Apocrypha*** was coined by the 5th-century Catholic Bible scholar Sophronius Eusebius Hieronymus, better known as Jerome, designating the books received by the Roman Catholic Church of his time that were a part of the Greek version of the Old Testament, yet, were not included in the Hebrew Bible. The actual word ***apocrypha*** is derived from the Greek word **"*abscondita*,"** which historically identified writings which had an obscure origin or which were heretical. In the Talmud the Jewish rabbis used this word to describe works that were not canonical Scripture. The term has come to be applied particularly to the books added to the Roman Catholic Bible and Orthodox Bible but ordinarily rejected by non-Catholics. Most of the Apocryphal books are also called the ***deuterocanonical books***. The word ***deuterocanonical*** means second list. "This name was first used in the sixteenth century by Sixtus Senensis and has since passed into common use in the Latin Church as a convenient label to cover the books Tobit, Judith, Wisdom, Ecclesiasticus, the two Maccabees, Baruch, and the Greek parts of Esther and Daniel. It was not intended to denote an inferior degree of authority, but only as recognition of the fact that the canonicity of these writings <u>had not</u> always met with universal consent in the Church." (*The Cambridge History of The Bible - Vol. 2* edited by G.W.H. Lampe; Cambridge University Press; p.92).

The *Apocrypha* is a series of books, written between B.C. 250 and B.C. 100, which exemplify the "superstitious" "traditions," "imaginations," and "commandments of men" which Jesus and Paul warned against (Acts 17:22, Matthew 15:9, Romans 1:21, Galatians 1:14). The Apocrypha consists of 15 books of Jewish literature written during the intertestamental period (the period between the Old Testament and the New Testament). Some of them have historic value, but all are spurious, of unknown authorship, and without claim of inspiration or authority. Some are legendary and fantasy. Many of them are written to reinforce post-exilic Jewish opposition to idolatry. All extant copies of the Apocrypha are written in Greek.

THE LIST OF THE APOCRYPHA

1. The First Book of Esdras (also known as Third Esdras)
2. The Second Book of Esdras (also known as Fourth Esdras)
3. Tobit
4. Judith
5. The Additions to the Book of Esther
6. The Wisdom of Solomon
7. Ecclesiasticus, or the Wisdom of Jesus the Son of Sirach
8. Baruch
9. The Letter of Jeremiah (This letter is sometimes incorporated as the last chapter of Baruch. When this is done the number of books is fourteen instead of fifteen.)
10. The Prayer of Azariah and the Song of the Three Young Men
11. Susanna
12. Bel and the Dragon
13. The Prayer of Manasseh
14. The First Book of Maccabees
15. The Second Book of Maccabees

Three of these fifteen books (I and II Esdras and the Prayer of Manasseh) are not considered canonical by the Roman Catholic Church. In Catholic Bibles the remaining twelve are interspersed among and attached to the undisputed thirty-nine books of the Old Testament: Tobit, Judith, Wisdom of Solomon, Ecclesiasticus, Baruch with the letter of Jeremiah, and I and II Maccabees which are arranged separately; the Additions to Esther are joined to Esther; and appended to the book of Daniel are the Prayer of Azariah and the Song of the Three Young Men (added after Dan.

3:23), and Susanna, and Bel and the Dragon. (I and II Esdras of the Catholic Bible are not the same as the I and II Esdras in the above list, but are different designations for our books Ezra and Nehemiah.) Since several of the apocryphal writings are combined with canonical books, the Catholic Bible numbers altogether forty-six books in its Old Testament. Non-Catholic editions of the English Bible since 1535, including early editions of the familiar King James Version, separate these apocryphal books from the canonical Old Testament.

The Roman Catholic Church, at the Council of Trent in 1546, decreed certain apocryphal writings to be canonical (authoritative). The books of the Apocrypha included were...
1. Tobit
2. Judith
3. Wisdom of Solomon
4. Sirach-Ecclesiasticus
5. Baruch
6. I and II Maccabees
7. Additions to Esther and Daniel which are absent from the Protestant Bible

I should note that Orthodox Christians (Greek, Russian, Serbian, Orthodox, etc.) usually include *3 Maccabees, 4 Maccabees,* and *Psalm 151.* Because of its brevity, I have chosen to include an English translation of **the Apocryphal Psalm 151** describing David's triumph over Goliath.

1 I was small among my brothers, and youngest in my father's house; I tended my father's sheep.
2 My hands made a harp, my fingers fashioned a lyre.
3 And who will declare it to my Lord? The Lord himself; it is he who hears.
4 It was he who sent his messenger and took me from my father's sheep, and anointed me with his anointing oil.
5 My brothers were handsome and tall, but the Lord was not pleased with them.
6 I went out to meet the Philistine, and he cursed me by his idols.
7 But I drew his own sword; I beheaded him, and removed reproach from the people of Israel.

WHO WAS THE FIRST PERSON TO BEGIN INCLUDING THE APOCRYPHAL BOOKS IN THE BIBLE?

It was Origen (circa 185-254) the heretic "who first included the Apocrypha with the Bible." *(Forever Settled* by Jack Moorman; Bible for Today; p.69). Origen was one of the greatest corrupting influences upon the early church as well as upon the copies of the Bible. He is thought to be the first to teach purgatory. His influence is considered to have led to the development of the Arian heresy a century later, which denied the full deity of Jesus Christ. Further, he taught infants should be baptized for the forgiveness of sin and many other heresies. As one author put it, "Origen freely acknowledged volitional alterations and corrections of the New Testament manuscripts in Alexandria (Ibid. p.69).

THE ENGLISH BIBLE AND THE APOCRYPHA

The Apocrypha had been introduced into the English version of the Coverdale Bible in 1535. However it noted – *"Apocrifa. The bokes & treatises which amonge the Fathers of old are **not rekened to be of authorite with the other bokes of the Byble**, neither are the foude in the Canon of the Hebrews."*

"The King James version in 1611 placed them between the Old and New Testaments. It began to be omitted from about 1629..." *(The Apocrypha also called Deutero-Canonical Writings* by Lloyd Thomas; http://ftp.iafrica.com/l/ll/ lloyd/Apocrypha.htm).

I turn your attention to the preface of the Geneva Bible of 1560 which includes this special advisory:

> "These bokes that follow in order after the Prophetes vnto the Newe testament, are called Apocrypha, that is bokes, which were not receiued by a comune consent to be red and expounded publikely in the Church, nether yet serued to proue any point of Christian religion, saue in asmuche as they had the consent of the other Scriptures called Canonical to confirme the same, or rather whereon they were grounded: but as bokes proceding from godlie men, were receiued to be red for the aduancement and furtherance of

the knowledge of the historie, & for the instruction of godlie maners: which bokes declare that at all times God had an especial care of his Church and left them not vtterly destitute of teachers and meanes to confirme them in the hope of the promised Messiáh, and also witnesse that those calamities that God sent to his Church, were according to his prouidence, who had bothe so threatened by his Prophetes, and so broght it to passe for the destruction of their enemies, and for the tryal of his children."

In other words, the Geneva translators were putting a disclaimer on these books, in the Reformation tradition of considering them (as Luther said) "useful and good for reading," but not equal to Scripture.

The decree of The Roman Catholic Council of Trent in 1546 declares everyone anathema, (cursed or condemned to destruction) who *"does not accept as sacred and canonical the aforesaid books* (the Apocrypha) *in their entirety and with all their parts."* So the question naturally comes up, <u>why were they included in virtually all the early English Bibles and yet they are not in our most non-Catholic Bibles today</u>? The influence toward crediting these writings with Bible authority did not begin until the 4th Century in the North African church.

As we have seen, the Jewish canon centered on the so-called Masoretic Text, which is written in Hebrew. The apocryphal books were not included in the original Hebrew Old Testament preserved by the Jews. These books were written during the 200 years preceding and the 100 years following the birth of Christ. **Romans 3:2** tells us that God entrusted His Word to the care of the Jews. Hence, since the apocryphal books were only a part of the Greek Septuagint Canon and not the Hebrew Canon, it is easy to see why the Jewish scribes believe that God guided them in the rejection of the Apocryphal books from the canon of Scripture.

"According to Torrey, the Jews not only rejected the Apocrypha, but after the overthrow of Jerusalem in 70 A.D., they went so far as to 'destroy, systematically and thoroughly, the Semitic originals of all extra-canonical literature,' including the Apocryphal. 'The feeling of the leaders at that time,' Torrey tells us, 'is echoed in a later

Palestinian writing (*Midrash Qoheleth*, 12,12): "Whosoever brings together in his house more than twenty-four books (the canonical scriptures) brings confusion.'" (*The King James Version Defended* by Dr. Edward F. Hills; Chapter 4).

But there are those who maintain that these extra books were part of a so-called Alexandrian Canon, for it was in that city that the Septuagint translation was produced. However, the famous Jewish philosopher, Philo of Alexandria (1st century), although quoting extensively from the Old Testament canon "never once quotes from any apocryphal books" (Archer 1974:73). In addition, the Jewish Aquila version of the Old Testament (early 2nd century), which supplanted the Septuagint, did not contain the Apocrypha." (*The Apocrypha also called Deutero-Canonical Writings* by Lloyd Thomas; http://ftp.iafrica. com/ l/ll/lloyd/ Apocrypha.htm).

Even, Josephus (A.D. 30-100), Jewish historian, explicitly excludes the Apocrypha, both by his count of the canonical books and his statement that <u>from the time of Malachi no further canonical writings were composed</u>, although records were kept - "*because the exact succession of the prophets ceased*" and "*no one has dared to add anything to them, or take anything from them, or alter anything in them.*" I also want to point out that the Jewish scholars of Jamnia (A.D. 70) did not recognize the Apocrypha. <u>No canon or council of the Church for the first four centuries recognized the Apocrypha as inspired</u>. Many, but not all, of the great church Fathers of the early church spoke out against the Apocrypha or confirm the exclusion of the Apocrypha by their count of the Old Testament books. Included are Athanasius, Cyril of Jerusalem, Bishop Melito of Sardis (170 A.D.), Tertullian, and Hilary of Poitiers.

So, why was the Apocrypha included in the early English Bibles? One key reason is that it was because of pressure by the Roman Catholic Church. Yet, we need to go way back to Jerome, translator of the Latin Vulgate in 405 A.D. for the answer. <u>He counseled that those books not available in Hebrew Canon were to be reckoned among the apocryphal writings</u>. Jerome at first refused even to translate the Apocryphal books into Latin, but later he made a hurried translation of a few of them. While he did include some of them in his translation, he noted that <u>they should not be used to establish doctrine</u>. In an article titled, *The Old Testament Canon,*

the author says, "Jerome produced the standard Latin translation of the Bible, the Vulgate, and he felt that it was important for this purpose that he learn Hebrew. He discovered the opinion of the Jews in the matter of the canon, the falsity of the legend of the translation of the LXX (Septuagint), and as a result made many disparaging remarks about the disputed books, calling them *apocrypha*."
(*The Old Testament Canon;* http://www.columbia.edu/cu/augustine/arch/sbrandt/canon.htm; section 3.2).

In fact, "after his death, and literally 'over his dead body,' the Apocryphal books were brought into his Latin Vulgate translation directly from the Old Latin Version." (*Outlines on Church History:The Collection of the Old Testament Scriptures - The Canon;* http://thechristian.org/church_history/ot_history.html; p.2).

You should know another thing. The *Way of Life Bible Encyclopedia* by David Cloud *says,* "Some Apocryphal books, though written as history, are actually fiction. This is a form of deception not found in divinely inspired books of the Bible. 'Ostensibly historical but actually quite imaginative are the books of Tobit, Judith, Susanna, and Bel and the Dragon, which may be called moralistic novels' (Oxford Annotated Apocrypha, p. xi). Noteworthy examples of ancient fiction they might be, but such books have absolutely no place among the seven-times purified Word of God **(Psalm 12:6-7)**."

At this point I want to share with you some information from an interesting little book I recently purchased called *The Scholastic History of The Canon of The Holy Scripture* written in 1657 by Dr. John Cosin of Cambridge University. The focus of this book is to make it clear to the Christian Church that the Apocrypha was not and is not a part of Holy Scripture. In the introduction, he begins by listing the books that make up the 39 books of our Old Testament.

Then he moves to the Apocryphal books next. He says, "...the other Books (as Jerome saith) the Church doth read for Example of Life, and Instruction of Manners; but yet doth it not apply them to establish Doctrine." Dr. Cosin then lists fourteen Apocryphal books. Finally he says, "All the Books of the New Testament, as they are commonly received, we do receive and accept them CANONICAL."

Next, the good Doctor cites Rome's, so-called, *"The New Canon of Scripture First set forth by The Councel of Trent, And after confirmed, and declared to be received with other Articles of Faith by BULLS of Pope PIUS the IV. Anno Dom. MDLX* (1560). (Note: I have kept the capitalization, wording and spelling as it appears in the original).

Both the Trent and the Pope declared anyone who rejected the Apocrypha as a part of the Bible's Canon *"Anathema"* or *"Damno...Anathematizo."* That simply means permanently condemned and damned to Hell.

From this point on, in the interest of easier reading, I have largely conformed the spelling to our modern standard but have, for the most part, left the capitalization as it appears in the book.

In his address "To the Reader" Dr. Cosin explains his purpose in writing this 225 page book. He says, and I quote...

> "In this Scholastical History I give an account of the Canonical and undubitate (not to be doubted) Books of Holy Scripture, as they are numbered in the VI Article of Religion set forth by the Church of England, and have been received by the Catholic Church in all several Ages since the time of the Apostles, till the Church of Rome thought fit to compose and dress up a New Additional Canon thereof for themselves in their late Council of Trent where it was one of the first things they did, to lay this Foundation for all their New Religion which they built upon it; That the Apocryphal Writings and Traditions of Men were nothing inferior, nor less Canonical, than the Sovereign Dictates of God as well for the Confirmation of Doctrinal Points pertaining to the Faith, as the ordering of Life and Manners; by that both One and the Other ought to be embraced with the same Affection of Piety, and received with the like religious Reverence; not making any difference between them.
>
> Those Writings of holy and learned men, who have been, next after the Prophets and Apostles, as the Shining Lights of the world in their Several Generations before us, we reverence and honor in their kind; and those Ecclesiastical

Traditions, which have been in use among us, and tend to the better preservation of Order and Piety in that Religion only which was once delivered to the Saints, we acknowledge and receive, as far as their own variable Nature and Condition requireth, with all due regard; but to make either of these Equal in Dignity or Authority with the Divine will and Word of God, as the Masters of the Assembly at Trent have done; and above all this, to Canonize a Tradition, which was not so much as a Tradition received in their own Church before, (as will appear by this present History,) nevertheless commanding it to be received as a necessary article of Faith, under the pain of their unhallowed Curse, and the Peril of damnation, this is so high and transcendent a presumption, as that God himself hath laid his Curse upon it; whereof it concerns them to take heed, least what they have vainly laid upon others, do not effectually reach to themselves, and fall on their own heads.

But, after this manner they began to set up their first doctrinal Tradition, in their last Council, at Trent; which they call an Oecumenical (Ecumenical) Council, as if all the Bishops in Christendom had been there present and voted in it; when it is well known, that the same time, wherein this their Additional Canon of Scripture was first made, (which was then done chiefly by the procurement of Catharin, and his Faction there, whose credit had otherwise been quite lost, having been much impaired already be his former and fierce opposition herein against the Writings of Cardinal Cajetan, the far more learned and Catholic Doctor of the two), it consisted not above fifty persons in all; among whom some of them were only Prelates Titular, and hired with pensions to serve the present turn.

And the rest of their Traditions that follow, (wherein now consisteth the very Life and Being of their particular and proper Religion, that differeth from Ours, and the true Catholic Religion of every Church, and every Age before them) having been confirmed by Pope Pius his Bull, and made so many New Articles of their Faith, (as the former was) are all alike.

As first (of these "New Doctrines" of Rome) –

That the Church of Rome is the MOTHER and Mistress of all other Churches; which is not only said Against the Truth of all Ecclesiastical History, and the public Declaration of an ancient General Council (the Second among the first four) received and approved by all good Christians but likewise against the expressed words of the Gospel it self (he notes Luke 24:47 in the footnotes), and against the common sense and knowledge of all persons that can but read or hear it.

That the Pope of Rome is the Monarch or Head of the Universal Visible Church, the Vicar of Deputy of Christ, and in that Sovereign Authority the true Successor of St. Peter, as Prince of the Apostles; by virtue whereof his Papal Determinations and Prescriptions are to be obeyed, in what matter so ever he shall be pleased to declare himself. I will not now mention the infamous Power, (that otherwhiles he hath assumed to himself), of deposing a just and lawful King of his rightful Inheritance; or of freeing his natural and sworn Subjects of their Bond of Faith and Allegiance towards him; (which are Dictates of Pope Hildebrand); But I note only at present the Authority he assumed over the Scripture of God (the Subject of all our History), which He and his Followers make to be greater than any those Scriptures have; for it is another of the same Pope's Dictates, confirmed by the Bull of Pius the IV in his Profession of the Tridentine Faith, 'That the Canonical Scriptures themselves shall be no Canonical Scriptures, unless he gives them Authority and Allowance so to be.' Which is to say, that when he pleaseth, he may take away all Authority from them.

Then, 'That all Scripture are to be expounded according to the Sense of this Roman Church; which must herein be held to be the only Judge; and to follow the unanimous consent of the Ancient Fathers.'

Next, that there are truly and properly Seven Sacraments, neither more nor less, instituted by Christ himself in the New Testament.

That in their Mass there is Real Transubstantiation of the Elements into the Body and Blood of Christ, remaining after Communion is done; and likewise a proper and propitiatory Sacrifice there offered up by the Priest for the Sinners of the Quick and the Dead, [is] the same that Christ offered upon the Cross.

That when the Priest receiveth the Sacrament alone, and when he giveth to others but under one kind only, (the bread only) yet it is lawful, and a complete Communion, notwithstanding that our Savior otherwise appointed it.

That after this Life there is a penal Purgatory to be undone for the Expiation as well of venial Sins, as the payment of temporal punishment due to mortal sins; as the payment of temporal punishments due to mortal sins; and that dead men's souls there detained are helped by the Suffrages of the Living, and the saying of Masses.

That the Saints above heaven (or any whom shall be the Popes pleasure to Canonize) ought to be religiously invocated (prayed to); and that they understand as well the minds as the words of those that pray to them.

That Whosoever will not fall down before Relics and Images, to kiss and worship them according to the present practice of the Church of Rome, and the Decrees of the Second Council at Nice, are to be accursed and damned.

That the penalty power and present use of Indulgences, was ordained and left by Christ in his Church, which anciently put the same into practice; and that the denial hereof ought to be anathemized.

And lastly, That all Definitions, Decrees, Canons, and Declarations made in their former Councils, and especially in this their Council of Trent, ought to be wholly and inviolately, undoubtedly and devoutly professed, taught, preached, and received as the true Catholic Faith, out of which none can be saved.

But, all these New Traditions, as they have no ground in the Scripture, so have they as little Testimony of Antiquity to be brought for them; out of both which we prescribe against them all.

The truth and strength of which their assertions, in one of their peculiar and prime Traditions, first set forth in their late Assembly at Trent, I examine in this History. Whereby I trust it will be made manifest to the Reader, That those Men, who do now so busily endeavor to seduce the Sons and Daughters of the Church of England for the Grounds of Truth of our Religion, which is no other than that we have received from Christ and his Universal Church, termed nevertheless by them a New Church, and a New Religion, that began in the days of King Henry VIII (which is as true, as if they should say, a sick person began then first to live, when he recovered from the disease and distemper that was before upon him; for we are the same Church still, [as he the same person] that we were before, though in a better estate and health of our souls, in greater soundness and purity of Religion, then indeed we were before when they had to do with it, and instructed us); Novelists, are in themselves the greatest Novelists of any in the world besides: And must be content (both in this peculiar Article of their Religion, which we now set forth and examine through the several Ages of the Church, and likewise in others, which we may, by the Grace of God, examine in the like manner hereafter), to come behind in time, after divers of those Novelists, and disturbers of true Religion, that now bear vogue among us.

It is a matter of Fact this, that is here tried, which may be put to a Jury of Twelve Men, that have no lawful Exception to be taken against them; but I give them more, and put it to many such, one after another; that there may be no want which in such case, as this is, will be the fairest way of Trial to find out the Truth, and leave the Reader to judge of it, on whose side it standeth.

In gathering my Witnesses together, and Collecting this Scholastic History, I must acknowledge to owe somewhat unto those learned Men, that have heretofore taken pains in this behalf, as well at home in our own Church, as abroad in others. Yet (let it be said without derogation for any of them), this Book hath been judged, by Him that first requested me to make it a part of my employment, (though he was a person well able to have more perfectly done it himself), and by other Men of knowledge, (Professors of true Religion and Learning), who have read it after him, and many time moved him to commit it to the Press; that it would give more ample satisfaction, and clear the passages in Antiquity from the Objections that some late Authors on the Roman side bring against us, then those other Writings of Home and Foreign Divines have done, that are extant in this kind. For besides the whole frame and order of the Book, insisting upon the right and best way of inquiry into this matter by the Historical Disquisition of the Universal Tradition and Testimony of God's Church herein unanimously delivered in all Ages form the Apostles Times (and before) to ours; My Observations as I passed along both through the Ancient and Latter Writers that I have said any thing of this subject, are many of them New; and where I have followed others, even there also I have added much of my own, to advance and manifest the Truth in them; having no other aim than herein to be serviceable to the Truth of God, set forth and professed by the Church of England; which Truth we endeavor, in these wavering and lapsing times, to preserve entire and upright among us.

My Discourse is continued, and not interrupted with quotations of Authors, which I have diligently searched, and placed, all the way, in the margin. The language that I use, is familiar, clear, and inoffensive, (which I trust will make it the more acceptable), for I neither , nor approve any other.

But if I may unwittingly have said anything, that shall be found to disagree either with any passage in the Holy Scriptures, or with the consent of Antiquity in the sense and Interpretation of those Scriptures, (which yet, I hope will, will not be found), I do here beforehand revoke and unsay it already.

At my Retirement in Paris this 17 Feb. 1657"

The remainder of the book moves to prove that there is no credible early church support for the Apocrypha being a part of the canon of the Scripture.

I will share just several brief examples.

102 A.D. - Clement the first – Rome called him Pope Clement. They quote him on "other matters" yet when he lists what is in the Canon of Scripture he does not include "Tobit and Judith, or any other of the books that are now in question." In fact, "there is no mention at all, which is a sign, that in those days they were to be no Canonical Parts of the Scripture."

157 A.D. - Polcrates – "Before St John died, (who died the last of all the Apostles), the Canon of the Scriptures was made perfect and delivered over to the Christian Church. Diverse years before his death he had made chief abode about Ephesus, and Sardis, and the other Churches in Asia, to which he wrote when he was banished into the Isle of Patmos by the Emperor Domitian. From this Banishment he was released by Nerva in the year of our Lord 97, and about three years after he quietly ended his days. It happened about 60 years from that time of his decease, there was some question made, by certain men that came and lived in those quarters, concerning the exact number of the Canonical Books of Scripture. For resolution herein Melito, who was then Bishop of Sardis (a man famous and venerable in his time, and of whom Polycrates the Metropolitan Bishop of Ephesus gave this honorable Testimony, that he was led and guided, in all things he did, by the Holy Ghost." He then lists all the books of the Old Testament and NONE of the Apocryphal books.

164 A.D. - Justin Martyr – "In all his works (he) citeth not so much as any one passage out of the Apocryphal Books, nor maketh the least mention of them all."

222 A.D. - Julius Africanus – Writes "eight several Arguments (where) he endeavoreth to prove it (the Apocryphal book of Susanna) a fable.

Some have asked me, "Is there any comment about the Apocrypha which was in the KJV 1611?" Alexander McClure, who was a biographer of the KJV translators, writes: "...the Apocryphal books in those times were more read and accounted of than now, though by no means placed on a level with the canonical books of Scripture" (*Translators Revived*, Alexander McClure, p. 185). He then lists several reasons assigned by the KJV translators for rejecting the Apocrypha as inspired.

The Thirty-nine Articles of the Church of England clearly states that the Apocrypha have no scriptural authority.

"...[the Church of England] doth not apply to them to establish any doctrine."

The Westminster Confession says, "The books commonly called Apocrypha, not being of divine inspiration, are no part of the canon of the Scripture; and therefore are of no authority in the Church of God, nor to be any otherwise approved, or made use of, than other human writings."

Luther included a note on the Apocrypha which stated, "These are books not to be held in equal esteem with those of Holy Scripture..."

So, returning to the question posed earlier: Why was the Apocrypha included in the early translations of the English Bible? **First**, the Roman Catholic influence played a major part. **Secondly**, the Apocrypha was considered to be of some literary and historical value. Some of the books do fill in some of the 400-year gap between the end of the Old Testament and the beginning of the New Testament.

WHY MANY REJECT THE APOCRYPHA

Despite the Roman Catholic decree at Council of Trent in 1546 which declares everyone anathema, (cursed or condemned to destruction) who *"does not accept* as *sacred and canonical the aforesaid books* (the Apocrypha) *in their entirety and with all their parts"* there are solid biblical reasons for rejecting them. Here are just a few.

1. As I have already mentioned, they are not included in the original Hebrew Old Testament preserved by the Jews. Therefore, it is

believed that God guided them in the rejection of the Apocryphal books from the canon of Scripture because, as we have seen, God had appointed the Jews as custodians of the Old Testament.

2. The New Testament churches did not receive them as inspired Scripture during the first four centuries after Christ. Here's why that is important. The Bible says in John 16:13 *Howbeit when he, the Spirit of truth, is come, he will guide you into all truth...* The Holy Spirit did not guide the Apostolic and Early New Testament Church to regard the Apocrypha as the inspired Word of God because it was not!

3. The Apocrypha contain teachings wholly contrary to the other books of the Bible. II Maccabees teaches <u>praying to the dead</u> and <u>making offering to atone for the sins of the dead</u>. Consider this quote from II Maccabees 12:43-45: He also took up a collection... and sent it to Jerusalem to provide for a sin offering...For if he were not expecting that those who had fallen asleep would arise again, it would have been superfluous <u>and</u> <u>foolish to pray for the dead...</u> Therefore <u>he made atonement for the dead,</u> that they might be delivered from their sin.

The Roman Catholic Church uses the above passage as support for purgatory. They teach that the faithful on earth can be of great help to persons who have died and are undergoing purgatory by offering for them the sacrifice of the Mass, prayers, almsgiving, and other religious deeds. STOP! That is not what the Bible teaches! <u>Consider the following questions and answer them.</u>

WHAT IS THE ONLY OFFERING THAT GOD WILL RECEIVE FOR SIN?

Hebrews 10:10-14 *By the which will we are sanctified through the offering of the body of Jesus Christ once for all. 11 And every priest standeth daily ministering and offering oftentimes the same sacrifices, which can never take away sins: 12 But this man, after he had offered one sacrifice for sins for ever, sat down on the right hand of God; 13 From henceforth expecting till his enemies be made his footstool. 14 For by one offering he hath perfected for ever them that are sanctified.*

1 Peter 3:18 *For Christ also hath once suffered for sins, the just for the unjust, that he might bring us to God, being put to death in the flesh, but quickened by the Spirit:*

It is only through Christ Jesus that atonement is made! **Romans 5:11** says," *And not only so, but we also joy in God through our Lord Jesus Christ, by whom we have now received the atonement."*

WHERE DO THE SAVED DEAD GO WHEN THEY DIE?

They do not go to purgatory; they go immediately to be with the Lord**. 2 Corinthians 5:6-8** points this out! *Therefore we are always confident, knowing that, whilst we are at home in the body, we are absent from the Lord: 7 (For we walk by faith, not by sight:) 8 We are confident, I say, and willing rather to be absent from the body, and to be present with the Lord." (See* also Philippians 1:20-23)

WHERE DO THE UNSAVED GO WHEN THEY DIE?

They do not go to purgatory; they go to Hades (Hell). **Luke 16:19-31** makes that very clear. There are no second chances after death. Those who do not believe on Christ are "*condemned already*" (**John 3:18**). **John 3:36** adds, *"He that believeth on the Son hath everlasting life: and he that believeth not the Son <u>shall</u> <u>not</u> <u>see life</u>: but the wrath of God abideth on him."*

Neither praying for the dead, nor saying masses for the dead will change the state of the ones who have died, You can pray for departed loved ones till you are blue in the face and spend every last penny you possess to get a priest to say masses for the dead but that will not change the eternal state of those who are unsaved. It will not even get them a cup of cold water in Hell.

Maccabees is not the only book with problems. There are major problems with the book of Tobit as well. Here are some of the problems.

THE ANGEL RAPHAEL TEACHES SORCERY & MAGIC WHICH GOD FORBIDS

Tobit 6:4,6-8 "Then the angel said to him, Cut open the fish and take the heart and liver and gall and put them away ... Then the young man said to the angel, Brother Azatias, of what use is the liver and heart and gall of the fish? He replied, As for the heart and the liver, if a demon or evil spirit gives trouble to any one, you make a smoke from these before the man or woman, and that person will never be troubled again. And as for the gall, anoint with it a man who has white films in his eyes, and he will be cured." What the angel suggests is nothing other than occult magic, which the Lord forbids! Deuteronomy 13:10-12 and Jeremiah 27:9 makes that clear.

TOBIT TEACHES THE FALSE DOCTRINE OF SALVATION BY WORKS

Tobit 12:9 "For almsgiving delivers from death, and it will purge away every sin."
Tobit 14:11 "So now, my children, consider what almsgiving accomplishes and how righteousness delivers."

Teaching that alleges that giving, or any other works, purges sin is inconsistent with the Bible. The Word of God says -**1 Peter 1:13-19** *"Wherefore gird up the loins of your mind, be sober, and hope to the end for the grace that is to be brought unto you at the revelation of Jesus Christ; 14 As obedient children, not fashioning yourselves according to the former lusts in your ignorance: 15 But as he which hath called you is holy, so be ye holy in all manner of conversation; 16 Because it is written, Be ye holy; for I am holy. 17And if ye call on the Father, who without respect of persons judgeth according to every man's work, pass the time of your sojourning here in fear: 18 Forasmuch as ye know that ye were not redeemed with corruptible things, as silver and gold, from your vain conversation received by tradition from your fathers; 19 But with the precious blood of Christ, as of a lamb without blemish and without spot:"*

Titus 3:5 *"Not by works of righteousness which we have done, but according to his mercy he saved us, by the washing of regeneration, and renewing of the Holy Ghost;"*

I could go on, but I will just point out one last example. The book of Judith contains the account of how a so-called godly widow destroyed one of Nebuchadnezzar's generals through deceit and sexual offers. It is also important to note that Judith's counsel regarding resisting Nebuchadnezzar was contrary to that given by God's prophet Jeremiah (see **Jeremiah 38:14**). God warned the Israelites to submit to Nebuchadnezzar rather than to resist, because the Babylonian captivity and destruction of Israel was a judgment from God upon the Jew's rebellion and idolatry.

In conclusion, there is clear evidence that the Apocryphal books are not inspired of the Lord. Neither Christ nor the apostles ever quoted from them, though they did quote from every other part of the Old Testament Scriptures. While there may be some historical value in some of the Apocryphal writings, they should not be considered inspired despite the decree of the Council of Trent and the inclusion of these books in almost all the early English versions of the Bible. Many of the Protestant Reformers warned that they were not on the level of the Bible and the Westminster Confession codified the Apocrypha's diminished value when it says, as I mentioned earlier, "The books commonly called Apocrypha, not being of divine inspiration, are no part of the canon of the Scripture; and therefore are of no authority in the Church of God, nor to be any otherwise approved, or made use of, than other human writings."

An increasing number of the modern versions of the Bible have included the Apocrypha and more will follow that perilous path in the future.

CHAPTER #3

THE GREEK NEW TESTAMENT CANON

Adysh Gospels Canon List

A - THE GREEK NEW TESTAMENT CANON - Ω

As the foundation of our Old Testament in the English Bible is the Hebrew Masoretic text, so the foundation of our New Testament of the English Bible is the Greek Traditional Text. I will briefly define the word **canon**, share my belief on **canonicity** and then we will consider the gathering and preservation of the New Testament Canon.

THE WORD "CANON" DEFINED

The word "**canon**" is of Christian origin, from the Greek word κανών, (kan-ohn; Strongs #2583). But, it was probably borrowed from the Hebrew word, קָנֶה, (kaw-neh'; Strongs #7070), meaning <u>a reed or measuring rod</u>, hence, norm or rule. Later "*canon*" came to mean <u>a rule of faith</u>, and eventually a catalog or listing. In **present usage** it signifies <u>a collection of religious writings inspired of God and hence, authoritative, normative, sacred and binding</u>. The Greek term occurs in **Galatians 6:16** – "*And as many as walk according to <u>this rule</u>, peace be on them, and mercy, and upon the Israel of God.*" It is also used in **2 Corinthians 10:13-16** (key verse 15). I should point out that "it is first employed of the books of Scripture, in the technical sense of a standard collection or body of sacred writings, by the church Fathers of the 4th century; one example is seen in the 59th canon of the Council of Laodicea (363 AD); in the Festal Epistle of Athanasius (365 AD); and by Amphilochius, archbishop of Iconium (395 AD). Yet, many years before it was given the official name "**canon**," the concept of "**canon**" was in place." (International Standard Bible Encyclopedia edited by James Orr, M.A., D.D.; the section on the canon)

MY VIEW OF CANONICITY

I hold to the conservative, non-higher critical view of canonicity. Those who hold this view believe **God established His canon, it was not established by "The Church."** The canon of Scripture does not derive its authority from the church, whether Jewish (Old Testament) or Christian (New Testament); but the office of the church merely recognized what God inspired. The church then became a witness and a custodian of what God ordained. In 1902 Dr. W. H. Green explained it this way: "No formal declaration of their canonicity was needed to give them (the books of the Bible) sanction. They were from the first not only eagerly read by the devout but believed to be Divinely obligatory....Each individual book of an acknowledged prophet of Yahweh, or of anyone accredited as inspired by Him to make known His will, was accepted as the Word of God immediately upon its appearance.... Those books and those only were accepted as the Divine standards of their faith and regulative of their conduct, which were written for this definite purpose by those whom they believed to be inspired of God.

It was this, which made them canonical. The spiritual profit found in them corresponded with and confirmed the belief in their heavenly origin. And <u>the public official action which further attested, though it did not initiate, their canonicity</u>, followed in the wake of the popular recognition of their Divine authority....The writings of the prophets, delivered to the people as a declaration of the Divine will, possessed canonical authority from the moment of their appearance....<u>The canon does not derive its authority from the church, whether Jewish or Christian; the office of the church is merely that of a custodian and a witness.</u>" (Underlining not in the original but added - *Pres. and Ref. Review*, April, 1902, p.182).

PRE-NEW TESTAMENT CANON

The New Testament Church was born on the Day of Pentecost, 50 days after the death of Christ (and Passover) around 36 A.D. We read about this in **Acts 2**. We know from the record that about 3,000 people received Christ as Savior on that day and were biblically baptized. In those early days the apostles, by their oral teachings, were the ones that guided the church. **Acts 2:42a** says, *"And they continued steadfastly in the apostles doctrine."*

The apostles were the ones who preached *Jesus*. **Acts 4:33** records, *"And with great power gave the apostles witness of the resurrection of the Lord Jesus: and great grace was upon them all."* When there were questions of major consequence concerning the doctrine and practice of the church they would send representatives to the apostles to clarify the matter (see **Acts 15:1-11**). God called others to advance the Christian faith as well. Paul encountered the risen Lord Jesus Christ on the Damascus Road (**Acts 9**) and was called to take the Gospel *to* the Gentiles (**Romans 1:13**).

Few people realize that **for the first 10 to 20 years of the Church's existence they had no New Testament writings**. The apostles taught what they had personally learned from the Lord Jesus. When the Disciples of Christ witnessed, they did so based on what they had learned from the apostles. In preaching, the Old Testament was used, bringing in Jesus' fulfillment of it. In other words, the Old Testament was interpreted Christologically (in light of Christ). A good example is found in **Acts 8:26-39**. **Isaiah 53 formed the basis of Philip's message**.

The New Church grew in numbers. As the time passed, the apostles, eye witnesses, and early disciples began to die, often by martyrdom. **The Holy Spirit moved on their hearts to leave a written record for future generations**. The Apostle John notes this in **John 20:30-31**. He wrote, *"And many other signs truly did Jesus in the presence of his disciples, which are not written in this book: 31 But these are written, that ye might believe that Jesus is the Christ, the Son of God; and that believing ye might have life through his name."*

I think it is important to note that neither the Gospels nor the New Testament is a comprehensive view of all the works of Jesus Christ, his disciples and the early church. We know this from what John wrote in **John 21:25**, *"And there are also many other things which Jesus did, the which, if they should be written every one, I suppose that even the world itself could not contain the books that should be written. Amen."*

So, what is included in the New Testament Canon is exactly what the Lord wanted included. It was written under His inspiration. Here is why I point that out. No doubt, the apostles, Paul and other disciples of Christ wrote other letters that were not included in the New Testament Canon because they were not inspired of God. What has come to be included in the New Testament Canon is inspired of God, as we shall see.

THE DEVELOPMENT OF THE NEW TESTAMENT CANON

Early New Testament Church history has left us with no exact record regarding how the New Testament Canon was formed. But, I will share the bits and pieces that are known. One thing I do know is this. The Lord Jesus Christ promised that the Holy Spirit would guide His disciples into all truth (**John 16:13**), and bring all things to remembrance so that they could accurately record what Christ deemed should be recorded (**John 14:26**). We know that is exactly what He did, though I must admit, we do not know all of the exact details of just how that transpired. True believers had the witness of the Holy Spirit to guide them in knowing which books were Holy Scripture and which were not. As we shall see, gradually all of the 27 New Testament books were collected and recognized by God's true Church.

Look at this chart. The first New Testament books penned were written by Paul - Galatians, 1 & 2 Thessalonians, 1 & 2 Corinthians and Romans. These were personal letters written to the churches that Paul had established on his three missionary trips. They were written between 49 and 58 A.D. Look further down on the chart. The last book written was Revelation, written somewhere just before the turn of the century (in the 90's A.D.).

I have included chart 2, *"Canon Lists of the New Testament from Early Times"* which I will be referencing in the section immediately following the chart, which is called **"Collecting the Letters."**

The New Testament Books Arranged
According To
The Time They Were Written

There is a dispute among scholars as to the dates the New Testament books were written. The dates in the chart reflect dates conservative Bible scholars believe the books were written.

BOOK	DATE WRITTEN	AUTHOR
GALATIANS	49 AD after the 1st missionary journey	Paul - Gal. 1:1
1 THESSALONIANS	50-51 AD after the 2nd missionary journey	Paul - 1 Thes. 1:1 & 2:18
2 THESSALONIANS	51 AD after the 2nd missionary journey	Paul - 2 Thes. 3:17
1 CORINTHIANS	54 or 56 AD	Paul - 1 Cor. 1:1 & 16:21

	during the 3rd missionary journey	
2 CORINTHIANS	55 or 57 AD during the 3rd missionary journey	Paul - 2 Cor. 1:1 & 10:1
ROMANS	55 or 58 AD during the 3rd missionary journey	Paul - Romans 1:1
JAMES: Not the Apostle James who was martyred 44 AD	45-50 AD	James, half-brother of our Lord - James 1:1
MARK	50's AD	John Mark
PHILEMON	60 or 61 AD	Paul - Philemon 1:1 & 19
COLOSSIANS	60 or 61 AD	Paul - Col. 1:1 & 4:18
EPHESIANS	60 or 61 AD	Paul - Eph. 1:1
LUKE	60 AD	Luke
ACTS	61 AD	Luke
PHILIPPIANS	61 AD	Paul - Phil. 1:1
1 TIMOTHY	62-63 AD	Paul - 1 Tim. 1:1
2 TIMOTHY	63 AD	Paul - 2 Tim. 1:1
MATTHEW	Mid 60's	Matthew Levi
TITUS	65 AD	Paul - Titus 1:1
1 PETER	65 AD	Peter - 1 Pet. 1:1
2 PETER	66 AD	Peter - 2 Pet. 1:1
HEBREWS	64-68 AD	Uncertain - traditionally Paul
JUDE	70-80's AD	Jude, half-brother of Jesus - Jude 1:1
JOHN	85-90 AD	John the Apostle
1 JOHN	90 AD	John the Apostle
2 JOHN	90 AD	John the Apostle
3 JOHN	90 AD	John the Apostle
REVELATION	90's AD	John the Apostle - Rev. 1:1, 4, 9; 21:2; 22:8

CANON LISTS OF THE NEW TESTAMENT FROM EARLY TIMES

White blocks: The book is not listed
Shaded blocks: The book was used.
Black blocks: The book is listed.

DATE	MARCION 140 AD	IRENAEUS 180 AD (See note 2)	MURATORIAN CANON 177 AD	EUSEBIUS 325 AD	ATHANASIUS 367 AD
MATTHEW			Note 3		
MARK			Note 4		
LUKE					
JOHN					
ACTS					
ROMANS					
1 CORIN.					
2 CORIN.					
GALATIANS					
EPHESIANS	Note 1				
PHILIPPIANS					
COLOSSIANS					
1 THESS.					
2 THESS.					
1 TIMOTHY					
2 TIMOTHY					
TITUS					
PHILEMON					
HEBREWS					
JAMES		?			
1 PETER					
2 PETER					
1 JOHN					
2 JOHN					
3 JOHN					
JUDE					
REVELATION				Note 5	
Shepherd of Hermes					

Wisdom of Solomon			■		
Revelation of Peter			■		

Note 1 – Maricon called this book **Laodiceans**

Note 2 – Compiled from references in Irenaeus' writings

Note 3 – In this list, the first two Gospels are missing, but Luke is called the 3rd Gospel so we assume Matthew is the first.

Note 4 – In this list, the first two Gospels are missing, but Luke is called the 3rd Gospel so we assume Mark is the second.

Note 5 – Eusebius says Revelation was still disputed in his time.

COLLECTING THE LETTERS

"At a very early period, probably before the end of the first, or the beginning of the second century, the books of the New Testament were collected into one volume, having before this been used separately as they were severally written, or could be procured in the different Churches." (*The Evidences of the Divine Origin, Preservation, Credibility and Inspiration of the Holy Scriptures* by S. Austin Alliborne; American Sunday School Union - 1871; p.21)

Early Christian letters, in fact, were the first documents distributed as collections. We find a trace of this in the New Testament itself. At the end of Peter's second letter, we read, *"And account that the longsuffering of our Lord is salvation; even as our beloved brother Paul also according to the wisdom given unto him hath written unto you; 16 As also in all his epistles, speaking in them of these things..."* **2 Peter 3:15-16**. This statement presupposes a collection of Paul's letters by about 66 A.D., since that is around the date that Peter wrote his second letter.

In 95 A.D., **Clement of Rome** wrote a letter in the name of the Christians of Rome to those at Corinth. In this letter he uses material found in Matthew and Luke, giving it a free rendering; he had been much influenced by the Epistle to the Hebrews. He knows Romans, Corinthians, and there are found echoes of 1 Timothy, Titus, 1 Peter and Ephesians.

The Epistles of Ignatius (115 A.D.) have correspondences with our gospels in several places (**Ephesians 5; Romans 6; 7**) and incorporate language from nearly all of the Pauline epistles. "*The Epistle to Polycarp* makes large use of Philippians, and besides this cites nine of the other Pauline epistles. Ignatius quotes from Matthew, apparently from memory; also from 1 Peter and 1 John. In regard to all these three writers—Clement, Polycarp, Ignatius—it is not enough to say that they bring us reminiscences or quotations from this or that book. Their thought is tinctured all through with New Testament truth." (*International Standard Bible Encyclopedia*; edited by Dr. James Orr; vol.1, p.564)

Quite early the desire to have the benefit of all possible Christian instruction led to the interchange of Christian writings. **Polycarp**, who lived about 110 A.D., writes to the Philippians, "I have received letters from you and from Ignatius. You recommend me to send on yours to Syria; I shall do so either personally or by some other means. In return I send you the letter of Ignatius as well as others which I have in my hands and for which you made request. I add them to the present one; they will serve to edify your faith and perseverance" (Epistle to Philippians, XIII).

This is an illustration of what must have happened toward furthering the knowledge of the writings of the apostles. "Just when and to what extent 'collections' of our New Testament books began to be made it is impossible to say, but it is fair to infer that a collection of the Pauline epistles existed at the time Polycarp wrote to the Philippians and when Ignatius wrote his seven letters to the churches of Asia Minor, i.e. about 115 A.D. There is good reason to think also that the four Gospels were brought together in some places as early as this." (*International Standard Bible Encyclopedia*; edited by Dr. James Orr; vol.1, p.564).

Next we come to **Justin Martyr**. It is during his lifetime that the beginning of the formation of the New Testament Canon is in position and authority given to the Gospels. Justin was born about 100 A.D. at Shechem, and died as a martyr at Rome in 165 A.D. His two Apologies and the Dialogue with Trypho are the sources for the study of his testimony. He speaks of the "Memoirs of the Apostles called Gospels" (*Apology.*, i.66) which were read on Sunday interchangeably with the prophets (i.67). Here emerges that equivalence in value of these "Gospels" with the Old Testament Scriptures, which may really mark the beginning of canonization. Whether these Gospels were our four Gospels as we now have them is yet a disputed question in the minds of some scholars, but the evidence is weighty that they were. (See Purves, *Testimony of Justin Martyr to Early Christianity*, Lect V.) What is interesting to note is that Tatian, one of Justin's pupils, made a harmony of the Gospels, i.e. of our four Gospels. Therefore, it is reasonable to assume that Justin's "Memoirs of the Apostles called Gospels" were indeed Matthew, Mark, Luke and John (see *The Diatessaron of Tatian;* Hemphill.) I should note that Justin also mentions the Apocalypse (Revelation); but he appears to have known the Acts, six epistles of Paul, Hebrews and 1 John, and echoes of still other epistles are perceptible. When he speaks of the apostles it is after this fashion: "By the power of God they proclaimed to every race of men that they were sent by Christ to teach to all the Word of God" (*Apology*, i.39).

Next in the development of the New Testament Canon we come to an "official list" by **Marcion the Gnostic** (85-160 A.D.). "MARCION was a rich shipowner of Sinope, the chief port of Pontus, on the southern shore of the Black Sea; he was also a bishop and the son of a bishop." (*Fragments of a Faith Forgotten;* by G.R.S. Mead; 3rd Edition 1931; p.241). He went to Rome (circa 140 A.D.), and at first he was in communion with the church at Rome, and contributed handsomely to its funds. But, he soon became at odds with the Roman Church and threatened to make a schism. He was excommunicated in 144 A.D. and became a dangerous Gnostic heretic, forming his own church, which became widespread and powerful. In support of his peculiar views, he formed a canon of his own. "He sought truth in his own truncated version of the New Testament, which included only 10 of the so-called Pauline Epistles and an edited version of St. Luke. He completely rejected the Old Testament. He explained in his *Antitheses* that since Jewish law was often opposed to St. Paul, all passages in the Bible that suggested the Jewish foundation of Christianity should be suppressed, even including such statements by St. Paul." (*The Columbia Encyclopedia*, Fifth Edition, Columbia University Press). Marcion's importance for us is twofold. He gives us the first clear evidence of the canonization of the Pauline epistles and secondly, he caused orthodox Christianity to clarify its canon.

By the time we come to the year 170 A.D., there is no longer any question as to a New Testament Canon; the only difference of judgment is as to its extent. **Irenaeus** is a good representation of these last years of the 2nd century. He has an apostolic connection as well, in that he was a pupil of Polycarp, who was a disciple of the Apostle John. Irenaeus was born in Asia Minor, lived and taught in Rome and finally became the bishop of Lyons. Because he had a wide acquaintance with the churches, he was uniquely competent to speak concerning the general judgment of the Christian world. Further, he was an earnest defender of "the faith which was once delivered to the saints," and therefore it is important to note that he makes the New Testament in great part his authority.

The only letters he does not mention or quote from are Philemon, Hebrews, 2 Peter, 2 and 3 John and Jude. He notes that some question whether James should be a part of the canon. Irenaeus dwells upon the fact that there are four gospels and that any attempt to increase or diminish the number is heresy. Tertullian, a contemporary, takes virtually the same position and Clement of Alexandria quotes all four gospels as "Scripture." I point this out to demonstrate that the position of Irenaeus was consistent with other Christian leaders of his time. In fact, by the end of the 2nd century, the canon of the gospels was settled. Matthew, Mark, Luke and John were recognized as the Gospels inspired of God, to the exclusion of the Gospels of Thomas, Nicodemus and James. I would also like to point out that it was Irenaeus who "gives for the first time the order of the four Gospels as we have it today: Matthew, Mark, Luke, and John." (*How We Got Our Bible: Christian History*, Issue *43;* 1997; p.28). The epistles of Paul were also clearly recognized as part of the New Testament Canon. Irenaeus makes more than two hundred citations from Paul, and looks upon his epistles as Scripture.

LVDOVICVS ANTONIVS MVRATORIVS
COLLEGII AMBROSIANI DOCTOR
DEINDE BIBLIOTHECÆ ESTENSI PRÆFECTVS

That brings me to what is called the **Muratorian Canon**. This fragment is named after a librarian from Milan, Italy who came across it while organizing some uncategorized materials. His name was Lodovico Antonia Muratori (1672-1750). In 1740 while organizing some uncatalogued materials he came across a document which is dated to near the end of the 2nd century which gives a list of the New Testament books. The first line of the document is missing, so the list actually begins with Mark (though Matthew is clearly implied). It is believed this list came from Rome and is the work of Hippolytus. This list does not mention Hebrews, James, 1 & 2 Peter and 3 John (though one scholar says 3 John might be implied). "In this list we have virtually the real position of the canon at the close of the 2nd century." (*International Standard Bible Encyclopedia*; vol.1, p.565).

Here is a translation of the Muratorian Canon —

"...at which *point*, he [Markus?] was present and thus set them down.
The third book of the gospel is the one according to Lukas. After the ascension of Christ, this physician Lukas composed it in his own name, since Paulus had taken him with himself as *a traveling companion. He wrote* what he thought, although he himself did not see the Lord physically. Therefore, he set down the events from the birth of John as far as he could ascertain it.

The fourth gospel is that of Johannes, one of the students. When his fellow students and overseers called him aside, he said, "Fast with me for three days from today, and let us relate to one another whatever might be revealed to each of us." During that same night it was revealed to Andreas, one of the envoys, that Johannes would write down in his own name what all of them remembered. [And therefore, although various *different things* are taught in the books of the gospel, this does not mean anything to the trust of believers, since everything is declared in all *of them* by the one and *genuine?* breath--about the birth; about the suffering; about the resurrection; about his discussions with his students; and about his two comings: first hated in humility (which has happened); second glorious with royal power (which is still to come). Why wonder then that Johannes (who was always true to himself) mentions certain points in his letters too, where he says of himself: "What we have seen with our eyes, and our ears heard, and our hands felt...we have written to you." For so he acknowledges *being* not only a witness who saw and heard but also a writer of all of the Lord's wonders, in order.]

Moreover, the Actions of the Envoys are included in one book. Lukas addresses them to the "most excellent Theophilus," the things that happened in his own presence. He makes this clear by the omission of Peter's suffering and of Paulus' journey when he left the city *of Rome* for Spain.

However, as for Paulus' letters: [They make it clear (to those who want to know) whose they are and from what place and why they were written. First of all, to the Korinthians, forbidding divisions by school of thought; then to the Galatians, forbidding circumcision; and then to the Romans, explaining that Christ is both the measure of the writings and also their principle—he wrote *here* at considerable length.]

[It is necessary to deal with these separately, since the blessed envoy himself followed the example of Johannes who preceded him,] and he wrote to not more than seven assemblies, in this order:

> the first to the Korinthians;
> the second to the Ephesians;
> the third to the Filippians;
> the fourth to the Kolossaeans;
> the fifth to the Galatians;
> the sixth to the Thessalonikans;
> the seventh to the Romans.

[Although he wrote one more time to the Korinthians and to the Thessalonikans for their correction, it is clearly recognizable that one assembly has spread across the whole land. For Johannes (in the Revelation) writes indeed to seven assemblies yet is speaking to all.]

He wrote besides these one to Philemon, one to Titus, and two to Timotheos. These were written in personal affection, but they have been *regarded as* holy in honor by the universal assembly, for the ordering of discipline in the assembly.

There are extant also a letter to the Laodiceans, and another to the Alexandrians, forged in Paulus' name to further the school of thought of Markion. And there are many others, which cannot be received into the universal assembly, for "it is not fitting for vinegar to be mixed with honey."

Indeed, the letter of Judah, and two entitled Johannes, are accepted in the universal assembly, along with the Wisdom, written by the friends of Solomon in his honor. We receive also the Revelations of Johannes and Peter, the latter of which some refuse to have read in the assembly.

But the Shepherd was written very recently in our time by Hermas in the city of Rome, when his brother overseer Pius was seated in the chair of the Roman assembly. Therefore indeed, it should be read, but it cannot be read publicly to the people in the assembly-- either *as* among the Prophets (since their number is complete) or among the envoys, to the end of time.

Now we accept nothing at all from Arsinous, or Valentinus and Miltiades, who also wrote a new book of songs for Markion, together with Basilides of Asia Minor, the founder of the Katafrygians." (*The Muratorian Canon;* www.friktech.com/rel/muratori.htm).

At this point I want to make a clarification concerning the term I have used several times in the above materials, and that term is, the "New Testament." The title "New Testament" appears to have been first used by an unknown writer against Montanism about 193 A.D. The term is regularly used by Origen (185-254 A.D.) and later writers.

Next we come to **Eusebius of Caesarea** (260-340 A.D.). "Early in the 4th century Eusebius, as a historian reviews the situation in his

Church History. He makes three classes; **first**, including the Gospels, Acts, Epistles of Paul, 1 Peter, I John is acknowledged; to these if one likes, one may add the Apocalypse (Revelation). The **second class** is questioned, but **accepted by the majority**; James, Jude, 2 Peter, 2 and 3 John. The **third class of works to be decidedly rejected**, contains the Acts of Paul, Hermes, Apocalypse of Peter, Barnabas, Didache..." (*Encyclopedia Britannica - 11th Edition of 1911*; vol. 3; p.887). Carsten Thiede puts it this way, "he is adamant that the Shepherd of Hermas, the Apocalypse of Peter, the Acts of Paul, the Letter of Barnabas and the Didache are 'not genuine,' that is, not of truly apostolic origin." (*How We Got Our Bible: Christian History, Issue 43*, 1997; p. 28).

True believers had the witness of the Holy Spirit to guide them in knowing which books were Holy Scripture and which were not. Gradually all of the 27 New Testament books were collected and recognized by God's saints. By the 4th century, the canon of Scripture was settled. The "frosting on the cake" comes in 367 A.D. when **Athanasius**, Bishop of Alexandria, a well-known defender of the faith, used the opportunity of his annual Easter Festal Letter (a letter to all the churches and monasteries under his jurisdiction) to publish a list of Old Testament and New Testament books which he said were "handed down and believed to be divine." In terms of the New Testament, he listed the same 27 texts we have today.

Here is an excerpt from that letter —

> In proceeding to make mention of these things, I shall adopt, to commend my undertaking, the pattern of Luke the Evangelist, saying on my own account: 'Forasmuch as some have taken in hand(4),' to reduce into order for themselves the books termed apocryphal, and to mix them up with the divinely inspired Scripture, concerning which we have been fully persuaded, as they who from the beginning were eyewitnesses and ministers of the Word, delivered to the fathers; it seemed good to me also, having been urged thereto by true brethren, and having learned from the beginning, to set before you the books included in the Canon, and handed down, and accredited as Divine; to the end that any one who has fallen into error may condemn those who have led him astray; and that he who has

continued stedfast in purity may again rejoice, having these things brought to his remembrance... this not tedious to speak of the [books] of the New Testament. These are, the four Gospels, according to Matthew, Mark, Luke, and John. Afterwards, the Acts of the Apostles and Epistles (called Catholic), seven, viz. of James, one; of Peter, two; of John, three; after these, one of Jude. In addition, there are fourteen Epistles of Paul, written in this order. The first, to the Romans; then two to the Corinthians; after these, to the Galatians; next, to the Ephesians; then to the Philippians; then to the Colossians; after these, two to the Thessalonians, and that to the Hebrews; and again, two to Timothy; one to Titus; and lastly, that to Philemon. And besides, the Revelation of John. (The Festal Letters of Athanasius; Letter 20; part 3-5; From: *The Christian Ethereal Classics Library,* located at - www.ccel.org/)

Athanasius wrote, "These are fountains of salvation, that they who thirst may be satisfied with the living words they contain. In these alone is proclaimed the doctrine of godliness. Let no man add to these, neither let him take ought from these." (The Festal Letters of Athanasius; Letter 20, part 6). Athanasius then says that the Shepherd of Hermas and the Teaching of the Apostles (the Didache) are 'indeed not included in the canon.' He does say, however, that they are helpful reading for new converts. (*How We Got Our Bible: Christian History, Issue 43,* 1997; p. 29).

While it would be accurate to say that there were still some groups, after Athanasius, that did not recognize the 27 New Testament books that we have today as the final New Testament Canon, the overwhelming majority of the Church did. In 393 A.D. the synod of Hippo recognized the Athanasian Canon. In A.D. 397 the Third synod of Carthage issued a catalog of books of the New Testament that are the same 27 we have in our New Testament today.

There is further affirmation of the New Testament Canon into the 5th century. In a letter in 414 A.D., Jerome accepts the New Testament books listed by Athanasius; a list that corresponds to today's New Testament. But he comments that he thinks the Letter of Barnabas should also be included, since the author was the companion of Paul and an apostle. Yet, what is important is that while holding that opinion, Jerome accepted what had come to be the consensus. In other words, Jerome confirms that by the beginning of the fifth century, the canon of the New Testament had achieved a kind of solemn, unshakable status; it could not be altered, even if one had different opinions. I should also point out that "Augustine (in his book on the Christian Doctrine), and Rufinus (in his Explication of the Apostles' Creed), also presented us with catalogs" all of which correspond to today's New Testament. (*The Evidences of the Divine Origin, Preservation, Credibility and Inspiration of the Holy Scriptures* by S. Austin Alliborne; American Sunday School Union - 1871; p.20).

Since the late 4th and early 5th centuries, history, tradition, and worship have approved the canon of our New Testament. While there were some attempts to exclude or add some books, these 27 books have remained the non-negotiable New Testament Canon of Christendom. These **27 New Testament books form the basis of our English New Testament**.

CHAPTER #4

THE FOUR TYPES OF NEW TESTAMENT MANUSCRIPTS

EARLY GREEK TRANSLATIONS

As we study the history of the English Bible, it is important that I remind you once again that the Old Testament was originally written mainly in Hebrew and the New Testament in Greek. Further, it must be remembered that <u>there are no original autographs of either the Hebrew Old Testament or the Greek New Testament</u>. But, the Old and New Testaments have been preserved in apographs (exemplars or copies) of the originals. Since our focus in this section is the New Testament, it is important to know that there are at least 5686 surviving Greek manuscripts (Norman Geisler & Peter Bocchino, *Unshakable Foundations,* (Minneapolis, MN: Bethany House Publishers, 2001) p. 256) that contain all or parts of the New Testament. New ones are being discovered regularly. In addition there are more than 19,000 ancient New Testament manuscripts in Latin, Syriac, Armenian, and other language versions. The oldest copies of the New Testament known to exist are not Greek copies but the Syriac and the Old Latin versions (pre-Jerome's Latin Vulgate). The Old Syriac "is a good translation from the Greek, and exists practically complete in about 46 manuscripts." (*General Biblical Introduction* by Herbert Miller, 1937; 240-41).

It used to be claimed that manuscripts of the New Testament were from the 4th or 5th century A.D. However recent discoveries have pushed that back to the 1st century. There is a fragment of the gospel of John that dates back to around 29 years from the original writing (John Rylands Papyri p52 - 125 A.D.). This is extremely close to the original writing date. This is simply unheard of in any other ancient writing and it demonstrates that the Gospel of John is a first century document.

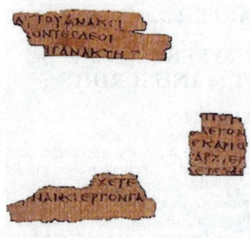

Then there is the exciting discovery of **The Magdalen** Papyrus. Dr. Carsten Peter Thiede, Director of the Institute for Basic Epistemological Research in Paderborn, Germany, uncovered it. I should note that Dr. Thiede is not a Textus Receptus (Traditional Text) supporter! Dr. Thiede examined three New Testament fragments called The Magdalen Papyrus because it was donated to Magdalen College in Oxford, England. These fragments were originally acquired in Luxor, Egypt in 1901. In 1953 they were dated to about 180-200 A.D. However, **Dr. Thiede carefully redated them and placed them at 66 A.D**., **making them the ONLY first century New Testament fragments extant**.

There is more! Using a very technical and accurate epifluorescent confocal laser scanning microscope, he found that the *Matthew 26:22* fragment revealed the Textus Receptus reading! It reads "**hekasotos auton**,"- *"every one of them,"* as the King James reads, as opposed to "**heis hakastos**,"- *"each one"* [one after another], as the critical texts read.

This fragment clearly documents the antiquity of the Textus Receptus text to the time of Peter, Paul, John the Apostle, etc. **Increasingly,** *the recension theory*, which we will explain later, **is being exposed for the sham that it is!**

THE FOUR DIFFERENT KINDS OF NEW TESTAMENT MANUSCRIPTS

"There are four kinds of Greek manuscripts that we have in our possession today: 1) **papyri**, 2) **uncials**, 3) **cursives**, and 4) **lectionaries**." (*Defending The King James Bible* by D. A. Waite; p. 53).

"The Greek manuscripts of the New Testament, so far as known, were written on papyrus, parchment, or paper. The autographs, both of the historical and epistolary writers, are supposed to have been written on papyrus. The great uncials copies and the most valued of the minuscules and lectionaries were written on parchment, while paper was employed largely in the making of the later lectionaries and the printed texts of the New Testament." (*Praxis In Manuscripts of the Greek New Testament* by Rev. Charles F. Sitterly; 1898; p.15).

PAPYRI MANUSCRIPTS

Papyrus is a brittle kind of paper made out of the papyrus plant, which grows in Egypt. To my knowledge there are about **97 papyrus fragment manuscripts of the New Testament**. Most of those surviving early texts only have a few verses on them. The most ancient example is the John Ryland papyrus fragment P52, seen at the left, which includes portions of John 18:31-33 & 37-38. It is housed in John Rylands Library, Manchester, England. The fragment is believed to have been written between 98 and 138 A.D. (*The Complete Text of the Earliest New Testament Manuscripts*; Philip W. Comfort & David P. Barrett; 1999 Baker Books; p.17-18).

There are six papyri of which I am aware, which record large portions of the New Testament. P45, dated around 200 A.D., contains portions of all four Gospels and Acts. P46, from the second century, has almost all of Paul's epistles and Hebrews. P47, also from the second century, contains Revelation 9-17. These are from what is called the **Chester Beatty Papyri** housed in Dublin Castle in Dublin, Ireland. Then there are three lengthy papyri from the

Bodmer Papyri. P66 is a second century papyrus that contains almost all of John. P72, a third or fourth century papyrus, contains all of 1 and 2 Peter and Jude. Finally, P75, dated between 175-200 A.D., contains the most of Luke through John 15.

THE UNCIALS OR MAJUSCULES

Uncial comes from the Latin word uncialis, which means inch-high. It is used to delineate a type of Greek and Latin writing which features capital letters. There are few, if any, divisions between words in uncial manuscripts and no punctuation to speak of. The word majuscule, meaning large or capital letter, is a synonym for uncial. There are some 267 uncials. Three of the most famous uncial New Testament manuscripts are the fourth century manuscripts, Sinaiticus and Vaticanus, and the fifth century, Codex Alexandrinus. As an example of an uncial I have included a picture of a portion of the corrupt Codex Vaticanus.

CURSIVES/MINUSCULES

Cursives or minuscules are Greek manuscripts written in lower case letters, more like handwriting. The letters flow together, much like writing of today. There are spaces between words and some degree of punctuation. There are at least 2,764 cursive New Testament manuscripts known today. On the left is a cursive manuscript of John 1 from about 1022 A.D.

78

LECTIONARY MANUSCRIPTS

The word lection comes from a Latin root word meaning, "to read." Lectionaries are portions of Scriptures in Greek (or Latin) Bibles that were read in the church services during the year. There are at least 2,143 known lectionaries in existence. I own a leaf from a 10th century lectionary. It is pictured below.

New discoveries are regularly coming to light and so it is difficult to have exact, up-to-date figures.

CHAPTER #5

TEXT STREAMS:
GROUPS OR TEXT FAMILIES

J. J. Griesbach identified three New Testament text-types calling them the Alexandrian, Western and Byzantine. He first published his findings in 1775. H. B. Swete writes that there are basically three types of manuscripts, the Constantinoplian or Textus Receptus; the Eusebio-Origen or Palestinian; the Hysychian or Egyptian text type. (*Introduction of the Old Testament in Greek* by H. B. Swete, pp. 76 & ff).

More recently men like Lightfoot, in his book *How We Got the Bible*, and Metzger in his book *The Text of the New Testament*, have broken down the divisions further and identify four text streams or text families; Alexandrian, Western, Caesarean, and Byzantine. While I agree that it is possible to divide and subdivide and micro-divide text types, depending upon the criteria you use, I have decided to look at the text streams issue simply and follow the path of Benjamin G. Wilkinson. He wrote, "anyone who is interested enough to read the vast volume of literature on this subject, will agree that down through the centuries there were only two streams of manuscripts. (*Which Bible* edited by Dr. David Otis Fuller; from the chapter - Our Authorized Bible Vindicated by Benjamin G. Wilkinson; p. 187).

THE TRADITIONAL, BYZANTINE, EASTERN, ECCLESIASTICAL OR APOSTALIC TEXT GROUP OF THE REFORMATION-PROTESTANT BIBLES

"The first stream which carried the Received Text in Hebrew and Greek, began with the apostolic churches, and reappearing at intervals down the Christian Era among enlightened believers, was protected by the wisdom and scholarship of the pure church in her different phases: precious manuscripts were preserved by such as the church at Pella in Palestine where Christians fled, when in 70 A.D. the Romans destroyed Jerusalem; by the Syrian Church of Antioch which produced eminent scholarship; by the Italic Church in northern Italy; and also at the same time by the Gallic Church in southern France and by the Celtic Church in Great Britain; by the pre-

Waldensian, the Waldensian, and the churches of the Reformation."
(Ibid. p.187).

Here is why this is important. Nearly all ancient English Bibles
(except the Wycliffe & Douay-Rheims Catholic Bible), and in fact **all
the Reformation English Bibles follow the same text family**.
That family is the **Received Text**, also called the **Textus
Receptus**. It must be noted that <u>Elzevir first gave the title, *Textus
Receptus,* to describe the Traditional Text in 1633</u>. This text type has
been called various names by Bible scholars...the Constantinoplian
text, Antiochian text, Byzantine text, Traditional text, Apostolic text,
the Ecclesiastical text, the Majority text and the Textus Receptus,
which is Latin for Received Text. I should note that some confusion
has resulted from the publishing of a Greek New Testament by
Thomas Nelson in 1892 by Hodges & Farstad that is called the
Majority Text. In 1991 Pierpont & Robinson published another.

The Textus Receptus belongs to the stream of early apostolic
manuscripts that were brought from Judea. The Textus Receptus was
the Bible of early Eastern Christianity. Dr. Hort admits this when he
says, "It is no wonder that the traditional Constantinopolitan text,
whether formally official or not, was the Antiochian text of the fourth
century. It was equally natural that the text recognized at
Constantinople should eventually become in practice the standard
New Testament of the East." (*Revision Revised*, John Burgon, p. 134.)

Regardless of where you stand on the "textual debate," this is the fact;
the foundational text of all English Bible New Testament translations
from 1525 to 1880 was from the Byzantine or Majority Text group of
which the Textus Receptus is a part. The sole exception was the Jesuit
Rheims New Testament of 1582.

I have used the term "Majority Text" numerous times now; therefore
I want to point out just how large this majority is. "This first
stream appears, with very little change, in the Protestant Bibles of
many languages, and in English, in that Bible known as the King
James Version, the one which has been in use for three hundred years
in the English-speaking world. <u>These manuscripts have in agreement
with them, by far the vast majority of copies of the original text</u>. So
vast is this majority that even the enemies of the Received Text admit
that <u>nineteen-twentieths of all Greek manuscripts are of this class.</u>"

(*Which Bible* edited by Dr. David Otis Fuller; from the chapter - Our Authorized Bible Vindicated by Benjamin G. Wilkinson; p. 187-88).

Indeed, the enormous majority of all Greek New Testament manuscripts in existence are from the so-called Byzantine or Traditional text group. When I began my study several years back, there were 5,255 known manuscripts and portions. Of that number 5,210 of them more closely matched the Majority Text group. Only 45 of them followed the minority, Egyptian or Westcott and Hort text group. So, more than 99% of all the manuscripts that exist are of the Byzantine text family, hence what was originally called the Majority text group. "The remainder, representing the Western stream of manuscripts, are clearly defective. **Yet it is these defective copies upon which almost all modern translators place their trust**. But the Reformers of the sixteenth and seventeenth centuries made no such error." (*Modern Bible Translations Unmasked* by Russell & Colin Standish; p.37).

In fact, there is enormous support for the Traditional Text found in Armenian, Ethiopic, Gothic, Latin, and Syriac translations, some predating the earliest Greek manuscripts we possess. But despite this fact, in the nineteenth century, following the texts of the Codex Vaticanus and the Codex Sinaiticus, many passages of the New Testament have been altered. Yet more recently discovered papyrus fragments have confirmed the Majority Text. "Nineteenth-century biblical scholars claimed that much of the first fourteen chapters of the Gospel of John was corrupted by scribes in the later Byzantine Era. This claim was shown to be utterly false by the discovery of Papyrus Bodmer II. Dated about A.D. 200, prior to the commencement of the Byzantine Era, this Papyrus verified many of the disputed passages attributed to late Byzantine copyists and demonstrated that these passages were present in very early manuscripts." (*Modern Bible Translations Unmasked* by Russell & Colin Standish; p.37-38).

EARLY WITNESS TO THE RECEIVED TEXT

Textual critics like D. A. Carson assert that, *"there is no unambiguous evidence that the Byzantine Text-type was known before the middle of the fourth century."* However, that just is not true. Edward Miller was an accomplished textual historian living at the end of the nineteenth century. His exhaustive research showed that portions of Scripture distinctive to the Received Text were quoted extensively by notable church leaders as early as the second century and onward. *(The Cause of The Corruption of The Traditional Text of the Holy Gospels; John Burgon and Edward Miller; P.64).*

Here are just a few specific examples of the leaders of the early church who support the readings of the Traditional or Received Text. I am indebted to Thomas M. Strouse, Ph.D. for the primary source material below.

The KJV — Mark 1:1-2 *"The beginning of the gospel of Jesus Christ, the Son of God; 2 As it is written in the prophets, Behold, I send my messenger before thy face, which shall prepare thy way before thee."*

In Sinaiticus and Vaticanus it reads, *"In the Prophet Isaiah."* The RV, ASV, RSV, NIV and 95% of all of the New Bibles read this way. But there is a problem. While **Mark 1:3 is a quotation of Isaiah 40:3, verse 2 is a reference to Malachi 3:1**. Therefore the KJV is right.

But, what about the early church? Is there any evidence that indicates whether the (erroneous) reading of the modern versions or the reading of the King James (which is based on the Received Text) is correct? The answer is yes. Irenaeus (130-202 A.D.) said this —*"Mark does thus commence his Gospel narrative 'The beginning of the Gospel of Jesus, Christ, the Son of God, as it is written in the prophets.' . . . Plainly does, the commencement of the Gospel quote the words of the holy prophets, and point out Him.., whom they confessed as God and Lord."* *(Against Heresies III: 10:5, :11:4, :16:3)*

Let's move on to another example. In my booklet called *"The Great (?) Uncials,"* I wrote how both Sinaiticus and Vaticanus omit Mark 16:9-20. Is there any support in the Early Church for this so-called "longer ending" of Mark 16? Again we look to a sermon of Irenaeus (130-202 A.D.). The longer reading must have been in the New Testament he was using because he references Mark 16:19, *"So then after the Lord had spoken unto them, he was received up into heaven, and sat on the right hand of God."* KJV. This is what Irenaeus writes —*"Also towards the conclusion of his Gospel, Mark* says: 'So then, after the Lord Jesus had spoken to them, He was received up into heaven, and sitteth on the right hand of God.'" (Against Heresies 111:10:6).

Consider **Luke 22:44**, *"And being in an agony he prayed more earnestly: and his sweat was as it were great drops of blood falling down to the ground."* There is the claim by those who hold the Critical Text position that verses 43-44 did not exist before the Byzantine Era (the 4th or 5th centuries). It that true? The answer has to be NO! Why? Because Justin (100-165 A.D.), says, *"For in the memoirs which I say were drawn up by His Apostles and those who followed them, it is recorded that His sweat fell down like drops of blood while He was praying, and saying, 'If it be possible, let this cup pass...'"* (Trypho 103:24)

Next, I turn your attention to **John 1:18** in the KJV. The verse says, *"No man hath seen God at any time; the only begotten Son, which is in the bosom of the Father, he hath declared him."* However, the NASB (New American Standard Bible) says "No man has seen God at any time; the only begotten God, who is in the bosom of the Father, He has explained Him."

The "older manuscripts" give us the reading of the NASB. This is a Gnostic perversion. They taught there were various levels of spiritual beings or lesser gods between God and man. J. P. Green clearly identifies the problem. He says, Vaticanus "in John 1:18 refers to Christ as the 'only begotten God.' How can anyone claim that one that is begotten is at the same time essential God, equal in every aspect to God the Father, and to God the Holy Spirit? This makes Christ to be a created Being. And it is a Gnostic twist given to the Bible by the heretic Valentinus and his followers, who did not regard the Word and Christ as one and the same; who thought of the Son of God and the Father as being one and the same Person. Therefore, they determined to do away with 'the only begotten Son' in order to accommodate their religion. (Unholy Hands on the Bible edited by Jay. P. Green, Sr.; Sovereign Grace Publishers; p.12).

Since several of the oldest manuscripts like Vaticanus read *"only begotten God"* and since these are before the Byzantine era, that must be the correct reading, right? My answer again is no! Twice Irenaeus (130-202 A.D.), in referring to the passage, says, *"the only begotten Son of God, which is in the bosom of the Father."* (Against Heresies 111:11:6, (IV:20:6).

John 3:13 is the next passage to be considered. The KJV reads *"And no man hath ascended up to heaven, but he that came down from heaven, even <u>the Son of man which is in heaven</u>."* I checked, and the NASB, NIV and the CEV leave this underlined phrase off. Others may as well. I did not check the other translations. But is there an early witness for the phrase <u>the Son of man which is in heaven?</u> Yes! Hippolytus (170-236 A.D.), in his sermon, *Against the Heresy of One Noetus,* says, *"And no man hath ascended up to heaven, but He that came down from heaven, even the Son of Man which is in heaven."* (Against the Heresy of One Noetus I: 1:4)

John 5:3-4 in the KJV reads *"In these lay a great multitude of impotent folk, of blind, halt, withered, waiting for the moving of the water. 4 For an angel went down at a certain season into the pool, and troubled the water: whosoever then first after the troubling of the water stepped in was made whole of whatsoever disease he had."* These verses are omitted in the NIV, again on the basis that they are only in the "less important manuscripts." By that they mean again the "older" ones. However, Tertullian (160-221 A.D.), in one sermon, On Baptism, makes it clear that the passage was in the early manuscript that he was using for he says, *"If it seems a novelty for an angel to be present in waters, an example of what was to come to pass has forerun. An angel, by his intervention, was want to stir the pool at Bethsaida. They who were complaining of ill-health used to watch for him; for whoever had been the first to descend into them, after his washing ceased to complain."* (On Baptism I: 1:5).

The list goes on and on. The critical scholars claim there is no early manuscript support for the verses and portions they delete, and yet a study of the sermons of the pastors in the early church quote the verses and portions the "scholars" omit, as they are in the Byzantine or Received text. Below are more examples.

John 6:69 KJV – *"And we believe and are sure that thou art that <u>Christ, the Son of the living God</u>."* This is supported by Irenaeus (130-202 A.D.) *"By whom also Peter, having been taught,* *recognized Christ as the Son of the living God.*" *(Against Heresies III: 11:6).*

Acts 8:36-37 KJV – "*And as they went on their way, they came unto a certain water: and the eunuch said, See, here is water; what doth hinder me to be baptized? 37 And Philip said, If thou believest with all thine heart, thou mayest. And he answered and said, I believe that Jesus Christ is the Son of God.*" Cyprian (200-258 A.D.) supports the inclusion of verse 36-37 Textus Receptus when he says, "*In the Acts of the Apostles: Lo, here is water; what is there which hinders me from being baptized? Then said Phillip, If thou believest with all thine heart thou mayest.*" *(The Treatises of Cyprian I: 1:17).*

Again, I assert, that since the reading of early church leaders match the Received/Byzantine text, that this text existed and was in use from a very early time!

1 Timothy 3:16 KJV – "*And without controversy great is the mystery of godliness: God was manifest in the flesh, justified in the Spirit, seen of angels, preached unto the Gentiles, believed on in the world, received up into glory.*" This passage is supported by Ignatius (35-116 A.D.) "*God was in the flesh.*" *(To the Ephesians 1:1:7),* by Hippolytus (170-236 A.D.) "*God was manifested in the flesh.*" *(Against the Heresies of Noetus I: 1:17),* and Dionysius (3rd cent.) "*For God was manifested in the flesh.*" *(Conciliations I: 1:853).*

1 John 5:7-8 KJV – "*For there are three that bear record in heaven, the Father, the Word, and the Holy Ghost: and these three are one. 8 And there are three that bear witness in earth, the Spirit, and the water, and the blood: and these three agree in one.*" This passage is supported by Cyprian (200-258 A.D.) who wrote "*The Lord says, 'I and the Father are one,* 'and *again it is written of the Father, and of the Son, and of the Holy Spirit,* 'and *these three are one.* '" *(The Treatises of Cyprian I:1:6).*

Revelation 22:14 KJV – "*Blessed are they that do his commandments, that they may have right to the tree of life, and may enter in through the gates into the city.*" Tertullian (160-221) wrote, "*Blessed are they who act according to the precepts, that they may have power over the tree of life, and over the gates, for entering into the holy city.*" *(On Modesty I: 19:2).*

Allow me to conclude with a pertinent statement from Tertullian (160-221 A.D.). He wrote, *Now this heresy of yours does not receive certain Scriptures; and whichever of them it does receives it perverts by means of additions and diminutions, for the accomplishment of its own purposes.* (On Prescriptions Against Heresies 1:17:1).

Wilbur Pickering gives the following abbreviated summary: "TR readings are recognized most notably by —
- 100-150 A.D.   The Didache, Diognetus, Justin Martyr
- 150-200 A.D.   Gospel of Peter, Athenagorus, Hegesippus, Irenaeus
- 200-250 A.D.   Clement of Alexandria; Tertullian, Clementines, Hippolytus, Origen
- 250-300 A.D.   Gregory of Thaumaturgus, Novatian, Cyprian, Dionysius of Alexandria, Archelaus
- 300-400 A.D.   Eusebius, Athanasius, Macaris Magnus, Hilary, Didymus, Basil, Titus of Bostra, Cyril of Jerusalem, Gregory of Nyssa, Apostolic Canons and Constitutions, Epiphanius, Ambrose." (*Forever Settled;* compiled by Dr. Jack Moorman; Dean Burgon Society Press; p. 95)

Why do the modern textual critics ignore the quotes of the early Church leaders? Do not their quotes demonstrate the existence of the Traditional Text or Received Text? Indeed they do! And what of the ancient translations that reflect that text? Why are they ignored? For the most part, advocates of the critical text have confined themselves to debating over existing Greek manuscripts of the New Testament. However, <u>they have largely ignored ancient translations of the New Testament which support the Received Text</u>. The logic at this point is simple. If these early translations of the New Testament reflect the Received Text, they must have been translated from it. The manuscripts underlying these translations therefore must be very early copies of the Received Text—maybe even the autographs themselves. Do such translations exist? Yes! But let's look at one Greek Codex before we move on to these other old manuscripts.

BODMER II – P66

This papyrus, (Papyrus Bodmer II (p66) – 125 A.D.) codex contains most of the Gospel of John and consists of 75 leaves and 39 unidentified fragments. The leaves are nearly rectangular, measuring 6.4 inches high and 5.6 inches wide. The written pages are numbered consecutively from 1 to 34, 35 - 38 are missing, and then from 39 to page 108.

"A prevailing chorus of the critical text position is that there is no historical record of the Byzantine Text (i.e., Received Text) to be found prior to the last half of the fourth century." (*Touch Not The Unclean Thing* by David H. Sorenson; p.76). However, nothing could be further from the truth. There is enormous support for the Traditional Text found in Armenian, Ethiopic, Gothic, Old Latin, Anglo-Saxon and Syriac translations, <u>many of them predating the earliest Greek manuscripts we possess</u>. But despite this fact, textual critics in the nineteenth century, following the texts of the Codex Vaticanus and the Codex Sinaiticus, have altered many passages of the New Testament. Further, I find it very encouraging that more <u>recently discovered papyrus fragments have confirmed the Majority Text</u>. "Nineteenth-century biblical scholars claimed that much of the first fourteen chapters of the Gospel of John was corrupted by scribes in the later Byzantine Era (330 to 1453 A.D.). This claim was shown to be utterly false by the discovery of Papyrus Bodmer II (also called P66). Dated about A.D. 200 originally, but after further examination, 125 A.D., **prior to the commencement of the Byzantine Era**, this Papyrus verified <u>many</u> of the disputed passages attributed to late Byzantine copyists and demonstrated that these passages were present in very early manuscripts." (*Modern Bible Translations Unmasked* by Russell & Colin Standish; p.37-38).

HERE ARE SOME EXAMPLES OF PASSAGES THAT VERIFY THE TEXT THAT UNDERLIES OUR KING JAMES BIBLE.

Reference	P66	Sinaiticus
John 4:1	κυριος (Lord)	Ιεσους (Jesus)
John 5:9	και ευτηεος (and immediately)	omitted
John 5:17	δε Ιεσους (but Jesus)	δε Ιεσους Κυειος (but Jesus Christ)
John 6:36	με (me)	omitted
John 6:46	και τεν μετερα (and the mother).	omitted
John 6:69	ο Χριστος (the Christ)	omitted
John 7:10	αλλ ος (but as)	αλλ (but)
John 7:39	πνευμα αγιον (Spirit Holy)	πνευμα (Spirit)

THE OLD SYRIAN TEXT OR PESHITTA

Brook Foss Westcott (1825-1903) and Fenton John Anthony Hort (1828-1892) alleged that the Alexandrian text, or the neutral text, as they called it, was that which most closely followed the originals. This false allegation is still repeated by so-called Fundamentalists such as W. Edward Glenny, formerly of Central Baptist Theological Seminary, but now at Northwestern College, a New Evangelical School. However, **you should be aware that Fenton John Anthony Hort conceded that there might be some evidence of the Syrian text** (i.e., Received Text) **as early as middle of the third century**.

So, let's take a look at the translation called the Old Syrian Peshitta New Testament, which is in the Aramaic language. First, the word Peshitta comes from the Syrian word **peshitla,** which means "common." It carries with it the implication that it was the version commonly used by the people.

The record of the Syrian versions is an important one. You will remember that Antioch in Syria is the birthplace of the word Christian. We read in **Acts 11:26** *"And when he had found him, he brought him unto Antioch. And it came to pass, that a whole year they assembled themselves with the church, and taught much people. And <u>the disciples were called Christians first in Antioch</u>."*

In fact, the church at Antioch was the home and sending church of the Apostle Paul. In the mid and latter portion of the first century, the church at Antioch no doubt was one of the pre-eminent churches in the Christian world. This church undoubtedly was the mother church for numerous other churches of Syria during that early period of church history. What I find interesting is that the tradition of the Syrian church is that the Peshitta was the work of St. Mark, while others claim the Apostle Thaddeus (Jude) translated it.

When was the Peshitta translated from Greek? A translation of the New Testament into Syrian was made about 150 A.D. according to Kenyon in his book, *Our Bible and the Ancient Manuscripts.* This early translation of the New Testament agreed with the Traditional Text or the Received Text. In fact, there is little question, even by proponents of the critical text, that the Peshitta Version was translated from a Greek text rooted in the Received Text. (*The King James Version Defended;* Dr. E. V. Hills' p.172).

John Burgon noted that the churches of the region of Syria have always used the Peshitta. There has never been a time when these churches did not use the Received-Text-based Peshitta. The greater point, however, is that one of the earliest churches of the Christian era used a translation of the New Testament based upon the Received Text. That is a clear indication that the Received Text was the true text of the New Testament with roots leading back to autographa.

THE OLD LATIN, ITALIC OR ITALA VERSION

Don't make the mistake that many people make. When they hear the word Latin used in conjunction with the Bible, or church, they automatically assume that it is to be associated with the Roman Catholic Church. However, that is not true because in northern

Italy, the Italic Church had begun in A.D. 120 according to Theodore Beza, the associate and successor of John Calvin, the great Swiss reformer. Its remoteness isolated it from the influence of the Church at Rome. The Italic Church was the forerunner of churches in this same region, which would later be called the Vaudois, or, the Waldenses. Both of these names simply mean "peoples of the valleys." The Italic, or pre-Waldensian Church, produced a version of the New Testament which was translated from the Received Text by the year 157 A.D. The noted church historian, Frederic Nolan, confirms this. This date is less than one hundred years after most of the books of the New Testament were written. The greater point is that the Itala (or Old Latin) was translated from the Received Text, indicating its existence to the earliest days of the New Testament church. Therefore, the Received Text clearly existed and was used by churches in early church history.

THE GOTHIC VERSION

Another early translation of the New Testament in a European language was, what has come to be known as, the Gothic Version. The Gothic language was used by Germanic tribes in central Europe in the fourth century. In about 350 A.D., a missionary to the Goths, named Ulfilas or Wulfilas, translated the New Testament into the Gothic language. Textual critic Frederic Kenyon wrote in 1912 that the Gothic Version "is for the most part that which is found in the majority of Greek manuscripts."(*Handbook to the Textual Criticism of the New Testament*; Frederick Kenyon).

In other words, Kenyon conceded that the Gothic Version was based upon the Received Text because we know that the vast "majority of manuscripts" are that which support the Received Text. The point of logic here again is simple. When the missionary Ulfilas translated the Gothic Version from the Received Text in about A.D. 350, it must have been in existence long before that date. When a missionary on the field had the Received Text with him, it certainly implied that it was the well-established, common text.

THE ETHIOPIC VERSION

This version dates to the beginning of the fourth century. While it does contain a mixed reading at times, it is classified as being basically Byzantine in origin. Thus the witnesses to Africa were also of the Traditional Text. Geisler and Nix state, "This translation adheres closely, almost literally, to the Greek text of the Byzantine type." They also classify the Armenian Version, Georgian Version, and the Slavonic Version of the same textual family, that of the Traditional Text. (*A General Introduction to the Bible* (Chicago: Moody Press, 1968); Norman L. Geisler and William E. Nix, 324-327).

"The clear historic indication is that the Received Text was the common text of the New Testament used throughout the civilized world from the earliest times of Christianity. Though we live in an age of relatively rapid editing, publishing, and distribution of new Bible translations, that was not the case in the first millennium of Christianity. For translations of the Bible to exist in the second to fourth centuries based upon what is distinctively the Received Text is *prima facie,* historic evidence that the Received Text was the commonly used, commonly translated, and commonly copied text of the New Testament. This is apparent." (*Touch Not The Unclean Thing;* David H. Sorenson; p. 82).

"The critical-text-position view that there is no record of any historic usage of the Received Text prior to the fifth century is simply wrong. There is a substantial historic record to the contrary. **The text used by the churches of Jesus Christ in the first five centuries was primarily the Received Text.** To be sure, there were localities which used the Alexandrian text, but they were limited largely to Alexandria and Rome." (*Touch Not The Unclean Thing;* David H. Sorenson; p. 82).

THE BYZANTINE TEXT-TYPE AND THE CHESTER BEATTY PAPYRI

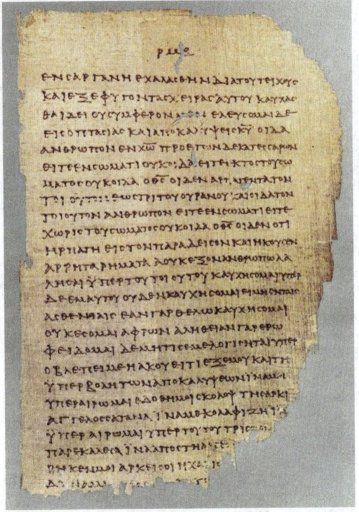

Chester Beatty Papyrus II: P46
2 Corinthians 11:33-12:9
150 to 200 A.D.

I am indebted to my Assistant Pastor, F. William Darrow, for the editing and preparation of this section of the book. It is gleaned from a book entitled, *"The Byzantine Text-Type and New Testament Textual Criticism"* by Harry A. Sturz. Copyright 1984.

Westcott and Hort propagated the idea that the Byzantine Texts were of such late date that they had to be corrupted text. Because of their teaching, the majority of textual critics follow their line of argument. In this book, Sturz attempts to prove Westcott and Hort were wrong and the Byzantine text should be used on an equal basis with the Alexandrian Texts, as well as the Western Texts. We would not put them on an equal basis, but believe the Byzantine Texts are the true texts and the Alexandrian and Western are corrupted. However, Sturz's reasons for elevating the Byzantine Texts are worth considering and that is what I am doing.

BACKGROUND

"Byzantine" refers to that type of text which characterizes the majority of the later Greek uncial, semi-uncial and minuscule manuscripts of the New Testament. It is also the type of text found in the Syriac Peshitta and Gothic versions and in the extant quotation of Church fathers from Chrysostom on.

The text derives its names from the provenance (origin) of most of its manuscripts: the Byzantine Empire. It has also been called "Antiochian," after the place of its origin, and the "Lucian Recension," after its supposed editor. It is Semler's "Oriental," Bengel's "Asiatic," Griesbach's "Constantinopolitan," Westcott and Hort's "Syrian" and Burgon's "Traditional." Other designations of the same text include: von Soden and Merk's "K" and Kenyon's "Alpha." It is largely the text which lies behind the "Textus Receptus" and the King James Bible. It was also called the Received Text, because it was received by all in the Byzantine Empire.

Karl Lachmann published a fourth-century text, which continued with Constantine Tischendorf. Westcott and Hort continued that and published a new Greek text with the intent of replacing the Textus Receptus. For the most part, the scholarly world has accepted the overthrow of the Textus Receptus and the Byzantine text-type; nevertheless, the agreement was not unanimous.

John William Burgon, Dean of Chichester, sought to refute the theory of Westcott and Hort and to support that text which lay behind the Textus Receptus; which he called the "Traditional" text. Two clear attitudes continue today. There are those who follow Westcott and Hort and there are some who adopt John Burgon's defense of the Traditional Text.

THE ARGUMENT THAT THE BYZANTINE TEXT IS SECONDARY

There appears to be a near consensus among modern New Testament scholars that the Byzantine text is practically useless for help in recovering the original text. This position is based on a century-old theory of textual history which contended that the Syrian text was derived from older text type. Westcott and Hort discerned what they felt to be the best text of the New Testament in two fourth-century manuscripts; the Sinaiticus and Vaticanus. They called this the "neutral" text. Their argument was that it was an early text. Putting these two together with some other texts, they called it "Alexandrian." Another text Westcott and Hort acknowledged to be early was called the "Western" text. Though they put most of their emphasis on the Alexandrian text, they did use the Western text some. The majority of textual critics still appear to agree that both the Alexandrian and the Western type texts originated earlier than did the Byzantine.

Three main arguments are used to this day to prove the Byzantine text was derived from others, making it later.

1. They theorize it was the putting of Alexandrian and Western texts together, called "conflate" readings.

2. They claim that no Church fathers are found attesting the Byzantine text in quotations of Scripture before the time of Chrysostom.

3. Westcott and Hort contend that when the readings of the Syrian text-type are compared with those of the other text-types, they are found to be not only conflate, but inferior in other matters involving content and style, thus indicating an editing process.

Bruce Metzger said, "Scholars today generally agree that one of the chief contributions made by Westcott and Hort was their clear demonstration that the Syrian (Byzantine) text is later than the other types of text."

THE ARGUMENT THAT THE BYZANTINE TEXT IS PRIMARY

Contrary to Westcott and Hort's theory is the concept that divine providence has preserved the Byzantine manuscripts as the best text. Other texts, then, would be considered deviations and corruptions of the true text.

John W. Burgon and Edward F. Hills say the Byzantine text is primary, or the basic text, the Traditional text and is therefore the norm by which all texts are to be judged. The basic premise of this view is that the agreement of a <u>large</u> <u>majority</u> of individual manuscripts constitutes the chief evidence for the true text because such plurality indicates the divinely preserved text.

In order to support this view at the outset, preservation is intimately linked with "inspiration." Edward F. Hills said, "If the doctrine of the divine inspiration of the Old and New Testament Scriptures is a true doctrine, the doctrine of the providential preservation of these scriptures must also be a true doctrine. It must be that down through the centuries God has exercised a special, providential control over the copying of the Scriptures and the preservation and use of the original text has been available to God's people in every age."

He also said, "The original New Testament manuscripts were written under special conditions, under the inspiration of God, and the copies were made and preserved under special conditions, under the singular care and providence of God."

Basically, he is saying the text of the majority of the manuscripts equals the best representative of the original and should be considered the standard text because it is the providentially preserved text.

Then, in contrast to Westcott and Hort, the Alexandrian manuscripts, together with those of the Western Text, are to be treated as deviations or corruptions of the true text.

A variation, or modification, of the Burgon-Hills' view discussed above has been put forth by Zane C. Hodges and Wilbur N. Pickering. The theory of the text, rather than arguing from "providence," defends the superiority of the majority number of manuscripts on the mathematical principle that is based on the reasoning that "the copies nearest the autograph will normally have the largest number of descendants." Thus, the Majority Text, upon which the King James Version is based, has, in reality, the strongest claim possible to be regarded as an authentic representation of the original text.

REASONS FOR CONSIDERING THAT THE BYZANTINE TEXT IS INDEPENDENT, BYZANTINE READINGS ARE OLD & DISTINCTIVELY BYZANTINE READINGS ARE FOUND IN EARLY PAPYRI

One of the chief reasons Westcott and Hort rejected the Byzantine text was the supposed late origin of its readings. In their opinion, readings which agreed with neither the Western nor the Alexandrian text-types and were not attested to by early Church fathers, but were found exclusively in the Byzantine and other late manuscripts, must be late in their formation. Therefore, they should be discarded automatically. Although the reasoning of Westcott and Hort seemed sound at the time they wrote, discoveries since then have undermined the confident appraisal that characteristically Byzantine readings are necessarily late.

When the Chester Beatty Papyri appeared, such arguments became too much for the theory to hold.

At this point, we need to explain what the Chester Beatty Papyri is. The Chester Beatty Biblical Papyri, or simply, the Chester Beatty Papyri, are a group of early papyrus manuscripts of biblical texts. The manuscripts are in Greek and are of Christian origin. There are eleven manuscripts in the group, seven consisting of portions of Old Testament books; three consisting of portions of the New

Testament (Gregory-Aland no. p[45], p[46] and p[47]) and one consisting of portions of the Book of Enoch and an unidentified Christian homily. Most are dated to the 3rd century. They are housed in part at the Chester Beatty Library in Dublin, Ireland, and, in part, at the University of Michigan, among a few other locations.

The papyri were most likely first obtained by illegal antiquity traders. Because of this, the exact circumstances of the find are not clear. One account is that the manuscripts were in jars in a Coptic graveyard near the ruins of the ancient city of Aphroditopolis. Other theories have proposed that the collection was found near the Fayurn instead of Aphroditopolis, or that the location was a Christian church or monastery instead of a graveyard. Most of the papyri were bought from a dealer by Alfred Chester Beatty, after whom the manuscripts are named, although some leaves and fragments were acquired by the University of Michigan and a few other collectors and institutions.

The papyri were first announced on November 19, 1931, although more leaves would be acquired over the next decades.

All the manuscripts are codices, which was surprising to the first scholars who examined the texts because it was believed that the papyrus codex was not extensively used by Christians until the 4th century. Most of the manuscripts dated to the 3rd century, with some as early as the 2nd century. The manuscripts also helped scholars understand the construction of papyrus codices.

Since all but two (P XI, XII) of the manuscripts are dated before the 4th century, they present significant textual evidence for the Greek Bible as it existed in Egypt prior to the Diocletianic persecutions where Christian books are said to have been destroyed and a century or more earlier than the Codex Vaticanus and the Codex Sinaiticus. (Information taken from the WIKIPEDIA, the free encyclopedia).

When the Chester Beatty Papyri came to light, a scholar named Francis Crawford Burkitt, an enthusiastic supporter of Westcott and Hort, made some interesting comments. The p[46] and p[45] contained Byzantine text. He refused to favor the Byzantine text, but had to admit it was early text. He stated, "And certainly it is not the Byzantine text, but an earlier ancestor of it, that has produced mixture. P[45], written about A.D. 240, is too early to be influenced by the Byzantine text, so that when it agrees with it the cause must be earlier."

Burkitt is sure of one thing – that in these instances, the Byzantine Text has not influenced the text of the papyrus, but he cannot answer how the reading of the papyrus got into the Byzantine Text.

C.C. Tarelli warns against the habit of taking for granted that certain readings, because they are in the late Byzantines but not in B or other earlier manuscripts, are therefore to be construed as improvements. He stated, "It is clear that evidence of p[45] changes the aspect of their problem." He said, "It is difficult to feel any greater certainty about the habitual superiority of B in the Gospels."

Bruce Metzger said, "During the past decades, several papyri have come to light which tend to increase one's uneasiness over Hort's reluctance to acknowledge the possibility that an ancient reading may have been preserved in the Antiochian text, even though it be absent from all the great uncial manuscripts. Since the discovery of the Chester Beatty Papyri (particularly p[45] and p[46]) and the Bodmer Papyrus II (p[66]), proof is available that occasionally the later Byzantine text preserves a reading that dates from the second or third century and for which there had been no other early witness."

He further stated, "Enough examples have been cited to suggest that some of the roots of the Antiochian text go back to a very early date, antedating Lucian by several generations. It does not follow, of course, that the Textus Receptus should be rehabilitated *en bloc*, or even that in the examples cited above, the Antiochian text is necessarily the original text. The lesson to be drawn from such evidence, however, is that the general neglect of the Antiochian readings, which has been so common among many textual critics, is quite unjustified."

Gunther Zuntz declared, "To sum up, a number of Byzantine readings, most of them genuine, which previously were discarded as 'late', are anticipated by p[46]. Our inquiry has confirmed what was anyhow probable enough: the Byzantines did not hit upon these readings by conjecture or independent errors. They produced an older tradition." He further stated, "It seems to me unlikely that the

Byzantine editors ever altered the text without manuscript evidence."

While Zuntz did not accept Burgon's belief of the superiority of the Textus Receptus, he said, "The chance that even so, they are far older than the manuscripts which attest them is none the less great." He went on to say, "Even so, we are now warned not to discard the Byzantine evidence *en bloc.*"

Several things should be observed concerning these "Distinctively" Byzantine readings found in the early papyri.

1. These 150 readings are early. They go back to the second century, for they are supported by papyri which range from the third to the second century in date. That such readings must be early is almost universally admitted by textual critics.

2. These readings were not edited in the fourth century. They were present in Egypt by the end of the second century.

3. The Old Uncials have not preserved a complete picture of the second century. The inadequacy of the "Old Uncials" to portray the second century textual picture is underscored further when p[45], p[66], p[72], p[75] are also seen to confirm the early and wide-spread existence of K readings which are neither Alexandrian nor Western. Westcott and Hort insisted that all pre-Syrian evidence for readings was to be found in the Alexandrian, Neutral and Western Texts, and they gave the complete second-century picture of the textual tradition. However, the distinctive Byzantine readings by early Egyptian papyri have proved that Westcott and Hort were wrong.

4. The Byzantine text-type has preserved second-century tradition not preserved by the other text-types. These readings are evidence that the Byzantine text has preserved at least portions of the second-century tradition of the New Testament independently of the Egyptian and Western text-type. Until the discovery of these papyri, the Byzantine text had been the sole repository of these readings from the second century. The Byzantine text-type can no longer be ignored in textual decisions.

5. Numerous distinctively Byzantine readings now proved early would seem to reverse the burden of proof. Instead of assuming that characteristically Byzantine readings are late, it may be more logical and more in accord with the facts, to assume that they are early. The burden of proof now appears to rest on whomever claims that a Byzantine reading is late. Furthermore, making textual decisions on the basis of how three or four "old" uncials read should be abandoned because they do not give a complete picture of the second-century traditions.

An interesting thought is that the Byzantine readings originated early in Antioch and found their way to Egypt and into early copies of manuscripts there. This seems logical for the early period because Antioch was the first missionary church. Such readings were then preserved in Antioch in the Byzantine text but became buried with the papyri in Egypt because they were rejected by the Alexandrian editors.

It is concluded that the papyri supply valid evidence that the distinctively Byzantine readings were not created in the fourth century but were already in existence before the end of the second century and that, because of this, Byzantine readings merit serious consideration.

BYZANTINE-WESTERN ALIGNMENTS GO BACK INTO THE SECOND CENTURY INDEPENDENTLY AND ORIGINATE IN THE EAST – NOT IN THE WEST

Westcott and Hort vigorously rejected the thought that Syrian text-type could add any weight of authority to the Western readings. However, in the Egyptian part of the Roman Empire there are Egyptian papyri, which read differently than the Alexandrian papyri, that agree with the Byzantine readings, thus attesting to an early origin of Byzantine readings. Gunther Zuntz said he found no instances in which any distinctively Western reading had ever affected the Eastern texts. His conclusion was that the readings in which the Byzantine text agrees with the Western text did not come from the West, but originated in the East. This is a blow to the Westcott and Hort theory. Zuntz sought to show that K-text, in each instance, to be the preserver of a very early form of the text as it was known and used in the East before it was adopted by the West.

Kuntz's work was with the p [46], the earliest of the Chester Beatty Papyri. He said, "Purely Byzantine readings, as we saw before, may be ancient. We can now add: Byzantine readings which occur in Western witnesses must be ancient. They go back to the time before the Chester Beatty papyrus was written; the time before the emergence of separate Eastern and Western traditions; in short, they reach back deep into the second century." His findings were that the Byzantine text furnishes an early and independent weight of evidence for readings where it and the Western text agree against the Alexandrian. He said the evidence now shows that in cases of Byzantine Western alignments, there has been independent preservation of such readings by each text-type from deep in the second century. Furthermore, such agreements did not result from an Eastern adoption of readings which originated in the West. The West got these readings from the East originally, which is attested by the Egyptian papyri.

Therefore, these papyrus-Byzantine-Western alignments opposed by the Alexandrian text-type reveal readings which were well nigh universally known in the second century. But, though they were eliminated from the Alexandrian text-type, they have been preserved independently in the Byzantine and in the Western traditions.

It is an intolerable thought for Westcott and Hort followers that the Antiochian text may have been the source rather than the recipient of the common material in such Byzantine-Western alignments.

THE SIGNIFICANCE OF THE BYZANTINE TEXT-TYPE

The significant provenance (geographical origin) of the Antiochian text-type raises further doubts about its dependence on Alexandria and the Western parts of the Empire. Why should the great apostolic and mission-minded church at Antioch send to Alexandria, or any other center, for Scripture copies by which to correct her own? Antioch was the third city of the Empire; a city with an independent and proud spirit; and something of this same independent spirit was part of its heritage as the "mother of all Gentile churches."

Antioch may well have been the prime source of the earliest copies of most of the New Testament Scriptures for newly established churches. Antioch was the place where the first Gentile missions originated. It was the home base for the Apostle Paul; Luke may have been there; Mark, Barnabas and Silas, Paul's companions, were there; Peter visited Antioch; Matthew may have written his Gospel there. Paul himself could have double-checked the local copies of his own epistles which were, thus far, possessed by the church at Antioch before he made his last journey from that place.

It should be remembered that the leadership of the Antiochian church was not characterized by illiteracy or a low level of education (Acts 13:1), and therefore, incapable of making copies of "Scriptures."

It is difficult to assume Antiochian dependence on other local texts for the improvement of her own. It might appear more logical to reason that if Antioch would send anywhere for copies of the New Testament Scriptures in order to purify its own text, they would most likely send to Ephesus, Galatia, Colosse, Thessalonica, Philippi, Corinth and Rome in order to acquire more perfect copies of the epistles originally sent to these locations.

Both Antioch and Alexandria had theological schools. Theophilus, who died before 188 A.D., was an advocate for the literal interpretation of Scriptures. He is considered a forerunner of the "School of Antioch." Antioch developed a school of literal interpretation which was almost diametrically opposed to the "School of Alexandria" with its principles of allegorical interpretation. This makes it difficult to believe that Antioch would look to Alexandria for help in either the earliest period or later when the differences between the schools became even more marked.

CONCLUSION

Westcott and Hort reasoned that the Byzantine text was made through an editorial process by using previously existing Western and Alexandrian texts. They argued that because the "Syrian" text was late, edited, and therefore secondary in origin, it should not be used as evidence in textual criticism of the New Testament.

Burgon and Hills, on the other hand, sought to controvert the Westcott and Hort theory by maintaining that the Byzantine text was the providentially preserved text; for this reason the Byzantine text was not secondary but primary. They refer to it as the "Traditional" text, the one which has descended in unbroken procession from the original because it was preserved by God's special care. In their opinion, the peculiar evidence for the primacy of the Byzantine text is its overwhelming superiority in numbers. For Burgon and Hills, the Alexandrian and Western texts are corruptions of the "Traditional" text and are, therefore, untrustworthy for the recovery of the original.

The thesis that the Byzantine text is late is now inadequate because of the Chester Beatty Papyri. Contrary to what Westcott and Hort held, distinctively Byzantine readings of every kind have been shown to be early as much as even in the second century.

Two conclusions are forthcoming: 1.) the Byzantine readings are early and 2.) the Byzantine text is unedited in the Westcott and Hort sense, and the conclusion which follows logically is that the Byzantine text is independent.

If the Byzantine text is not "secondary" but is "independent" in its attestation to early readings, it appears reasonable to conclude that the Byzantine text should be followed.

THE MINORITY, WESTERN, ALEXANDRIAN OR EGYPTIAN TEXT FAMILY & THE SO-CALLED GREAT UNCIALS

The second stream is a small one of a very few manuscripts, about 45. Less than 1% of all Greek New Testament manuscripts fit into this group. Here is a brief overview of the three manuscripts considered to be the most important within this group.

CODEX ALEXANDRINUS (A)

1. Codex Alexandrinus (A) – This codex was the first of the so-called "great uncials" to become known to western paleographers. "Walton, in his polyglot Bible, indicated it by the letter **A** and thus set the fashion of designating Biblical manuscripts by such symbols." (*The Catholic Encyclopedia* online; *Codex Alexandrinus*; http://www.newadvent.org/ cathen/04080c.htm). The codex came to the knowledge of the western world when Cyril Lucar, the Patriarch of the Greek Catholic (Greek Orthodox) Church in Alexandria was transferred in 1621 A.D. to become the new Patriarch of Constantinople. He sent the codex as a gift to King James I of England, but James I died before the gift was presented. Finally, in 1627 A.D. Charles I accepted it in James I's stead. It seems probable that Cyril Lucar had brought it with him from Alexandria. Concerning the provenance of the volume, there is "a note by Cyril Lucar states that it was written by Thecla, a noble lady of Egypt, but this is probably merely his interpretation of an Arabic note from the 14th century which states the MS was written by Thecla, the martyr (shortly after the Council of Nicaea in 325 AD)." The article goes on to say that "another Arabic note by Athanasius (probably Athanasius III., patriarch c. 1308 A.D.) states that it was given to the patriarch of Alexandria, and a Latin note of a later period dates the presentation in 1098." Upon careful examination, scholars say it is clear that more than one person worked on the volume. Actually, at some time in its history the work was bound into four volumes, three Old Testament Volumes and one containing the New Testament and 1 and 2 Clement. The Catholic Encyclopedia says, "two hands are discerned in the New Testament by Woide, three by Sir E. Maunde Thompson and Kenyon" and, "the greater part of Volume III (last volume of the Old Testament) is ascribed by Gregory to a different hand from that of the others." (*The Catholic Encyclopedia* online; *Codex Alexandrinus*). The text of Alexandrinus is in double columns of 49 to 51 lines. It is the first codex to contain the major chapters with their titles. A new paragraph is indicated by a large capital. But, there are some paleographers that believe **that the principal scribe who prepared this codex could not even read Greek**, because spaces sometimes appear in the middle of a word.

THE OLD TESTAMENT OF ALEXANDRINUS

I have often read that Alexandrinus contains a complete Old Testament. But that is not an accurate statement. There are about 30 Psalms missing, Psalm 49:19 to 79:10, because along the line some place, ten leaves of the Old Testament were lost. There are various other lacunas (gaps) in the Old Testament as well. "Genesis

14:14-17; 15:1-5, 16-19; 16:6-9; I Kings 12:20-14:9" are missing as well. (*The Catholic Encyclopedia* online; *Codex Alexandrinus*). The order of the Old Testament books is peculiar.

Not only are there Old Testament deletions, but there are numerous Old Testament **additions** as well. It contains deuterocanonical books and in addition to 1 and 2 Maccabees it adds 3 and 4 Maccabees which are apocryphal books of a very late origin. I find it interesting that *The Epistle to Marcellius,* which is attributed to Athanasius, is inserted as a preface to the Psalter, together with Eusebius' summary of the Psalms. It contains Psalm 151 as well as 14 Odes or Liturgical Canticles.

THE NEW TESTAMENT OF ALEXANDRINUS

The New Testament has lost from 19 to 25 leaves of the Gospel of Matthew, as far as Matthew 25:6. Strangely there are two leaves missing from the Gospel of John (John 6:50 to 8:52) which cover the much disputed passage about the adulterous woman. But, what is amazing is that the Gospels follow the so-called Syrian type text, the ancestor of the Textus Receptus, which is evidence that the traditional text type did have an early origin! There are three leaves missing in 2 Corinthians containing 4:13 to 12:6. This manuscript ends with Mark 16:8, therefore leaving out 9-20. It omits John 5:4 (For an angel went down at a certain season into the pool, and troubled the water: whosoever then first after the troubling of the water stepped in was made whole of whatsoever disease he had.) and 1 John 5:7 *(For there are three that bear record in heaven, the Father, the Word, and the Holy Ghost: and these three are one.).*

There are additions to the New Testament as well. According to the table of contents the New Testament once contained the Psalms of Solomon, though it is now missing. Also added to the New Testament are the Epistle of St. Clement of Rome and the II Epistle of Clement. In these two letters "Clement of Alexandria teaches that: [1] Men are saved by works (2 Clement 2:12,15); [2] Christians are in danger of going to Hell (2 Clement 3:8); [3] Christians don't get new bodies at the resurrection (2 Clement 4:2); [4] He was a prophet who wrote Scripture (2 Clement 4:11); [5] The male and female in 1 Corinthians 11:9 were anger and concupiscence (when they were speaking of Christ's being the head, then the husband, followed by the wife in order or chain of authority). Not believing the Bible literally, Clement both fantasized and spiritualized the Scriptures." (*Which Version is The Bible?* By Floyd Jones Th.D., Ph.D.; Published by Global Evangelism of Goodyear Arizona; p.69).

In conclusion, I have to wonder why Codex A is considered so valuable textually when it has so many problems. Copyist's errors are frequent. I remind you that numerous paleographers believe that whoever prepared the text could not even read Greek. Likewise it is agreed that two or three different people worked on the manuscript. One author says it "is considered one of the most valuable witnesses to the Septuagint." But, "it is found, however, to bear a great affinity to the text embodied in Origen's Hexapla and to have been corrected in numberless passages according to the Hebrew." And in fact, "the text of the Septuagint codices is in too chaotic a condition...to permit of a sure judgment on the textual value of the great manuscript." (*The Catholic Encyclopedia* online; *Codex Alexandrinus*). The New Testament is not much better because of its mixed origin, not to mention the extra biblical material included in the volume. This early 5th century copy of the Bible (with some mutilations) is in the British Library in London. Many scholars consider it to be 3rd of importance only to the next two...

CODEX VATICANUS (B)

2. Codex Vaticanus (B) – This codex is an uncial manuscript thought to be from mid-4th century. It is made up of 759 leaves written in three columns and has 42 lines to the column, except for the poetical books where there are two columns per page. "It was written by three scribes" according to the Encyclopedia Britannica which goes on to state that later and then much later changes were made by two other scribes (*Encyclopedia Britannica - 11ᵗʰ Edition; vol.3*; p879). It went unnoticed in the Vatican library for many years until it became known to textual scholars in 1475. However, it was used by Rome. "Pope Sixtus V made it the basis of an edition of the Greek Old Testament in 1580" (*The New Archeological Discoveries and Their Bearing Upon the New Testament* by Camden M. Cobern; published by Funk and Wagnalls 1922; p.136).

It was not published to scholars until it was issued in different volumes between 1828 to 1838 in 5 volumes which proved to be very inaccurate. In fact, the Vatican kept the manuscript sequestered and took great pains to be sure it was not readily available to outsiders for about another 400 years! From 1843-1866, leading scholars Constantine von Tischendorf and S.P. Tregelles were allowed to look at it for a few hours, but not allowed to copy the MS.

How is this manuscript viewed? Though I cannot figure out why, **many consider this to be the greatest of Codex witnesses to the New Testament**. In fact, this parchment manuscript "was reckoned <u>as the chief authority among MSS. for the Greek Testament of Westcott and Hort</u>." (*The New Archeological Discoveries and Their Bearing Upon the New Testament* by Camden M. Cobern; published by Funk and Wagnalls 1922; p.136). But there are those who have questioned this evaluation and with good reason! In 1860, while a temporary chaplain of an English congregation at Rome, <u>John Burgon made a personal examination of it and found some major problems within the manuscript</u>. This has been confirmed by many others. Here are just a few of the problems. "The entire manuscript has had the text mutilated, <u>every letter has been run over with a pen, making exact identification of many of the characters impossible</u>." (*Vaticanus and Sinaiticus* - ww.waynejackson. freeserve. co.uk/kjv /v2.htm).

Dr. W. Eugene Scott, who owns a large collection of ancient Bible manuscripts and Bibles says, "the manuscript is faded in places; scholars think it was overwritten letter by letter in the 10th or 11th century, with accents and breathing [marks] added along with corrections from the 8th, 10th and 15th centuries. **All this activity makes precise paleographic analysis impossible**. <u>Missing portions were supplied in the 15th century by copying other Greek manuscripts</u>." (*Codex Vaticanus* by Dr. W. Eugene Scott, 1996). I question the "great witness" value of any manuscript that has been overwritten, doctored, changed and added to for more than 10 centuries.

THE OLD TESTAMENT OF VATICANUS

The first 46 chapters of Genesis are missing through Genesis 46:28. 2 Kings 2:5-7, 10-13 are missing as well. Psalm 105:27 to Psalm 137:6 are omitted as well. "The order of the books of the Old Testament is as follows: Genesis to Second Paralipomenon, First and Second Esdras, Psalms, Proverbs, Ecclesiastes, Canticle of

Canticles, Job, Wisdom, Ecclesiasticus, Esther, Judith, Tobias, the Minor Prophets from Osee to Malachi, Isaias, Jeremias, Baruch, Lamentations and Epistle of Jeremias, Ezechiel, Daniel; the Vatican Codex does not contain the Prayer of Manasses or the Books of Maccabees." (*The Catholic Encyclopedia* online; *Codex Vaticanus*)

THE NEW TESTAMENT OF VATICANUS

Coming to **the New Testament**, Barry Burton writes in his book *Let's Weigh the Evidence* — "it omits...Matthew 3, the Pauline Pastoral Epistles (1 & 2 Timothy, Titus, Philemon), Hebrews 9:14 to 13:25, and all of Revelation... in the gospels alone it leaves out 237 words, 452 clauses and 748 whole sentences, which hundreds of later copies agree together as having the same words in the same places, the same clauses in the same places and the same sentences in the same places." Floyd Jones further notes that Matthew 16:2-3 and Romans 16:24 are missing.

There is yet another strange thing about Vaticanus that John Burgon tells us about relating to the last twelve verses of Mark.

"To say that in the Vatican Codex (B), which is unquestionably the oldest we possess, St. Mark's Gospel ends abruptly at the eighth verse of the sixteenth chapter, and that the customary subscription (Kata Mapkon) follows, is true; but it is far from being the whole truth. It requires to be stated in addition that the scribe, whose plan is found to have been to begin every fresh book of the Bible at the top of the next ensuing column to that which contained the concluding words of the preceding book, has at the close of St. Mark's Gospel deviated from his else invariable practice. He has left in this place one column entirely vacant. It is the only vacant column in the whole manuscript. Why did he leave that column vacant? What can have induced the scribe on this solitary occasion to depart from his established rule? The phenomenon (I believe I was the first to call distinct attention to it) is in the highest degree significant, and admits only one interpretation. The older manuscript from which Codex B was copied must have infallibly contained the twelve verses in dispute. The copyist was instructed to leave them out — and he obeyed; but he prudently left a blank space *in memoriam rei*. Never was a blank more intelligible! Never was silence more eloquent! By this simple expedient, strange to relate, the Vatican

Codex is made to refute itself even while it seems to be bearing testimony against the concluding verses of St. Mark's Gospel, by withholding them; for it forbids the inference which, under ordinary circumstances, must have been drawn from that omission. It does more. By leaving room for the verses it omits, it brings into prominent notice at the end of fifteen centuries and a half, a more ancient witness than itself." (*The Last Twelve Verses of the Gospel of St. Mark* by John William Burgon; p. 86-87).

That's not all. I turn your attention to **John 1:18** — *"No man hath seen God at any time; the only begotten Son, which is in the bosom of the Father, he hath declared him."* Notice the phrase I have underlined, "the only begotten Son." Both Vaticanus (B) and Sinaiticus (Aleph) read "the only begotten **God**" instead of "the only begotten **Son**." That clearly reflects the Arian heresy! In fact, many textual authorities have identified Vaticanus and Sinaiticus, the manuscripts so revered by modern textual critics, as two of the copies of the Greek New Testament made by Eusebius. Frederick Nolan and other authorities have charged Eusebius with making many changes in the Scripture. Nolan wrote, "As it is thus apparent that Eusebius was not wanting in power, so it may be shown that he wanted not the will, to make those alterations in the sacred text, with which I have ventured to accuse him." (*An Inquiry into the Integrity of the Greek Vulgate* by Frederick Nolan; p. 35). I bring this to your attention because, "it is no less true to fact than paradoxical in sound, that the worst corruptions to which the New Testament has ever been subjected, originated within a hundred years after it was composed; that Irenaeus (A.D. 150), and the African Fathers, and the whole Western, with a portion of the Syrian Church, used far inferior manuscripts to those employed by Stunica, or Erasmus, or Stephens thirteen centuries later, when moulding the Textus Receptus." (Scrivener, *Introduction to New Testament Criticism*, 3rd Edition, 511, quoted in Wilkinson, p.18.).

Here is another interesting fact. "It contains the Epistle of Barnabas...which teaches that water baptism saves the soul." (*Which Version is The Bible?* by Floyd Jones; published by Global Evangelism of Goodyear Arizona; p. 68).

Finally, there are two important points that I want to make before moving on. "Erasmus knew about Vaticanus B and its variant readings in 1515 A.D. while preparing the New Testament Greek text. Because they read so differently from the vast majority of mss which he had seen, Erasmus considered such readings spurious." (*Which Version is The Bible?* by Floyd Jones; published by Global Evangelism of Goodyear Arizona; p. 68). Further, as I understand it, Vaticanus was available to the translators of the King James Bible, but they did not use it because they knew it is unreliable. It wasn't until 1889-1890 that a complete facsimile was made. The manuscript remains in Vatican City to this day.

One more note of interest. There is a note in Hebrews 1, between the two columns. A corrector had erased a word in what would be verse 3 and substituted another word in its place. A second corrector came along, erased the change, reinstated the original word, and wrote this comment – "Fool and knave, leave the old reading, don't change it."

CODEX SINAITICUS (A OR ALEPH)

3. **Codex Sinaiticus (a or ALEPH)** – This codex (also mid-4th century) was discovered by Tischendorf at St. Catherine's Monastery at the foot of Mt. Sinai on his third visit there in 1859. Today, most of this codex is housed in the National British Library. "The original provenance of the codex is debatable, but the two likeliest contenders seem to be Egypt and Caesarea. It was certainly present in the library at Caesarea sometime between the fifth and seventh centuries, where it was corrected at one point against a manuscript that had been corrected against the original Hexapla of Origen by the martyr Pamphilius. Although it has frequently been suggested, it is unlikely that Sinaiticus (or Codex Vaticanus, a very similar manuscript) was one of the fifty parchment books ordered by the Emperor Constantine. The text of the OT reflects the Old Greek (where it has been determined), though it is inferior to Vaticanus in most books. In the NT, Sinaiticus is frequently cited as an Alexandrian witness. However, in John 1-8, at least, it contains a text more closely related to the Western tradition." (*Codex Sinaiticus* by James R. Adair, Jr. - Expanded by the author from his article in *Eerdmans Dictionary of the Bible*).

This manuscript is written on thin vellum. The portion of the manuscript that resides at the British Library contains 346½ leaves; of that number 199 are Old Testament leaves. There are another 43 leaves at the University Library at Leipzig and yet another 3 partial leaves at Leningrad. In 1975 the monks at St. Catherine's monastery discovered several leaves from Genesis, believed to be from Sinaiticus, in a room whose ceiling had collapsed centuries ago. The leaves measure 13 x 15½ inches and are written in uncial characters, without accents or breathings, and with no punctuation except, at times, the apostrophe and the single point for a period. It is written in four columns to the page, except in the poetical books, which are written in two wide columns. There are 48 lines per column except in the Catholic Epistles, which have 47 lines per column. Originally it must have contained the whole Old Testament, but it "has suffered severely from mutilation, especially in the historical books from Genesis to Esdras (Ezra) inclusive. A curious oddity that occurs is that Esdras (Ezra) 9:9 follows 1 Parlipomen (1 Chronicles) 19:17 without any break." (*The Catholic Encyclopedia* online; *Codex Sinaiticus*). The article goes on to say that one of the many later correctors has added a note that states that the seven leaves of 1 Parlipomen (1 Chronicles) were copied into the Book of Esdras (Ezra) because the manuscript from which Sinaiticus was copied was incorrect as well. One has to wonder about the scribe(s) doing the copying. Either he (or they) did not know the Bible or he did not know the language or he was careless. Perhaps it was a combination of all of these. But, I must say that errors like this lead me to doubt that statement of the "scholars" who claim that this is one of the "best" manuscripts. Speaking of scribes, Konstantin Von Tischendorf identified the handwriting of four different scribes in the writing of the original text. But that is not the end of the scribe problem! "He recognized seven correctors of the text..." (*The Catholic Encyclopedia* online; *Codex Sinaiticus*). Others say there were as many as ten scribes who altered the text. James R. Adair, Jr., author of the article on Sinaiticus in the *Eerdmans Dictionary of the Bible* says at one point the codex was "corrected against the original Hexpala of Origen by the martyr Pamphilius." He arrived at this conclusion because of a note that is in the manuscript. It reads —

"This codex was compared with a very ancient exemplar which had been corrected by the hand of the holy martyr Pamphilus [died 309 AD]; which exemplar contained at the end of the subscription in his own hand: 'Taken and corrected according to the Hexapla of Origen: Antonius compared it: I, Pamphilus, corrected it.'"

The problem is that Origen was a Bible corrupter, who "was moving away from the pure text of Scripture which had come from the Apostles hands." *(Rome and The Bible;* by David Cloud; published by Way of Life Literature, 1996; p. 22). And there is good reason to come to this conclusion. Origen "cited the versions of Aquila, Symmachus, and Theodotion, on the former part of the Canon, he appealed to the authority of Valentinus and Heracleon on the latter. While he thus raised the credit of those revisals, which had been made by heretics, he detracted from the authority of that text which had been received by the orthodox. Some of the difficulties which he found himself unable to solve in the Evangelists, he undertook to remove..." *(Inquiry into the Integrity of the Greek Vulgate* by Frederick Nolan; published 1815; p.432).

My point is simply this. The early corrections of the manuscript are made from Origen's corrupt source. But that was just the beginning of the tampering! As many as nine other scribes tampered with the codex. Consider the observations of Tischendorf once again. He "counted 14,800 corrections in Sinaiticus." *(Codex Sinaiticus* by Navida Shahid; www.beyond-the-illusion.com/files/Religion/Islam/research/codx0894.html).

Alterations, and more alterations and more alterations were made, and, in fact, most of them are believed to have been made in the 6th and 7th centuries. "On nearly every page of the manuscript there are corrections and revisions, done by 10 different people." *(Which Is The Right Version of the Bible*; www.waynejackson. freeserve.co.uk/kjv/v2.htm). He goes on to say, "...the New Testament...is extremely unreliable...on many occasions 10, 20, 30, 40, words are dropped...letters, words even whole sentences are frequently written twice over, or begun and immediately canceled; while that gross blunder, whereby a clause is omitted because it happens to end in the same word as the clause preceding occurs no less than 115 times in the New Testament."

There is one particular omission that made a real impact upon my mind that I want to draw your attention to. Several years back I went to the British Museum, specifically to take a look at Sinaiticus. To my surprise I discovered Mark 16:9-20 indeed was missing. This accounts for the New International Version saying— "The two most reliable early manuscripts do not have Mark 16:9-20." It should be noted that the Sinaiticus New Testament omits Matthew 16:2-3; John 5:5, John 8:1-11; Acts 8:37; Romans 16:24; 1 John 5:7 and about a dozen other entire verses. "The most significant fact regarding these MSS is that in both Vaticanus B and Sinaiticus a, John 1:18 reads that Jesus was the only begotten 'God' instead of the only begotten 'Son'–which is the original Arian heresy! This means that God had a little God named Jesus who is thus a lesser God than the Father– that at first there was a big God and He created a little God. Thus, Jesus comes out to be a God with a little 'g'. But at the incarnation **a god was not begotten**. God begat a son who, insofar as his deity is concerned, is eternal (Micah 5:2).This reading renders these MSS as UNTRUSTWORTHY and DEPRAVED! This Arian heresy resulted from Origen's editing the Greek manuscripts encountered in his travels and appears in Vaticanus B and Sinaiticus a, which were derived from copying his work." (*The Septuagint: A Critical Analysis* by Floyd Jones; published by Global Evangelism 1998; p. 10).

There are numerous other problems with this codex as well. For instance, it includes two uninspired books in the New Testament. The entire Epistle of Barnabas, except six leaves, (which teaches baptismal regeneration), and the Shepherd of Hermas, which is incomplete.

Finally, I must point out something ironic about these two alleged "oldest and best" manuscripts. They do not agree with each other! "There are 3036 differences between the readings in Vaticanus and Sinaiticus in the Gospels alone" (*Codex B and Its Allies* by Herman Hoskier; volume 2, p.1). John Burgon points out that it is easier to find two consecutive verses in which the two manuscripts differ, than two consecutive verses in which they entirely agree. We should find that very disturbing. My research has led me to conclude **that the three "Great Uncials" are at best unreliable**. I am thankful that the Bibles of the martyrs, that is to say, the Bibles of the Reformation, were based on the **majority text family**.

CHAPTER #6

"CHRISTIAN" GNOSTICISM'S CORRUPTION OF THE WESTERN/ALEXANDRIAN MANUSCRIPTS

There is a *Gnostic Revival* going on today. It has been fueled by the Gnostic fairy tale, *The Da Vinci Code*, the National Geographic Society's sponsorship, television special and publication of the Gnostic Gospel of Judas and a renewed interest in The Nag Hammadi Codices.

Please note that the word "Christian" is between quotation marks. By using the quotation marks I am indicating to the reader that I am saying that the "Christianity" of the Gnostics is not really Christianity at all. In fact, the only way that the Gnosticism I am speaking of can be considered Christian, is in the sense that they scrounged words, writings and ideas from Christianity, and then redefined, rearranged, edited and rewrote them to fit their own purposes and to advance their own false teachings. I present this to you, so that you will realize that the "scholarly" community is all in a frenzy about the so-called Gnostic Gospels, and are in the process of rewriting early Christian History with a Gnostic spin to reflect the findings at Nag Hammadi, Egypt and the recently discovered Gospel of Judas. I trust this information will be helpful.

Let me tell you a little bit about the Nag Hammadi manuscripts...

THE GNOSTIC DISCOVERY AT NAG HAMMADI, EGYPT & THE DA VINCI CODE

Nag Hammadi is a village in Egypt near the Nile River. In 1945, six Bedouin camel drivers were digging for fertilizer when one of them uncovered a human skeleton. Next to the skeleton was an earthenware jar. Inside the jar, they found thirteen leather-bound volumes containing fifty-two treatises; hence they were called the Nag Hammadi codices. This library of ancient documents, dated around 350 A.D. contained texts relating to an early Christian heresy called Gnosticism. Dan Brown's book, titled, *The Da Vinci Code,* falsely characterizes these writings as "the earliest Christian records" and the "unaltered gospels."

These thirteen leather-bound volumes contained fifty-two treatises including The Gospels of Thomas and Philip. Also found were the Acts of Peter and the Twelve Apostles, The Letter of Peter to Philip and the Apocalypses of Peter and Paul. In his book, *The Gnostic Discoveries,* Marvin Meyer makes it clear all of the writings were Gnostic in nature, and they were **all written in Coptic**. Now, there is another important fact you need to know. The Nag Hammadi texts were all written in the second and third centuries A.D. In *The Da Vinci Code*, Teabing claims that the Nag Hammadi texts are "the earliest Christian records (*DVC* p.245). **The truth is that <u>every book in the New Testament was written in the first century A.D.</u>**! In fact, Gnostic beliefs did not begin to be mixed with Christianity until about 150 A.D. and so-called Christian Gnostic sects virtually disappeared by the 6th century. The only known exception was the Mandaean sect of Iran/Iraq.

There is also something further I should draw to your attention. <u>Scholars regard the Gnostic gospels as not genuine, spurious, and counterfeit.</u>

A BRIEF DEFINITION AND EXPLANATION OF GNOSTICISM

Peter Jones, professor of New Testament at Westminster Seminary California, and director of *Christian Witness to a Pagan Planet,* says this about Gnosticism –

"Gnosticism is formed from the Greek term ***gnosis*** meaning knowledge, but it means here a particular form of knowledge, namely 'spiritual experience.' Like all pagan spirituality, so-called

'Christian' Gnosticism engages in 'sacred technologies' (occult meditations, chanting mantras, drumming, etc.) to access the higher, spiritual self, the self that is part of God. In this essentially out-of-body experience, all physical and this-worldly restraints, like rational thinking and a sense of specific gender, fall away. In a word, the experience of 'enlightenment' is both the rejection of the goodness of the physical creation and an acquisition of the knowledge of the divinity of the human soul."

Basically, Gnostics see the human soul as divine. You look within for God.

There was <u>no consensus on a Gnostic canon of scriptures</u>. Gnostic groups had no scruples about rewriting and adapting other religions' sacred writings to fit their fancy. Many of their own works were circulated in different versions. Various sects had their own <u>preferred rendition.</u> Further, Gnostic groups had <u>no unified doctrinal statement within Gnostic groups</u>. In fact, the Nag Hammadi find revealed that <u>a variety of different beliefs existed among different groups and individuals</u>. For instance, some taught celibacy and others did not.

THE EARLY CORRUPTION OF THE NEW TESTAMENT

Purposeful efforts to alter and corrupt the New Testament began almost immediately after each Gospel and letter was written. Look at **2 Corinthians 2:17** *"For we are not as many, <u>which corrupt the word of God</u>: but as of sincerity, but as of God, in the sight of God speak we in Christ."* The word **corrupt** here is a translation of the Greek word kapaleuontes (kap-ale-loo-entace) which means, a huckster. One scholar said this about the word – The word was used to describe shady "wine-dealers *playing tricks with their wines*; mixing the new, harsh wines, so as to make them pass for old. They not only sold their wares in the market, but had *wine-shops* all over the town..." where they peddled their corrupt wine claiming it was genuine. They made a bundle of money by their deception.

So, <u>how is this word used in reference to the Word of God</u>? Gnostic hucksters, and others, took the pure word of God and, like the shady wine dealers, mixed in their own philosophies, opinions and perversions, and they peddled it all over as the real thing.

We know that false gospels and false letters were written and circulated while the apostles were still alive. Look at **2 Thessalonians 2:2** *"That ye be not soon shaken in mind, or be troubled, neither by spirit, nor by word, nor by letter as from us, as that the day of Christ is at hand."* It is obvious that someone had written a letter and was circulating it, claiming that it was from the Apostle Paul and other disciples. Paul says the letter is bogus, fake, a fraud.

2 Peter 2:1-3 says, *"But there were false prophets also among the people, even as there shall be false teachers among you, who privily shall bring in damnable heresies, even denying the Lord that bought them, and bring upon themselves swift destruction. 2 And many shall follow their pernicious ways; by reason of whom the way of truth shall be evil spoken of. 3 And through covetousness shall they with feigned words make merchandise of you: whose judgment now of a long time lingereth not, and their damnation slumbereth not."* These false prophets and teachers are said to **"privily...bring in damnable heresies."** That is, they secretly introduced spurious (unauthentic, counterfeit or bogus) teachings that were "damnable heresies" or perversions of the truth. They sought to peddle these heresies among believers. And how would they do that? Certainly by their slick teachings, but likely also in their writings and corruptions of what God had given in the New Testament.

AN OVERVIEW OF GNOSTIC HERESIES

Let's look at some of the early heresies that developed in the days of the apostles, and shortly afterwards. The beginnings of these heresies are alluded to in the Epistles of John, Paul and Jude.

Galatians 1:6-8 *"I marvel that ye are so soon removed from him that called you into the grace of Christ unto another gospel: 7 Which is not another; but there be some that trouble you, and would pervert the gospel of Christ. 8 But though we, or an angel from heaven, preach any other gospel unto you than that which we have preached unto you, let him be accursed."*

Someone was promoting a false perverted letter or letters, and many in the church of Galatia were buying into the lie.

1 John 4:3 in the King James Bible —*"And every spirit that confesseth not that Jesus Christ is come in the flesh is not of God...."*

The NIV says, "Every spirit that does not acknowledge Jesus is not from God...." You see that the NIV leaves out the word "**Christ.**" Why? It is because it was translated from the Alexandrian line of Greek texts that had been corrupted by the Gnostics. The so-called "Christian" Gnostics believed in a dualistic Jesus Christ. Jesus was the physical Jesus and Christ was the spiritual Jesus. This will be explained more fully later in this book. However, suffice it to say that this corrupt teaching influenced some of the scribes who changed the Apostolic texts to reflect their Gnostic beliefs.

Jude 1:3-4 *"Beloved, when I gave all diligence to write unto you of the common salvation, it was needful for me to write unto you, and exhort you that ye should earnestly contend for the faith which was once delivered unto the saints. 4 For there are certain men crept in unawares, who were before of old ordained to this condemnation, ungodly men, turning the grace of our God into lasciviousness, and denying the only Lord God, and our Lord Jesus Christ."* This verse makes it obvious that "ungodly men" were turning the "grace of our God into lasciviousness." That is what Gnostics did. They taught that the flesh is evil and therefore, it does not matter what you do with it.

Next, we are going to look at three early heresies – **Gnosticism in general, Docetism, and Marcionism.** Docetism and Marcionism are types of Gnosticism. There are others, but I will only address these. But, know this: Gnosticism had a big influence on early Christianity and also had a major influence on the transmission of the New Testament, and accounts for many of the differences between the Apostolic-Traditional line and the Alexandrian-Western line of manuscripts.

GNOSTICISM IN GENERAL

I remind you of what was mentioned earlier in this book: There was no unified doctrinal statement among Gnostic groups. There was no consensus on a Gnostic canon of scriptures. Gnostic groups had no scruples about rewriting and adapting other religions' sacred writings to fit their fancy. Many of their own works were circulated in different versions. Various sects had their own preferred rendition.

While my research indicates that Carpocrates was the founder of the "Christian" Gnostics in the first half of the second century A.D., I do not know for sure that there were not others that preceded him. There were sects of Gnostics before him that used other religions and philosophies as their basis. However, we know that Carpocrates corrupted Christian teachings because of what Irenaeus wrote. The earliest and most vivid account of the Carpocratian Gnostics can be found in Irenaeus' (130-202 A.D.) work titled *Against Heresy.* This sect did **not** believe Jesus was divine. His followers did not believe they had to follow the Law of Moses or any moral law. They were very licentious (immoral) in their behavior.

Gnosticism, in all of its varieties, was the most influential heresy faced by the early Church. Not only did the Gnostics corrupt many readings found in the New Testament, but also offered their own writings as inspired scriptures, such as the *The Gospel of Thomas, The Gospel of Peter, The Gospel of Philip, The Gospel of Judas, The Gospel of the Ebionites, The Gospel of The Twelve, The Gospel According To The Hebrews* (also called *The Gospel According To Matthew,* not to be confused with the real Gospel of Matthew), *The Gospel According to the Egyptians, The Gospel of Mary (Magdalene), The Acts of Andrew, The Acts of Peter, The Acts of John,* etc. Gnosticism had a variety of forms and sects, which broadened its base and growth. Historian Will Durant calls Gnosticism "the quest of godlike knowledge (gnosis) through mystic means" (*The Story Of Civilization* Vol. III, p. 604).

Durant is correct. **Gnosticism is thinly veiled Pantheism**. Pantheism is the doctrine that identifies God with and in the whole universe; every particle, tree, table, animal, and person are part of GOD. Or, to explain it in a very basic way, the Greek word **pan** = all. The Greek word **theos** = God. Therefore it literally means "God is All" and "All is God."

The Gnostics taught that the physical (material) is evil and the spiritual (non-material) is good. Thus, a good god (spiritual) could not have created a physical world, because good can not create evil (that is the spiritual would not create the physical). So the Gnostic god created a being (or a line of beings called *aeons*) removing himself from direct creation. One of these aeons, or gods, created the world. The so-called **Christian Gnostics** believed that Jesus was one of these aeons who created the world. Some Gnostics taught that Jesus did not have a physical body. When he walked on the earth, he left no footprints because he never really touched the earth (he being spiritual and the world physical). Others taught that only our spiritual bodies were important, so the physical body could engage in whatever acts it desired because only the spiritual body would be saved. Still other Gnostics taught that the physical body was so evil that it must be denied in order for the spiritual body to gain salvation, thus shunning marriage and certain foods (**1 Timothy 4:1-3**).

The influence of Gnosticism can be seen in some of the heresies of today. **For example**, many of the teachings stated above are found, in revised form, in the teachings of the Jehovah's Witnesses. To the Jehovah's Witness, Jesus is a created god, not God manifest in the flesh. It is no wonder that the Watchtower's New World Translation *changes* "God was manifest in the flesh" in **1 Timothy 3:16** and replaces it with "He was made manifest in flesh." The TR Greek, which underlies our King James Bible, reads ψεοϖ *(theos)* (God) <2316> εϕανερωψη *(Ephanerothe)* (was manifested/revealed) <5319> (5681) εν (in) <1722> σαρκι *(sarki)* (the flesh) <4561>. However, the Greek text which underlies the NWT has made a change, so it is natural for the Jehovah's Witnesses to choose the reading which reflects their false doctrine. What is interesting is that the NIV, NASB, ESV, and perhaps others say "*He*" instead of "God," thus following part of the Gnostic corruption. Why? Because the NWT, NASB, NIV and ESV have as their base the corrupt Alexandrian text.

The same is true of **John 1:18** where the NWT reads, "the only-begotten god" (Gk. *monogenes theos*). Again, this is because the Greek text of the NWT reads differently from the Textus Receptus Greek text that the King James Bible was translated from – "*only begotten Son*" (Gk. *monogenes heios*).

1881 Westcott & Hort - θεον ουδεις εωρακεν πωποτε <u>μονογενης θεος</u> ο ων εις τον κολπον του πατρος εκεινος εξηγησατο.

1894 Scrivener - θεον ουδεις εωρακεν πωποτε ο <u>μονογενης υιος</u> ο ων εις τον κολπον του πατρος εκεινος εξηγησατο.

Again, in both of these examples, the NASV and ESV agree with the NWT because <u>they are both based on the same Greek text</u>. It is clear that Gnostic false doctrine has influenced the various Western/Alexandrian manuscripts, and as a result of the modern translations using Greek texts based on Western manuscripts, Gnosticism influences translations today.

Before I move on, I want to point out that the phrase "*only begotten god*" is supported by Clement of Alexandria, Origen, Jerome, papyrus 66 and the Alexandrian (Western) line of manuscripts. The phrase "*only begotten Son*" is quoted by Chrysostom, Tertullian, Basil, the Old Latin and Old Syrian translations and the majority of all Greek manuscripts. Hence, you can see that the Western line of manuscripts, that underlies the modern translations, was corrupted by the Gnostics who introduced those corruptions in the texts originally. However, the Eastern or Traditional lines of manuscripts, which underlie our King James Bible, were not corrupted.

DOCETISM

Docetism is one of many types of Gnosticism. It dates back to Apostolic times. The name comes from the Greek word *dokesis*, "appearance" or "semblance," because they taught that Christ only "**appeared**" or "**seemed**" to be a man, to have been born, to have lived and suffered. This particular type of Gnosticism taught that Christ's body was a phantom and that he did not have a real physical body. Some denied the reality of Christ's human nature altogether, some only the reality of His human body or of His birth or death. The word *Docetae* which is best rendered by "**Illusionists**," first occurs in a letter of Serapion, Bishop of Antioch (190-203 A.D.) to the Church at Rhossos, where troubles had arisen about the public reading of the **apocryphal *Gospel of Peter***. Serapion, at first unsuspectingly, allowed it to be read, but soon after forbade it, saying that he had borrowed a copy from the sect who used it, "whom we call Docetae."

Another variety of **Docetism** taught that the nature of Christ was dualistic (two-fold), spiritual and physical. **Jesus** was the physical, **Christ** was the spiritual. The Christ departed Jesus at the crucifixion, and left him on the cross to suffer and die. There was no literal bodily resurrection, just a spiritual resurrection. This certainly differs from what the New Testament teaches. Consider the following passages of Scripture –

Colossians 2:6-9 *"As ye have therefore received Christ Jesus the Lord, so walk ye in him: 7 Rooted and built up in him, and stablished in the faith, as ye have been taught, abounding therein with thanksgiving. 8 Beware lest any man spoil you through philosophy and vain deceit, after the tradition of men, after the rudiments of the world, and not after Christ. 9 For in him dwelleth all the fulness of the Godhead bodily."*

Hebrews 10:5-12 *"Wherefore when he cometh into the world, he saith, Sacrifice and offering thou wouldest not, but <u>a body hast thou prepared me</u>: 6 In burnt offerings and sacrifices for sin thou hast had no pleasure. 7 Then said I, Lo, I come (in the volume of the book it is written of me,) to do thy will, O God. 8 Above when he said, Sacrifice and offering and burnt offerings and offering for sin thou wouldest not, neither hadst pleasure therein; which are offered by the law; 9 Then said he, Lo, I come to do thy will, O God. He taketh away the first, that he may establish the second. 10 By the which will we <u>are sanctified through the offering of the body of Jesus Christ once for all</u>. 11 And every priest standeth daily ministering and offering oftentimes the same sacrifices, which can never take away sins: 12 But this man, after he had offered one sacrifice for sins for ever, sat down on the right hand of God."*

Luke 24:39 *"Behold my hands and my feet, that it is I myself: handle me, and see; for a spirit hath not flesh and bones, as ye see me have."*

The Docetic Gnostics wrote their own *Gospels* including **The Acts of John** and, as mentioned above, **The Gospel of Peter**. The Gospel of Peter was cited by Justin Martyr, Origen, and Eusebius, but was not discovered by scholars until 1886. While excavating the grave of a monk, a French archaeological team discovered this manuscript in Egypt. Only a small portion of it remains, but what does remain, gives a differing account of the crucifixion than the four Gospels. This separation of the Christ from Jesus is seen in the following quotation – "And many went about with lamps, supposing that it was night, and fell down. And the Lord cried out, saying, 'My power, my power, thou hast forsaken me.' And when he had said it he was taken up. And in that hour the veil of the temple of Jerusalem was rent in twain." (Gospel of Peter, verse 5) Thus, according to the Docetics, the power of Jesus, that is the Christ was taken up, but Jesus was left to die on the cross and be buried in the tomb. There was no bodily resurrection!

I point this out because we see the same idea in **Matthew 8:29**. The King James Bible reads *"And, behold, they cried out, saying, What have we to do with thee, Jesus, thou Son of God? art thou come hither to torment us before the time?"*

The NIV says, **Matthew 8:29** "What do you want with us, Son of God?" This reading is from Nestle-Aland 21 and reflects the Alexandrian reading. Note that the NIV does not deny the exorciser is the "Son of God," but denies that He is **JESUS the Son of God**. This reading clearly reflects Gnostic dualistic teaching about Jesus Christ as we see exemplified in their false Gospel of Peter.

There is another interesting fact that you should know. The **Docetic Gnostics** used an altered version of the Gospel of Mark according to Irenaeus. He wrote —"Those who separate Jesus from Christ and say that Christ remained impassible while Jesus suffered, and try to bring forward the Gospel According to Mark, can be corrected out of that, if they will read it with a love of the truth." (Irenaeus' **Against Heresies**, cited from Early Christian Fathers Vol. 1; translated by Cyril C. Richardson and published by The Westminster Press, page 382).

MARCIONISM

Marcion was born in between 85 to 110 A.D. No one knows for sure. He founded his own Gnostic-oriented heretical sect about 144 A.D. He taught that the God of the Old Testament could not have been the Father of Jesus Christ, because Christ speaks of His Father as a God of love, but the God of the Jews was a God of wrath. Marcion taught that Jehovah, the God of the Old Testament, created the world, but that all created flesh was evil. The soul/spirit of man was created by a greater god, one who was above Jehovah. This greater god created the spiritual realm and was the true Father of Jesus Christ. To release man's soul from his flesh, this greater god sent Christ. Christ appeared, in the form of a thirty-year-old man, in a spiritual body that appeared to be physical but was not a physical body. **Salvation was gained by renouncing Jehovah and all things physical**. Marcion rejected the Hebrew Scriptures, and the quotations of those Hebrew Scriptures in the New Testament. **The followers of Marcion issued their own New Testament composed of Luke and Paul's letters revised to their liking**. The followers of Marcion made their revisions to support and reflect their doctrines. Ultimately, these Marcionian revisions reflected their private interpretations, and these perversions have survived in some of the ancient Greek New Testament manuscripts and account for the differences between the eclectic Greek text and the Textus Receptus.

Let me explain. Irenaeus points out that "Marcion cut up that Gospel According to Luke" (Irenaeus' *Against Heresies*, p. 382). This would account for the large number of changes found in varying manuscripts of Luke and the large number of verses that are left out. It is, for example, understandable why the phrase *"And when he had thus spoken, he shewed them his hands and his feet."* (**Luke 24:40**) would be omitted by Marcion, since he did not believe in the physical resurrection of Jesus but only in a spiritual resurrection. In fact, the apparatus of the United Bible Society's Greek text points out **that this verse is omitted by both Marcion and Codex D** (UBS, 2nd ed., p. 317). This verse is omitted from the text of the NEB and RSV. Thus we see that Codex D, which is a Western line of manuscripts in the Gospels, and the RSV reflect some of the tampering done by Marcion and his followers.

There were many other "Christian" Gnostic sects that existed between about 150-300 A.D. besides the two I have named above— The Valentinians, Simonians, Ophites, Basilidianians, Cainites, Nicolaites, Mandaeisites and many more. Many of the Gnostic corruptions of New Testament Scripture have made their way into the alleged "**oldest and best**" manuscripts.

[Source materials include: 1911 Encyclopedia Britannica; *Inspiration, Preservation and the KJV* by Dr. J. Michael Bates; *World Magazine* April 29 & May 20, 2006; *Early Heresies* by Thomas Holland; *The Gnostic Discoveries* by Marvin Meyer; *Jung and the Lost Gospels* by Stephan A. Hoeller]

CHAPTER #7

THE LATIN VULGATE

LATIN VERSIONS BEFORE JEROME

Let's look at the subject of the Latin Bible before the time of Jerome. The manuscripts which have survived from the earlier period are known by the general designation of **Old Latin**. When we ask where these first translations came into existence, we discover a somewhat surprising fact. **It was not at Rome**, as we might have expected. **The language of Christian Rome was mainly Greek, down to the 3rd century**. Paul wrote the Epistle to the Romans in Greek. When Clement of Rome, in the last decade of the 1st century, wrote an epistle in the name of the Roman church to the Corinthians, he wrote in Greek. Justin Martyr, and the heretic Marcion alike, wrote from Rome in Greek. Out of 15 bishops who presided over the Roman Church down to the close of the 2nd century, only four have Latin names. Even the pagan emperor Marcus Aurelius wrote his Meditations in Greek. If there were Christians in Rome at that period whose only language was Latin, they were not sufficiently numerous to be provided with Christian literature; at least none has survived.

THE OLD LATIN IN NORTH AFRICA

It is from North Africa that the earliest Latin literature of the church that we know of has come down to us. The church of North Africa had a distinguished list of Latin authors. One of the most eminent of these Africans was Cyprian, bishop of Carthage, who was martyred 257 A.D. His genuine works consist of a number of short treatises, or tracts, and numerous letters, filled with Scripture quotations from the Latin. It is certain that he used a version then and there in use, and it is agreed that "his quotations are carefully made and thus afford trustworthy standards of African Old Latin in a very early though still not the earliest stage" (Hort, *Introduction to the New Testament in Greek*, 78).

CYPRIAN'S BIBLE

Critical investigation has made it clear that the version used by Cyprian survives in a fragmentary copy of Mark and Matthew, now at Turin in North Italy, called Codex Bobbiensis (k), and in the fragments of the Apocalypse (Revelation) and Acts contained in a palimpsest at Paris called Codex Floriacensis (h). It has been found that another MS, Codex Palatinus (e) at Vienna, has a text closely akin to that exhibited in Cyprian, although there are traces of mixture in it. The text of these manuscripts, together with the quotations of the so-called *Speculum Augustini* (m), is known among scholars as **African Old Latin**. Another manuscript with an interesting history, Codex Colbertinus (c) contains also a valuable African element, but in many parts of the Gospels it sides also with what is called the **European Old Latin** more than with k or e.

It is clear to see that a Latin Bible existed at least a century and a half before Jerome's work.

TERTULLIAN'S BIBLE

Next, we move half a century nearer to the fountainhead of the African Latin Bible when we take up the testimony of Tertullian who flourished toward the close of the 2nd century. He differed from Cyprian in being a competent Greek scholar. He was thus able to translate for himself. Some scholars maintain that before 210-240 A.D. there was no Latin Bible, and that Tertullian, with his knowledge of Greek, just translated as he went along. Yet, far more scholars disagree, and the view generally is that while Tertullian's knowledge of Greek is a disturbing element, his writings, with the copious quotations from both Old Testament and New Testament, do testify to the existence of a version which had already been in circulation and use for some time.

THE EASTERN ORIGIN OF OLD LATIN

While many favor the origin of the first Latin Bible being from Africa, recent investigation into what is called the Western text of the New Testament has yielded results pointing elsewhere. **It is clear from a comparison that the Western type of text has**

close affinity with the Syriac witnesses originating in the eastern provinces of the empire. The close textual relation disclosed between the Latin and the Syriac versions has led some authorities to believe that, after all, the earliest Latin version may have been made in the East, and possibly at Antioch. An increasing number of discoveries are being made that point to the East, Antioch, as being the origin.

CLASSIFICATION OF OLD LATIN MANUSCRIPTS

We have already identified the African group, so designated from its connection with the great African Fathers, Tertullian and especially Cyprian, and comprising k, e, and to some extent h and m. The antiquity of the text here represented is attested by these African Fathers.

When we come down to the 4th century, we find in Western Europe, and especially in North Italy, a second type of text, which is designated **European group**. This group consists of the Codex Vercellensis (a) and Codex Veronensis (b) of the 4th or 5th century at Vercelli and Verona respectively, and there may be included also the Codex Vindobonensis (i) of the 7th century at Vienna. These give the Gospels, and *a* gives for John the text as it was read by the 4th century Father, Lucifer of Cagliari in Sardinia. The Latin of the Greek-Latin manuscript D (Codex Bezae) is known as d, and the Latin of the translation of Irenaeus, are classed with this group.

There is also a third type of Latin, called *Italic,* because of its more restricted range. It is represented by Codex Brixianus (f) of the 6th century, now at Brescia, and Codex Monacensis (q) of the 7th century, at Munich. The speculation is that this text is probably a modified form of the European, produced by revision, which has brought it more into accord with the Greek, and has given it a smoother Latin aspect. The group has received this name because the text found in many of Augustine's writings is the same, and as he expressed a preference for the **Itala**, the group was designated accordingly.

INDIVIDUAL CHARACTERISTICS

It is possible that all these groups, comprising, in all, 38 codices, go back to one original. When Jerome's revision took hold of the church, the Old Latin representatives for the most part dropped out of notice. <u>Some of them, however, held their ground and continued to be copied down to the 12th and even the 13th century</u>. Codex c is an example of this; it is a manuscript of the 12th century, but as Professor Burkitt has pointed out (*Texts and Studies*, IV, "Old Latin," 11) "it came from Languedoc, the country of the Albigenses. Only among those called heretics by Rome, and who were isolated from the rest of Western Christianity could an Old Latin text have been written at so late a period."

An instance of an Old Latin text copied in the 13th century is the Gigas Holmiensis, quoted as Gig, now at Stockholm, and so called from its great size. It contains the Acts and the Apocalypse of the Old Latin and the rest of the New Testament according to the Vulgate. It must be remembered that in the early centuries complete Bibles were unknown. Each group of books, Gospels, Acts and Catholic Epistles, Pauline Epistles, and Revelation for the New Testament, and Pentateuch, Historical Books, Psalms and Prophets for the Old Testament, has to be regarded separately. It is interesting, also, to note that when Jerome revised, or even retranslated from the Septuagint, Tobit and Judith of the Apocrypha, the greater number of these books, Wisdom, Ecclesiasticus, 1 and 2 Maccabees, and Baruch were left unrevised, and were simply added to the Vulgate from the Old Latin version.

[I have adapted this section from a report written by Thomas Nichols. The information comes from Wordsworth and White, *Old Latin Biblical Texts*, 4 volumes; F.C. Burkitt, "The Old Latin and the Itala," *Texts and Studies*, IV; "Old Latin VSS" by H.A.A. Kennedy in Hastings' *Dictionary of the Bible* (five volumes); "Bibelübersetzungen, Lateinische" by Fritzsche-Nestle in *PRE*[3]; *Introductions to Textual Criticism of the New Testament* by Scrivener, Gregory, Nestle, and Lake. - http://www.bible-researcher.com/oldlatin.html]

JEROME'S LATIN VULGATE

John 3:16 in the Latin Vulgate – sic enim dilexit Deus mundum ut Filium suum unigenitum daret ut omnis qui credit in eum non pereat sed habeat vitam aeternam.

"Make knowledge of the Scripture your love and you will not love the views of the flesh." Jerome

THE TRANSLATOR

His name was actually Sophronius Eusebius Hieronymus, but he chose to go by Jerome. He was born in about 340 to 342 A.D. according to the Catholic Encyclopedia. Other sources put his birth at about 347 A.D. The place of his birth was at Stridon, a small town in north Italy near today's Italian-Yugoslavian border. He was given an excellent classical education by his parents and was tutored in Rome by Donatus, the famous pagan grammarian. The result was that Jerome became an expert in the Greek and Latin languages. In 360 A.D., at about the age of eighteen, he was baptized into Roman Catholicism by Liberius, bishop of Rome. From Rome, he went to visit to Trier, famous for its schools, and there began his theological studies. Later he went to Aquileia, and towards 373 A.D. he set out on a journey to the East. He settled first in Antioch, where he heard Apollinaris of Laodicea, one of the first exegetes (verse by verse explainers of the Scripture) of that time and not yet separated from the Church. In 374 A.D. he went to Antioch. There, in a dream, he saw himself in judgment before Christ, who rebuked him for his vain pursuit of worldly wisdom. For penance, Jerome withdrew into the desert of Chalcis, southwest of Antioch, to live as a hermit and follow the false teaching of asceticism. He testifies that he was beset by temptations of many kinds. From 374 to 379 A.D. he followed this ascetic lifestyle, that is a solitary life of contemplation, austere self-denial, self-torture and poverty. To occupy himself, he began an intense study of Hebrew. He found this study extremely difficult. Jerome increasingly found life as an ascetic hermit in the deserts of Syria an unhappy experience so went to Antioch where he continued to study Greek and Hebrew. It was there that he was ordained as a Catholic priest. From there he moved to Constantinople about 380 or 381 A.D. where he studied under Gregory of Nazianzus, also called Gregory Theologus. We will look at some of the errors he picked up from Gregory a little bit later in our study. Around 382 A.D., Jerome returned to Rome where he was secretary to Pope Damasus I, and spiritual director of many noble Roman ladies who were becoming interested in the monastic life. It was Damasus, in about 382 A.D., who set him the task of making a new translation of the Bible into Latin — into the popular form of the language, hence the name of the translation: the Vulgate. After the death of Damasus on December 11, 384 A.D., Jerome found his position became a very difficult one. His harsh criticisms had made him many bitter enemies. After a few months he was compelled to leave Rome. By way of Antioch and Alexandria, he reached Bethlehem in 386 A.D. He settled there in a monastery near a convent founded by two Roman ladies, Paula and Eustochium, who had followed him to Palestine. He completed his Latin Bible in 405 A.D. He died at Bethlehem after a long illness on September 30, 420 A.D. He is buried at St. Mary Major in Rome.

JEROME AND HIS BELIEFS

Jerome picked up many bad teachings from Gregory of Nazianzus. Jerome erroneously taught, "If anyone disbelieves that Holy Mary is the Mother of God, such a one is estranged from the Godhead." One key problem that would taint Jerome's Bible translation was his rejection of the pure text of Scripture, which had come from the Apostles, and his acceptance of the corrupted Eusebian text. As we will see, Eusebius incorporated into his text the corrupted text of Origen. Jerome "was brought up (by Nazianzus) with a dislike for the vulgar [common] edition of the Greek, and with a predilection [a preconceived liking] for the corrected text of Eusebius." (*An Inquiry into the Integrity of the Greek Vulgate or Received Text of the New Testament, in which Greek manuscripts are newly classed, the integrity of the Authorized Text vindicated, and various readings traced to their origin;* by Frederick Nolan (1784-1864); Published in London by F.C. and J. Rivington, 1815; p.151). The problem here is that Eusebius, according to Nolan, made changes in the Greek text that was commonly used. Nolan states that "it is probable

Eusebius derived most of the peculiar readings from Origen." (Ibid. p.460) and further, Eusebius "suppressed those passages (Mark 16:9-20 and John 8:1-11) in his edition" (Ibid. p. 240) of the Greek New Testament.

Herein lies a major problem. "Eusebius worshipped at the altar of Origen's teachings... (*and*) used Origen's six-column Bible, the Hexapla, in his Biblical labors... Origen's corrupt manuscripts of the Scriptures were well arranged and balanced with subtlety." (*Alford's Greek New Testament: Volume 1, Part II - Publisher's Foreword*; Published by Guardian Press).

Church historian Philip Schaff referred to Origen as a Christian Gnostic and Platonist saying, "His predilection for Plato (the pagan philosopher) led him into many grand and fascinating errors." Origen (185-253 A.D.) was tainted on two accounts; by the Platonists and by the Gnostics! His native city was Alexandria, likely the greatest center of Gnostic sects and heretical in the Roman Empire. In fact, numerous textual critics "have accumulated evidence indicating that a vast majority of variant readings due to deliberate scribal corruption of the text were in existence by A.D. 250. Many corrupt manuscripts were produced under the auspices of Gnostic sects or by individual Gnostic teachers. Direct attacks on Scripture were made almost from the beginning, and are documented in the cases of Basilides, Marconi, the Ebionites, the Valentinians, and numerous others. These Gnostic heretics mutilated and altered Scripture to suit their own fancies. They were followed in this abominable practice in the 2nd century and early in the 3rd century by Justin Martyr (who as an apologist greatly modified Christianity by Greek philosophy), Tatian (the pupil of Justin Martyr who became a Gnostic and then produced the Diatessaron), Clement of Alexandria, and Origen (both clearly within the pale of Gnosticism)...The damage done to orthodox Christianity by these heretics can hardly be overestimated." (Ibid. p. iv). Dr. Benjamin G. Wilkinson demonstrates the folly of adopting Origen as a primary textual witness. He writes, "When we come to Origen, we speak the name of him who did the most of all to create and give direction to the forces of apostasy down through the centuries. It was he who mightily influenced Jerome, the editor of the Latin Bible known as the Vulgate."

When you closely examine Jerome, it becomes obvious that he was deeply infected with false teaching. Not only did Jerome follow the false teaching of asceticism, but he also believed the demonic doctrine that all church leaders should be celibate (1 Timothy. 4:1-3). James Heron, author of *The Evolution of Latin Christianity,* also tells us Jerome was at the forefront of Mariolatry (Mary worship), teaching that through Mary's obedience she became instrumental in helping redeem the human race. Further, he taught that Mary was a perpetual virgin, despite the biblical evidence to the contrary (Matthew 13:55-56; John 2:12). Heron writes further that Jerome was a leading influence in advocating "the invocation of the saints," teaching that the saints in heaven hear the prayers addressed to them by people on earth and then intercede for those who pray to them, sending help from heaven. This is wholly unbiblical, being a combination of necromancy and a usurpation of the mediatorial, high priestly office of the Lord Jesus Christ (1 Timothy 2:5; Hebrews 7:25-26). While we neither have time nor space to discuss the extent of his errant teachings, I will conclude by stating that he believed in the veneration of holy relics, including the bones of dead Christians, and in the blessing of so-called "holy" water. Obviously, Jerome was deeply infected with false teaching.

There is another issue that we need to look at before we move on, and that is the spirit and character of Jerome. Schaff writes of his "irritability and bitterness of temper, such vehemence of uncontrolled passion, such intolerant and persecuting spirit, and such inconstancy of conduct." (*History of The Christian Church* by Philip Schaff; vol. 3, p.206) One of Jerome's contemporaries said, "He had a fetid mouth, fraught with a putrid stench..." Armitage writes, "The pen of Jerome was rendered very offensive by his grinding tyranny and cragged temper. No matter how wrong he was, he could not brook (put up with) contradiction." (*A History of Baptists* by Thomas Armitage; p.207).

His pen was filled with venom. In fact, "Jerome had a particularly hateful attitude toward those who followed the simple apostolic Faith." (*Rome and The Bible* by David Cloud; p.24). On one hand you have genuine New Testament Christians who are seeking to "*earnestly contend for the faith which was once delivered unto the saints*" (Jude 1:3), and stand against apostasy. On the other hand, there are the apostates like Jerome, who are fearlessly adding their extra-biblical traditions and practices to what is clearly revealed in the Word of God. My point is simply this. It was impossible that Jerome possessed the Holy Spirit discernment necessary to produce a pure translation of the Scriptures.

JEROME'S TRANSLATION

There were numerous other Latin translations of the Scriptures in circulation before Jerome's version, such as the Old Latin and Italic versions. In fact, the separated Christians kept their old Latin versions, some of them still in use in the 12th century. Why? As we have already mentioned, Jerome's New Testament work used Greek manuscripts that moved away from the pure text of the Scriptures, those of Eusebius of Caesarea (270-340 A.D.) who based his Greek translation upon the corrupted translation of Origen (185-254 A.D.). When you begin with corrupt manuscripts, you produce a corrupt version. That is exactly what happened.

How was the "Vulgate" received by the Roman Catholic Church once it was finished? His translation was not universally received in the church. In fact, it was not even called the *Vulgate* until the 13th century. Vedder writes, "Jerome was reviled throughout the West for his labors, and...it was not until after Gregory the Great had given his formal approval (about 600 A.D.) that his recension (translation) came into general use in the Roman Church." (*Our New Testament* by Henry Vedder; 1908; p. 297).

Another problem with the Latin Vulgate is that it was constantly being changed. The Roman hierarchy made a translation, which they called The Ancient Vulgate, which was composed of earlier Latin versions and some of Jerome's version. Then even more corrupt revisions came into general use. "The Romanists pretended that this Vulgate translation was the very same with St. Jerome's, and that, whatever variations were found, they were occasioned by the negligence of the transcribers. However this may be, it cannot be denied that it has considerable faults, that it abounds with barbarous words, and that in many passages the sense of the original is corrupted, and in some entirely lost. Still the Council of Trent (1545-1563) thought fit to declare that 'the same ancient and vulgate Version, which has been approved and used in the Church for many ages past, shall be considered the authentic Version in all publick lectures, sermons, and expositions, which no one shall presume to reject, under any pretence whatever.'" (*The Holy Bible;* printed at Oxford for The Society for Promoting Christian Knowledge in 1817; Quote from the General Introduction to the Bible).

Forty years after the Council of Trent proclaimed the Vulgate the sole authentic edition of the Scriptures, Pope Sixtus V made a corrected version of the Latin Vulgate, calling it "true, legitimate, and authentic." But, in September of 1590 the College of Cardinals declared it to be full of errors. Another edition of the Latin Vulgate appeared in 1592 which contained more than 3,000 alterations from the text of Sixtus, whole passages being omitted or introduced, and verses being divided differently. In fact, the alleged "authentic edition of Scriptures" bears little resemblance to Jerome's original work and never was a trustworthy translation. The Roman Catholic Church in England used it for hundreds of years. Likewise, it served as the basis for the first English translation of the Bible, the hand-written Wycliffe Bibles in the 1380's and the English Catholic Bible Douay-Rheims version of 1609. **The Latin Vulgate was not used in any of the Bibles that brought about the Protestant Reformation.**

CHAPTER #8

EARLY BUILDING BLOCKS OF THE ENGLISH BIBLE IN THE BRITISH ISLES

EARLY INTRODUCTION OF CHRISTIANITY TO THE BRITONS

"The literary history of the English Bible may be said to begin with John Wiclif, to whom is ascribed the honour of having given to his own countrymen, in or about the year 1382, the first complete Bible in their own tongue." (*A Brief Sketch of The History of The Transmission of the Bible Down To The Revised English Version of 1881-1895* by Henry Guppy; Published by Manchester University, 1936; p.8) Yet long before Wycliffe's time, portions of the Bible had been translated or paraphrased in rhyme, in both Anglo-Saxon, Anglo-Norman and in a number of dialects, which were used in various parts of the country. But before we look briefly at some of these "building blocks," we need to discover when and how Christianity was introduced into Britain, because it was Christianity that was eventually responsible for introducing the Bible to the British Isles.

Caesar conquered Britain in 55 B.C., and for the better part of 500 years after that, Rome had a strong presence there. Faded traces of Rome's presence are still evident across the British landscape today. None the least of these is the remains of Hadrian's Wall that once divided England from Scotland. Christianity was introduced early into England. "There is evidence that evangelists from the East had penetrated to Britain by the middle of the second century; as not long after, Tertullian (197 A.D.) writes – 'There are places of the Britons, which were unaccessible to the Romans, but yet subdued to Christ.'"(*The Church History of Britain* by Thomas Fuller, D.D.; Volume 1, p. 28).

Origen likewise wrote, "The power of God our Saviour is even with them which in Britain are divided from our world." (Ibid.). Despite this early exposure to Christian teaching, the Bible was not available to the people. "Irenaeus (180 A.D.) refers to the Barbarians (Britons) who have believed without having a knowledge of the letters (New Testament Epistles), through oral teaching merely."(*History of The Christian Church*; by George Park Fisher; 1907 Charles Scribner's Sons; p.46).

While God certainly ordained that the Gospel be preached so men might believe on Christ, He also commanded believers to search and study the Bible that they might grow and understand the things of the Lord. When the Bible is not readily available, that presents BIG PROBLEMS! **Acts 17:11** reveals why the absence of the Scriptures is such a problem. It says, *"These* [the Berean believers] *were more noble than those in Thessalonica, in that they received the word with all readiness of mind, and searched the scriptures daily, whether those things were so."* When the Bible is not accessible or not able to be understood, people cannot search the scriptures for themselves and therefore cannot ascertain whether the things they are being taught by their pastors and teachers are correct. With the absence of the Holy Scriptures and in the presence of Barbarian invasions, progressively the darkness of Scriptural ignorance resettled on the Britons. The last of the Roman legions left the shores of Britain in 410 A.D. They had been the defenders against the barbarian invasions. The result was a series of Saxon invasions of Britain, which took place from the middle of the 5th century and onward, and virtually cut off communication with the rest of the Roman Empire. The Saxons wreaked havoc on the cities and countryside from the east sea to the west. "Public and private edifices were destroyed, priests slain at the altars, and chieftains with their people: some part of the population flying to monasteries, others to the forests and mountains, and many to foreign parts, imply the successful ravages...against the unprepared and astonished natives. (quote from Bede, lib.1.c.15. p.53 as recorded in *The History of the Anglo-Saxon: Comprising The History of England* by Sharon Turner; 4th edition printed in London in 1823; Vol. III p.252).

The Saxons were pagans and the result was that almost the whole southern part of the island turned to idolatry. "Christianity, such as it was, could only be found in the western edges of South Britain." (*An Historical Account of the English Versions of The Scriptures;* in the preface to the English Hexapla of 1841; p.1).

THE GOTHIC VERSIONS

At this point, before we look at how and when Christianity was reintroduced into Britain, I want to focus on the Gothic versions of the Bible, particularly the translation of Ulphilas. The great ecclesiastical historian, Robert Robinson, writes, "Certain it is, they (the Goths) had a translation of the Scriptures into their own language so early as the time of Ulphilas, who lived in the reign of Constantine, many years before they dismembered the empire." (*Ecclesiastical Researches* by Robert Robinson; Cambridge England, 1792; p. 201).

Perhaps you are wondering why I am including the Gothic translations of the Bible as one of the building blocks in our English Bible. Here is why. "The Gothic is a language of Low German origin, as well as the Anglo-Saxon and English." (*The Gospels Gothic, Anglo-Saxon, Wycliffe and Tyndale Versions* by Joseph Bosworth; published by Gibbings and Company in London - 1907; p. iii). To put it more clearly, one of the primary roots of the Anglo-Saxon and English language is the Gothic language. This is readily seen when we compare the Gothic with the Anglo-Saxon and the English as we see in the chart below.

GOTHIC ENGLISH AND ANGLO-SAXON VERSES COMPARED

Bible Passage		Gothic	English	Anglo-Saxon
Luke 20:42		In bokom Psalmo	**In the book of Pslams**	On tham Sealme
John 10:9		Ik im thata daur	**I am the door**	Ic eom geat
Luke 18:4		Langai wheilai	**For a (long) while**	Langre tide
John 7:33		Nauh leitila wheila	**Now a little while**	Gut sume hwile*
Luke 20:28		Whis brothar	**Whose brother**	Hwaes brother

John 12:24		Kaurno whaiteis	**A corn of wheat**	Hwaetene corn
Mark 10:5		Hardu- hairtei	**Hardness of heart**	Heortan heardness
John 6:60		Hardu ist thata waurd	**Hard is that word>**	Heard is theos spraec^
Luke 20:29		Sibun brothryus	**Seven brothers**	Seofon gebrothur
Mark 9:3		Wheitos swa snaiws	**White as snow**	Swa hwite swa snaw
Luke 1:19		Yuke auhsne	**Yokes of oxen**	An getyme oxena+
Luke 8:30		Wha ist namo thein?	**What is thy name?**	Hwaet is thin nama?
Luke 6:48		Galeiks ist mann	**He is like a man**	He ys gelic men

*Yet some while or time; >After the Wiclif not KJV; ^Hard is this speech;
+*Literally* a team of oxen

The heathen Goths settled in Dacia, to the northwest of the Black Sea, at an early period. While they lived in that area many were converted to Christianity. Their leader was Bishop Theophilus, who is known to have been present at the Council of Nicea in 325 A.D. according to his signature on records of that council. Ulphilas (also called Ulfilas, Ulfila, Wulfila in various documents) was appointed head of the Gothic Church in that area when he was but 30 years old, in 348 A.D. "His eminent talents, learning, and benevolence gave him unbounded influence over his countrymen. It, therefore became a proverb among the Goths, *'Whatever is done by Ulphilas, is well done.'"* (*The Gothic Anglo-Saxon, Wycliffe and Tyndale Gospels* by Joseph Bosworth and George Waring; 4th Edition 1907; p. iii).

Ulphilas wrote in Latin, Greek and Gothic and "the cherished desire of his heart" (Ibid.) was to translate the New Testament from the original Greek into the Gothic language "that every one of his

142

countrymen might read the word of God in his own tongue." (Ibid.). It is believed that his work was completed before 360 A.D. He faithfully preached and taught his people from the Gothic Scriptures. "Ulphilas drew his water of life from the pure fountain, and delivered it to his people uncontaminated. He imbibed the doctrines of the Gospel at the fountainhead, the original Greek, and preached those doctrines to the Goths in their own nervous and expressive tongue." (Ibid.)

The first building block of the English Bible, which was laid upon the foundation of the apostles and prophets, Christ being the corner stone, was the Gothic language Bible.

HOW WAS CHRISTIANITY REINTRODUCED INTO BRITAIN?

Some people would like to attribute the reintroduction of Christianity to Gregory. We are told that one day the Catholic monk saw two fair-haired, blue-eyed boys being sold in the Roman slave market. He promptly asked who they were. "They are Angles" was the reply (because they came from Angleland later called England). Gregory said, "Not Angles, but angels and they ought to be joint-heirs with the angels in heaven." (*The Indestructible Book* by Ken Connolly; Baker Books; p.53).

When Gregory became pope he remembered the boys he had seen in the slave market and in 596 A.D. he commissioned Augustine and forty monks to take Roman Catholicism to Britain. Augustine and company arrived in Kent in 597 A.D. just a few months before Colum Cille died in Scotland. Shortly after arriving in England, King Ethelbert gave them the use of an old Romano-British church in Canterbury as a mission base. While Augustine did have considerable influence in Britain, he was not the first to reintroduce Christianity into Britain. Thirty-four years before Augustine arrived in Kent, England, Colum Cille, or Saint Columba, and company established a college and church on a Scottish isle. It was this man and his companions, not Augustine, that were first responsible for the reintroduction of Christianity to the Scots and Britons. Yet, it is impossible to properly understand the person and work of Colum Cille unless you know a little something about another person who

143

laid the groundwork for biblical Christianity in Ireland. That person was Maewyn Succat.

WHO WAS MAEWYN SUCCAT?

In about 430 A.D. a young man from Britain named Maewyn Succat began to evangelize Ireland. He is more commonly known as Patricius or Saint Patrick. It is believed that he took the Latin name Patricius (Patrick) when he began his missionary work in Ireland. Part of the problem you encounter researching the life of Patrick is that there is very little authentic information available. In spite of that fact, I have confined my research to what scholars consider to be authentic information relating to Patrick. Historians indicate that there are two authentic documents composed by Patrick. The first is his *Epistle to the Irish,* more commonly called, *The Confession of Patrick.* It begins, *I Patrick, a sinner...."* It is his testimony, written later in his life, which tells us about his life, his salvation, his beliefs, and his call to missionary service. It also includes a brief accounting of his missionary trials and triumphs. The second authentic document that Patricius authored is his *Letter to Coroticus.* This is an open letter to British Christians living under the rule of cruel King Coroticus.

There is one hymn that may have originally been authored by Patrick, but most historians believe there have been numerous additions and changes throughout the years so that it is impossible to distinguish between what is Patrick's and what was added later. It is called *The Loric* or *Hymn of Patrick,* but is also known as *The Breastplate (or Shield) of St. Patrick* and *The Deer's Cry.* I only mention this hymn for the record. I have not used it in this research.

THE LIFE OF PATRICK

Patrick was born sometime between 385 and 415 A.D. No one knows for sure. He was not Irish at all, but was a "free born" son of a Roman-British *decurio.* A *decurio* was an area magistrate, a nobleman who was the leader of ten others. His father, Calpurnius or Calpornius, had been "chosen by the Romans to be a government official for the town of Bannavem Taberniae." (*Saint Patrick - Pioneer Missionary to Ireland* by Michael J. McHugh; Christian Liberty Press; p. 7) He "also owned a farm nearby in the city of Dumbarton," Pictland, which today is Scotland. At the time this city was under British control (Ibid. p.7). Thus, he was a Roman Brit. His father's primary job was overseeing the collecting of taxes for Rome. Calpurnius was also a deacon in their local church. His mother's name was Conchessa. His grandfather, Potitus, was a presbyter, or a pastor. Patrick lived in Britain during a very turbulent time. For 470 years, the Roman legions had held off the foreign barbarians from pillaging the English countryside. But everything changed when the last legion sailed from Britain in 410 A.D. Immediately Irish warlords and others raided the once peaceful coastal towns of England. These roving bands of pirates looted, pillaged, raped and captured huge numbers of English citizens to sell as slaves to the highest bidder back in their homeland. When Patrick was about 16 years of age, a fleet of 50 *currachs* (longboats) weaved their way toward the English shore where Patrick and his family lived. "The warriors quickly demolished the village, and as Patricius darted among the burning houses and screaming women, he was caught." (*Christian History* Magazine -- Issue 60; *Patrick The Saint;* p.10).

We learn more by reading Patrick's Confession. "*I was taken into captivity to Ireland with many thousands of people, and deservedly so, because we turned away from God, and did not keep His commandments, and did not obey our pastors, who used to remind us of our salvation. And the Lord brought over us the wrath of his anger and scattered us among the nations...*" Patrick was sold as a slave to Miliucc, a Druid tribal chieftain, and put to work herding pigs and/or sheep. He lived like an animal himself, having no shelter and being constantly with the animals day and night, often in hunger and thirst. He felt helpless and hopeless. Put yourself in his shoes. Imagine what it was like to go from being a privileged nobleman's son to being a swine-herding slave overnight.

Patrick had ignored the Lord up to this point in his life. In his mind, he had not really needed the Lord. But things were different now; very different. His mind went back to some things that his preacher grandfather had taught him. The despair of slavery and the solitude of his occupation compelled him to see his need for Christ and remember his Christian upbringing. He writes in his confession, "*I was about sixteen but did not know the true God, but in a strange land, the Lord opened my unbelieving eyes, and I was converted.*" (*Patrick of Ireland: The Untold Story* by Rev. Roy D. Warren, Jr.). Patrick came to know Christ as his personal Savior and was freed from his slavery to sin, though it would be several more years before he escaped from his captors. But, Patrick grew in the Lord. *"His devotion to the Lord Jesus Christ brought upon him a nickname, 'Holy-Boy" from his fellow slaves. Through the years, he learned to pray whether he was working or resting."* (*The Real Saint Patrick* by H. A. Ironside; FBC Press, Corona, NY; p.11).

It is evident by his own testimony he learned to practice 1 Thessalonians 5:17 which says, *"Pray without ceasing."* He writes this in his Confession: *"After I came to Ireland, every day I had to tend sheep, and many times a day I prayed. The Love of God and His fear came to me more and more, and my faith was strengthened. And my spirit was moved so that in a single day I would say as many as a hundred prayers, and almost as many in the night, and this even when I was staying in the woods and on the mountains; I used to get up and pray before daylight, through snow, through frost, through rain, and I felt no harm, and there was no sloth in me...because the spirit within me was then fervent."*

Patrick remained a slave to Miliucc for six years. Then, one night, when he was 22 years old, he testifies, *"I heard a voice while I was sleeping say, '...soon you will go to your own country. See, your ship is ready."* That night he fled. Assured God was leading him, he plunged through the bogs and scaled the mountains that separated him from the sea. In his confession he says he traveled, *"perhaps 200 miles."* He goes on, *"I went in the strength of God who directed my way to my good, and I feared nothing until I came to that ship."* It is obvious that Patrick believed the truth of Psalms 37:23 *"The steps of a good man are ordered by the LORD: and he delighteth in his way."* At first, the sailors would not allow him to come on the ship, but as he turned to walk to the hut where he was staying he began to pray. He says, *"before I had ended my prayer, I heard one of them shouting behind me, 'come, hurry, we shall take you on in good faith; make friends with us in whatever way you like.' And so on that day I...hoped they would come to the faith of Jesus Christ because they were pagans."*

Three days later they landed on the coast of Gaul (today called France) but found only devastation. "Goths or Vandals had so decimated the land that no food was to be found in this once fertile area." (*Christian History* Magazine -- Issue 60; *Patrick The Saint;* p.11). For almost a month they walked searching for food until hunger overcame them. The pagan captain, who had mocked Patrick's faith finally came to him and said, "You say your God is great and all-powerful? Then pray for us. We are all starving to death, and we may not survive to see another soul."

Patrick responded, *"Be converted from your faith to the Lord my God, to Whom nothing is impossible, that He may send you food in you way, even until you are satisfied; because everywhere there is abundance with Him."* (*The Real Saint Patrick* by H. A. Ironside; FBC Press, Corona, NY; p.11). Patrick believed the truth of Luke 1:37 *"For with God nothing shall be impossible."* Patrick writes in his Confession, *"With the help of God, so it came to pass: suddenly a herd of pigs appeared on the road before our eyes, and they killed many of them."* God indeed had provided. After quite some time, Patrick made it back to Britain and his family. He was home at last – free. But, this is not the end of the narrative.

PATRICK'S CALL TO EVANGELIZE IRELAND

Acts 16:9 is commonly called Paul's "Macedonian Call." — *"And a vision appeared to Paul in the night; There stood a man of Macedonia, and prayed him, saying, Come over into Macedonia, and help us."* Paul responded and went to Macedonia to proclaim the Gospel. Patrick received his Ireland Call in a similar fashion. Victoricus urged Patrick in a dream, "We beg you, holy youth, to come and walk among us once more." (*Saint Patrick - Pioneer Missionary to Ireland* by Michael J. McHugh; Christian Liberty Press; p. 86) The Lord made it clear to Patrick that he was calling him back to Ireland to preach the Gospel. The problem was that his family did not want him to go. It was well known that escaped slaves were woven into giant wicker baskets, suspended over fires, and roasted alive in sacrifice to the Druids gods. But Patrick was called of God and returned to Ireland, beginning his missionary work about 430 A.D. "Patrick was really a first – the first missionary to barbarians beyond the reach of Roman law." (*How The Irish Saved Civilization* by Thomas Cahill; Doubleday; p.108). Cahill goes on to say, "Patrick's gift to the Irish was his Christianity — the first de-Romanized Christianity in human history, a Christianity without the sociopolitical baggage of the Greco-Roman world... Ireland is unique in religious history for being the only land into which Christianity was introduced without bloodshed." (Ibid.). To be sure, <u>Patrick was not a Catholic</u>, though that did not stop the Roman Catholics from claiming him later and making him over in their own image. In fact, his name is nowhere to be found in Catholic writing until almost two centuries after he had died. (I think it is important to note one important clarification concerning Cahill's remark. The first de-Romanized Christianity in human history was the Christianity of the apostles which is recorded in the New Testament and which was spread throughout the known world for the first 150 or so years after the death, resurrection and ascension of the Lord Jesus Christ.)

Biblical, Apostolic, New Testament Christianity was the message Patrick preached to the Irish pagans. He taught the Gospel message of salvation by grace through faith in Christ, not the spurious, works-oriented version of salvation propagated by the Roman Church. Likewise, he taught believer's baptism. In fact, God so blessed his efforts spreading the Gospel that one source says, *"he planted over 200 churches and had over 100,000 truly saved converts."* (*Patrick of Ireland: The Untold Story* by Rev. Roy D. Warren, Jr.).

Archbishop Usher says, "We read in Nennius that...St. Patrick founded 365 churches, and ordained 365 bishops, and 3,000...elders." There is no way of determining which figures are correct. But we do know that Patrick was mightily used in reaching Ireland for Christ! He says, *"I am greatly a debtor to God, who has bestowed his grace so largely upon me, that multitudes were born again to God through me. The Irish, who never had the knowledge of God and worshipped only idols and unclean things, have lately become the people of the Lord, and are called the sons of God."* (*History of the Christian Church* by Philip Schaff; Volume 4, p.46). Schaff goes on, "He speaks of having baptized many thousands of men..." (Ibid.). Patrick died on March 17th somewhere between 465 to 493 A.D.

That brings us back to the man I spoke of at the beginning of this section, Colum Cille. There can be no doubt that Colum Cille was taught, believed and preached the pure, Apostolic, de-Romanized, New Testament Christianity that Patrick had firmly established in Ireland. It is also true that Colum Cille, with his twelve companions, reintroduced New Testament Christianity, first to western Pictland (Scotland) and then to Northern England, called Northumbria.

WHO WAS COLUM CILLE OR COLUMBA?

Historical tradition holds that Crimthann was his Irish name at birth. Crimthann means fox. Anna Ritchie writes in her book *Iona*, "it is possible that he took the name Columba (Latin for dove) on entering the Church. The Irish name Colum or Colm was relatively common, and thus in later times Columba became known as Colum Cille (church-dove) to distinguish him from the rest." (Iona by Anna Ritchie; Batsford Book; p.31).

Schaff says, "He received in baptism the symbolical name *Colum*, or in the Latin *Columba* (Dove, as a symbol of the Holy Ghost), to which afterwards was added *cille* (or *kille*), i.e. "of the church," or "the dove of the cells," on account of his frequent attendance at public worship, or, more probably, for his being the founder of many churches." (*History of the Christian Church* by Philip Schaff; Volume 4, p.65).

Colum Cille was born in Gartan, in County Donegal in 521 or 522 A.D. According to Rev. T. V. Moore in his book, *The Culdee Church*, he was "of the family of the Kings of Ulster, and related to a royal family in Scotland." His father, Fedilmid mac Ferguso, also known as Phelim, was of the Uí Néill clan and descended from the famous Niall of the Nine Hostages. His mother was Eithne, descended from a king of Leinster. Columba had a brother and three sisters. He received a very thorough classical education and also had a sound education in the Bible and New Testament Christianity. His first teacher was a preacher named Cruithnechan and then he was mentored by Bishop Finnio or Finnen. Not much else is known about his early life. More comes to light when he was in his early 40's. He is said to have established his first church and college at Derry, Ireland in 548 A.D. Others followed, notably Durrow in County Offaly, Ireland, which <u>became famous for the Celtic artistry of its illuminated manuscripts</u>.

Perhaps you are wondering what any of this has to do with our study on the history of the English Bible. Let me explain. Just as Patrick carried de-Romanized, New Testament, Apostolic Christianity to Ireland, so Colum Cille (Columba) carried the same de-Romanized, pure, New Testament, Apostolic Christianity to Scotland and England. Here's how it is said to have happened. During a visit to

Moville, Columba is said to <u>have secretly copied a book of Psalms</u> belonging to Finnian. When Finnian discovered this, he insisted the copy belonged to him since it was copied from his Psalter. Colum Cille refused to hand it over, and their dispute was referred to the high king, Diarmuid, to settle. He ruled: ***"To every cow her calf, and to every book its copy."*** This is perhaps the first copyright case in history, and prototype of our modern day copyright laws.

BATTLE FOR THE BIBLE

Colum Cille did not want to give up the book of Psalms he had copied. And, he already resented Diarmuid for slaying a youth to whom he had given sanctuary. In 561 A.D. he persuaded his kinsmen to wage war against King Diarmuid. They defeated the King and his army at Cuildreimhne in County Sligo, Ireland. As a result, Colum Cille took possession of the *Cathach,* the Psalter written on vellum, which he had copied. The word *Cathach* means Battler. That Psalter still exists today and this is a picture of one of the surviving leaves.

Though he retained possession of the Psalter he had copied, the war he had started to keep it was not acceptable to the Culdee church. "Tradition holds that 3001 men died fighting to gain possession of..." the *Cathach*. (*Christian History* Magazine; Issue 60; p.28). A church council gathered and exiled him from his beloved Ireland. The council called on him to make amends by converting an equal number of pagans to Christianity as had been killed in the battle. In 563 A.D., he and 12 missionary companions sailed to the little island of Hy, commonly called Iona, which is off the coast of Scotland. "It is an inhospitable island, three miles and a half long and a mile and a half broad, partly cultivated, partly covered with hill pasture, retired dells, morass and rocks." (*History of the Christian Church* by Philip Schaff; Volume 4, p. 66-67). There he established a Christian community, which consisted of a Church and a Christian College. This served as a base for training missionaries who spread the Christian faith to Scotland, the northern part of England and even to the Continent of Europe. Iona was a light-house in the darkness of heathenism. The Picts, who got their name from painting their bodies, were pagans, and still painting their bodies and fighting their battles, naked. Columba preached the Gospel first among the Picts. Bede writes, "He converted them by example as well as by word." (*History of the Christian Church* by Philip Schaff; Volume 4, p.69).

Before I continue, I must warn you about the tainted material you will find relating to either Columba or Iona. Most all of the modern material will refer to Iona's Christian community as a <u>monastery</u>. But, as Dr. Moore says, "the name (monastery) is calculated to mislead." (*The Culdee Church* by Rev. T.V. Moore, D.D.; published by the Presbyterian Committee of Publication in 1868).

The Christian church and college of Iona, established by Colum Cille, were not in the Roman Catholic tradition. The Catholics have gone to great lengths in their efforts to revise history and claim them. Further, the so-called "monks" need not be celibate either. The missionaries of Iona were allowed to marry, and in fact many did marry. *"The institutions of Iona were not designated to cultivate eremites (religious hermits) and solitary ascetics, <u>but to train Christian scholars and missionaries</u>, who would go forth as soldiers of Christ, trained to conquer and occupy the outlying territory of heathenism."* (Ibid.) In fact, missionaries trained at Colum Cille's Iona did more to carry the pure Gospel to Great Britain, France, Germany and Switzerland than any other group. It is *"not generally known, that it is to this Culdee Church that England owes some of the first efforts to Christianize her people, after the Saxons had restored Paganism there."* (Ibid.) The reference to the *Culdee Church* refers to churches made up of those who had been taught and who believed the pure Gospel of the New Testament. It was the de-Romanized New Testament faith taught by Colum Cille and his followers. Colum Cille's high standing, both in secular Celtic society and as a Christian, uniquely qualified him to carry out this mission. In addition to the works he had started in

Derry, Darrow and Kells, Ireland, he established missionary outposts in Scotland and England at St. Andrews, Melrose, and Lindisfarne on Holy Island, and others.

On June 9th, 597 A.D., Colum Cille (later called St. Columba) died at the age of 75. From the small island Christian community that Colum Cille established has come an immense outflow of Christian missionary work, culture, art, literature and academic learning. Over 300 manuscript books are said to have been produced personally at his hand. Only one exists that scholars are sure is the work of his hand and that is the *Cathach*, the Psalter written on vellum. Yet, many, including myself, believe the Book of Kells is his work. The Book of Kells, one of the world's most famous illuminated manuscripts, was almost certainly written on Iona, and if not by the hand Colum Cille, then it surely was done by one of his missionary-scribes.

Before we move on to the Book of Kells, it should be noted that the Celtic (Keltic) or Culdee faith, that de-Romanized, pure Gospel faith taught by Colum Cille and his followers, flourished until the Synod of Whitby in 664 A.D. In 664, the King of Northumbria, Oswy, summoned the Synod of Whitby to decide the dating of Easter and the tonsure (type of haircut) of monks. Oswy's queen, Enfleda, came from Essex and favored the practices of the Roman Catholic Church. The arguments were presented and the King chose in favor of the Roman Catholic position. The old Culdee church, founded by Colum Cille, put up a gallant struggle for the pure Apostolic, New Testament faith for the next 500 years and was finally visibly overthrown with the suppression of the Culdees church and Bible college at St. Andrews in 1297 A.D. *"As Romish influence advanced it became necessary to silence the continual protest which these men (the Culdees) maintained against the doctrines and pretensions of the Romish Church."* (The Culdee Church by Rev. T.V. Moore, D.D.; published by the Presbyterian Committee of Publication in 1868).

From this point on the Culdees worked clandestinely. In fact, principles of the old Culdee Church were never completely eradicated from Great Britain and reappear in the teachings of Wycliffe and the Reformers.

THE BOOK OF KELLS

For centuries this beautiful Gospel codex was revered as The Great Gospel Book of Colum Cille. In 1655, Samuel O'Neale wrote that the belief of the townspeople of Kells was that the manuscript was *"written as they say by Columbkill's own hand."* The New Testament Gospels continued to be associated with St. Colum Cille, for when the book was shown to Queen Victoria in 1849, it was introduced to the queen as St. Columba's book. But, among so-called scholars, it is doubted that this is the case. They refer to it as The Book of Kells. To my knowledge, Bishop James Ussher was the first to refer to it as The Book of Kells, because it had been kept at the Abby of Kells in Ireland from around 807 to about 1650 A.D.

Modern scholarship places the writing of The Book of Kells around the year 800 A.D. It is one of the most beautifully illuminated manuscripts in the world. It contains the four gospels, preceded by prefaces, summaries, and canon tables or concordances of gospel passages. It is written on vellum and contains a Latin text of the Gospels in insular majuscule script accompanied by magnificent and intricate whole pages of decoration with smaller painted decorations appearing throughout the text. The Latin text is a combination of the Latin Vulgate intermixed with the old Latin translation. It contains 340 folios (680 pages), which include decorative initials, portraits of the Evangelists, carpet pages (decorative leaves without text) and scenes from the life of Christ that are vividly illuminated in rich colors. If it was not written by Colum Cille, it then was wholly written by the missionary scribes of Colum Cille's Church and college on the western Scottish Island of Iona and brought to Kells, County Meath, Ireland to escape Viking raiders, where it was finished. It was stolen in 1006, stripped of its gold cover, which was probably inlaid with precious stones, and thrown into a ditch. The outer leaves and margins of the vellum pages were damaged by water before it was found some time afterwards. The book was then kept in Kells until 1654. In that year the governor of the town sent the book to Dublin for safety because Oliver Cromwell's cavalry was quartered in the church of Kells. Some years later the Bishop of Meath gave it to Trinity College where it resides today. Later in the 19th century, additional damage was done to the manuscript when some of these damaged pages were over trimmed during rebinding. In 1953 it was bound into four volumes.

Colum Cille and his Gospel book (the Book of Kells) are important building blocks in the development of the English Bible. It was Colum Cille who first reintroduced New Testament Christianity to Scotland and England and it was his missionary scribes who meticulously reproduced Psalms, Gospels and other Scripture portions, primarily in Latin, for use in teaching Bible truths and public worship.

The next major building block is getting the Scripture into the English language. As you will see, this was a long slow process. The problem is that the English language was in transition. But, as the language took shape there were many who attempted to translate portions of the Bible into the vulgar (common) language of their time.

CAEDMON'S PARAPHRASE OF THE SCRIPTURES IN ANGLO-SAXON — 650'S A.D.

"The first attempt, of which we have certain knowledge, at anything like a paraphrase of Scripture in the Anglo-Saxon tongue to which a date can be assigned, is the poet of Caedmon in the seventh century." (*The English Hexapla;* Preface: *An Historical Account of the English Versions of the Scriptures* by Samuel Bagster and Sons, 1841; p.2). Caedmon was a lay monk from Whitby. Caedmon "has been described as 'the first Saxon poet,' and 'the Milton of our forefathers,' whose gifts had been discovered while he was a poor cow-herd on the neighboring downs." (*A Brief Sketch of The History of the Transmission of the Bible Down To The Revised English Version of 1881-1895* by Henry Guppy, M.A., Litt.D.; 1934

Manchester University publication; p.9). Caedmon composed a metrical version of large portions of Old Testament history. It opens with the fall of the angels, moves to creation, and then the deluge (flood) and on to the history of the children of Israel in their departure from Egypt and entering into the promised land. To this he adds information about Nebuchadnezzar and Daniel. Here is a translation of a small portion of his work —

"Now must we praise the author of the heavenly kingdom, the Creator's power and counsel, the deeds of the Father of glory: how He, the eternal God, was the author of all marvels —He, who first gave to the sons of men the heaven for a roof, and then, Almighty Guardian of mankind, created the earth." (*The Encyclopedia Britannica - 11th Edition;* vol.4; p.934).

He also composed material that dealt with the main facts in the life of Our Lord Jesus Christ, and the preaching of the apostles. In addition, many of his other poems dealt with, as Guppy says "the Divine benefits and judgments, by which he endeavoured to turn all men from the love of vice, and to excite in them the love of, and application to, good actions." (Ibid. p.9). The people learned and sang these religious poems or paraphrases and for a time they were their sole source of Bible knowledge. These poems are the earliest Anglo-Saxon works presenting Scripture in any form, though it must be remembered that they can by no means be considered a translation of the Scripture. Caedmon died in 680 A.D.

ALDHELM AND GUTHLAC THE HERMIT - THE EARLIEST TRANSLATORS OF SCRIPTURE INTO ANGLO-SAXON —EARLY 700'S A.D.

"It is impossible to ascertain with any exactness how soon there was a translation of the Holy Scriptures into the language of the inhabitants of Britain." (*The Holy Bible - The Authorized Version;* Quote from the General Introduction by Rev. D'Oyly & Rev. Mant; Oxford 1817). The first "English" translators of whom we have any information are Aldhelm and Guthlac, both in the early 700's A.D. There is no record of when <u>Aldhelm</u> was born, but we do know that he was the Abbot of Malmesbury and Bishop of Sherborne. He made a literal translation of the Psalms into Anglo-Saxon about 706 A.D. to be used in the daily services of the church. He died in 709 A.D.

Guthlac of Crowland, Crowland being a village near Peterborough, England, was born in 674 A.D. According to historians, he was the first Saxon anchorite hermit. He made a translation of the Psalms into Anglo-Saxon in the early 700's A.D.

LINDISFARNE GOSPELS, ST. CUTHBERT'S GOSPELS OR THE BOOK OF DURHAM

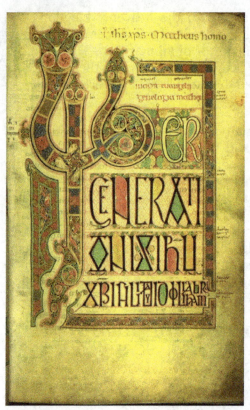

The Lindisfarne Gospels is one of the most cherished treasures of the British Library. It is a Latin translation of Matthew, Mark, Luke and John after Jerome's Vulgate with the Anglo-Saxon translation added later. It is named for the monastery of Lindisfarne founded by followers of Colum Cille about 635 A.D. It was established on a rocky island off the coast of Northumberland, which is today called Holy Island. "Four men are named in Aldred's colophon as contributors to the making of the Lindisfarne Gospels." The **first** is Bishop **Eadfrith** of Lindisfarne. He is said to have written the manuscript in honor of St. Cuthbert, who died in 687 A.D. His part in this work is believed to have taken place around 698 A.D. The **second**, credited with illuminating and binding it, is Bishop **Etherwald** of Lindisfarne, who succeeded Eadfrith, 724-740 A.D. The **third** is **Billfirth** the Anchorite, who provided ornaments of gold, silver and jewels for its outer casing. "The **fourth** is **Aldred** himself, who inserted the Anglo-Saxon translation or gloss" sometime after 995 A.D. (*The Lindisfarne Gospels*; by Janet Backhouse; Phaidon Press; p.12). A gloss differs from a translation in that it translates the text word for word between the lines, without much regard to the grammatical arrangement.

In 793 A.D., without warning, Lindisfarne was raided and sacked by Vikings. Writing from the court of Charlemagne to King Ethelred of Northumbria, Alcuin of York exclaimed: '... never before has such terror appeared in Britain as we have now suffered from a pagan race, nor was it thought that such an inroad from the sea could be made.' Although the community soon returned to the island, it was with an increasing sense of uneasiness as monastery after monastery suffered the same fate. The Gospel volume remained at Lindisfarne (Holy Island) until the Viking (Danish) invasion of Northumbria in 875 A.D. At that point Bishop Eardulf took the relics of Saint Cuthbert and other treasures of the monastery, including the Lindisfarne Gospels and the bones of the two men who had made it, his predecessors Eadfrith and Ethelwald, and set off in search of a safer home. All the inhabitants of the island, seven of whom were given special charge over the relics, accompanied him. Their wanderings, chronicled at the beginning of the twelfth century by Symeon of Durham, lasted about seven years. There was a time when it seemed that their final destination would be Ireland. But we are told that, as the bishop and his party tried to put out to sea, a terrible storm arose. Three great waves swept over the ship and the copy of the Four Gospels, richly bound in gold and jewels, was swept overboard and lost. This was taken as a sign of St. Cuthbert's displeasure. Therefore, the voyage was immediately abandoned. Saint Cuthbert then appeared in a dream to Hunred, one of the seven bearers, and told him where the manuscript could be found. Upon investigation, the Gospel book is said to have been found washed up, unharmed, on the sands at a low tide. According to Symeon of Durham, the manuscript was the Lindisfarne Gospels. Not long after this episode, the party finally settled at Chester-le-Street, in County Durham, where Saint Cuthbert's relics remained until 995 A.D., and it was there that Aldred the priest added his Anglo-Saxon gloss and colophon to the manuscript. This was probably done during the third quarter of the tenth century. It was subsequently restored to Lindisfarne, where it remained until the dissolution of the monastery in 1534. Sir Robert Cotton purchased it in the seventeenth century, through whom it passed into the keeping of the British Museum, where it is deservedly regarded as one of the nation's most treasured possessions. (above paragraph adapted from material in *The Lindisfarne Gospels* by Janet Backhouse).

"THE VENERABLE" BEDE'S GOSPEL — 735 A.D.

Not long after the Lindisfarne Gospels, "Bede translated the whole Bible..." according to notes in the front of an 1817 Bible I purchased in an antique store in England. (*The Holy Bible - The Authorized Version*; Quote from the General Introduction by Rev. D'Oyly & Rev. Mant; Oxford 1817). But, most other scholars disagree. However, there is agreement on this much. Bede, a native of Durham, spent most of his life studying and writing in a monastery in Jerrow (Yerrow). He did write a series of commentaries on the entire Bible as well as an important work entitled, *Ecclesiastical History of Britain*. But, far and away his most important work was his translation of the Gospel of John into the Anglo-Saxon language, which was completed in the last hours of his life. This is the account of its completion.

"The illness of Bede increased, but he only laboured the more diligently (in the translation of St. John). On the Wednesday, his scribe told him that one chapter alone remained, but feared that it might be painful to him to dictate. 'It is easy,' Bede replied; 'take your pen and write quickly.' The work continued for some time. Then Bede directed Cuthbert to fetch his little treasures from his casket (capsella) that he might distribute them among his friends. And so he passed the remainder of the day till evening in holy and cheerful conversation. His boy scribe at last found an opportunity to remind him, with pious importunity, of his unfinished work. 'One sentence, dear master, still remains unwritten.' He answered, 'Write quickly. The boy soon said, 'It is completed now.' 'Well,' Bede replied, 'thou hast said the truth; all is ended. Support my head with thy hands; I would sit in the holy place in which I was wot to pray, that so sitting I may call upon my Father.' Thereupon, resting on the floor of his cell, he chanted the Gloria [Glory be to the Father, through the Son, in the Holy Spirit], and his soul immediately passed away, while the name of the Holy Spirit was on his lips." (*A General View of the History of the English Bible* by Brooke Foss Westcott; 1916 MacMillan).

To my knowledge, there are no extant portions of Bede's Gospel of John. I have been able to find what **John 3:16** would have looked like from a 955 A.D. **Anglo-Saxon Gospel** –

God lufode middan-eard swa', daet he sealde his 'an-cennedan sunu, daet nan ne forweorde de on hine gelyfp, ac haebbe dact 'ece lif.

Remember, the English language was in transition until the King James Bible. It was a mixture of Gothic, Anglo-Saxon, Anglo-Norman, and French. I should also point out that Bible portions were not widely available. The only Bible most people were acquainted with were the Psalms they sang in church or portions they had memorized after hearing it by word of mouth.

📖 ALCUIN OF YORK—LATE 700's A.D.

Sometime around the late 700's or early 800's, Alcuin, the schoolmaster of York, translated the first five books of the Old Testament into the prevailing dialect. We can set the date because there are records that indicate that Alcuin died in 804 A.D. Guppy quotes a portion of a sermon written by Alcuin, which seems to indicate that the distribution of the Scriptures at this time must have been much more extensive than is generally supposed. The quote reads, "The reading of the Scriptures is the knowledge of everlasting blessedness. In them man may contemplate himself as in some mirror, what sort of person he is. The reading cleanseth the reader's soul, for, when we pray, we speak to God, and when we read the Holy Books, God speaks to us." (*A Brief Sketch of The History of the Transmission of the Bible Down to the Revised English Version of 1881-1895*; by Henry Guppy; Manchester University, 1934; p.10). If the Scriptures were available and read in this era, it would have been confined to the sons of nobility. The common people would neither have had the money nor the ability to read the manuscripts.

📖 ALFRED THE GREAT—MID 800's A.D.

Alfred the Great lived and ruled in the late 800's A.D. and died in 901 A.D. In the preface to his translation of Gregory's "Pastoral Care," which is considered to be the first of Alfred's literary works, the king gives expression to the wish that **"all the free-born** youth of my people . . . may persevere in learning . . . until they can perfectly read the English Scriptures." (Ibid. Guppy; p.10). Alfred translated the Decalogue or Ten Commandments, and passages from Exodus 21, 22 and 23. This served as the introduction of his Book of Laws, by which he ruled the country, which was popularly known as "Alfred's Dooms." It is likely that he also translated other portions of the Bible into Anglo-Saxon as well but it is not certain. William of Malmesbury says, "He began a version of the Psalter which was interrupted by his death."

☐ RUSHWORTH GLOSS OF THE GOSPELS —850 A.D.

The Rushworth Gospels, so called, were written in Latin by an Irish scribe named MacGregol in about 850 A.D. The interlinear Anglo-Saxon gloss was added by a scribe named Owun (Owen), and a priest named Faerman. The Gospels of Mark, Luke and John in the Rushworth book are so nearly identical with those of the Lindisfarne manuscript that it suggests that the translation contained may represent a publicly circulated version. It is called the Rushworth Gloss after the man who owned the book before it passed into the Bodleian Library at Oxford. John Rushworth, of Lincoln's Inn, was Deputy Clerk to the House of Commons during the Long Parliament.

☐ AELFRIC THE GRAMMARIAN PARAPHRASE — LATE 900'S A.D.

Aelfric the Grammarian was a monk at Winchester and later was the abbot of both Cerne and Eynsham at the same time. While there are no exact records known to exist relating to his birth and death, historians speculate that he died about 1020 A.D. Probably in the late 900's A.D. he wrote a summary account of both the Old and New Testaments. But, his principle work was the Anglo-Saxon translation or paraphrase of the first seven books of the Bible, known as "Aelfric's Heptateuch." Several manuscripts of this work are known, the most famous of which is preserved in the British Museum. The Heptateuch is partly translated literally and partly paraphrased. "He appears to have done this work with the express intention of enabling his countrymen to read the Scriptures for themselves." (An Historical Account of the English Versions of The Scriptures;

in the preface to the English Hexapla of 1841). In one of his sermons on the importance of reading the Bible he says, **"Happy is he, who reads the Scriptures, if he convert the words into action."**

📖 ANOTHER ANGLO-SAXON VERSION OF THE GOSPELS —1050'S A.D.

Shortly before the Norman Conquest there was another translation of the Gospels into the Anglo-Saxon language. Historians do not know who the translator was. What is interesting about this Gospel manuscript is that, in large part, it was translated from a Latin version before the time of Jerome.

📖 THE ANGLO-NORMAN VERSION OF THE GOSPELS

When the Normans, under William the Conqueror, conquered England in 1066 A.D., the translation of the Scriptures into the language of the English people (Anglo-Saxon) came to a halt for all practical purposes. The conquerors made every effort to impose their Norman French language upon the conquered nation. Norman French became the language of the schools and the justice system, such as it was. It was the language of the King and his court. But, the Anglo-Saxon language retained its hold, for the most part, on the market-place, in the homes and in the everyday proceedings of the common people.

While there was scarcely any translation activity, "there appears to have been an Anglo-Norman version of the Gospels, or at least a transcript of the Gospels into the dialect which was now displacing the genuine Anglo-Saxon: there are at least three such manuscripts known to be in existence, one of which is attributed to the time of William the Conqueror, the other two to the time of Henry the Second. These three manuscripts all exhibit the same translation, although with variations made by the copyists." (Ibid. Bagster's English Hexapla).

The contest for supremacy between the two languages had far-reaching effects. The Anglo-Saxon language spoken in England became so corrupted by its contact with the Norman French that new dialects sprang up all over the country. As time went on, the people in the northern part of the country could not understand the dialect spoken by the people in the south, and vice versa. There was no longer a common English tongue and therefore, it appears that no attempt was made to translate a complete version of the Bible or even a New Testament. Obviously, before there could be a common English Bible, there must be something approaching a common English speech. Some unifying ground had to be found. Slowly but surely a common English language began to take shape. But it will not be till the latter part of the 14th century that the English people get their first complete Bible in their own language called Middle English.

Let's move on to the people who paraphrased or translated portions of the Scriptures in this chaotic time of the development of the English Language.

📖 THE ORMULUM METRIC GOSPEL PORTIONS — 1100's A.D.

An Augustinian monk named Orm, Orme, or Ormin made a metric paraphrase, in the style of Saxon poetry without rhyme, of the Gospels and Acts of the Apostles of each days reading. He then elaborately expounded on his paraphrase, based on the writings of Aelfric, Bede, and St. Augustine. His work shows us the development of the English language in its early state. Fragments of this poetic work are preserved in the Bodleian Library in Oxford. I was unable to get a first-hand look at his work when I visited the library. I plan to make arrangements ahead of time on my next trip. But I do know this: no date is associated with this work, but the language indicates that it likely belongs to the 1100's A.D.

📖 GENESIS, EXODUS — 1250'S A.D.

Another interesting Scripture portion from this time of transition is housed in the British Museum. It is the story of Genesis and Exodus which scholars believe was written in the Suffolk area sometime around 1250 A.D. The author is unknown.

📖 *SURTEES PSALTER, MIDLANDS OR NORTHERN (YORKSHIRE) — 1250-1300*

Around the same time there is a Psalter (book of Psalms) called the Surtees Psalter dated between 1250-1300 A.D. What makes this Psalter unique is that it is the first known work attempting <u>a literal translation of the scriptures into Middle English</u> in this early stage. To this point, what we have seen are paraphrased in Middle English, but no actual word for word translations.

INSTRUCTIONS FOR READING MIDDLE ENGLISH

While it is not possible for me to duplicate exactly the Middle-English alphabet, I have reproduced it as near as possible to enable you to see and hear what Middle-English sounded like. But before you can read the Psalm 23 from the Surtees Psalter in Middle English, some instruction needs to be given. When you read Middle English, it is almost imperative that you do so *out loud*. This will help you to make intellectual sense of the strange-looking words; what looks strange to the eye is often more familiar to the ear. In fact, one of the chief delights of reading 700-year-old English is the *aha!* of understanding that comes with this ongoing revelation: Middle English is a foreign language *that you already know*. If you have no formal training in Middle English phonology, that's all right. It is believed that medieval English vowel sounds were more or less the same as those in modern European languages. Early Middle English was written before (or in the earliest stages of) the "Great Vowel Shift." Therefore give vowels the sounds they have in Spanish, or especially German: "**a**" is always pronounced "**ah**" as in "**fa**ther." The "**e**" is always pronounced "**ay**" as in "break," except when it occurs at the end of a word, in which case it is pronounced like the unaccented schwa "**uh**" sound as in the German "bitte"); The "**i**" and "**y**" are always pronounced "**ee**" as in "fiend"; "**o**" is always pronounced "**oh**" as in "poem." The "**u**" is always pronounced "**oo**" as in "fruit"; "**ai**" or "**ay**" are diphthongs pronounced "eye." Medieval consonants have more or less their modern values, with a few exceptions: "**gh**" (whether spelled thus, or sometimes with the archaic **yogh**) is the guttural sound of the German or Scottish "**ch**," a sound no longer used by most English speakers. Rolle and some others mainly used the archaic *thorn* to render the voiced "**th**" (as in "this" or "that"), as distinct from the unvoiced "th" of "think" or "thorn"; modern writers of English don't seem much impoverished by the lost distinction, and neither will readers of transliterated medieval texts. There are no silent consonants, so pronounce the "**k**" and the "**gh**" in "knight" as "kuh-neeght." (Adapted from information located at-www.dutchgirl.com/foxpaws/biographies /Ghostly_Gladness/ rollelyrics.html).

SURTEES PSALTER —PSALM 23

1. Lauerd me steres, noght wante sal me:
   In stede of fode þare me louked he.

2. He fed me ouer watre ofe fode,
   Mi saule he tornes in to gode.

3. He led me ouer sties of rightwisenes,
   For his name, swa hali es.

4. For, and ife .I. ga in mid schadw ofe dede,
   For þou wiþ me erte iuel sal .i. noght drede;

5. Þi yherde, and þi stafe ofe mighte,
   Þai ere me roned dai and nighte.

6. Þou graiþed in mi sighte borde to be,
   Ogaines þas þat droued me;

7. Þou fatted in oli me heued yhite;
   And mi drinke dronkenand while schire es ite!

8. And filigh me sal þi mercy
   Alle daies ofe mi life for-þi;

9. And þat .I. wone in hous ofe lauerd isse
   In lengþe of daies al wiþ blisse.

📖 *THE SHOREHAM PSALM —EARLY 1300's*

"The earliest English version in prose of an entire book of Scripture appears to have been a translation of the Psalter and Canticles (Proverbs), side by side with the Latin, made by William of Shoreham or Scorham, who in 1320 was appointed vicar of Chart Sutton, Sevenoaks, Kent, where he had been a monk." (*The Brief Sketch of The History of The Transmission of the Bible Down To The Revised English Edition of 1881-1895;* by Henry Guppy; Manchester University; p. 13).

Here is Psalm 23 in the Shoreham Version —

1. Our Lord gouerneþ me, and noþyng shal defailen to me; in þe stede of pasture he sett me þer.

2. He norissed me vp water of fyllyng; he turned my soule fram þe fende.

3. He lad me vp þe bisti3es of ri3tfulnes for his name.

4. For 3if þat ich haue gon amiddes of þe shadowe of deþ, y shal nou3t douten iuels; for þou art wyþ me.

5. Þy discipline and þyn amendyng conforted me.

6. Þou madest radi grace in my si3t o3ayns hem þat trublen me.

7. Þou makest fatt myn heued wyþ mercy; and my drynk makand drunken ys ful clere.

8. And þy merci shal folwen me alle daies of mi lif;

9. And þat ich wonne in þe hous of our Lord in lengþe of daies.

(*The Earliest Complete English Prose Psalter, Together with Eleven Canticles and a Translation of the Athanasian Creed.* Ed. Karl D. Bülbring. London, 1891)

📖 *TRANSLATIONS OF RICHARD ROLLE, THE HERMIT OF HAMPOLE — 1300's*

A key person in the history of the English Bible is a man named Richard Rolle. He "was born near the end of the 13ᵗʰ century, at Thorton (now Thornton Dale), near Pickering, Yorkshire." (*The Encyclopedia Britannica - 11ᵗʰ Edition;* vol. R*; p.466). The following tells us of his early life.

"Richard was a clever lad. His parents were sure he was the brightest lad in Thornton-le-Dale and were prepared to invest in his abilities. Though poor they saw that he had a good education —the only means he had of making his way in the world. The readiness of Thomas Neville, of the greatest family in the North and Archdeacon of Durham, to sponsor him through Oxford must have convinced them that their faith in their son was justified. For the devout scholar with a good brain and a powerful patron a career in the

Church in the fourteenth century held the promise of immense prestige, power and even wealth. The new and very successful University of Oxford was the gateway to all that. They knew their Richard would do well. He would become a priest and great preferments would follow. Archdeacon —perhaps Bishop! He would not be the first from as poor a home as theirs to achieve such eminence. And he would not forget that it was his parents' sacrifices that had made it all possible.

"Then wholly unexpectedly, he was back home at Thornton. Suddenly he had left Oxford. There had been no scandal. He hadn't been expelled. He hadn't failed his exams. Indeed, for some years 'he made great progress in his study'. And then he knew that that for him was not the progress that mattered. He feared 'to be caught in the snare of sinners'. The best explanation of his decision comes from a sentence in his greatest book 'The Fire of Love'. He writes, 'An old wife is more expert in God's love than the great divine who studies for vanity that he may appear glorious and so be known and may get rents and dignities.' The north-country puritan was outraged by the worldliness of Christian and ecclesiastical Oxford." (A Saint for South Yorkshire: A Brief History of Richard of Hampoke; at www.dutchgirl.com/foxpaws/biographies/Ghostly_Gladness/rollebylunn.html; p.2)

So, at age 19 he returned home intending to become a hermit. "At first he dwelt in a woods near his home, but fearing his family would put him under restraint, he fled from Thornton and wandered about till he was recognized by John de Dalton, who had been his fellow student at Oxford, and who now provided him with a cell and the necessaries for a hermit's life." (*The Catholic Encyclopedia; Richard Rolle de Hampole;* by Edwin Burton; online edition).

After a time "he left the Daltons, and wandered from place to place, resting when he found friends to provide for his wants.... After some years of wandering he gave up his more energetic propaganda (preaching), contenting himself with advising those who sought him out. He began also to write songs and treatises by which he was to exert his widest influence. He settled in Richmondshire...." (*The Encyclopedia Britannica - 11th Edition;* vol. R*; p.466). Carl McColman says his writings were "intensely personal, somewhat dramatic, and passionate both in describing the depths of his faith and experiences of God, and in attacking his detractors." (*Richard Rolle, Hermit of*

Hampole by Carl McColman; online article). Many of his works are in Latin. His English works were written later in his life, probably between 1340 and his death. Rolle translated many parts of the Scripture into the northern dialect of English, which include a Psalter together with a commentary, the Lord's Prayer, the Seven Penitential Psalms, and portions of the Book of Job. Here is his translation of...

PSALM 23

Lord gouerns me and nathyng sall me want; in sted of pasture thare he me sett.
On the watere of rehetynge forth he me broght; my saule he turnyd.
He led me on the stretis of rightwisnes; for his name.
ffor whi, if i had gane in myddis of the shadow of ded; i. sall noght dred illes, for thou ert with me. Thi wand and thi staf; thai haf confortyd me.
Thou has grayid (vr. ordand) in my syght the bord; agayns thaim that angirs me.
Thou fattid my heued in oyle; and my chalice drunkynand what it is bright.
And thi mercy sall folow me; all the dayes of my lif.
And that i. won in the hows of lord; in lenght of dayes.

Some consider his greatest work to be "*The Pricke of Conscience*," a lengthy poem of 9624 lines in the old Northern English dialect. While I am not knowledgeable enough of his works to give my opinion one way or the other, I can say this with confidence: Richard Rolle, outrage with the worldliness of the Church and ecclesiastical education, his preaching and writing against sin, his calling others to a holy life, his exaltation of the spiritual side of religion over its dead rituals, his enthusiastic love of Christ and his declaration of individual soul liberty led to the foundation of the Lollard movement that taught that the Scripture was the final authority for faith and practice, above the Church.

When he was nearly 50 he moved to Hampole, near Doncaster in South Yorkshire England. He died September 29th, 1349 A.D. in the Black Death, which killed perhaps 1/3 of the total population of England. **He had a great influence on his own and the next** generation, laying the foundation for the first complete translation of the Bible, John Wycliffe's translation, and its distribution by the Lollards.

CHAPTER #9

ROME'S WAR AGAINST THE BIBLE AND BIBLICAL CHRISTIANITY

WHY THE BIBLE AND NT CHRISTIANITY WERE BANNED BY THE ROMAN CATHOLIC ECCLESIASTICAL ESTABLISHMENT

The Roman Catholic Church had everything to gain and nothing to lose by keeping the people in the dark about the truths of the Bible. Through ignorance of the Word of God, they were able, through *"cunningly devised fables,"* to control and manipulate the people. Why? Because knowing and obeying the Word of God brings great stability into the life of an individual. **Matthew 7:24-25** equates the man who hears the words of Jesus and does them with a wise man who builds his house upon a rock. In verses 26-27 of the same chapter, the man who hears but does not do His sayings is compared to one who builds his house upon the sand. When the storms come, the house left standing was the one built on the rock. Throughout His earthly ministry the Lord Jesus Christ stressed the importance of continuing in His Word. But why did he urge them to do that? He declared, *"Ye shall know the truth, and the truth shall make you free."* **John 8:32**. A person's spiritual freedom begins when that person trusts Christ as Savior. The Apostle John indicates that this is the reason he wrote his Gospel. He says, *"But these are written, that ye might believe that Jesus is the Christ, the Son of God; and that believing ye might have life through his name."* John 20:31. The importance of the Word of God cannot be underestimated. Paul writes that it is what our faith must be based on! He says, *"So then faith cometh by hearing, and hearing by the word of God."* There can be no saving faith without the Word of God! But there is more. There can be no spiritual growth without the studying of the Bible.

Believers have been commanded to grow spiritually. The Apostle Peter, under the inspiration of the Holy Spirit wrote, *"But grow in grace, and in the knowledge of our Lord and Saviour Jesus Christ. To him be glory both now and for ever. Amen."* **2 Peter 3:18**. But how is spiritual growth facilitated? The key to Christian growth and development is personally studying and obeying the Word of God. This is clearly taught in both the Old and New Testaments. For example, **Psalms 119:9-16** says, *"Wherewithal shall a young man cleanse his way? by taking heed thereto according to thy word. 10 With my whole heart have I sought thee: O let me not wander from thy commandments. 11 Thy word have I hid in mine heart, that I might not sin against thee. 12 Blessed art thou, O LORD: teach me thy statutes. 13 With my lips have I declared all the judgments of thy mouth. 14 I have rejoiced in the way of thy testimonies, as much as in all riches. 15 I will meditate in thy precepts, and have respect unto thy ways. 16 I will delight myself in thy statutes: I will not forget thy word."* New Testament examples include 2 Timothy 2:15-16 and Acts 1:11 – *"Study to show thyself approved unto God, a workman that needeth not to be ashamed, rightly dividing the word of truth. 16 But shun profane and vain babblings: for they will increase unto more ungodliness."* **2 Timothy 2:15-16**. *"These were more noble than those in Thessalonica, in that they received the word with all readiness of mind, and searched the scriptures daily, whether those things were so."* **Acts 17:11**

The Scriptures are clear. Knowing the truth of the Word of God and obeying the truth, as recorded in the Bible, brings spiritual growth to be sure, but it also affects mental freedom and inner peace! People who know and practice God's Word are not easily intimidated or manipulated. That is exactly why <u>the Roman Catholic Ecclesiastical establishment did not want people to know truths of the Bible</u>. They wanted to control and manipulate the people for their own advantages and did not want them to be exposed to verses like we find in **Acts 5:29** – *Then Peter and the other apostles answered and said, We ought to obey God rather than men.* The truth is, "the Roman Catholic Church kept Europe in the Dark Ages by hindering vernacular translations from being made and distributed, by bitterly persecuting any Christian who attempted to do this, by shrouding the Bible with its own traditions, and by placing its priesthood between the Bible and the people."(*Rome And The Bible;* by David W. Cloud; Way of Life Literature; p.51).

Throughout Europe the corrupt ecclesiastical leaders of the Roman Catholic Church issued decrees aimed at forcing people to stop reading, preaching, teaching, listening to or believing the Bible in their own language. Though these decrees were made on the

European continent, their impact was definitely felt in England, particularly after Innocent III's triumph over King John in 1213 A.D.

The following quotes from historians give us a clear indication of Ecclesiastical Rome's hatred for the Bible and biblical Christianity.

"The reading of the Bible by laymen was subject to so many restraints, especially after the rise of the Waldenses, that, if not absolutely forbidden, it was regarded with grave suspicion." (*History of The Christian Church*; by George Park Fisher; 1907 Charles Scribner's Sons; p.219).

In 1181 A.D., Lucius III issued a decree, stating, "We declare all Puritans, Paterians, Poor of Lyons, etc., to lie under a perpetual curse for teaching baptism and the Lord's Supper otherwise than the Church of Rome." (*A Concise History of Baptists from the Time of Christ their Founder to the 18th Century*; by G. H. Orchard; Published 1885; p. 194). In addition, Lucius called a special Council at Verona in 1183-84, in the presence of Emperor Frederick Barbarossa, "to bind in chains of perpetual anamatha those who presumed to preach, publicly or privately, without the authority of the bishop." (*History of the Baptists*; Thomas Armitage, D.D.; 1890; p.297).

In 1229 A.D. the persecution against Bible believers is amplified even further. "The Council of Toulouse (1229), the same that established the Inquisition (1231), struck at the whole matter by an edict forbidding laymen to read the Scriptures, whether in Latin or the vernacular." (*A Handbook of Church History*; Rev. Samuel G. Green D.D.; Fleming H. Revelle; p.511). The edict read – "Prohibemus etiam, ne libros Veteris Testamenti aut Novi laici permittantur habere; nisi forte Psalterium, vel Breviarium pro divinis officiis, aut horas B. Mariae aliquis ex devotione habeant in vulgari translatos, arctissime inhibeamus." (Ibid.) Here is my basic translation of the edict – "**We prohibit laymen, and refuse them permission to have the books of the Old and New Testament; except perhaps they might desire to have the Psalter, or some Breviary of the divine service, or the Hours of the blessed Virgin Mary, for devotion but expressly forbid their having other parts of the Bible translated into the vulgar tongue.**" Three years later, "In 1234 a synod at Tarragona extended the prohibition of the Scriptures in the vernacular to the clergy."

And in addition "ordered all vernacular versions to be brought to the Bishop to be burned." (*The Bible From The Beginning;* by Paris Marion Simms; The MacMillan Company – 1929; p.162).

THE INQUISITION ESTABLISHED

POPE INNOCENT III

Pope Innocent III (1160 to 1216 A.D.) is the father of the Inquisition. He laid much of the groundwork for the Inquisition, which officially started fifteen years after his death. "Born Lotario de' Conti di Segni at the castle of Gravignano, he came from an ancient noble family with powerful connections. He studied theology at the University of Paris and Canon Law at the University of Bologna, thus receiving the best education his age offered. Although not yet a priest, he was, at the age of 37, unanimously elected pope by the College of Cardinals on the day of his predecessor's death." (*Microsoft Encarts – Funk & Wagnall's Corporation;* Article: Innocent III).

There had been "Inquisition" type atrocities going on for multiplied decades. "Papal documents, as well as the Second (1139), Third (1179) and Fourth Lateran Councils (1215), prescribed imprisonment and confiscation of property as punishment for heresy and threatened to excommunicate princes who failed to punish heretics." (*Grolier Electronic Publishing – 1992;* Inquisition). But these atrocities were amplified many times when Lotario (Innocent III) was elected pope. In fact, shortly after he was elected to the papal office he **"declared that as by the old law, the beast touching the holy mount was to be stoned to death, so simple and**

uneducated men were not to touch the Bible or venture to preach its doctrines." (*History of the Christian Church*, Volume VI; Philip Schaff; Eerdmans Publishing, 1910; p.723). In 1215 A.D. he issued a papal decree commanding "that they shall be seized for trial and penalties who engage in the translation of the sacred volumes, or who hold secret conventicles, or who assume the office of preaching without the authority of their superiors; against whom process shall be commenced, without any permission of appear." (*Illustrations of Popery: The Mystery of Iniquity Unveiled* by J. P. Callender; published in New York in 1838; p.387).

The "examinations" to determine guilt or innocence instituted under Innocent III were horrifically hideous and barbaric. Thieleman J. van Braght says there was 1) **trial by red-hot iron**, 2) **examination by hot water** and 3) **trial by cold water**. Here is how each of these was applied, according to *The Bloody Theater or Martyrs Mirror of the Defenseless Christians* by Thieleman J. van Braght; first English edition 1837 - this addition 1996.

• *TRIAL BY RED-HOT IRON*

A person who was charged with holding sentiments contrary to the doctrine of the Roman Catholic Church would be brought to the priest for examination. The priest, dressed in sacerdotal attire marched to the altar chanting the song of the three Hebrew children in the fiery furnace (Daniel 3) and laid a piece of iron on the hot coals to be heated red-hot. As the iron was heated, with great pomp, the priest would repeatedly sprinkle holy water on the iron and coals while saying the Mass. Then as the priest took the wafer into his hand he prayed, "Lord God we pray Thee that Thou wouldst clearly manifest the truth in this Thy servant; Thou, O God, who hast in former times done great and wonderful signs by fire among Thy people...who didst preserve Lot, Thy servant, when Sodom and Gomorrah were justly laid in the ashes by fire; who, in the sending of the Holy Ghost by the light of fiery and flaming tongues, did separate the believers from the unbelievers; grant us grace while we make this trial, that through this red-hot fire we may discover the truth...that the innocent may be acquitted; but the guilty detected and punished." (*Martyrs Mirror* by Thieleman J. van Braght; pp. 310-311).

The priest then blessed the red-hot iron, sprinkled it lightly with holy water, picked it up with tongs and placed it into the hand of the accused who then had to carry it nine paces. The hand was then tightly wrapped up with cloth by the priest, and sealed for three days. At the end of the third day the hand was unwrapped and if there was a wound, the accused was judged guilty but if there was no evidence of a burn, he was acquitted.

• *EXAMINATION BY HOT WATER*

As in trial by hot iron, a person who was charged with holding sentiments contrary to the doctrine of the Roman Catholic Church would be brought to the priest for examination. At his option the priest would sometimes choose to use a kettle of boiling water for the examination instead of a hot iron. After the ceremonial prayers, etc. the accused would have to thrust his arm into the boiling water up to the elbow. If the accused was not scaled or the skin did not peel off from the arm he was judged innocent. If there was harm, this "proved" guilt. This brutal procedure was sometimes called Ketel-vang, particularly in the Netherlands.

• *TRIAL BY COLD WATER*

Trial by cold water served the same purpose as the other two examinations. The accused person was marched ceremoniously with a priest, one of the judges and a train of onlookers to the brink of some deep body of cold water, usually a canal or river. The accused was then given a cup of holy water to drink. As the accused drank the water, the priest would say, "This holy water be for a test to thee this day." Then turning to the water the accused was to be thrown into the priest would say, "I adjure thee, O Water, in the name of God the Father, who created thee in the beginning, and would have thee serve to meet the necessities of man, and be separated from the waters above."

Then he appealed to the water in the name of Christ, then in the name of the Holy Ghost and finally in the name of the Holy Trinity with shockingly stern words. Then the accused was addressed sternly and then unceremoniously stripped completely naked and thrown into the water. If he sank, he was considered innocent, but if he floated he was immediately condemned and burned at the stake as being guilty.

It is clear that Innocent III, Father of the Inquisition, was determined to do away with all Bible believers who dared preach, teach, read or believe the Bible. He went to great lengths to exterminate these Bible reading, Bible believing, Bible preaching pests. One of his most successful exterminations he used was for Crusades. But these Crusades were not against the Moslems to reclaim Christian territory. They were to exterminate Bible believing Christians. The great English Baptist Historian G. H. Orchard writes of one such crusade –

"In the year 1209, a formidable army of cross-bearers, of forty days' service, was put into motion, destined to destroy all heretics. ...The cruelties of these Crusades appear to have no parallel; in a few months there were sacrificed about two hundred thousand lives, and barbarities practiced, before unheard of, all which met the approbation of Innocent the 3rd. Two large cities, Beziers and Carcassone, were reduced to ashes, and thousands of others, driven from their burning houses, were wandering in the woods and mountains, sinking daily under the pressure of want." (*A Concise History of Baptists from the Time of Christ their Founder to the 18th Century;* by G. H. Orchard; Published 1885; p.211).

Though it may not seem possible that the persecution against Bible believers could get worse, it did. The prevailing spiritual darkness becomes pitch black when Pope **Gregory IX** (nephew of Innocent III) came to power. He "forbade laymen possessing the Bible, and suppressed translations. Translations among the Albigenses and Waldenses were burned, and the people burned for having them." (*Halley's Bible Handbook;* by Henry Halley; Regency Reference Library Edition by Zondervan; p.783). He formally instituted the official papal Inquisition in 1231. He began by adopting a law that Holy Roman Emperor Frederick II had enacted for Lombardy in 1224 and extended to the entire empire. This law "ordered convicted heretics to be seized by secular authorities and burned." (*Grolier Electronic Publishing – 1992;* Inquisition). Schaff adds that Frederick II condemned heretics either to be burned or to have their tongues torn out at the discretion of the judge. (*History of the Christian Church,* Volume V; Philip Schaff; Eerdmans Publishing, 1910; p.521).

Church historian William Blackburn writes, "No legalized institution (the Inquisition) has ever done more to crush intellectual and religious liberty, or added more to the unspoken miseries of the human race. Every layman daring to possess a Bible, now first forbidden to the laity by this council, was in peril of the rack, the dungeon, and the stake." *(History of the Christian Church from its Origin to The Present Time* by William Maxwell Blackburn; published by Walden and Stowe in 1880; p.309).

THE KEY ENFORCERS OF THE INQUISITION

DOMINIC DE GUZMAN

But how was the Inquisition carried out? Who instituted the Pope's orders? The orders started by Dominic de Guzman and Francis of Assisis played a major role in the papal Inquisition. Italian friar Francis of Assisi (1181-1226 A.D.) started the order of the Grey Friars or Franciscans. Dominic de Guzman of Spain (1170-1221 A.D.) started the Black Friars or Dominicans. "The seat of the Inquisition in each district was the monastery of the order (Dominicans or Franciscan) to which the inquisitors for that part belonged." (*The Encyclopedia Britannica - 11th Edition;* Vol. 14. P.589). In fact, "The office of inquisitor was entrusted almost exclusively to the Franciscans and, especially, the Dominicans" (*Microsoft Encarts – Funk & Wagnall's Corporation;* Article: The Inquisition) because of their tenacity and superior training in Catholic ecclesiastical dogma. Dominic especially sought to "increase the power of the church and to perpetuate the integrity of Catholic doctrine. Dominic was cold, systematic, austere. He was a master disciplinarian. Dominic was called the hammer of the heretics. (*History of the Christian Church* by Philip Schaff; volume 5, pp.380-381). In fact "the blood-thirst of the Dominicans earned for themselves the stigma of (being labeled) **Domini Cannes** or the Lord's Dogs." (*History of the Baptists;* Thomas Armitage, D.D.; 1890; p.311-312). Armitage says,

"The horrible Inquisition was formed for the expressed purpose of planting an iron foot upon the throat of the most hallowed rights of man... The tribunal of infernal origin clothed certain monks with limitless power to torture the Waldensians and lead them to execution without legal forms or the rights of trial. Many of them... were cast from high precipices and dashed to pieces. Some were driven into caverns, and by filling the mouths of their caves with fagots were suffocated. Others were hanged in cold blood, ripped open and disemboweled, pierced with prongs, drowned, racked limb from limb till death relieved them; were stabbed, worried by dogs, burned, or crucified with their heads downward...four hundred mothers who had taken refuge in the Cave of Castelluzzo, some 2,000 feet above the valley, entered by a projecting crag, were smothered with their infants in their arms. And all the time that this gentle blood was flowing, the sanctified beauty known as Innocent III drank it in like nectar of Paradise... The very sentences which they (the Dominicans) pronounced in mockery of trial and justice were a Satanic compound of formality and heartlessness, sanctimony and avarice, obsequiousness and arrogance." (*History of the Baptists;* Thomas Armitage, D.D.; 1890; p.311-312).

All this was done to true Christians by those who claimed they were the only Christians because these true Christians dared possess, read, believe, teach and preach from a Bible they understood.

THE ALLEGED BIBLICAL BASIS RATIONALIZA-TION FOR THE INQUISITION ATROCITIES

Have you ever wondered how a church that claims to exist by apostolic authority (the claim is false) could perpetrate such atrocities upon people? I have. In my research I found the answer and it is mind-boggling. **St. Augustine** (354 to 430 A.D.) taught that it was appropriate, even necessary, for people to be compelled to worship and obey the directives of the official, approved church. He based this on **Luke 14:23** which says, *And the lord said unto* *the servant, Go out into the highways and hedges, and <u>compel</u> <u>them to come in</u>, that my house may be filled.* He interpreted this verse "as endorsing the use of force against heretics." (*Grolier Electronic Publishing – 1992;* Inquisition).

An heretic was defined as anyone who disagreed with and or refused to adopt the doctrines and practices of the official church, the Roman Catholic Church. If the heretic could not be persuaded to conform to the Church, he believed the Bible taught that the heretic should be punished as God punishes sinners...by being burned with fire. Augustine based this teaching on **John 15:6** which says – *If a man abide not in me, he is cast forth as a branch, and is withered; and <u>men gather them, and cast them into the fire, and they are burned</u>.*

Historian H. G. Wells records the words of Dominic as he tells the "heretics" he is through trying to convince them of their errors and now will torture them into capitulating to Roman Catholic dogma. Dominic writes this in his last discourse to the Bible believing "heretics" before he unleashes the full fury of his hellish Inquisition atrocities upon them – "For many years I have exhorted you in vain, with gentleness, preaching, praying, and weeping. But according to the proverb of my country, 'Where blessing can accomplish nothing, blows may avail,' we shall rouse against you princes and prelates, who, alas! Will arm nations and kingdoms against this land...and thus blows will avail where blessings and gentleness have been powerless." (*The Outline of History* by H. G. Wells; p.547).

This is the official position of the Catholic Church regarding heretics. I want you to realize that the Roman Catholic Church has never rescinded the bulls calling for the burning of heretics. There has never been an official apology for the Inquisition though recently there has been some beating around the bush about being sorry for Roman Catholic persecution in general!

Augustine held an unbiblical position. I believe that man's first obligation is to God, not to human leaders in any church. Peter reminds us in **Acts 5:29** *"We ought to obey God rather than men."* The Bible teaches that we all have the freedom of conscience. We all have the right and responsibility to study the Bible and interpret for ourselves what it means. Further, we will be required to give account of ourselves to God. Therefore, no other man and no church can or should try to act as our conscience (1 John 2:27; Romans 14:5 & 12; 1 Thessalonians 5:21; Acts 17:11; 2 Timothy 2:15). Yet, despite the genuine truths of the Word of God, the Roman Catholic Inquisition "machine" ploughed ahead devouring everyone in its path who disagreed with her.

CHAPTER #10

THE ROOT OF THE CONFLICT BETWEEN THE CHURCH OF ROME AND THE CHRISTIANS SHE PERSECUTED AND MARTYRED

In Stirling, Scotland, about two hundred yards outside the main gate of Stirling Castle, is a strange looking pyramid structure that stands in Holyrood Church Cemetery. The pyramid is a monument dedicated to all those who gave their lives in pursuit of religious freedom. As I stood there silently, my thoughts turned to thankfulness for those who were martyred for the true New Testament faith, paving the way for the religious freedom that I enjoy in my country, the United States of America. The roots and trunk of that struggle are recorded in the pages of *The Ecclesiastical History: Containing The Acts and Monuments of Martyrs: With A general Discourse of these latter Persecutions, horrible Troubles and Tumults, stirred up by Romish Prelates in the Church* by John Foxe. In 1563, England was stirred by the appearance of this book, which was dedicated to Queen Elizabeth.

"From the halls of royalty to the humblest village, there was no level of English society that escaped the commotion aroused by the work. While the book was spurned by the enemies of the English Reformation, it was met with the admiration and approval of many, including the Queen herself. So impressed was she with the work, that she ordered copies to be placed in the hands of every church and college official in the nation, and that a copy be placed in every parish church for the use of all the people." (*The History and Legacy of Foxe's Book of Martyrs* by Robert Liddell; in U-TURN Volume 6 Number 1 Autumn 1998; p.5).

What I find ironic, no, in fact pathetic, is how little attention this work receives in Christian churches, colleges and seminaries today. I have talked with numerous students and professors from a variety of Christian educational institutions and find that, for the most part, the work commonly called *Foxe's Book of Martyrs* receives, at the most, just a passing reference in this generation. No other book, apart from the Bible, fueled the fires in the hearts of Englishmen to reject Papism and promote the biblical Gospel than this book. In fact, within thirty-three years of Foxe's death, Pilgrims, Puritans and other nonconformists were setting out across the Atlantic with their Geneva English Bibles and copies of Foxe's Book of Martyrs with the goal of establishing biblical focused settlements and evangelizing the heathen. "Sadly, the power of the message that Foxe was attempting to convey in his work is lost in the current versions which have been greatly abridged." (Ibid.).

Today's versions highlight the dramatic accounts of the martyrs and their suffering. Yet, what is just as important is an explanation of the biblical truths that they refused to compromise and were willing to suffer and die for. I have found the unabridged work of John Foxe, which is nearly 3,000 pages long, to be valuable in amplifying my zeal to stand for Bible truth as well as helping me to understand the development of the struggle for freedom of religion and freedom of conscience that I enjoy today.

THE ROOT OF THE CONFLICT BETWEEN "HOLY MOTHER CHURCH" AND THE MARTYRS

- ### THE CHARACTERIZATION OF "HOLY MOTHER CHURCH" VS. THE TRUE NEW TESTAMENT CHURCH

The Roman Catholic Church had been in the seat of power and had claimed universal dominion and authority in Christendom for centuries. But, as the centuries rolled on, the Church of Rome moved further and further away from the doctrine given to them by the Apostle Paul in his letter to the Romans, and the New Testament model of the Church and Christianity. They, like the Pharisees of old (see Matthew 15:1-9), tampered with the biblical model, adding mountains of human traditions and man-made inventions until genuine worship of God was well-nigh impossible. Further, in an effort to cover up their own trespasses, they endeavored to keep the people from the Bible and the Bible from the people. To add insult to injury, when anyone, be it nobleman, priest or plebeian, returned to the New Testament model of Christianity, they were condemned as heretics and dealt with in a most brutal manner.

John Foxe gives us a rather graphic characterization of "Holy Mother Church," as the Papists refer to their church, contrasted to the New Testament Church as defined in the Bible –

"Although it cannot be sufficiently expressed with tongue or pen of man, into what miserable ruin and desolation the Church of Christ was brought in those latter days; yet partly by the reading of these stories afore past, some intelligence may be given to those who have judgment to mark, or eyes to see, in what blindness and darkness the world was drowned, during the space of these four hundred years heretofore and more. By the viewing and considering of which times and histories, thou mayest understand (gentle reader) how the religion of Christ, which only consisteth in spirit and verity, was wholly turned into, outward observations, ceremonies, and idolatry. So many saints we had, so many gods; so many monasteries, so many pilgrimages. As many churches, as many relics forged and reigned we had. Again, so many relics, so many lying miracles we believed. Instead of the only living Lord, we worshipped dead stocks and stones. In place of Christ immortal, we adored mortal bread. Instead of his blood, we worshipped the blood of ducks; how the people were led, so that the priests were fed, no care was taken. Instead of God's Word, man's word was set up. Instead of Christ's Testament, the pope's testament, that is, the Canon Law. Instead of Paul, the Master of Sentences took place, and almost full possession. The law of God was little read, the use and end thereof was less known; and as the end of the law was unknown, so the difference between the gospel and the law was not understood, the benefit of Christ not considered, the effect of faith not expended: through the ignorance whereof it cannot be told what infinite errors, sects, and religions crept into the church, overwhelming the world as with a flood of ignorance and seduction. And no marvel; for where the foundation is not well laid, what building can stand and prosper? The foundation of all our Christianity is only this; The promise of God in the blood of Christ his Son, giving and promising life to all that believe in him [Romans 3:22]: Giving (saith the

Scripture) unto us, and not bargaining or indenting with us. And that freely (saith the Scripture) for Christ's sake, and not conditionally for our merit's sake. [Romans 4:5]

"Furthermore, freely (saith the Scripture) by Grace, [Romans 4:6] that the promise might be firm and sure, and not by the works that we do, which are always doubtful. By Grace (saith the Scripture) through promise to all and upon all that believe [Romans 3:22], and not by the law, upon them that do deserve. For if it come by deserving, then it is not of Grace: If it be not of Grace, then it is not of Promise [Romans 11:6], and contrariwise, if it be of grace and promise, then is it not of works, saith St. Paul. Upon this foundation of God's free promise and grace first builded the patriarchs, kings, and prophets: upon this same foundation also Christ the Lord builded his church: upon which foundation the apostles likewise builded the Church Apostolical or Catholical.

"This Apostolical and Catholic foundation so long as the church did retain, so long it continued sincere and sound: which endured a long season after the Apostles' time. But after, in process of years, through wealth and negligence crept into the church, so soon as this foundation began to be lost, came in new builders, who would build upon a new foundation a new church more glorious, which we call now the church of Rome; who, not being contented with the old foundation, and the Head-cornerstone, which the Lord by his word had laid, in place thereof hid the groundwork upon the condition and strength of the law and works. Although it is not to be denied, but that the doctrine of God's holy law, and of good works according to the same, is a thing most necessary to be learned, and followed of all men; yet it is not that foundation whereupon our salvation consisteth; neither is that foundation able to bear up the weight of the kingdom of heaven, but is rather the thing which is builded upon the foundation; which foundation is Jesus Christ, according as we are taught of St. Paul, saying; "No man can lay any other foundation beside that which is laid, Christ Jesus," etc. [1 Corinthians 3:11]

"But this ancient foundation, with the old ancient church of Christ, as I said, hath been now of long time forsaken, and instead thereof, a new church with a new foundation hath been erected and framed, not upon God's promise, and his free grace in Christ Jesus, nor upon free justification by faith, but upon merits and deserts of men's working. And hereof have they planted all these their new devices, so infinite, that they cannot well be numbered; as masses-trecenaries, dirges, obsequies, mattens (matins), and hours-singing-service, vigils, midnight-rising, bare-foot-going, fish-tasting, Lent-fast, ember-fast, stations, rogations, jubilees, advocation of saints, praying to images, pilgrimage-walking, works of supererogation, application of merits, orders, rules, sects of religion, vows of chastity, willful poverty, pardons, relations, indulgencies, penance, satisfaction, auricular confession, founding of abbeys, building of chapels, giving to churches: and who is able to recite all their laborious buildings, falsely framed upon a wrong ground; and all for ignorance of the true foundation, which is the free justification by faith in Christ Jesus the Son of God.

"Moreover note, that as this new-found Church of Rome was thus deformed in doctrine, so no less was it corrupted in order of life and deep hypocrisy, doing all things only under pretenses and dissembled titles. So, under the pretense of Peter's chair, they exercised a majesty above emperors and kings. Under the visor of their vowed chastity, reigned adultery; under the cloak of professed poverty, they possessed the goods of the temporality; under the title of being dead to the world, they not only reigned in the world, but also ruled the world; under the color of the keys of heaven to hang under their girdle, they brought all the states of the world under their girdle, and crept not only into the purses of men, but also into their consciences: they heard their confessions; they knew their secrets; they dispensed as they were disposed, and loosed what them listed: And finally, when they had brought the whole world under their subjections, yet neither did their pride cease to ascend, nor could their avarice be ever satisfied. And if the example of cardinal Wolsey and other cardinals and popes cannot satisfy thee, I beseech thee (gentle reader) turn over the aforesaid book of 'the Ploughman's Tale' in Chaucer, above-mentioned, where thou shalt understand much more of their demeanour than I have here described.

"In these so blind and miserable corrupt days of darkness and ignorance, thou seest, good reader (I doubt not) how necessary it was, and high time, that reformation of the church should come, which now most happily and graciously began to work, through the merciful and no less needful providence of Almighty God; who, although he suffered his church to wander and start aside, through the seduction of pride and prosperity a long time, yet at length it pleased his goodness to respect his people, and to reduce his church into the pristine foundation and frame again, from whence it was piteously before decayed. Hereof I have now consequently to entreat; intending by the grace of Christ to declare how, and by what means this reformation of the church first began, and how it proceeded, increasing by little and little unto this perfection which now we see, and more I trust shall see." (*The Ecclesiastical History: Containing The Acts and Monuments...* 1641 Edition; by John Foxe; Volume 2, Book 7; pp. 56-57; Scripture references in [ ] added by author of this book.)

Obviously, no words are minced by Foxe in contrasting the true "Church of Christ...which the Lord by his Word" founded with the "falsely framed...new-found church of Rome" which had "been erected and framed, not upon God's...free grace in Christ Jesus, nor upon free justification by faith, but upon merits and deserts of men's working" and "thus deformed in doctrine." In fact, it is clear to me, that the root of conflict between the church of Rome and those she labeled heretics can be boiled down to this basic issue – how "the church" is defined and who or what is the final authority?

• *THE CHURCH OF ROME AND HER VIEW OF FINAL AUTHORITY*

There are sentences and phrases scattered throughout Foxe's work that could be lifted out to give Rome's definition of "Holy Mother Church" and her assertion of authority. One example is found in an exchange between Archdeacon Dr. Harpsfield and Master John Bradford. Hapsfield asserts "that by baptism then we are brought, and, as a man would say, begotten of Christ: for Christ is our Father, and the church his spouse is our mother...so all spiritual men have Christ for their father, and the church for their mother." (*The Third Volume of the Ecclesiastical History: Containing the Acts and Monuments of Martyrs...*1684 Edition; by John Fox; Volume 3, p.242).

By contrast, Lady Jane Grey believed that the way into the family of God, the church, was by faith in Christ and his shed blood as recorded in the New Testament Scriptures. In an exchange between her and Mr. Fecknam, he asks what is necessary for a man (or woman) to become a Christian. She responds, "That he should believe in God the Father, the Son, and the Holy Ghost, three persons and one God." (ibid.; p.26). Fecknam asks if there is anything else necessary and claims that works are necessary for salvation. Jane clearly responds – "I deny that, and I affirm that faith only saveth: but it is meet (right) for a Christian, in token that he followeth his master Christ, to do good works; yet may we not say that they profit to our salvation. For when we have done all, yet we be unprofitable servants, and faith only in Christ's blood saveth us." (Ibid. p.26).

Jane was a student of the Bible. She knew it well. It is obvious that her biblical view of how a person becomes a part of "the church," and the Roman Catholic view differ. But the differences are wider and deeper than indicated in these two brief passages I have related. For a better understanding I turn your attention to a section at the end of volume one in the ninth edition (1684 edition) that is composed of extracts from the pope's canon law that defines the Roman Catholic view of the "church" as well as what their view of final authority is.

"Forasmuch as it standeth upon necessity of salvation, for every, human creature to be subject unto me the pope of Rome, it shall be therefore requisite and necessary for all men that will be saved, to learn and know the dignity of my See and excellency of my domination, as is here set forth according to the truth and very words of mine own laws, in style as followeth: First, my institution began in the Old Testament, and was consummated and finished in the New, in that my priesthood was prefigured by Aaron; and other bishops under me were prefigured by the sons of Aaron, that were under him; neither is it to be thought that my church of Rome hath been preferred by any general council, but obtained the primacy only by the voice of the Gospel, and the mouth of the Savior, and hath in it neither spot nor wrinkle, nor any such like thing. Wherefore, as other seats be all inferior to me, and as they cannot absolve me, so have they no power to bind me or to stand against me, no more than the ax hath power to stand or presume above him that heweth with it, or the saw to presume above him that ruleth it. This is the holy and apostolic mother-church of all other churches of Christ; from whose rules it is not meet that any person or persons should decline; but like as the Son of God came to do the will of his Father, so must you do the will of your mother the church, the head whereof is the church of Rome; and if any other person or persons shall err from the said church, either let them be admonished, or else their names taken, to be known who they be, that swerve from the customs of Rome. Thus then, forasmuch as the holy church of Rome, where of I am governor, is set up to the whole world for a glass or example, reason would what thing so-ever the said church determineth, or ordaineth, that to be received of all men for a general and a perpetual rule for ever. Whereupon we see it now verified in this church, that was fore-prophesied by Jeremy, saying, "Behold, I have set thee up over nations and kingdoms, to pluck up and to break down, to build and to plant," etc. Whoso understandeth not the prerogative of this my priesthood, let him look up to the firmament, where he may see two great lights, the sun and the moon, one ruling over the day, the other over the night: so in the firmament of the universal church, and hath set two great dignities, the authority of the pope, and of the emperor; of which two, this our dignity is so much more weighty, as we have the greater charge to give account to God for kings of the earth, and the laws of men. Wherefore be it known to you emperors, who know it also right well, that you depend upon the judgment of us: we must not be brought and reduced to your will. For, as I said, look what difference there is betwixt the sun and the moon, so great is the power of the pope ruling over the day, that is, over the spirituality, above emperors and kings, ruling over the night; that is, over the laity. Now, seeing then the earth is seven times bigger than the moon, and the sun eight times greater than the earth it followeth that the pope's dignity fifty-six times doth surmount the estate of the emperors. (*Acts and Monuments of Matters Most Special and Memorable Happening in the Church...* 1684 Edition; by John Fox; Volume 1, Book 6; p. 887).

Clearly, from the Roman Catholic perspective, "the church" was the Church of Rome headed by "the pope of Rome...and other Bishops" under him. By papal decree, it was "necessary for all men that will be saved" to be subject to the Pope of Rome, "to learn and know the dignity" of the Pope's authority, and "whose rules it is not meet (right) that any person or persons should decline (disobey)."

Is there any doubt about their view of final authority when you read statements like – "What thing soever the said church determineth, or ordaineth, that (is) to be received of all men for a general and a perpetual rule forever" or that the power of the pope is alleged to be "fifty-six times" more powerful than any emperor's power. Rome demand was, "so must you do the will of your mother church, the head whereof is the church of Rome." In short, the Church of Rome fabricated her own definition of "the church" and then established herself as the sovereign final authority over it and all Christendom.

• *THE MARTYR'S VIEW OF FINAL AUTHORITY AND "THE CHURCH"*

The martyr's view of final authority is clearly seen to be the Bible. For example, I point you to a portion of the letter that Laurence Saunders sent to the Bishop of Winchester. I will begin with the section of the letter where Saunders quotes Acts 24:16 –

"And herein study I to have always a clear conscience towards God and towards men: so that (God I call to witness) I have a conscience. And this my conscience is not grounded upon vain fantasy, but upon the infallible verity of God's word, with the witnessing of his chosen church agreeable unto the same...Wherefore I, in conscience weighing the Romish religion, and, by indifferent discussing thereof, finding the foundation unsteadfast, and the building thereupon but vain: and, on the other side, having my conscience framed after a right and uncorrupt religion, ratified and fully established by the word of God, and the consent of his true church, I neither may, nor do intend, by God's gracious assistance, to be pulled one jot from the same; no, though an angel out of heaven should preach another gospel [Galatians 1:8] than that which I have received of the Lord." (*The Third Volume of the Ecclesiastical History: Containing the Acts and Monuments of Martyrs...*1684 Edition; by John Fox; Volume 3, p.111; Scripture references in [ ] added by author of this book.)

The position of Laurence Saunders was this: the Bible alone is the final authority, not the Church of Rome and her vain, corrupted teachings. The true church conforms to the Word of God. The false church, Roman Catholic Church, refused to conform to the Bible. Therefore he could not conform to a church that was built on an "unsteadfast" foundation and preached a false gospel. Saunders position is not unique among the martyrs, but in fact is shared by most of them.

There is one particular story of the transformation of a Romanist to the position of biblical authority that I find helpful. It is the story of John Rogers, who would ultimately be the first martyr in the reign of so called "Bloody Mary." Cambridge educated Rogers had been an ardent Romanist. For many years he was a Roman Catholic chaplain to the English merchants in Antwerp. But all that changed when he began to keep "company with that worthy servant and martyr of God William Tyndale, and with Miles Coverdale." (Ibid. p.98) Both Tyndale and Coverdale bore a hatred for "popish superstition and idolatry, and love to true religion. In conferring with them the Scriptures, <u>he came to great knowledge in the gospel of God</u>, insomuch that he cast off the heavy yoke of popery, perceiving it to be impure and filthy idolatry, and joined himself with them two in that painful and most profitable labor of translating the Bible into the English tongue, which is entitled, The Translation of Thomas Matthew." (Ibid. p.98).

John Rogers' life changed dramatically when he began to read, study, believe and talk about the truths of the Bible with Tyndale (English Bible translator 1526 & 1536) and Miles Coverdale (English Bible translator 1537). He took Christ as Savior and the Bible became his final authority. The specific basis of his conviction concerning the necessity of believing the New Testament Gospel of Jesus Christ, believing the Bible to be the final authority in all matters of faith and practice, and the necessity of propagating its teachings is seen in material he wrote while he was in prison for his so-called heresy. He points to Peter, the alleged first Pope of Rome, who, with the other apostles, said that when laws of God and man conflict, God is to be obeyed. Here is what he wrote:

"I say, it is not only lawful for any private man, which bringeth God's word for him, and the authority of the primitive and best church, to speak and write against such unlawful laws; but it is his duty, and he is bound in very conscience to do it. Which thing I have proved by divers examples before, and now will add but one other, which is written in Acts 5, where it appeareth that the high priests, the elders, scribes, and pharisees, decreed in their council, and gave the same commandment to the apostles, that they should not preach in the name of Christ, as ye have also forbidden us. Notwithstanding, when they were charged therewithal, they answered 'Obedire oportet Deo magis quam hominibus:' that is, 'We ought more to obey God than man: [Acts 5:29] even so we may, and do answer you; God is more to be obeyed than man; and your wicked laws cannot so tongue-tie us, but we will speak the truth.

"The apostles were beaten for their boldness, and they rejoiced that they suffered for Christ's cause. Ye have also provided rods for us, and bloody whips: yet when ye have done that which God's hand and council hath determined that ye shall do, be it life or death, I trust that God will so assist us by his holy Spirit and grace, that we shall patiently suffer it, and praise God for it. And whatsoever become of me and others, which now suffer for speaking and professing of the truth, yet be ye sure that God's Word will prevail, and have the over hand, when your bloody laws and wicked decrees, for want of sure foundation, shall fall in the dust. And that which I have spoken of your acts of parliament, the same may be said of the general councils of these latter days, which have been within these five hundred years, where the Antichrist of Rome, by reason of his usurped authority, ruled the roost, and decreed such things as made for his gain, not regarding God's glory: and therefore are they to be spoken, written, and cried out against, of all such as fear God and love his Truth." (Ibid; p.104; Scripture references in [ ] added by author of this book.)

Is it not ironic that John Rogers' belief in the final authority of the Bible was rooted in the words spoken by the Apostle Peter in Acts 5:29, while the Roman Catholic church, which claims to be founded on Peter, wholly ignored Peter's words and proclaimed that her own decrees, which often contradicted the Bible, outranked the Bible? Indeed!

Throughout the pages of Foxes' work we see the conflict between the final authority of Rome and the final authority of the Bible. There was a willingness on the part of the "heretics" to be corrected, but only if that correction came from the Scriptures. But the papists refused to bow to the authority of the Scriptures. One example is the case of John Bradford. A Spanish priest was seeking to persuade Bradford to accept the papist authority. Bradford denied that the Romanist's teachings were biblical. Alphonsus the priest said, "Why? Will you believe nothing but that which is expressly spoken of in the Scriptures?" John responded, "I will believe whatsoever you shall by demonstration out of the Scriptures declare unto me." (*The Third Volume of the Ecclesiastical History: Containing the Acts and Monuments of Martyrs*...1684 Edition; by John Fox; Volume 3, p.248).

Allow a second illustration before we conclude this point. I return to John Rogers for a moment. He ardently denied that he was an heretic. Stephen Gardiner, the Lord Chancellor, alleged that Rogers was an heretic because he would "not receive the bishop of Rome to be the supreme head of the catholic church." (Ibid. p.99). Rogers said, "I know no other head but Christ of his catholic church, neither will I acknowledge the bishop of Rome to have any more authority than any other bishop hath by the Word of God, and by the doctrine of the old and pure catholic church four hundred years after Christ." (Ibid. p.99) He went on to say that, if it could be proved from the Bible that he was in error, he would change his mind. At this point, Chancellor Gardiner becomes angry and spits out, what I believe to be the Roman Catholic position of the Bible. He says, "thou canst prove nothing by the Scripture. The Scripture is dead: it must have a lively (living) expositor." (Ibid. p.99). Rogers quickly responds, "NO, the Scripture is alive," (Ibid. p.99) no doubt having Hebrews 4:12 in mind.

- ## *THE ROOT OF THE CONFLICT RESTATED SIMPLY*

Hence, the root of the conflict can clearly be seen. The martyrs believed the Bible defined the church and that the Bible was the final authority in all matters of belief and practice. For the Roman Catholic establishment, she defined "the church" however she saw fit and Canon Law was the final authority. Since the Romanists had the "might," she insisted that she was "right" and anyone who disagreed with her was charged with heresy and punished severely. So, as Foxe pointed out earlier, "Instead of God's Word, man's word was set up. Instead of Christ's Testament, the pope's testament, that is, the canon law. Instead of the only living Lord, we worshipped dead stocks and stones. In place of Christ immortal, we adored mortal bread." (*The Ecclesiastical History: Containing The Acts and Monuments...* 1641 Edition; by John Foxe; Volume 2, Book 7; pp. 56).

Now that the root of the conflict has been identified we can move on to the next point.

AN OVERVIEW OF THE CHARGES OF HERESY BROUGHT AGAINST THE MARTYRS BY THE ROMAN CATHOLIC CHURCH, CONTRASTED WITH THE DEFENSE OR REPLY OF THE MARTYRS

- ## *THE HERESY OF DENYING TRANSUBSTANTIA-TION AND THE PROPITIATORY SACRIFICE OF THE MASS*

In my reading of Foxe's work, the basis most often used for declaring an individual an heretic was the denial of transubstantiation and the mass. This is noted in the preface of the ninth edition (1684) at the beginning of "The Third Volume and Tenth Book, Beginning with the Reign of Queen Mary." It says,

"FORASMUCH as we are come now to the time of queen Mary, when so many were put to death for the cause especially of the Mass, and The Sacrament of the Altar (as they call it), I thought it convenient, upon the occasion given, in the ingress of this foresaid story, first, to prefix before, by the way of preface, some declaration collected out of divers writers and authors, whereby to set forth to the reader the great absurdity, wicked abuse, and perilous idolatry, of the popish mass; declaring how, and by whom, it came in, and how it is clouted and patched up of divers additions: to the intent that the reader, seeing the vain institution thereof, and weighing the true causes why it is to be exploded out of all churches, may the better thereby judge of their death, who gave their lives for the testimony and the Word of Truth." (*The Third Volume of the Ecclesiastical History: Containing the Acts and Monuments of Martyrs*...1684 Edition; by John Fox; p.1).

I should point out that the usual course followed in convicting people of heresy was to charge them with multiple heresies. Consistently, in multiple charges of heresy, one of the key charges related to denial of transubstantiation. This was the case with Dr. Rowland Taylor, pastor of the Hadley church. He was charged with the heresy of preaching (and practicing) that priests could be married, denying transubstantiation and the propitiatory nature of the sacrifice of the mass.

Before we look at the charge relating to the latter, we need to consider the **three basic views of the Lord's Supper** held within Christendom – **Transubstantiation, Consubstantiation** and **Commemoration**. Those who believe in transubstantiation teach that at the moment of the prayer of consecration, **magically** the bread and wine change substance and become, literally, the body and blood of Christ. Those who believe in consubstantiation teach that at consecration something **mysteriously** happens, bringing the presence of Christ to the elements. Those who believe in commemoration believe in neither magic nor mystery, but in **memorial**. They look back and remember the suffering and death of Christ for us.

The latter position was that for which Dr. Rowland Taylor was convicted of heresy. Dr Taylor writes,

"My second cause why I was condemned an heretic is, that I denied Transubstantiation and Concomitation [meaning that the bread/wine body/blood of Christ literally coexist together with one another at the same time], two juggling words of the papists, by the which they do believe, and will compel all other to believe, that Christ's natural body is made of bread, and the Godhead by and by to be joined thereunto; so that immediately after the words called 'the words of consecration,' there is no more bread and wine in the sacrament, but the substance only of the body and blood of Christ together with his Godhead: so that the same being now Christ, both

God and man, ought to be worshipped with godly honor, and to be offered to God, both for the quick and the dead, as a sacrifice propitiatory and satisfactory for the same. This matter was not long debated in words: but because I denied the aforesaid papistical doctrine (yea rather, plain, most wicked, idolatry, blasphemy and heresy), I was judged a heretic. I did also affirm the pope to be antichrist, and popery antichristianity. And I confessed the doctrine of the Bible to be sufficient doctrine, touching all and singular matters of Christian religion, and of salvation." (*The Third Volume of the Ecclesiastical History: Containing the Acts and Monuments of Martyrs...1684 Edition; by John Fox; Volume 3, Book11, p.141; Information in [ ] is added by the author.*)

Taylor was burned at the stake as an heretic. But, how did these martyrs defend their position against Rome's teaching? We see a concise statement of their defense recorded in the ninth edition of Foxe. He is referring to George Bucker, also called Adam Damlip, who was drawn, hanged and quartered for his preaching against transubstantiation and the propitiatory sacrifice of the mass. Foxe writes –

"This godly man, by the space of twenty days or more, once every day, at seven of the clock, preached very godly, learnedly, and plainly, the truth of the blessed sacrament of Christ's body and blood, mightily inveighing against all papistry, and confuting the same; but especially those <u>two most pernicious errors or heresies, touching transubstantiation, and the pestilent propitiatory sacrifice of the Romish mass, by true conference of the Scriptures, and applying of the ancient doctors</u>; earnestly therewith oftentimes exhorting the people to return from their popery; declaring how popish he himself had been, and how, by the detestable wickedness that he did see universally in Rome, he was returned so far homeward, and now became an enemy, through God's grace, to all papistry." (*The Second Volume of the Ecclesiastical History...1684; Vol. 2, Book 8, p. 470*).

John Damlip used the Scriptures and the teaching of the early church father to support his position. Indeed, this was the pattern of the martyrs. They would hold up the biblical model and then support that model with the teachings of the early church. A good example is the defense put forth by **Cranmer, the Archbishop of Canterbury**. He wrote, **"<u>this monstrous paradox of</u>**

transubstantiation was never induced or received publicly in the church, before the time of the Lateran council, under pope Innocent III, A. D. 1216; or at most before the time of Lanfranc, the Italian, archbishop of Canterbury, A. D. 1070." (Ibid. p.373).

He goes on to assert that Tertullian and Augustine both taught the sacrament was a "figure, a sign, a memorial, and a representation of the Lord's body, and knew no such transubstantiation" (Ibid.). and yet were neither considered traitors nor heretics. He continues that Ambrose and Theodoret knew nothing of transubstantiation. In 780 A.D. the words of Bede make it clear "that no transubstantiation as yet in his time was received in the church of England." (Ibid. p.374). I would like to note the words of the Lateran Council in 1216 A.D. that codified the "monstrous paradox of transubstantiation."

"There is one universal church of the faithful, without which none can be saved; in which church the selfsame Jesus Christ is both priest and also the sacrifice; whose body and blood are truly contained in the sacrament of the altar, under the forms of bread and wine, the bread being transubstantiated into the body, and the wine into the blood, by the power and working of God: so that to the accomplishing of this mystery of unity, we might take of his, the same which he hath taken of ours. And this sacrament none can make or consecrate, but he that is a priest lawfully ordained, according to the keys of the church, which Jesus Christ hath left to his apostles, and to their successors, etc." (Ibid. p.385).

Certain papists did try to prove that transubstantiation was of an early origin by misquoting early church fathers. In fact they were lying! But credible men like Erasmus exposed that lie by writing, **"In the sacrament of the communion, the church concluded transubstantiation but of late days. Long before that, it was sufficient to believe the true body of Christ to be present either under the bread, or else by some other matter."**(Ibid. p.386).

So, the pattern is clear. The Roman Catholic Church had the "might," concocted her own "right," and then brutally persecuted and martyred those who would not yield to her.

- *THE HERESY OF REJECTING THE SUPREME POWER AND AUTHORITY OF THE POPE AND HIS PRELATES, PRIESTS, & HIS CHURCH, ETC.*

Rome claims that by authority of the Council of Constance "it standeth upon necessity of our salvation, to believe, <u>the bishop of Rome to be supreme head of the church</u>." (Ibid. book 7, p.51). But, John Wycliffe did not agree. He asserted that, "It is not necessary to salvation to believe the Church of Rome to be supreme head over other churches." (*Acts and Monuments of Matters Most Special and Memorable Happening in the Church...* 1684 Edition; by John Fox; Volume 1, Book 5, p.513).

Martyr John Rogers, as mentioned earlier, refused to acknowledge the Bishop of Rome as supreme. He said, "I know none other head but Christ of his catholic church, neither will I acknowledge the bishop of Rome to have any more authority than any other bishop hath by the Word of God, and by the doctrine of the old and pure catholic church four hundred years after Christ." (*The Third Volume of the Ecclesiastical History: Containing the Acts and Monuments of Martyrs...*1684 Edition; by John Fox; Volume 3, Book 11, p.99). He said, if he could not find it in the Scriptures, he would not accept it. Likewise, George Marsh denied that the Bishop of Rome was the supreme head of the Church. Dr. Coats pressed him to admit the pope was head of the church and the church was founded on the pope's laws. Marsh responded, "Jesus Christ himself being the head corner-stone; and <u>not</u> upon the Romish laws and decrees, the bishop of Rome being the supreme head." (Ibid. p.189).

Over and over again in Foxe's work we see Rome and the martyrs clashing on this point. Martyr John Bradford sums it up well. "I render and give my life, being condemned as well for not acknowledging the antichrist of Rome to be Christ's vicar-general and supreme head of his catholic and universal church here or elsewhere upon earth." (Ibid. p.256-257). So we see again, the Roman Catholic Church had the "might," concocted her own "right," and then brutally persecuted and martyred those who would not yield to her.

- ### *THE HERESY OF BELIEVING A PERSON SHOULD ONLY CONFESS TO CHRIST AND PRAY TO HIM, NOT THE DEPARTED SAINTS*

Space will not allow me but to mention just briefly these last "heresies" for which people were condemned and give a quick quote or two.

Alice Potkins "was condemned to be burned, for she was not, neither would be confessed to the Priest, for that she received not the Sacrament of the Altar, because she would not pray to the Saints." (Ibid. p.637). Many others also believed what Alice believed. Miles Coverdale believed this as did Robert Ferrar, Rowland Taylor, John Philpot, John Bradford, John Wigorn, John Hooper, Edward Crome, John Rogers, Laurence Saunders, Edmund Laurence, and others. On the 8th day of May, A.D. 1554 all of these preachers drafted and signed a declaration of their beliefs. Article six stated, "We confess and believe that God only by Christ Jesus is to be prayed unto and called upon; and therefore we disallow invocation or prayer to saints departed this life." (Ibid. p.83). Coverdale is the only one who escaped martyrdom.

- ### *THE HERESY OF DENYING THE EXISTENCE OF PURGATORY & DENYING THAT THOSE MASSES DELIVER SOULS FROM PURGATORY*

These same preachers mentioned above denied the existence of Purgatory. They wrote,

"We confess and believe, that as a man departeth this life, so shall he be judged in the last day generally, and in the mean season is entered either into the state of the blessed for ever, or damned for ever; and therefore is either past all help, or else needs no help of any in this life. By reason whereof we affirm <u>purgatory</u>, masses of "Scala coeli," trentals, and such suffrages as the popish church doth obtrude as necessary, <u>to be the doctrine of Antichrist</u>." (Ibid. p. 83).

Few people know that the origin of the false belief that masses release a soul from purgatory is a dream. Foxe records –

"The opinion to think the mass to help souls in purgatory, was confirmed by Pope John 17 by reason of a dream, wherein he dreamed that he saw (and heard the voices of) devils lamenting and bewailing, that souls were delivered from them by the saying of masses and diriges. And therefore he did approve and ratify the feast of All Souls, brought in by Odilo. Moreover he adjoined also to the same the feast of Allhallows, about the year of our Lord 1003." (Ibid. Book 10, p.9).

The denial of purgatory and the power of the mass to release a soul from purgatory was heresy.

• *THE HERESY OF BELIEVING ONLY BAPTISM AND THE LORD'S TABLE TO BE SACRAMENTS*

At different times during history, the Roman Catholic Church taught that there were from seven to eleven Sacraments. People who recognized only the two Bible ordinances were condemned as heretics. The same group of preachers, as I have mentioned before, wrote that they believed the "Sacraments of Christ" were "Baptism and the Lords Supper."

Likewise, when Fecknam asked Jane Grey, "How many sacraments are there?" She responded, "Two. The one the Sacrament of Baptism, and the other the Sacrament of the Lords Supper." To which Fecknam asserted, "No, there are seven." At this point Jane challenges the Master Fecknam, "By what Scripture find you that?" The man never does support his position from the Holy Scriptures but tells Jane that she should base her teachings not on the Bible but upon "the Church to whom you ought to give credit." (Ibid. p.26).

Thus, we are back to the same root problem, are we not? The Church of Rome rejected the Bible's authority and set herself up as the authority. The Romanists had "might," concocted their own "right," and then brutally persecuted and martyred those who would not yield to her debauched and twisted authority.

- ### THE HERESY OF REJECTING THE PRACTICE OF GRANTING INDULGENCES & PRIESTS FORGIVING SINS

There were preachers who clearly taught their congregations the New Testament truth of 1 Timothy 2:5 that Christ alone is our mediator and confession should only be made to Him (1 John 1:9; Romans 3:25), for God alone can forgive sins, through Christ alone. One such preacher was Thomas Beele. Under examination Elizabeth Stamford said that, "Thomas Beele did many times and oft teach her this aforesaid lesson, that she should confess her sins to God, and that the pope's pardons and indulgences were naught worth, and profited not, and that worshipping of images and pilgrimages is not to be done." (*The Second Volume of the Ecclesiastical History*...1684; Book 7; p.17).

Teaching against indulgences infuriated the Roman church. She needed money to complete St. Peters in Rome. In 1581 Pope Leo sent a new edict in which he declared indulgences to be accepted. He wrote,

"...the catholic doctrine of the holy mother-church of Rome, prince of all other churches, that the bishops of Rome, who are the successors of Peter and vicars of Christ have this power and authority given to release and dispense, also to grant indulgences, available both for the living and for the dead lying in the pains of purgatory: and this doctrine he charged to be received of all faithful Christian men, under pain of the great curse, and utter separation from all holy church." (*Acts & Monuments - Volume 4*; Ages CD; p. 407-408).

Rome sold untold millions of dollars' worth of indulgences claiming you could buy forgiveness of sins past, present and future and for the living and the dead. This practice was particularly prevalent and so noxious in Germany that Foxe writes, "true piety is almost extinct in all Germany, while every evil-disposed person promiseth to himself, for a little money, license and impunity to do what him listeth: whereupon follow fornication, incest, adultery, perjury, homicide, robbing and spoiling, rapine, usury, with a whole flood of all mischief's, etc." (Ibid. p.462).

It was heresy to buck the system and indulgences were the order of the day. But there were those, like Luther, who did go against the system.

The above heresies are not an exhaustive list. There were many other charges of heresy leveled against people. It was heresy to believe that priests may marry. It was heresy to preach in English or any other language of the people. Only Latin was to be used. It was heresy to deny that worshipping images had no spiritual merit. It was heresy to believe that pilgrimages had no spiritual merit. It was heresy to believe that abstaining from meat on Friday and fasting had no spiritual merit. It was heresy to believe that "the Keys" were not given to Peter alone. It was heresy to preach against the wicked living of priests and prelates. It was heresy to believe the pope's excommunication was worthless. It was heresy to speak against the pope for any reason. People were convicted as heretics because they did not attend mass.

- ### *THE HERESY OF READING, POSSESSING, TEACHING, OR PREACHING THE BIBLE IN ENGLISH*

It should come as no surprise to the reader that the Romanists took steps to suppress the Bible in the vulgar or common tongue of the people as well as any other books that were written that would advocate the biblical view. During the reign of Henry V (1413-1422), an act was confirmed by which the "English sheriffs were forced to take an oath to persecute the Lollards, and the justices must deliver a relapsed heretic to be burned within ten days of his accusation...No mercy was shown under any circumstances." (*A History of the Baptists* by Thomas Armitage D.D.; 1890; pp.323, 325).

In that day, the Lollards were the "heretics" who were distributing the manuscript English Bible of Wycliffe, and other material of his, and preaching biblical truths. In 1414 the English Parliament under Henry V joined in asking for harder measures against the Lollards. The 1563 version of Foxe's work records...

"For, in the said parliament, the king made this most blasphemous and cruel act, to be as a law for ever: That whatsoever they were that should read the Scriptures in the mother tongue (which was then called Wickliff's learning), they should forfeit land, cattle, body, life, and goods, from their heirs for ever, and so be condemned for heretics to God, enemies to the crown, and most arrant traitors to the land." (*The Ecclesiastical History: Containing The Acts and Monuments...*1563 Edition; by John Foxe; p.274).

In 1416, Archbishop Chichele at Oxford required "the clergy (to do) a thorough search in every parish twice a year, for all persons that 'hold any either heresies or errors, or have any suspected books in the English tongue,' or harbor any heretics." (*History of the Christian Church from Its Origin to the Present Time,* by William Maxwell Blackburn; 1880; p.346).

To be sure, there is record of this law being brutally enforced. The first example I put forth is that of Sir John Oldcastle Lord Cobham. He was responsible for numerous copies of Wycliffe's English Bible being copied and distributed among the people. According to Foxe, The Chronicle of St. Alban's notes that Thomas Arundel, the archbishop of Canterbury, called together all the Romanist clergy of the realm for the primary purpose of repressing "the growing and spreading of the Gospel, and especially to withstand the noble and worthy Lord Cobham, who was then noted to be a principal favorer, receiver, and maintainer of those whom the bishop misnamed to be Lollards" (*Acts and Monuments of Matters Most Special and Memorable Happening in the Church...*1684 Edition; by John Fox; Volume 1, p.635). He was arrested and charged with heresy, escaped and arrested again. Shortly before he was barbarously martyred for his faith in the Word of God, a papist representative, a lawyer, tried to get him to return to the beliefs of Romanism. He utterly rejected that by saying,

"My belief is, as I said before, <u>that all the Scriptures of the sacred Bible are true. All that is grounded upon them I believe thoroughly</u>, for I know it is God's pleasure that I should so do; <u>but in your lordly laws and idle determinations have I no belief</u>. For ye be no part of Christ's holy church, as your open deeds do show; but ye are very Antichrists, obstinately set against his Holy Law and will. The laws that ye have made are nothing to his glory, but only for your vain glory and abominable covetousness." (Ibid. p.640).

Further, when this faithful old knight was brought to the place of where he would be roasted like a pig in the fire, he warned the people, "to obey God's commands written down in the Bible, and always shun such teachings as they saw to be contrary to the life and example of Christ." (*History of the Christian Church* Vol. 2 by Henry C. Shelton; 1895/Reprint 1994; p.426). Thus we see the end of one who financed the distribution and preaching of the Word of God in English.

To be sure, in the eyes of Rome, Sir John Oldcastle Lord Cobham was a major threat. But, what about the common people who were without wealth and influence? How were they treated for lesser infractions relating to reading, teaching and possessing portions of the Bible in English? In fact, they fared no better. Their story can be seen, beginning on page 181 of the ninth edition (1684) of Foxe's work. Here we find the account of seven who were martyred as heretics at Coventry in the year 1519. And what was their heresy? "The principal cause of the apprehension of these persons was for teaching their children and family the Lord's Prayer and the Ten Commandments in English." (*The Second Volume of the Ecclesiastical History*...1684, Vol.2, Book 8; p.181). At first, one of the seven was released. Let me pick up the story as Foxe records it,

"Upon Palm Sunday the fathers of these children were brought back again to Coventry, and there, the week next before Easter (because most of them had borne faggots in the same city before), were condemned for relapse to be burned. Only Mistress Smith was dismissed for that present, and sent away. And because it was in the evening, being somewhat dark, as she should go home, the aforesaid Simon Mourton, the Sumner, offered himself to go home with her. Now, as he was leading her by the arm, and heard the rattling of a scroll within her sleeve; 'Yea,' saith he, 'what have ye here?' And so took it from her, and espied that it was the Lord's Prayer, the Articles of the Faith, and the Ten Commandments in English. When the wretched Sumner understood this; 'Ah sirrah!' said he, 'Come, as good now as another time;' and so brought her back again to the bishop, where she was immediately condemned, and so burned with the six men before named, the 4th of April, in a place thereby, called The Little Park, A.D. 1519." (Ibid. pp.181-182).

It was heresy to possess, read, and teach the Bible in English. The Roman Catholic Church had the "might," concocted her own "right," and then brutally persecuted and martyred those who would not yield to her.

I conclude this section by sharing <u>Lord Cobham's characterization of the Pope and the Roman Catholic ecclesiastical establishment</u>. He said,

"Touching the pope and his spirituality, I owe them neither suit nor service, forasmuch as I know him, by the Scriptures, to <u>be the great Antichrist, the son of perdition</u>, the open adversary of God, and <u>the abomination standing in the holy place</u>...And let all men consider well this, that Christ was meek and merciful; <u>the pope is proud and a tyrant</u>: Christ was poor and forgave; <u>the pope is rich and a malicious manslayer</u>, as his daily acts do prove him: <u>Rome is the very nest of Antichrist</u>; and <u>out of that nest come all the disciples of him; of whom prelates, priests, and monks, are the body, these pilled (shaved) friars are the tail behind</u> ...Then said Cobham unto them all: 'Christ saith in his gospel, Matthew 23. Wo unto you Scribes and Pharisees, hypocrites; for ye close up the kingdom of heaven before men, neither enter ye in yourselves, nor yet suffer any others that would enter into it, but ye stop up the ways thereunto with your own traditions, and therefore, are <u>ye the household of Antichrist</u>: ye will not permit God's verity to have passage, nor yet to be taught by his true ministers, fearing to have your wickedness reproved. But by such flatterers as uphold you in your mischiefs, ye suffer the common people most miserably to be seduced.'" (Ibid. pp.611-612).

Rome did all within her power to suppress and even extinguish Biblical Christianity and keep the Bible and Bible knowledge from the people. Once again, the Roman Catholic Church had the "might," concocted her own "right," and then brutally persecuted and martyred those who would not yield to her. But the tide would turn thanks in part to men like John Wycliffe and his Lollard preachers and later Gutenberg's invention of the printing press with movable type. As we shall see, printing the truth of the Word of God, the Bible, and the truth of Roman Catholic atrocities as recorded in Foxe's Book of Martyrs, the truth revealed would turn the tide.

CHAPTER #11

JOHN WYCLIFFE AND THE FIRST ENGLISH BIBLE

TIME LINE OVERVIEW OF WYCLIFFE'S LIFE

Before we look at the life and times of John Wycliffe I want to lay before you a basic time line of events that may help you better understand the era of Wycliffe and the Lollards.

Year - AD	Event
1215	Magna Carta signed by King John
1252	Pope Innocent VI officially sanctions the use of torture to obtain confessions from heretics
1324	Most scholars believe John Wycliffe was born about this year
1340	John Wycliffe is believed to have enrolled in Balliol Hall at about this time
1343	Pope Clement VI officially sanctions indulgences
1347	The Black Death infects Europe
1348	The Black Death kills 2.5 million people in England
1351	The Plague stops after killing 25 million people in Europe
1353	John Wycliffe's father dies and he becomes lord of the manor or estate
1361	John Wycliffe is ordained to the ministry
1372	A Doctors of Divinity degree is awarded to Wycliffe
1374-1376	John Wycliffe is chosen by the English Crown to go to Burnges to negotiate with the papists. From 1376 to 1378 Wycliffe is the clerical advisor of John of Gaunt the Duke of Lancaster
1377	Charges of heresy are brought against Wycliffe and he appears at St. Paul's in London to be tried. The trial is broken up when John of Gaunt and Lord Percy insist that Wycliffe be seated and the Bishop demands that he stand. A riot breaks out Wycliffe slips out uncharged and unharmed. Pope Gregory XI issues 5 papal bulls against Wycliffe.
1378	The beginning of the "Great Papal Schism" which last for the next 40 years with a pope and college of cardinals in Avignon, France and another in Rome, Italy with each pope excommunicated and anathematizing the other. Wycliffe called to Lambeth Palace to be tried on charges of heresy, but the Queen Mother, Joan of Kent, warns the Bishops not to pass judgment on Wycliffe

1381	Wycliffe falsely accused to being responsible for the Peasants Revolt
1382	The Entire Bible is translated into English for the first time. An earthquake stops a synod called to condemn Wycliffe, his writings and his Bible translation
1384	Wycliffe dies peacefully on New Years Eve
1401	First English statute passed legalizing the burning of heretics
1414	Reading the English Scriptures is outlawed upon the pain of forfeiture "of land, cattle, life and goods from their heirs forever."
1415	Council of Constance condemns Wycliffe as an heretic and his student John Hus is burned at the stake
1428	Remains of Wycliffe are exhumed, burned to ashes and scattered in the stream near the Lutterworth parish

The Acts of the Apostles records the birth and spread of the Christian faith in the first century. At a very early period, likely before the end of the first, or the beginning of the second century, the books of the New Testament had been collected into one volume. The New Testament was then repeatedly hand copied and carried by Christians wherever they went. In fact, for the first five or six centuries, the Bible, and particularly the New Testament, was translated into more than 100 languages, according to Dr. Craig Lampe, curator of one of the world's largest private collections of ancient Bibles. But, the Church of Rome increasingly usurped the autonomy of the local churches and dominated the realm of Christendom. With the growth and consolidation of popish power, the Bible, in the language of the people, declined in importance while the opinions and judgments of the prelates and priests became the law. The Bible went from being available in more than 100 different languages to just one language, Latin. Why? It was because "the aim of the Romish prelacy was no less, than the entire monopoly of all ecclesiastical and secular rule." (*The English Bible – History of the Translation of the Holy Scriptures Into the English Tongue* by H. C. Conant; 1856; p.15).

The Roman Church intended to rule the secular and sacred world. In order to accomplish that goal, Rome had to consolidate her power. Since knowledge is the vital element of power, the control of knowledge was paramount. Knowledge of the Word of God leads to freedom. Our Lord said, *"ye shall know the truth, and the truth shall make you free."* **John 8:32**. Therefore, the Bible had to be taken away from the people, if they were to be controlled. So, "instead of God's Word, man's word was set up. Instead of Christ's

Testament, the pope's testament, that is, Canon law" was substituted. (*The Ecclesiastical History: Containing The Acts and Monuments...1641 Edition; by John Foxe, Volume 2, Book 7, p.56*). Gradually, access to biblical knowledge (and secular knowledge for that matter) was withdrawn from the people and wholly held in the greedy, bloody hands of the Roman Catholic establishment. Slowly but surely the Bible, in the language of the people, was taken away. The light of the Word of God was virtually extinguished all over the Roman dominated world, including Britain.

Here is but one example of the distressing state of biblical knowledge. "In 1353, three or four young Irish priests came over to England to study divinity; but were obligated to return home because <u>not a copy of the Bible was to be found at Oxford</u>." (*The English Bible: History of the Translation of the Holy Scriptures Into The English Tongue; by H. C. Conant; 1856; p.45*).

How did the Catholic ecclesiastical establishment view this sad state of affairs? "It has frequently been made the subject of praise to the papal clergy, that they alone were the depositaries of learning, at a period when all other classes of society were sunk into ignorance and barbarism." (*Ibid. p.15*) That is a travesty! If the Roman priesthood would have encouraged and facilitated the spreading of the Bible and secular knowledge it would have been an age of light! But, instead they hid the light of knowledge within their cloisters, and history now records this period as "The Dark Ages." When the Bible was taken away from the common people, "they lost the charter of their rights as men." (*Ibid. p.16*). As time went on, the people became the mere tools and bond-slaves of the priesthood. They became "the rabble, the vulgar herd, the mob, to be used or abused without limits or mercy, for the benefit of their masters." (*Ibid. p.16*).

J. C. Ryle characterizes the state of English Christianity this way –

"The three centuries immediately preceding our English Reformation...were probably the darkest period in the history of English Christianity. It was a period when the Church of this land was thoroughly, entirely, and completely Roman Catholic – when the Bishop of Rome was the spiritual head of the Church – when Romanism reigned supreme form the Isle of Wright to Berwick-on-

Tweed, and from the Land's End to the North Foreland, and ministers and people were all alike Papists. It is no exaggeration to say that for these three centuries before the Reformation, Christianity in England seems to have been buried under a mass of ignorance, superstition, priestcraft, and immorality. The likeness between the religion of this period and that of the apostolic age was so small, that if St. Paul had risen from the dead he would hardly have called it Christianity at all." (*Light From Old Times of Protestant Facts and Men;* by J. C. Ryle; first published in 1890; p. 22).

It is into this sad state of affairs that God raised up a man named John Wycliffe, commonly called "the Morning Star of the Reformation."

WYCLIFFE: HIS BIRTH AND LIFE

As we begin to examine the life of "the Morning Star of the Reformation" I must point out that his last name has a variety of different spellings – Wycliffe, Wycliff, Wicliffe, Wiclif, Wicklif, Wyclif or De Wycliffe. I note this because the quotes included in this section include different spellings. I have not made an error in spelling, but have merely spelled his name consistently with the author from where the quote originated.

No one knows for sure the exact date or place of Wycliffe's birth. It falls within a ten-year span between 1320 and 1330. One writer notes, "The date and place of Wyclif's birth are alike uncertain. We place it (the date of his birth) about 1320. As to the place, the only information we have is from Leland, who, writing two centuries after the event, tells us that he was <u>born at Spreswell</u>, and elsewhere says that he sprang from the village of Wycliffe-on-Tees. No such village as Spreswell exists..." (*The English Works of Wyclif Hitherto Unprinted* by F. D. Matthew; 1880; Published for The Early English Tract Society; p. b).

There are those who propose that the name was Ipreswell which is today called Hipswell and therefore say that John was born in Hipswell. In my thinking, the best explanation that I have read is offered by Dr. Vaughan. He says that "Spreswell, or Speswell, stood close to the river Tees, half a mile from (the village of) Wycliffe, and on the same side of the river." (Ibid.) His authority for this statement is "John Chapman, a gentleman of respectable position in Gainsford, whose great-grandfather was the last person married in the chapel which stood there till, soon after his marriage it fell down." (Ibid.) While there is no trace of Spreswell existing today, and therefore the exact location of Wycliffe's birth cannot be fixed, the general area is not in doubt.

"The Wycliffe family were lords of the manor of Wycliffe and patrons of the rectory, from the time of the Conquest (of William). In agreement with the prevailing custom, they took their name from the place of their residence. Representatives of the family continued to live in the Manor house, which may still be seen situate on a high bank not far from the parish church, until the beginning of the 17th century; when the estate was carried by marriage into the family of the Tonstalls. After the Reformer's death, his family, perhaps as a protest against his career, seem to have distinguished themselves by their firm attachment to the papacy. Even after the Reformation, they, together with half the population of the village, remained Romanists; and their conduct bears fruit to the present day. The old church on the bank of Tees belongs to the English Protestant Establishment, while the Roman Catholic inhabitants of Wycliffe worship in their own chapel adjoining the Manor-house." (*Life and Times of John Wycliffe The Morning Star of the Reformation* (no author given); The Religious Tract Society; 1884; pp. 23-24). The grave of John Wycliffe's father may still be seen near the village of Wycliffe-upon-Tees.

KNOWN FACTS ABOUT THE LIFE JOHN WYCLIFFE

While there has been a great deal of speculation about John Wycliffe's early life, there is no documented evidence revealing anything about his childhood through his mid-teen years. The first mention about anything in his life is when he was about seventeen years old. "The older tradition concerning Wycliffe's residence in the University of Oxford, was that he entered first, in his seventeenth year, Queen's College; that afterwards he was transferred to Merton...being made a Fellow of Merton." *(Life and Times of John Wycliffe The Morning Star of The Reformation;* 1884; The Religious Tract Society; p.27). Later investigation has proved beyond a shadow of a doubt that in about 1340 he enrolled at Balliol Hall (college), which had been founded by the noble family of Balliol from Barnard Castle 1260-1282 near where Wycliffe lived and not Queens College. The greater part of John's life was spent studying or teaching at the colleges of Oxford.

There is another bit of information that we do know for sure. In 1342 Wycliffe's family village and manor came under the lordship of John of Gaunt (see the picture adjacent), more commonly called the Duke of Lancaster (1340–1399). Gaunt was England's most powerful political figure in the late 1300's. The Duke was virtually the ruler of England during the last years of the 50-year reign of his father, King Edward III, who was said by some to have become senile. He continued to be in a place of power even during the early years of the reign of his elder brother's young son, his nephew, Richard II. His brother, Edward the Black Prince (so called because of black armor he wore into battle) died the year before his father when his son Richard II was just nine. This wealthy, powerful leader no doubt knew the prominent Wycliffe family and in the coming years the duke was to become John Wycliffe's patron and protector.

Now back to some particulars on Wycliffe's University education. Like many other details of John's life there is some degree of confusion about which of the individual schools of Oxford University he attended. Let me begin with this quote. "In 1356 he graduated from Merton College. Five years later, in 1361, he added his Master of Arts, and eight years later, in 1369, when he was in his forties, he was awarded his Bachelor of Divinity degree. Then in 1372 he earned his doctorate in divinity." *(The Indestructible Book* by Ken

Connolly; Baker Books 1996; p. 69). However, Lechler says, "He was all along a Balliol man, from his first coming up to Oxford in 1335 to his election to the mastership of his college." (*John Wiclif and His English Persecutors – Vol. 1* by Professor Lechler and translated by Peter Lorimer; 1887; p.185).

How do scholars explain the confusion over the college issues? The "John Wiclif of Balliol was a different man from the John Wiclif of Merton." (Ibid. p. 186). The purpose of this study is not to unravel the confusion over Wycliffe's college education. Yet it is plausible, that within the extended Wycliffe family, there were two Johns that were related and about the same age. But let me be clear about what we know for sure. John Wycliffe the Reformer was a student at Balliol Hall (college) and likewise was elected as the Master (president) of Balliol College. Of this there is no dispute.

I would be remiss if I did not bring up the so-called "Black Death" at this point. It had a marked influence on Wycliffe personally and his times. The outbreak of the plague was "preceded by many earthquakes," (*Fighters & Martyrs for the Freedom of Faith* by Luke S. Walmsley; 1912; p. 31) and then first appeared in Constantinople in 1347. The first outbreak in England was at Dorchester in June of 1348 and continued for ten months. While there were other outbreaks in 1361, 1369 and 1375, the plague killed off half of the population of England, that is two and a half of the five million people, according to Eadie in his *History of the English Bible.*

"During this terrifying plague, Wycliffe experienced a profound spiritual revival that reached to the core of his being. The holy fear of God that came upon him brought a disregard for human popes and potentates: it seemed that he held communion with the citizens of the invisible world. He rearranged his priorities and became more earnest in his theological studies." (*The Indestructible Book* by Ken Connolly; Baker Books 1996; p.69). It is at this point that a transformation took place in Wycliffe's life that proved to be permanent. It is highly probable that this is when John came to a saving knowledge of Jesus Christ. In 1353 John's father died, making John the lord of the Wycliffe family manor and overseer of the family properties.

In 1361 Wycliffe was ordained to the ministry. He "received a rich college living from Fillingham in Linconshire, which provided income for his continued studies at Oxford" and he also taught there. (*Christian History*, Volume II, No.2, Issue 3; p.11). The Church of Fillingham supported him until 1368 when he exchanged it for the Ludgarshall Church, which was also in the diocese of Lincoln.

LUDGARSHALL CHURCH.
THE SCENE OF WYCLIFFE'S MINISTRATIONS, 1368–1374.

The Ludgarshall Church supported him until King Edward III appointed him to the Church of Lutterworth in 1374. While it sounds strange to us today, Wycliffe neither lived nor preached in the Fillingham or Ludgarshall Church that paid him. In fact, he neither lived nor preached at the Lutterworth Church until he retired. In those days absentee pastors were common. It was acceptable for the parson to arrange for someone to take his place.

So, what was John Wycliffe doing with his time since he was not pastoring? "By 1371 he was recognized as the leading theologian and philosopher of the age at Oxford, thus second to none in Europe..." (Ibid.) In point of fact, "the splendour of Wyclif's talents, learning and character attracted hosts of students, said to be <u>thirty thousand</u>, who imbibed his opinions. They made him the hero and idol of the University. He was awarded the honorable title of 'The Gospel

Doctor.' To the intense chagrin of the ecclesiastics, he was elected and installed its Professor of Divinity." (*Fighters & Martyrs for the Freedom of Faith* by Luke S. Walmsley; 1912; p.28). In 1372 he began a series of lectures as a part of the divinity course at Oxford. It was not long before the lecture hall was filled to overflowing.

There were many who were jealous of Wycliffe's popularity and others who were diametrically opposed to his biblical teaching. One of his adversaries was Henry Knighton. If anyone would think that Wycliffe's talents and abilities were overstated it would be one of his enemies, would it not? That is why it is important to take notice of his evaluation of "The Gospel Doctor." Knighton writes, "as a theologian, the most eminent of his time; in philosophy, second to none; as a schoolman, incomparable. No man excelled him in the strength and number of his arguments; and he excelled all men in the irresistible power of his eloquence." (*The English Bible – History of the Translation of the Holy Scriptures Into the English Tongue* by H. C. Conant; 1856; p.54).

"Walden, another of Wycliffe's arch enemies, wrote a letter to Pope Martin V complaining about the ability and success of Wycliffe. He said, "that he had often stood amazed beyond measure at the excellence of his learning, the boldness of his assertions, the exactness of his authorities, and the strength of his arguments." (Ibid.) But, I must make something clear. The secret of John Wycliffe's power was not his academic learning. His secret was that he had drunk deeply at the fountain of Eternal Truth, the Bible, and he led others to the same fountain also.

THE POLITICAL INFLUENCE OF JOHN WYCLIFFE

In order to understand Wycliffe's involvement in politics, you must know the political climate of the times. To facilitate that you need to go back to 1294 when Boniface VIII was elected Pope. When he came to the throne he had a quarrel with Philip the Fair, the King of France. The Pope wrote Philip a haughty letter in which he "asserted that all kings whatever, the King of France as well as other, by divine command owed allegiance to him not only in religious matters but also in secular and human affairs." (*A History of Heresy* by David Christie-Murray; Oxford University Press; 1976; p.112). The King wrote a fiery letter bitterly disagreeing! As a result, the Pope retorted by issuing a papal bull (decree) called *Unam Sanctum,* in which he asserted that <u>the whole human race was subject to the Roman pontiff and that all who differed from this doctrine were heretics and could not be saved</u>. There was a power struggle between the King and the Pope. The king accused the Pope of heresy, simony (selling spiritual benefits and or offices), dishonesty and practicing occult magic. In turn, Pope Boniface excommunicated the King and all those loyal to him. The wrangling between Philip and Boniface characterized the political climate of the day, and not just in France.

There was a power struggle going on between kings and popes in England as well. It had been going on since the days of King John in 1213 when the pope had imposed a huge tax on England, which she refused to pay. In Wycliffe's day, the pope demanded the tax be paid with arrears. But this tax was not the only money the Roman Catholic Church was extracting from England. The popes gave "the best English prebends (payments from a church to one officiating) and deaneries (payments from a University to one in an administrative position) to Italian Cardinals, and other foreigners also held fat English livings. On a Bishop's death the Popes not only extracted the first year's fruits (first year's wages) from his successor, but, by the device of promotion of several Bishops, blandly took over also several first fruits. Electoral rights of cathedrals, chapters, abbeys, convents were also usurped to this end. The Papal collector lived in London like a prince always hostile to English interests, and his entourage ever the secret spy for the Roman Curia. From Church dignities alone some historians affirm the Pope took English gold five times as much as the King got in taxes. J. R. Green says the Pope 'made the clergy pay and the clergy the people, but of a population of little more than two million the ecclesiastics (those in religious orders) numbered between twenty and thirty thousand, owning landed property more than a third of the soil; their spiritualities in dues and offerings amounting to twice the royal revenues.' The nation had often growled and kicked at this impoverishing, unchristian prostitution and degrading yoke. In these high affairs Wyclif was summoned by the King to answer important questions of law and policy..." (*Fighters & Martyrs for the Freedom of Faith* by Luke S. Walmsley; 1912; p.28-29).

Let me be more specific. Pope Urban V demanded that England pay not only the 1000 marks yearly that had been demanded in King John's day, but that the payment of all arrearages, principle and interest for the past thirty years be paid immediately. In 1365 King Edward the III called Wycliffe to join Parliament in responding to this matter. Wycliffe argued, "The Pope cannot claim, as the representative of Christ anything beyond that Christ claimed for himself. But Christ's office was purely spiritual; he refused all secular dominion; nay, so far was he from exercising temporal lordship, that he subsisted on charity, and had not where to lay his head. He concludes, therefore, that England owes no civil allegiance to the Pope, and may properly repel his aggressions upon her temporal sovereignty. On the same general ground he maintained also, that the secular possessions of the Clergy are held on the same tenure with that of the other subjects of the realm, and are liable to control, of if abused, to forfeiture by the secular powers which first bestowed them; and in all civil cases, the persons of ecclesiastica should, as in the case of the laity be subject to the civil courts." (*The English Bible – History of the Translation of The Holy Scriptures Into The English Tongue* by H.C. Conant; 1856; pp.52-53). King and Parliament rejected Urban's demand and the King was cited to appear before the pontiff to give answer for his conduct.

In 1371, John of Gaunt, King Edward III's youngest son, with a secular, noble council, took power from his aging father. Wycliffe was again called to Parliament to give his counsel concerning the Pope's view of dominion, that view being, that he was supreme both politically and spiritually. We find Wycliffe connected with a parliamentary movement for an additional reform in respect to the clergy, particularly with respect to their exclusion from secular offices. As I pointed out earlier, the clergy nearly had a monopoly of all places of honor and profit in the State joined to their ecclesiastical power. This gave them a most dangerous predominance in the government. In addition, because they were clergy, they claimed that they were not subject to civil law. It was

Wycliffe who questioned their perfect rights on both accounts. He claimed that "crimes of the priests were punishable by the law of England." (*The English Works of Wyclif* by F. D. Matthew; 1880; p.292).

Further, he opposed the admixture of the spiritual and temporal on purely religious grounds. He believed that such a coalition was incompatible with the New Testament conception of the sanctity and high responsibility of the sacred office. He based that on 2 Timothy 2:4 (the Wycliffe edition reads – "No man holding knighthood to god wlappith (entangleth) him self with worldly needs." His favorite axiom was, "He that warreth, entangleth not himself with this life". He complained that "prelates and great religious possessioners, are so occupied in heart about worldly lordships and pleas of business, that no habit of devotion, of praying, of thoughtfulness on heavenly things, on the sins of their own hearts or those of other men, may be preserved; neither are they found studying and preaching the Gospel, nor visiting and comforting of poor men." (*The English Bible – History of the Translation of The Holy Scriptures Into The English Tongue* by H.C. Conant; 1856; p.53).

For these reasons, Wycliffe concludes that, "neither prelates nor doctors, priests nor deacons, should hold secular offices." (Ibid.) Both John of Gaunt and Parliament concurred with the teachings of Wycliffe on this subject. They resisted the pressures of the Pope to manipulate English government and refused to pay papal taxes.

But, Pope Gregory XI was not one to take "NO" for an answer. In 1372, he tried to re-impose a tax on the English clergy again; the English royal government, and Edward III's council forbade compliance. There was increasing tension between the English crown and the Pope. So in 1372 an ambassador was sent by the English crown asking that the taxes and penalties against them be set aside. Gregory XI finally agreed to discuss the grievances. "Thus a conference was arranged for at Bruges. Wycliffe was appointed as a delegate of the Crown." (*John Wycliffe: Christian History, Issue 3*, 1997; p.12). The year was 1374; two years after Wiclif became the professor of Divinity at Oxford. The bishop of Bangor and others joined him. "The place at which the negotiation was to be carried on was Burnges; where the commissioners appear to have arrived in or about the month of August, 1374. The proceedings were lengthened out for a considerable time, so that Wiclif does not appear to have left Burnges till July, 1376; having thus been for nearly two years in contact with the utter corruption of the Papal emissaries." (*The English Hexapla Preceded by An Historical Account of the English Translations* printed by Samuel Bagster and Sons in 1841; p.14).

It is obvious that the Crown was pleased with Wycliffe's service to England because, "during his absence (November, 1375,) [he] was presented by the king with the prebend of Aust in the collegiate church of Westbury, and subsequently with the rectory of Lutterworth." (*The English Hexapla* by Samuel Bagster and Sons; 1841, p.14). These facts show pretty plainly the Crown was pleased with how he carried out his mission.

Again in 1377 Wycliffe was called upon by the Crown and Parliament and asked whether it was lawful to withhold payment to Rome, and again he responded that it was. But why did Wycliffe believe this was true? While it is difficult to give a short answer, I will attempt to give a brief overview. Wycliffe wrote a work called *On Civil Dominion.* "The mediaeval theory of the papacy had assimilated the feudal conception of "dominium" and mediate ownership: just as, in the state, all land belonged to the king, and through him to his tenants-in-chief, mesne (middle) tenants, and the peasants who cultivated it, so the papacy had become the final claimant of all spiritual dominion, – the head of the ladder of grace, which descended through the archbishops and bishops to the parish priests. Wycliffe's theory...discarded the idea of mediate dominion or ownership, and not merely with regard to spiritual powers, but temporal possessions. He taught that all dominion, power or ownership, came from God, and that every man was His tenant-in-chief, owing no vassalage to any mesne tenant. Those who disregard the laws of God were *ispo facto* dispossessed of dominion, – temporal ownership or spiritual power." (*The Lollard Bible and Other Medieval Biblical Versions* – by Margaret Deanesly, M.A.; Cambridge University Press 1920; pp.226-227).

To be sure the Pope was not happy with Wycliffe's disagreement with him and support of the English Crown. Consequently, seven months after he returned from Bruges, he was called to appear before a convocation of bishops at St. Paul's in London to answer the charges of heresy brought against him by William Courtaney, Bishop of London. Simon Sudbury, archbishop of Canterbury called the Synod. On February 19, 1377 Wycliffe appeared to answer the charges made against him. He appeared at St. Paul's accompanied by four friars from Oxford, under escort of Gaunt, who was the real target of these proceedings, and Henry Lord Percy, the Lord Marshall of England. Here is how Wycliffe was described. This description is based on several portraits of unquestioned originality still in existence: "... a tall thin figure, covered with a long light gown of black colour, with a girdle about his body; the head, adorned with a full, flowing beard, exhibiting features keen and sharply cut; the eye clear and penetrating; the lips firmly closed in token of resolution—the whole man wearing an aspect of lofty earnestness and replete with dignity and character." (*John Wycliffe: Christian History, Issue 3,* 1997; p.12).

While Wycliffe was upstanding in his deportment, not as much could be said for John of Gaunt and Lord Percy. It must be remembered that Wycliffe was Gaunt's clerical advisor between 1376-1378 and so the Duke felt an obligation to protect him.

St. Paul's was crowded with people. Wycliffe was one of the most renowned figures in all England. People wanted to see him and witness the showdown. Lord Percy was clearing the way for Wycliffe and that made Bishop Courtenay angry. The Bishop said sarcastically, "Lord Percy, if I had known it I had known beforehand what masteries (weapons) you would have kept in the church, I would have stopped you out from coming hither." John of Gaunt responded, "He shall keep such masteries here, though you say, 'Nay.'" Lord Percy turned to Wycliffe and said, "Wyckliffe, sit down; for, you have many things to answer to, and you need to repose yourself on a soft seat." Bishop Courtenay flared, "It is unreasonable, that one, cited before his ordinary, should sit down during his answer. He MUST and SHALL stand." John of Gaunt asserted, "The Lord Percy's motion for Wyckliffe is but reasonable. And as for you, my lord bishop, who are grown so proud and arrogant, I will bring down the pride, not for you alone, but for all the prelacy in England."

The power struggle between the Crown and the English Catholic hierarchy cannot be missed. I believe this is exactly what the ecclesiastical establishment wanted and they were willing to use Wycliffe to get to the King.

Bishop Courtenay called Gaunt's bluff by saying, "Do your worst, sir." He knew that the mob of people packed into St. Paul's could overwhelm even the entourage with Wycliffe. John of Gaunt shot back, "Thou bearest thyself so brag upon thy parents, (his father was Hugh Courtney, Earl of Devonshire), who shall not be able to help thee; they shall have enough to do to help themselves." Courtenay retorted, "My confidence is not in my parents, nor in any man else, but only God, in whom I trust, by whose assistance I will be bold to speak the truth." Gaunt upped the stakes by foolishly saying, "Rather than I will take these words at his hands, I will pluck the bishop by the hair out of the church." (Note: the above account is from *Fullers Church History of Britain – Vol. 1* by Thomas Fuller; 1842; pp. 446-447).

Though these last words were quietly whispered by the duke, into the ear of the one next to him, the Londoners became so enraged that they had offended their Bishop that a riot broke out, and Gaunt and Percy barely escaped serious harm at the hand of those who overheard them. All the while John Wycliffe and Archbishop Sudbury said not a word. Sudbury slipped out at the beginning of the riot. The other bishops saw what they were up against as well. With two such powerful protectors aligning themselves with Wycliffe, they knew that if they condemned him, Gaunt and Percy may well bring an army after them. So, they simply instructed Wycliffe to quit preaching and writing his doctrine. There is no historical record that he agreed to their demands. But we do know that John Wycliffe quietly slipped out unharmed and went on to preach and write many volumes.

God had worked this fiasco for good, because in the future He had more important things for Wycliffe to do. But, three months after the altercation at Saint Paul's Cathedral, on May 22, 1377, Pope Gregory XI issued five scathing bulls or decrees against Wycliffe. Three of the bulls were sent jointly to Simon Sudbury, the Archbishop of Canterbury who held ecclesiastical power in England, and to William Courtenay, the Bishop of London, who was enthusiastic about carrying out the Pope's wishes and Edward III of England. The reason that one was sent to the King was because the Pope needed political support in order to carry out his orders. But, Edward III died on June 21, before he received it, leaving his only living son, John of Gaunt, in power. He sent another to the Chancellor of University of Oxford, where Wycliffe taught, attempting to pressure them to arrest their most famous "heretical" professor. This is a translation of the bull condemning Wycliffe sent to the university –

"Gregory, bishop, servus servorum dei, (the servant of God's servants) to his beloved sons the Chancellor and University of Oxford, in the diocese of Lincoln, grace and apostolic benediction.

"We are compelled to wonder and grieve that you, who, in consideration of the favors and privileges conceded to your University of Oxford by the apostolic see, and on account of your familiarity with the Scriptures, in whose sea you navigate, by the gift of God, with auspicious oar, you, who ought to be, as it were, warriors and champions of the orthodox faith, without which there is no salvation of souls, – that you through a certain sloth and neglect allow tares to spring up amidst the pure wheat in the fields of your glorious University aforesaid; and what is still more pernicious, even continue to grow to maturity. And you are quite careless, as has been lately reported to us, as to the extirpation of these tares; with no little clouding of a bright name, danger to your souls, contempt of the Roman Church, and injury to the faith above mentioned. And what pains us the more, is that this increase of the tares aforesaid is known in Rome before the remedy of extirpation has been applied in England where they sprang up. By the insinuation of many, if they are indeed worthy of belief, deploring it deeply, it has come to our ears that John de Wycliffe, rector of the church of Lutterworth, in the diocese of Lincoln, Professor of the Sacred Scriptures (would that he were not also Master of Errors), has fallen into such a detestable madness that he does not hesitate to dogmatize and publicly preach, or rather vomit forth from the recesses of his breast, certain propositions and conclusions which are erroneous and false. He has cast himself also into the depravity of preaching heretical dogmas which strive to subvert and weaken the state of the whole church and even secular polity, some of which doctrines, in changed terms, it is true, seem to express the perverse opinions and unlearned learning of Marsilio of Padua of cursed memory, and of John of Jandun, whose book is extant, rejected and cursed by our predecessor, Pope John XXII, of happy memory. This he has done in the kingdom of England, lately glorious in its power and in the abundance of its resources, but more glorious still in the glistening piety of its faith, and in the distinction of its sacred learning; producing also many men illustrious for their exact knowledge of the Holy Scriptures, mature in the gravity of their character, conspicuous in devotion, defenders of the Catholic Church. He has polluted certain of the faithful of Christ by sprinkling them with these doctrines, and led them away from the right paths of the aforesaid faith to the brink of perdition.

"Wherefore, since we are not willing, nay, indeed, ought not to be willing, that so deadly a pestilence should continue to exist with our connivance, a pestilence which, if it is not opposed in its beginnings, and torn out by the roots in its entirety, will be reached too late by medicines when it has infected very many with its contagion; we command your University with strict admonition, by the apostolic authority, in virtue of your sacred obedience, and under penalty of the deprivation of all the favors, indulgences, and privileges granted to you and your University by the said see, for the future not to permit to be asserted or proposed to any extent whatever, the opinions, conclusions, and propositions which are in variance with good morals and faith, even when those proposing strive to defend them under a certain fanciful wresting of words or of terms. Moreover, you are on our authority to arrest the said John, or cause him to be arrested and to send him under a trustworthy guard to our venerable brother, the Archbishop of Canterbury, and the Bishop of London, or to one of them.

"Besides, if there should be, which God forbid, in your University, subject to your jurisdiction, opponents stained with these errors, and if they should obstinately persist in them, proceed vigorously and earnestly to a similar arrest and removal of them, and otherwise as shall seem good to you. Be vigilant to repair your negligence which you have hitherto shown in the premises, and so obtain our gratitude and favor, and that of the said see, besides the honor and reward of the divine recompense.

"Given at Rome, at Santa Maria Maggiore, on the 31st of May, the sixth year of our pontificate."

THE CONDEMNED CONCLUSIONS OF JOHN WYCLIFFE

Note: I have taken the Middle English and modified the spelling to enable the reader to better understand it. John Wycliffe was accused of being an heretic because he believed the following...

All the whole race of mankind here on earth, besides Christ, hath no power simply, to ordain that Peter and all his offspring should politically rule over the world forever.

God cannot give to any man for him and his heirs any civil dominion forever.

All writings invented by men, as touching perpetual heritage, are impossible.

Every man being in grace justifying, hath not only right unto, but also for his time hath indeed all good things of God.

A man can but only ministratoriouslie (ministerially) give any temporal or continual gift, either to his natural son, or to his son by imitation. [This is a particularly hard point to understand. But, I believe that it refers to the truth that a person can only give temporal gifts to his children or others. It is not possible for a man to give eternal gifts to anyone, such as the release from purgatory, a certificate of indulgence (i.e. to commit sin), etc.]

If God be, the temporal lords may lawfully meritoriously take away the riches from the church when they do offend (break the law) habitually.

We know that Christ's vicar cannot, neither is able by his bulls (decrees), neither by his own will and consent, neither by the consent of his college, neither to make able (qualify) or disable (disqualify) any man. [That is, to qualify them for Heaven or disqualify them].

A man cannot be excommunicated to his hurt or undoing, except he be first and principally excommunicated by himself.

No man ought, but in Gods cause alone, to excommunicate, suspend, of forbid, or otherwise to proceed to revenge by any ecclesiastical censure.
A curse or excommunication do not simply bind but in case it be pronounced and given out against the adversary of God's law.

There is no power given by any example, either by Christ or by his apostles, to excommunicate any subject, especially for denying to [pay] any temporalities (revenues, fees, secular possessions), but rather counterwise.

The disciples of Christ, have no power to extract by any civil authorities, temporalties (revenues, fees, secular possessions) by censures.

It is not possible by the absolute power of God, that if the pope, or any other Christian do pretend by any means to bind or to loose, that thereby he so bind or loose.

We ought to believe that the vicar of Christ, doth at such times only bind and loose, when as he worketh conformably by the law and ordinance of Christ.

This ought to universally to be believed, that every priest rightly and duly ordered, according unto the law of grace, hath power according to his vocation, whereby he may minister the sacraments, and consequently absolve any man confessing his fault, being contrite and penitent for the same.

It is lawful for kings, in causes licensed by the law, to take away the temporalities (revenues, fees, secular possessions) from the spirituality (priests, prelates, friars, etc.) sinning habitualiter, that is, which continue in the custom of sin, and will not amend. Whether they be temporal lords, or any other men whatsoever they be, which have endowed any church with temporalities (secular possessions); it is lawful for them to take away the same temporalities, as were by way of medicine, for to avoid sin, notwithstanding any excommunication or other ecclesiastical censure, forasmuch as they are not given but under condition.

An ecclesiastical minister, and also the bishop of Rome may lawfully be rebuked of his subjects, and, for the profit of the church, be accused either of the clergy or of the laity.

(Ecclesiastical Biography or Lives of Eminent Men Connected with the History of Religion in England; from the Commencement of the Reformation to the Revolution by Christopher Wordsworth; 1853; Volume 1 pp.203-208).

The above were the specific charges of heresy brought against John Wycliffe by Pope Gregory XI.

HOW DID OXFORD UNIVERSITY RESPOND?

The University refused to condemn her outstanding scholar. Instead, Wycliffe consented to a form of "house-arrest" in Black Hall in order to spare the university further punitive action by the Pope. Wycliffe refused to appear again at St. Paul's in the prescribed thirty-day period. He did agree to appear at Lambeth Palace, the London residence of the Archbishop of Canterbury and in 1378 he faced the bishops there.

When Dr. Wycliffe was called to give account to the court concerning the charges that were brought against him, he began his *Protestatio* with:

"I profess and claim to be by the grace of God a sound (that is, a true and orthodox) Christian and while there is breath in my body I will speak forth and defend the law of it. I am ready to defend my convictions even unto death. In these my conclusions I have followed the Sacred Scriptures and the holy doctors, and if my conclusions can be proved to be opposed to the faith, willingly will I retract them."

He then continued:

"I deny that the Pope has any right to political dominion: that he has any perpetual civil dominion: that he can qualify or disqualify simply by his bulls." (*Christian History* Volume II, No 2, Issue 3; p. 18).

In the middle of his testimony a message was received from the Queen Mother, Joan of Kent. She was the widow of the legendary warrior-hero, Edward the Black Prince, and the mother of the young King Richard II. It was obvious that the Crown intended to protect Dr. Wycliffe. After all, he had rendered patriotic service to the Crown whenever he had been called upon and in fact, the Queen Mother was an advocate of his teachings. Sir Lewis Clifford, suspected of being a Lollard (follower of Wycliffe's teachings) himself, spoke with authority when he delivered the Queen Mother's message warning the counsel not to pass judgment on the Gospel Doctor. The Commissioners took the hint, seeing the futility of continuing the trial. They contented themselves with prohibiting Wycliffe from further exposition of his ideas. Wycliffe later wrote, "As they ought to be, the papal bulls will be superseded by the Holy Scriptures. The veneration of men for the laws of the papacy, as well as for the opinions of modern doctors ... will be restrained within due limits. What concern have the faithful with writings of this sort, unless they are honestly deduced from the fountain of Scripture? By pursuing such a course, it is not only in our power to reduce the mandates of prelates and Popes to their just place, but the errors of these new religious orders also might be corrected and the worship of Christ well purified and elevated." (Christian History Volume II, No 2, Issue 3; p. 18)

Wycliffe's last recorded political involvement took place in 1378. He testified that civil authorities had the right to enter the church and apprehend criminals who had taken sanctuary in church. Heretofore ecclesiastical officials declared that secular authorities had no authority in the church. These are the circumstances that led to Wycliffe's appearance before Parliament. John of Gaunt Duke of Lancaster had "violated the sanctuary" of Westminster by sending a band of armed men into the church to apprehend two men guilty of a crime who had taken refuge there. One of the men was caught. The other was killed while resisting arrest. And a "servant of the church" was killed while attempting to keep the soldiers from arresting the men. "At the parliament held at Gloucester in October, in the presence of the legates of Pope Urban VI, Wycliffe read an apology for the duke's actions at Westminster, pleading that the men were killed in resisting legal arrest. The paper, which forms part of the *De Ecclesia,* lays down the permissible limits of the right of asylum and maintains the right of the civil power to invade the sanctuary in order to bring escaped prisoners to justice." (*Encyclopedia Britannica, 11th Edition of 1911;* Volume 28; p. 868).

While Wycliffe increasingly withdrew from the public affairs of England, it is reasonable to say that <u>the last seven years of his life were the most productive spiritually</u> because it was in these years that he boldly stood against the Roman ecclesiastical establishment and for biblical Christianity. He clashed with Rome in three major doctrinal areas – The Church, Communion and The Bible in the language of the people. We will look at these doctrinal areas more closely a little bit later in our study. Suffice it to say that his biblical stance against Transubstantiation, circulated in 1379 and 1380 and the Peasants Revolt cost him the support of John of Gaunt and his teaching position at Oxford. He was banished from the university in 1381 and moved to his parish church in Lutterworth where he and his friends worked on the vernacular translation of the Scriptures.

Before I move on, a brief overview of the Peasant's Revolt it in order. This was the first major popular rebellion in English history.

"It lasted less than a month. It failed completely as a social revolution. The passage of a poll tax, which hit hardest at the poorest, was the final spark igniting growing general unrest among the peasants, both in the city and in the countryside. Workers were still seething against the fixing of maximum wages following the Black Death. The wealth and worldly attitude of the higher clergy incensed the people. Dreams of a better way of life following the French wars urged others on. John Ball preached the freedom of the individual. And disgust with the weakness and poor management of the government angered others. Rebels under Wat Tyler reached London on June 13, 1381. They killed Flemish merchants and razed the palace of the unpopular John of Gaunt. On the 14th, King Richard II met with the rebels outside London at Mile End and promised cheap land, free trade, the abolition of serfdom and forced labor. While the king was gone, rebels inside the city captured the Tower of London and beheaded the Archbishop of Canterbury, Simon of Sudbury. On the following day, the king met at Smithfield with Wat Tyler and unexpectedly the enraged mayor of London killed Tyler. But the king made further promises to the rebels if they would disperse. They left London. Once the rebellions ended in the provinces, all promises were forgotten. The only gain was the prevention of further poll taxes." (*Christian History, John Wycliffe;* Volume II, No2, Issue 3; 1997 p. 9).

Wycliffe's enemies tried to blame him for stirring up the unrest. To be sure, he was in agreement with many of the peasants' concerns and even pleaded their cause once the violence ceased. But he had not encouraged their violence, and, in fact there was no solid evidence that connected him directly to the uprising. But that did not stop his opponents from making the accusations.

Now that the political popularity of John Wycliffe had diminished, it should come as no surprise to the reader that the Roman ecclesiastical establishment would, at last, seize the opportunity to get back at the man who was responsible for undermining their position, power and wealth. Their two previous attempts to silence Wycliffe proved fruitless. In 1382 Archbishop William Courtenay wrote a letter to church leaders calling them to London to pass judgment on Wycliffe and twenty-four of his beliefs that Courtenay had drawn up.

The archbishop stated that Wycliffe believed...

1. That the material substance of bread and of wine remains, after the consecration, in the sacrament of the altar.
2. That the accidents do not remain without the subject, after the consecration, in the same sacrament.
3. That Christ is not in the sacrament of the altar identically, truly and really in his proper corporeal presence.
4. That if a bishop or priest lives in mortal sin he does not ordain, or consecrate, or baptize.
5. That if a man has been truly repentant, all external confession is superfluous to him or useless.
6. That it is not founded in the gospel that Christ instituted the mass.
7. That God ought to be obedient to the devil.
8. That if the pope is fore-ordained to destruction and a wicked man, and therefore a member of the devil, no power has been given

to him over the faithful of Christ by any one, unless perhaps by the Emperor.

9. That since Urban VI, no one is to be acknowledged as pope; but all are to live, in the way of the Greeks, under their own laws.

10. To assert that it is against sacred scripture that men of the Church should have temporal possessions.

11. That no prelate ought to excommunicate any one unless he first knows that the man is excommunicated by God.

12. That a prelate thus excommunicating is thereby a heretic or excommunicate.

13. That a prelate excommunicating a clerk who has appealed to the king, or to a council of the kingdom, on that very account is a traitor to God, the king and the kingdom.

14. That those who neglect to preach, or to hear the word of God, or the gospel that is preached, because of the excommunication of men, are excommunicate, and in the day of judgment will be considered as traitors to God.

15. To assert that it is allowed to any one, whether a deacon or a priest, to preach the word of God, without the authority of the apostolic see, or of a Catholic bishop, or of some other which is sufficiently acknowledged.

16. To assert that no one is a civil lord, no one is a bishop, no one is a prelate, so long as he is in mortal sin.

17. That temporal lords may, at their own judgment, take away temporal goods from churchmen who are habitually delinquent; or that the people may, at their own judgment, correct delinquent lords.

18. That tithes are purely charity, and that parishioners may, on account of the sins of their curates, detain these and confer them on others at their will.

19. That special prayers applied to one person by prelates or religious persons, are of no more value to the same person than general prayers for others in a like position are to him.

20. That the very fact that any one enters upon any private religion whatever, renders him more unfitted and more incapable of observing the commandments of God.

21. That saints who have instituted any private religions whatever, as well of those having possessions as of mendicants, have sinned in thus instituting them.

22. That religious persons living in private religions are not of the Christian religion.

23. That friars should be required to gain their living by the labor of their hands and not by mendicancy.

24. That a person giving alms to friars, or to a preaching friar, is excommunicate; also the one receiving.
(Taken from: *Internet Medieval Sourcebook;* at www.fordham.edu/halsall/sbook.html)

"As the archbishop and suffragants (assistant bishops), with the other doctors of divinity, and lawyers with a great company of babbling friars, and religious persons were gathering together to consult, concerning John Wickliffe's books, and the whole sect (of the Lollards), at Gray Friers in London, upon Saint Dunstans Day (May 19th, 1382) after dinner, about two o'clock, the very hour and instant that they should go forward with their business, a wonderful and terrible earthquake fell." *(Ecclesiastical Biography or Lives of Eminent Men Connected with the History of Religion in England; from the Commencement of the Reformation to the Revolution* by Christopher Wordsworth; 1853; Volume 1 pp.221). Hence, this is called the "Earthquake Council." To be sure the earthquake was strong enough to dislodge some of the large stone blocks out of castle walls. Wycliffe insisted that this was the judgment of God upon their efforts. The archbishop claimed it was God's judgment upon Wycliffe and his Lollards. His assertion did meet with some success. Local magistrates did back area bishops in restraining the followers of Wycliffe, called the Lollards, at Oxford. Numerous key Lollards recanted of their biblical beliefs when severely threatened and Wycliffe's writings were banned. But, these depressing circumstances worked in favor of his most important contribution, the translation of the Bible into the vernacular English.

WHAT WYCLIFFE BELIEVED, TAUGHT AND PREACHED

While it is true that Dr. John Wycliffe was politically active in fighting the abuses in the papal establishment, it is important to see that he was, all the while, advancing biblical truth in his teaching, preaching and writing. "Wycliffe first denounced the corrupt practices and then the corrupt doctrines of Romanism leading to those practices." *(History of the Church of God from the Creation to A.D. 1885* by Cushing Biggs Hassell; p.457).

He began preaching, teaching and writing against the unbiblical doctrines and practices of Roman Catholicism when he was about 35 to 37 years old. Wycliffe exposed the errors of transubstantiation, sacramentalism, purgatory, indulgences, tradition being equal in authority with the Scriptures, the papacy, infant baptism, praying to the saints, and many other false teachings of Roman Catholicism. That is why he is called the "Morning Star" of the Reformation, because he believed, taught, wrote and preached doctrines that were not advanced until 100 years later by the Reformers. But, when you make a careful study of his writings, at least the ones that remain, because Catholic authorities destroyed many of his works, it becomes obvious that he went far beyond the  Reformers of the 1500's in his rejection of unscriptural Roman Catholic doctrines and practices and his advocacy of New Testament Christianity.

Where did John Wycliffe get his biblical ideas? Without a doubt, his careful study of the Scriptures increasingly molded his thinking. But it is also fair to say that there is a strong possibility that he was influenced by the Baptists of his day. I have in my library a book called the *Martyr's Mirror*. As it turns out there were many Baptists (Waldensian separatists Anabaptists) living in England in 1391. They had been there at least 30 years. We read in the account that 443 of these believers were brought up on charges of heresy. "From this it appears...that the Saxon countries were full of Waldenses, that is, orthodox Christians before the time of Huss. For it can easily be computed, that when 443 Waldenses were examined at once, there must have been incomparably greater numbers who were not examined in regard to their faith, but concealed themselves, or took to flight, in order to escape danger. And truly, those who are noticed in the book, as having been examined, frequently mention very many others of their faith who were not present." (*Martyrs Mirror*, Thieleman J. van Braght; p.325).

Joseph Milner, the Anglican historian, believed that there was a connection between the Waldensians and John Wycliffe: "The connection between France and England, during the whole reign of Edward III, was so great, that it is by no means improbable, that Wickliffe himself derived his first impressions of religion from [Raynard] Lollard [a Bible-believing Waldensian leader who was burned at the stake at Cologne]" (Milner, *The History of the Church of Christ*, 1819, III, p. 509).

Baptist historian William Jones adds the following observations: "Thomas Walden, who wrote against Wickliff, says, that the doctrine of Peter Waldo was conveyed from France into England – and that among others Wickliff received it. He is joined in this opinion by Cardinal Bellarmine, also, is pleased to say that 'Wickliff could add nothing to the heresy of the Waldenses'" (Jones, *A History of the Christian Church*, II, p. 91). Further Joseph Ivimey references Joshua Thomas' *History of the Welsh Baptists*, and says that John Wycliffe "received much of his light in the gospel" from the 14th century Baptists who lived in Olchon in Herfordshire (*History of the English Bapitsts* by Joseph Ivimey; 1811, Vol. 1, pp.65-66).

As I have studied the beliefs of John Wycliffe I believe that he was, as David Cloud says, "powerfully influenced, even directly instructed, in his Bible-believing views by separatist Baptist Christians then living in and about England." (*John Wycliffe and The First English Bible* by David W. Cloud; p.5).

OVERVIEW OF HIS BELIEFS

• *HIS VIEW OF THE MONASTIC ORDERS*

The Pope had given a special commission to the Mendicant Friars. They answered directly to him and not to area Bishops or parish priests. This gave the friars a great advantage. These begging friars would wander from parish to parish and diocese to diocese pedaling their wares. The parish priests had nearly quit preaching altogether and confined themselves to conducting mass and hearing confessions. The Friars seized the opportunity to exploit the neglected people. The traveling, barefoot friar would "announce in some neglected hamlet that he had come to offer pardons, indulgences, the redemption of their deceased friends from purgatory, and all the precious wares of the church, at a price within the reach of the poorest laborer or beggar. It seemed to the deluged people like good tidings of great joy. He could, moreover, by certain old rags, pigs' bones, rusty nails, bits of rotten wood, and similar rubbish which he carried about with him under the name of relics, ensure them good crops, and fruitful herds, and fruitful wives, all for a very reasonable consideration." (*The English Bible* by H.C. Conant; p.33). The begging friars wormed their way into the hearts of the common people. In about 1360 John Wycliffe began opposing the Mendicant (begging) Friars and other Catholic clergy for their anti-biblical lifestyle and doctrine.

"It is an evidence both of his ability and courage, that, single-handed, he (John Wycliffe) dared to attack a Monastic order of such power and authority in the Romish Church. Two of these orders, the Dominican and Franciscan, ruled the Roman Catholic Church throughout Europe for nearly three centuries, with an absolute sway. ... Day by day Wycliffe used greater plainness of speech in portraying the scandalous conduct of the friars." (*The History of the English Bible* by Blackford Condit; 1881, pp. 55, 58).

This is what Wycliffe said:

"Friars be worse enemies and slayers of man's soul, than is the cruel fiend of hell by himself. For they under the habit of holiness lead men and nourish them in sin, and be special helpers of the fiend to strangle men's souls." (*Old England's Worthies Being Full and Original Biographies* by Lord Brougham and other distinguished authors; 1887; p.14).

"Friars draw children from Christ's religion into their private Order by hypocrisy, lies and stealing. ... And so they steal children from father and mother ... sometime such as should sustain their father and mother by the commandment of God; and thus they are blasphemers taken upon full counsel in doubtful things that are not expressly commanded nor forbidden in holy writ; since such counsel is appropriated to the Holy Ghost, and thus they are therefore cursed of God as the Pharisees were of Christ...Friars shew not to the people their great sins firmly as God biddeth, and namely to mighty men of the world; but flatter them or nourish them in sin. Also, Friars are thieves ... For without authority of God they make new religions of errors of sinful men" (*The Life of Dr. John Wiclif*, John Lewis, pp. 7,24, 27).

- ## *HIS VIEW OF THE POPE, HIS INFALLIBILITY, SPIRITUAL AUTHORITY AND THE PAPAL CHURCH*

Wycliffe fervently opposed the teaching of the infallibility of the pope. An anonymous writer whom Wycliffe calls Mixtus Theologus or Motley Divine, asserts "the authority and infallibility of the pontiff in the strongest terms. He declared, according to Wycliffe, that as the pope could not commit mortal sin, whatever he ordained must be just. To that Wiclif replied, that if so, he might remove any book from the Scripture, and introduce any novelty in its place; and thus, making the very Scripture heresy, establish heresy in its stead."

Wycliffe spoke advisedly because that is exactly what the Papal establishment was doing. They substituted man-made doctrines, Canon Law, for the Word of God. Wycliffe amplified his attacks on papal infallibility when the "Great Schism" broke out in 1378. The two rival popes hurled bulls at each other, excommunicated each other, and damned each other to Hell. There was little need of that, seeing that both of them were unsaved and went to Hell on their own, in my opinion.

Wycliffe further exposed the error of the church and papal tradition being equal in authority with the Scriptures. "He boldly taught that a papal decree has no validity except so far as it is founded on the Scriptures and that the exercise of the power to bind and loose has no effect save when it is conformed to the judgment of Christ." (*History of The Christian Church*; by George Park Fisher; 1907 Charles Scribner's Sons; p.273).

He said that the Catholic practice of establishing universities and granting masterships and doctorates had been inherited from the heathen, and "are altogether of as much use to the church as the devil" (*Martyrs Mirror* by Thieleman van Braght, p. 324). Wycliffe spoke out boldly against the pope, contending that "it is blasphemy to call any head of the church, save Christ alone" (*History of the English Baptists* by Thomas Crosby, I, 1740, p. 7).

He further stated "I deny that the Pope has any right to political dominion: that he has any perpetual civil dominion: that he can qualify or disqualify simply by bulls." (*Christian History Volume II No 2, Issue 3;* page 18). In fact he said that papal bulls "as they ought to be... will be suspended by the Holy Scriptures." (Ibid.) He also warned men against venerating the pope and his laws. He said that the Scriptures and the worship of Christ purified and elevated should correct the errors of the pope, prelates, priests and doctors.

Wycliffe stated, "It is supposed, and with much probability, that the Roman pontiff is the great Antichrist...How than shall any sinful wretch, who knows not whether he be damned or saved, constrain men to believe that he is head of holy Church? Certainly, in such a case they must sometimes constrain men to believe that a devil of hell is head of holy Church, when the Bishop of Rome shall be a man damned for his sins." (*History of The Christian Church* by Shelton, II, p. 415).

Dr. Wycliffe asserted that whoever pretended to amend Christ's religion, in fact denies it, and is an apostate from the faith. "Christ's religion is the most true, because it was confirmed of God and not of sinful men; and because by it the Pope and every other man must be confirmed, or else he shall be damned; while the new Orders [are] being confirmed only by the Pope, may turn out to have been confirmed by a devil." (*The English Bible* by H.C. Conant; p.51).

• *HIS VIEW OF THE OFFICES OF THE CHURCH*

John Wycliffe viewed the ecclesiastical hierarchy as being wholly the development of men and not only was it against the Bible, it was also against the model of the early Church. He boldly "asserted that in the primitive Church there were but two sorts of clergy, and was opposed to the existence of the multiplied ranks of the priesthood – popes, cardinals, patriarchs, monks, canons, etc." (*History of The Christian Church*; by George Park Fisher; 1907 Charles Scribner's Sons; p.274) In fact, these are the exact words of Wycliffe recorded in his *Trialogus* – "From the faith of the Scriptures it seems to me to be sufficient that there should be presbyters and deacons holding the state and office which Christ has imposed on them, since it appears certain that these degrees and orders have their origin in the pride of Caesar. I boldly assert one thing, namely, that in the primitive church, or in the time of Paul, two orders of the clergy were sufficient, that is, a priest and a deacon. In like manner, I affirm that in the time of Paul, the presbyter and bishop were names for the same office." (*The Life and Times of John Wycliffe The Morning Star of The Reformation* by the Religious Tract Society; p.140).

- ## ON SAINT-WORSHIP, PRAYERS TO THE SAINTS & FESTIVALS

"Whoever entreats a saint, should direct his prayers to Christ as God, not to the special Saint, but to Christ. Nor doth the celebration or festival of a saint avail anything, except in so far as it may tend to magnify Christ, inciting us to honor Him, and increasing our love for Him. If there be any celebration in honor of the saints, which is not kept within these limits, it is to be ascribed, without doubt, to cupidity (covetousness), or some other evil motive. Hence, not a few think it would be well for the Church, if all festivals of that nature were abolished, and those only retained which have respect immediately to Christ. For then, they say, the memory of Christ would be kept more freshly in the mind, and the devotions of the common people would not be unduly distributed among the members of Christ...For the Scriptures assure us that Christ is the Mediator between God and man." (*The English Bible* by H.C. Conant; p.56).

- ## ON THE SUPPOSED DISTINCTION BETWEEN MORAL AND VENIAL SIN

Wycliffe taught his students that "the distinction between moral and venial sin, 'about which the prelates babble so much,' is merely a priestly contrivance for making gain."

- ## ON CONFESSION, ABSOLUTION AND INDUL-GENCES

"It is not confession to man but to God, who is the true Priest of souls, that is the great need of sinful man. Private confession and the whole system of medieval confession was not ordered by Christ and was not used by the Apostles, for of the three thousand who were turned to Christ's Law on the day of Pentecost, not one of them was confessed to a priest...It is God who is the forgiver." (*Christian History* Magazine; Volume II, No 2, Issue 3; p. 25).

"There is no greater heresy for a man than to believe that he is absolved from sin if he gives money, or because a priest lays his hand on his head and says: 'I absolve you;' for you must be sorrowful in your heart, else God does not absolve you." (Ibid. p.24).

The doctrine of priestly absolution and indulgences is an impious invasion of the prerogatives of God, who is alone able to forgive sin. The great churchmen who were so free with their dispensations, were, in his exact words, "blasphemers of the wisdom of God, pretending in their own avarice and folly, to understand what they know not; sensual simonists, who chatter on the subject of grace as if it were something to be bought and sold like an ox or an ass." (Ibid. p.55).

"Many think that if they give a penny to a pardoner, they shall be forgiven the breaking of all the commandments of God, and therefore they take no heed how they keep them. But I say to thee for certain, though thou have priests and friars to sing for thee, and though thou each day hear many masses, and found chauntries and colleges, and go on pilgrimages all thy life, and give all thy goods to pardoners; all this shall not bring thy soul to heaven." (*English Hexapla* by Samuel Bagster & Sons; 1841; Introduction p.13).

• *ON SALVATION*

Concerning salvation he wrote, "For as much as the Bible contains Christ, that is all that is necessary for salvation, it is necessary for all men, not for priests alone. It alone is the supreme law that is to rule Church, State and Christian life, without human traditions and statutes." (*Christian History* Magazine; Volume II, No 2, Issue 3 – Wycliffe Commemorative Edition; p. 26).

"Trust wholly in Christ; rely altogether on His suffering; beware of seeking to be justified in any other way than by His righteousness. Faith in our Lord Jesus Christ is sufficient for salvation. There must be atonement made for sin, according to the righteousness of God. The Person to make this statement (atonement) must be God and man." (Translation from Latin appears in *The Prosecution of John Wyclyf* by Joseph H. Dalmus – 1952; Yale University Press).

In one of his sermons Wycliffe illustrates saving faith by using the Bible account of the brazen serpent lifted up before Israel. He said, "As a right looking on the adder of brass saved the people from the venom of serpents, so a right-looking by full belief on Christ saveth His people. Christ died not for His own sins, as thieves do for theirs; but as our Brother, who Himself might not sin (was not able to sin) He died for the sins that others had done." (*The Life and Times of John Wycliffe The Morning Star of the Reformation* by The Religious Tract Society; 1884; p.133).

- ## *ON INFANT BAPTISM & BAPTISMAL REGENERATION*

There were Catholic leaders alive at the time of Wycliffe who charged him with denying infant baptism. Catholic authorities Thomas Walden and Joseph Vicecomes said that Wycliffe rejected infant baptism and they charged him with Anabaptist views. Walden, who wrote against the Wycliffites or Hussites in the early part of the 1400s, called Wycliffe "one of the seven heads that came out of the bottomless pit, for denying infant baptism, that heresie of the Lollards, of whom he was so great a ringleader." (Danver's *Treatise*, p. 2, 287, cited in *History of the English Baptists*, by Joseph Ivimey, 1811, I, p. 72). Walsingham, another Catholic authority, identified Wycliffe with the "cursed opinions of Berengarius" and said that "<u>his followers did deny baptism to infants.</u>" (Ivimey, I, p. 72). Berengarius lived in France in the 11th century and was charged by the Catholic authorities with such "heresies" as denying transubstantiation and infant baptism. <u>The Berengarians practiced believer's baptism</u> and were charged with being Anabaptists. The trial held at Blackfriars in June, 1382 to condemn Wycliffe brought many articles of accusation, including the charge "that the children of believers might be saved without baptism." (Ivimey, I, p. 73). The *Martyrs Mirror*, also states that in 1370 Wycliffe issued an article "declared to militate against infant baptism." (*Martyrs Mirror* by Thieleman J. van Braght; p. 322). Jacob Mehrning, in his *History of Baptism*, said that Wycliffe "taught, among other things, that baptism is not necessary to the forgiveness of original sin; thereby sufficiently opposing, or, as H. Montanus says, rejecting, infant baptism, which is founded upon the forgiveness of original sin. On this account, forty-one years after his death, his bones, by order of the pope, were exhumed, burnt, and the ashes thrown into the water." (*History of Baptism* by Jacob Mehrning; pp. 737,738). It is clear that John Wycliffe rejected infant baptism. But, we do not know for sure whether he practiced believer's baptism and if he did, if it was by immersion.

• *ON TRANSUBSTANTIATION*

The Fourth Lateran Council had declared transubstantiation a dogma of the Catholic Church. They maintained that when the bread and the cup are blessed they literally become the body and blood of Christ. Therefore, Christ's body is broken and His blood flows again and again as often as the Mass is conducted. This is contrary to the "once for all" teaching in Hebrews 9 & 10. Wycliffe "attacked the doctrine of transubstantiation, maintaining that the bread and the wine remain unchanged..." (*History of The Christian Church*; by George Park Fisher; 1907 Charles Scribner's Sons; p.273). He cited the statement of Berengarius of Tours in 1059 given to establish his orthodoxy. This statement: "The same bread and wine ... placed before the Mass upon the alter remain after consecration both as sacrament and as the Lord's Body." To put it in his own words, "The nature of the bread is not destroyed by what is done by the priest...it remains bread substantially.... The consecrated Host we priests make and bless is not the body of the Lord but an effectual sign of it. It is not to be understood that the body of Christ comes down form heaven to the Host consecrated in every church." (*Christian History* Magazine; Volume II, No 2, Issue 3; p.24)

• *ON CHRISTIANS CONTENDING FOR THEIR FAITH*

"All Christians should be the soldiers of Christ. But it is plain that many are chargeable with great neglect of this duty; being prevented by fear of the loss of temporal goods and worldly friendships, and apprehensive about life and fortune, from faithfully setting forth the cause of God, from standing manfully in its defense, and if need be, from suffering death in its behalf. From the like source comes that subterfuge of Satan, argued by some of our modern hypocrites, that it cannot be a duty now, as in the primitive church, to suffer martyrdom, since in our time the great majority of men being believers, there are none to persecute Christ to the death in his members. But this is, without doubt, a device of Satan to shield sin. For the believer, in maintaining the law of Christ, should be prepared, as his soldier, to endure all things at the hands of the satraps of this world; declaring boldly to Pope and Cardinals, to Bishops and Prelates, how unjustly, according to the teaching of the Gospel, they serve God in their offices, subjecting those committed to their care to great injury and peril, such as must bring on them speedy destruction. All this applies, indeed, to temporal lords, but not in so great a degree as to the clergy; for as the abomination of desolation begins with a perverted clergy, so the consolation begins with a converted clergy. Hence we Christians need not visit pagans to convert them, by enduring martyrdom in their behalf; we have only to declare with constancy the Word of God before Caesarean Prelates, and straightway the flower of martyrdom will be ready to our hand!" (*The English Bible* by H.C. Conant; p.58-59)

• *ON THE IMPORTANCE OF PREACHING*

John Wycliffe was a powerful preacher and he believed that preaching was the very best way to spread the Word of God among the people. In fact, he spent a great deal of time training his "poor preachers" to travel across England reading and preaching the Bible to the people. He would provide the men with Scripture tracts, Scripture portions and sermon outlines so that they could accomplish their task. And, we must remember that all this was done in the English language, not in Latin.

Wycliffe taught that "the highest service to which man may attain on earth is to preach the law of God." And he lamented the fact that in his day there "...priests are found in taverns and hunting; and playing at their tables, instead of learning God's law and preaching." (*Christian History* Magazine; Volume II, No 2, Issue 3; p.24).

He was also very particular about the content of what was being preached. He wrote, "Some men who preach tell the tales that they find in the saints' lives without teaching Holy Writ. And such things often please more the people. But we believe there is a better way— to avoid such that please and, instead, to trust in God and to tell surely His law and specially His Gospel. And, since these words are God's words, they should be taken as believed, and God's words will give men new life more than the other words that are for pleasure." (Ibid.)

Wycliffe believed in the transforming power of the Holy Word of God, when the Holy Spirit of God energized it. He said, "O marvelous power of the Divine Seed which overpowers strong men in arms, softens hard hearts, and renews and changes into divine men, those men who had been brutalized by sins, and departed infinitely far from God. Obviously such miraculous power could never be worked by the word of a priest, if the Spirit of Life and the Eternal Word did not, above all things else, work with it." (Ibid.).

• *ON THE AUTHORITY OF THE BIBLE*

John Wycliffe believed that the **Bible** was the sole authority for all of life, and Christ was the only way of Salvation. He wrote, **"Holy Scripture is the preeminent authority for every Christian, and the rule of faith and of all human perfection."** (*Christian History* Magazine; Volume II, No 2, Issue 3; p. 26).

"The authority of the Holy Scriptures infinitely surpasses any writing, how authentic soever it may appear, because the authority of Jesus Christ is infinitely above that of all mankind. The authority of the Scriptures is independent on any other authority, and is preferable to every other writing, but especially to the books of the Church of Rome." (*John Wycliffe and The First English Bible* by David Cloud; p.2).

"I am certain, indeed, from the Scriptures, that neither Antichrist, nor all his disciples, nay, nor all fiends, may really impugn any part of that volume as it regards the excellence of its doctrine. But in all these things it appears to me that the believing man should use this rule—If he soundly understands the Sacred Scripture, let him bless God; if he be deficient in such perception, let him labour for soundness of mind. Let him also dwell as a grammarian upon the letter, but be fully aware of imposing a sense upon Scripture which he doubts the Holy Spirit does not demand." (Ibid.).

"We ought to believe in the authority of no man unless he say the Word of God. It is impossible that any word or any deed of man should be of equal authority with Holy Scriptures. ... For the laws made by prelates are not to be received as matters of faith, nor are we to confide in their public instructions, nor in any of their words, but as they are founded in Holy Writ, since the Scriptures contain the whole truth." (Ibid.).

"The chief cause of the existing state of things is our want of faith in the Holy Scriptures. We do not sincerely believe in the Lord Jesus Christ, or we should abide by the authority of His Word, especially of the Evangelists, as of infinitely greater weight than every other. It is the will of the Holy Spirit, that the books of the Old and New Law should be read and studied, as the one sufficient source of instruction; and that men should not be taken up with other books, which, true as they may be, and they even containing Scripture truth, are not to be confided in without caution and limitation. Hence Augustine often enjoins it on his readers, not to place any faith in his word or writings, except so far as they have their foundation in Scripture. Of course we should judge thus of the writings of other holy doctors; much more of the writings of the Roman Church and her doctors, in these later times. If we follow this rule, the Scriptures will be held in becoming reverence. The papal bulls will be superseded, as they ought to be. The veneration of men for the laws of the papacy, as well as for the opinions of our modern doctors, which, since the loosing of Satan, they have been so free to promulgate, will be restrained in within due limits. What concern have the faithful with writings of this sort, except as they are honestly deduced from the fountain of Scripture? By such a course, we can not only reduce the mandates of popes and prelates to their proper place, but the errors of these new religions might be corrected, and the worship of Christ well purified and exalted." (*The English Bible* by H.C. Conant; p.57).

"That the New Testament is of full authority, and open to understanding of simple men, as to the points that are most needful to salvation. ... That men ought to desire only the truth and freedom of the holy Gospel, and to accept man's law and ordinances only in as much as they are grounded in Holy Scripture... That <u>if any man in earth, either angel of heaven teacheth us the contrary of holy Writ</u>, or any thing against reason and charity, <u>we should flee from him in that as from the foul fiend of hell</u>, and hold us steadfastly to, life and death, the truth and freedom of the holy Gospel of Jesus Christ, and take us meekly men's sayings and laws, only in as much as they accord with holy Writ and good consciences, and no further, for life neither for death." (*John Wycliffe and The First English Bible* by David Cloud; p.2).

- ***ON THE NECESSITY OF THE PEOPLE TO HAVE THE BIBLE IN THE COMMON TONGUE***

Wycliffe lamented about Oxford Universities denying their students access to the Word of God until they had studied worldly subjects for nine or ten years. This comes from the General Prologue of a handwritten Wycliffe Bible. "Alas, alas, alas, the most abomination that ever was heard among Christian clerks is now purposed in England, in the chief university of our realm, as many true men tell with great wailing; that no man shall learn divinity, neither holy writ, no but he that hath done his fourme in art; this would be nine year or ten year before that he learn holy writ, after that he can commonly well his grammar." (*The Lollard Bible and Other Medieval Biblical Versions* by Margaret Deanesly, M.A.; Cambridge University Press 1920; p.257).

"Those Heretics who pretend that the laity need not know God's law but that the knowledge which priests have had imparted to them by word of mouth is sufficient, do not deserve to be listened to. For Holy Scriptures is the faith of the Church, and the more widely its true meaning becomes known the better it will be. Therefore since the laity should know the faith, it should be taught in whatever language is most easily comprehended...Christ and His apostles taught the people in the language best known to them." (*Speculum Seculum Dominous, Opera Minora;* by John Wycliffe; Wycliffe Society, John Loserth - editor; 1913; p. 74).

Wycliffe New Testament

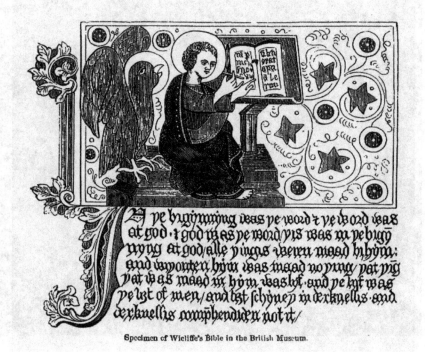

Specimen of Wicliffe's Bible in the British Museum.

THE TRANSLATION OF THE FIRST ENGLISH BIBLE

This is a portion of a page of a Wycliffe Bible that is in the British Museum in London. It is John 1:1-5. It is hard to read in the black letter style so I have typed out the text, which reads –

"In the bigynnynge was ye word and ye word was at god, and god was ye word. This was in ye bigynnynge at god. All thingis weren maaedby hym: and withouten hym was maad no thing that think that was maad in him was liif, and ye liif was ye ligt of men, and the ligt schyneth in derknessis, and derknessis comprehendiden not it."

I remind you that each manuscript is different because they were all handwritten. Some are very plain. Some are very ornate. I have facsimile samples of four different types of Wycliffe manuscript Bibles in my collection. Each one is very different from the other.

"To Wyclif we owe, more than to any one person who can be mentioned, our English language, our English Bible, and our reformed religion," said Professor Montague Burrows in his 1881 lecture series. Without a doubt, that is true. As I mentioned earlier, the greatest and most enduring accomplishments, for the cause of Christ, took place in the last ten years of Wycliffe's life. "Wycliffe became convinced that everyone had the right and duty to read the Scriptures in their own language – and that only the Word of God could break the bondage of Romanism which enslaved the people." (*Zion's Fire* Magazine - March/April, 1991 Special Edition; p.8). Walmsley writes of the undertaking, "Wyclif had long yearned to open the Word of God to the common folk in their 'modir tonge,' (mother tongue) and now, retired to the quiet parsonage of Lutterworth, he plodded, oft with tired brain and hand, for years over piles of old Latin manuscripts and commentaries, and at last, in 1382-83, for the first time in her history, England possessed the complete Holy Bible in the tongue of the people." (*Fighters & Martyrs for the Freedom of Faith* by Luke S. Walmsley p.32).

In fact, in 1380 Wycliffe, with the help of his personal secretary, John Purvey, the New Testament appeared. Two years later (1382), again with the help of Nicholas of Hereford and John Purvey the Old Testament was completed and the entire handscribed Bible was issued. "From Genesis to Baruch 3:20 the work was the translation of Hereford, the most violent of the early Lollards, and the most prominent in the university after Wycliffe himself. (*The Lollard Bible and Other Medieval Biblical Versions* by Margaret Deanesly, M.A.; Cambridge University Press 1920; p.253).

We can get a little glimpse as to intentions of the translators, the pressures brought to bear upon them, and the problems they encountered by reading the General Prologue found written in one of these ancient Wycliffe Bibles.

"For though covetous clerks be wooed by simony, heresy, and many other sins to dispise and stop holy writ, as much as they may: yet the lewid (lay) people crieth after holy writ, to con it and keep it, with great cost and peril of their life. For these reasons and others, with common charity to save all men in our realm, which God would have saved, a simple creature hath translated the Bible out of Latin into English. First, this simple creature had much travail, with diverse fellows and helpers, to gather many old Bibles, and other doctors, and common glosses, and to make one Latin Bible some deal true; and then to study it of the new, the text with the gloss, and other doctors, as he might get, and specially Lyra on the Old Testament, that helped full much in this work; the third time to counsel with old grammarians and old divines, of hard words, and hard sentences, how they might best be understood, and translated; the fourth time to translate as clearly as he could to the sentence, and to have many good fellows and cunning at the correcting of the translation. First, it is to know, that the best translating is out of Latin into English, to translate after the sentence by as open, or opener, in English as in Latin, and go not far from the letter; and if the letter may not be used in the translating, let the sentence ever be whole and open, for the words ought to serve to the intent and sentence, and else the words be superfluous or false.

"At the beginning I purposed, with God's help, to make the sentence as true and open in English as it is in the Latin, or more true and more open than it is in Latin; and I pray, for charity and for common profit of Christian souls, that if any wise man find any default of the truth of translation, let him set in the true sentence and open of holy writ, but look that he examine truly his Latin Bible, for no doubt he shall find full many Bibles in Latin full false, if he look, namely, many new; and the common Latin Bibles have more need to be corrected, as many as I have seen in my life, than hath the English Bible Late translated. And whether I have translated as openly or openlier in English as in Latin, let wise men deem, that know well both languages, and know well the sentence of Holy Scripture. And whether I have done this or nay, no doubt they that con well the Scripture of holy writ and English together, and will travail, with God's grace, thereabouts, may make the Bible as true and open, yes and open, yea and openlier in English than it is in Latin." (*The Lollard Bible and Other Medieval Biblical Versions* by Margaret Deanesly, M.A.; Cambridge University Press 1920; pp.258-259).

We should pay tribute to Wycliffe and his helpers because producing this Bible was no small task. After the initial translation work was done, scribes had to individually copy each volume. **It took a scribe 10 to 12 months to produce one handwritten Bible**.

HOW DID THE ENGLISH PEOPLE ACCEPT A BIBLE IN THEIR OWN LANGUAGE?

The people loved the Wycliffe translation. For the first time the English people had an opportunity of reading the Bible in their own language. And read it they did. "The forbidden book was often read by night, and those who had not been themselves educated listened with eagerness to the reading of others; but to read it, and to hear it read, were alike forbidden. Copies of the New Testament were also borrowed from hand to hand through a wide circle, and poor people gathered their pennies and formed copartneries (partnerships) for the purchase of the sacred volume. Those who could afford it gave five marks for the coveted manuscript (a very large amount of money in that day), and others in their penury gave gladly for a few leaves of St. Peter and St. Paul a load of hay. ... Some committed portions to memory, that they might recite them to relatives and friends. Thus Alice Colins was commonly sent for to the meetings, 'to recite unto them the Ten Commandments and the Epistles of Peter and James.'" (*History of the English Bible* by John Eadie, I, pp. 91, 92).

"The knowledge of divine truth, received by the reading of the Scriptures, was transmitted by a succession of pious men for more than a century after Wycliffe's death. ... Readers of the manuscript Bible were numerous in London, where they had several places of meeting; and they abounded also in the counties of Lincoln, Essex, Norfolk, Suffolk, Buckingham, and Hereford. ... These Bible readers called themselves 'brothers' or 'sisters' in Christ, and at an early period they took the name of 'just-fast men,' or 'known men,' and 'known women'" (Ibid. 94-95).

My personal friend Dr. Kenneth Connolly helped me to understand just how much a Wycliffe Bible would cost. He said, "the cost for purchasing one was about 40 pounds sterling. There were 240 pennies in a pound. 40 pounds would be 9600 pennies. Let me give you an idea of how much money that was. Two pennies could buy a chicken and 4 pennies could buy a hog in that day. There were men who would work in the field for an entire month and then bring that entire month's wages to buy one single page of Wycliffe's Bible."

HOW DID THE ECCLESIASTICAL ESTABLISHMENT RESPOND TO THE BIBLE BEING TRANSLATED INTO ENGLISH?

They were furious. After all, translating the Bible into the common tongue of the people was considered heresy, because the Roman Catholic Church believed that only the "sacred" tongue of Latin was acceptable. Catholic chronicler Henry Knighton of Wycliffe's era gives us a glimpse of Rome's view of Wycliffe and his Bible –

"Christ gave His Gospel to the clergy and the learned doctors of the Church so that they might give it to the laity and to weaker persons, according to the message of the season and personal need. But this Master John Wyclif translated the Gospel from Latin into the English – **the Angle not the angel language**. And Wyclif, by thus translating the Bible, made it the property of the masses and common to all and more open to the laity, and even to women who were able to read...And so the pearl of the Gospel is thrown before swine and trodden underfoot and what is meant to be the treasure both of the clergy and laity is now become a joke to both. The jewel of the clergy has been turned into the sport of the laity, so that what used to be the highest gift to the clergy and the learned members of the Church has become common to the laity." (*Christian History Magazine*; Volume II, No 2, Issue 3; p.26).

The established church opposed the Bible in the common tongue for "about the next five generations." They went to great lengths to wrest the English Bible out of the hands of the people. For example, "in 1429 Margery Backster was indicted because she asked her maid Joan to 'come and hear her husband read the law of Christ out of a book he was wont to read by night.' ... The means employed to discover the readers and possessors of Scripture were truly execrable in character. Friends and relations were put on oath, and bound to say what they knew of their own kindred. The privacy of the household was violated through this espionage; and husband and wife, parent and child, were sworn against one another. The ties of blood were wronged, and the confidence of friendship was turned into a snare in this secret service. Universal suspicion must have been created; no one could tell who his accuser might be, for the friend to whom he had read of Christ's betrayal might soon be tempted to act the part of Judas towards himself, and for some paltry consideration sell his life to the ecclesiastical powers." (*History of the English Bible* by John Eadie, I, p.93).

"The English Catholic Church's opposition to a vernacular translation was predictable. The authority of the priests rested solely in the Church. The Church's grasp on the laity depended on biblical ignorance. Therefore, they vehemently opposed Wycliffe's translation. Any free use of the Bible in worship and thought signaled a deep threat to the Church's authority." (*The New Testament In English* Translated by John Wycliffe – First Exact Facsimile with introduction by Donald L. Brake; p. xvii).

The English Catholic church pressured the English parliament to action. In 1381 A.D. "the English Parliament passed the first English statute against heresy, enjoining arrest, trial and imprisonment." (*History of the Church of God from the Creation to A.D. 1885;* by Cushing Biggs Hassell; p. 459). Soon after this law was enacted, as I pointed out earlier, Archbishop Courtney gathered 47 bishops, monks and religious doctors to examine Wycliffe's teachings in May of 1382. They judged 10 of his teachings as heresy and 16 others were ruled erroneous and ruled that his writings were forbidden to be read in England. The King called for the imprisonment of all who believed the condemned doctrines and teachings of Wycliffe. When the ruling was made, "a powerful earthquake shook the city. Huge stones fell out of castle walls and pinnacles toppled." (*Rome And The Bible;* by David W. Cloud; Way of Life Literature; p.57). As I mentioned earlier, "Wycliffe called it a judgment of God and afterwards described the gathering as the Earthquake Council." (*John Wycliffe:The Dawn of The Reformation;* by David Guy Fountain; Mayflower Christian Books 1984; p.39).

Many phrases from our King James Bible of 1611 originate with Wycliffe's handwritten Bible, including **"straight is the gate and narrow the way," "born again," "worship the father in spirit and truth," "the spirit of adoption of sons," "a living sacrifice," "the deep things of God," "the cup of blessing which we bless," "what fellowship hath light with darkness," "we make known to you the grace of God," "and upbraideth not," "whited sepulchres," "revelation of the mystery," "be it far from thee," "despise ye the Church of God," "the world and all that dwell therein is the Lord's," "who is this King of glory?" "he taught them in parables."**

PSALM 23 IN THE WYCLIFFE BIBLE

The Lord govereneth me, and no thing schal faile to me; In the place of pasture there he hath set me. He nurschide me on the water of refreischying; he conuertide my soule. He ledde me forth on the pathis of righteousness; for his name. For whi thoug Y schal go in the myddis of schadewe of deeth; Y schal not drede yuels, for thou art with me. Thi gerde and thi staf; thou han coumfortid me. Thou has maad redi a boord in my sigt; agens hem that troblen me. Thou hast maad fat myn heed with oyle; and my cuppe, fillinge, is ful cleer. And thi merci schal sue me; in alle the daies of myh liif. And that Y dwelle in the hows of the Lord; in to the lengthe of daies.

Translating the Bible from Latin into English was a massive undertaking. An equally daunting task was hand writing each copy. But, all of that would be little use if the Bible were not distributed to the people. How was this accomplished? To answer that question we need to look at Dr. Wycliffe's preachers.

WYCLIFFE'S LOLLARD PREACHERS

John Wycliffe, the Gospel Doctor, was a great teacher. You will remember that people came from all over Europe to sit under his teaching. When he was expelled from Oxford many of these young men followed him to Lutterworth. There Wycliffe established a group  of itinerant preachers he called "evangelical men" to get the Word of God out to the people. Others referred to this group as "Wycliffites" or "poor preachers." Archbishop Courtenay officially called them "Lollards" in 1382 when he banned the teachings of Wycliffe. "Lollard" was intended to be a term of derision. There are differences of opinion as to its origin and meaning. Some say it is from the Dutch *lillaerd*, which means a mumbler (of prayers and hymns). Others say it is derived from the Latin word *lolium* meaning a cockle or tare. Despite the derision, men flocked to be taught by him. Why? Because he gave them something they would never get in the colleges of their day or even at a modern Bible college or seminary. Here's what he taught them.

He taught them how to live. He instilled in them a very strong work ethic. When they left him and went out to preach they had no shoes on their feet. They were barefooted. They wore coarse clothing. They were specifically told they were not to beg. If their needs were not provided they were to work.

He taught them how to preach. John Wycliffe was the greatest theological mind of his generation. People came from all over England and Europe to sit under the teaching of Wycliffe. Wycliffe trained these men to preach the Bible clearly and accurately. He trained them how to refute the lies and errors being advanced by the priesthood of that day. He provided them with sermon outlines, Bible tracts and Scripture portions, all in the language of the people.

He taught them how to spiritually reproduce. Wycliffe urged his evangelical men to capture England for Christ. And they must have learned the lesson of spiritual reproduction because one historian wrote that 10 years after Wycliffe was dead "you cannot travel anywhere in England, but of every two men you meet one will be a Lollard." (*Zion's Fire* Magazine - March/April, 1991 Special Edition; p.9) But that is not all. "Wyclif was a pioneer of vast force in popular education. It is known that between 1363-1400 the Lollards founded and conducted no less than twenty five Grammar Schools free from ecclesiastical control." (*Fighters & Martyrs for the Freedom of Faith* by Luke S. Walmsley p.31).

He taught them how to die. Wycliffe plainly told these men that if they preached the biblical truths that they had learned from his English Bible they would likely die. Many of them did die. Here is what the Lollards believed. In fact, they had carefully presented their beliefs to Parliament in what is called...

THE TWELVE CONCLUSIONS OF THE LOLLARDS

The Twelve Conclusions of the Lollards are preserved in their original English form (other Latin summaries survive) in Roger Dymok's *"Against the Twelve Heresies"* of the Lollards, an elaborate refutation of each of the heresies, written in 1396-97 for Richard II. The original conclusions were presented to parliament (which took no action) and posted at St. Paul's Cross.

The text that follows is literally translated from the Middle English, at the cost of some archaisms and obscurities, a few of which are explained in italicized glosses.

"We poor men, treasurers of Christ and his Apostles, denounce to the Lords and the Commons of the Parliament certain conclusions and truth for the reformation of the Holy Church of England, the which has been blind and leprous many years by the maintenance of the proud prelacy, borne up with flattering of private religion, the which is multiplied to a great charge and onerous [to] people here in England.

THE FIRST CONCLUSION: STATE OF THE CHURCH

When the Church of England began to dote in temporality after her stepmother, the great Church of Rome, and churches were slain by appropriation to diverse places. Faith, Hope, and Charity began for to flee out of our Church. For Pride with his sorry genealogy of deadly sins challengeth it by title of heritage. This conclusion is general and proved by experience, custom, and manner, as you shall after hear.

THE SECOND CONCLUSION: THE PRIESTHOOD

The Second Conclusion is this: Our usual priesthood, the which began in Rome feigned of a power higher than angels, is not the priesthood the which Christ ordained to his Apostles. This conclusion is proved: for the priesthood of Rome is made with signs, rites, and bishops' blessings, and that is of little virtue. nowhere ensampled in the Holy Scripture, for the bishops ordinals in the New Testament be little of record. And we cannot see that the Holy Ghost, for any such signs, gives any gifts, for he and his noble gifts may not stand with deadly sin in no matter person. The corollary of this conclusion is that it is full uncouth to many that be wise to see bishops play with the holy ghost in making of their orders, for they give crowns in characters instead of white harts, and that is the livery of Antichrist, brought into Holy Church to color idleness.

THE THIRD CONCLUSION: CLERICAL CELIBACY

The Third Conclusion, sorrowful to hear, is: That the law of continence annexed to priesthood, that in prejudice of women was first ordained, induces sodomy in Holy Church; but we excuse us by the Bible, for the suspect degree that says we should not name it. Reason and experience prove this conclusion. For delicious meats and drinks of men of Holy Church will have needful purgation or worse. Experience for the privy assay of such men is that they like not women. The corollary of this conclusion is that the private religions, beginners of this sin, were most worthy to be annulled but God, for his might, of privy sin send open vengeance.

THE FOURTH CONCLUSION: TRANSUBSTANTIA-TION

The Fourth Conclusion that most harms the innocent people is this: That the sacrament of bread induces all men but a few to idolatry, for they ween that Christ's body, that never shall out of heaven, by virtue of the priest's word should be essentially enclosed in a little bread, that they show to the people. But would God that they would believe that the Doctor Evangelicus says in his Trialogue, *quod panis materialis est habitudinaliter corpus Christi.* For we suppose that on this wise may every true man and woman in God's law make the sacrament of the bread without any such miracle. The corollary of this conclusion is that if Christ's body be endued with everlasting joy, the service of Corpus Christi made by Friar Thomas is untrue and painted full of false miracles, and that is no wonder, for Friar Thomas that same time, holding with the Pope, would have made a miracle of a hen's egg, and we know well that every lie openly preached turns itself to villainy that ever was true and without lack.

THE FIFTH CONCLUSION: EXORCISMS AND HALLOWINGS

The Fifth Conclusion is this: that exorcisms and hallowings, made in the church, of wine, bread, and wax, water, salt, oil and incense, the stone of the altar, upon vestment, miter, cross, and pilgrim staffs be the very practice of necromancy rather than of the holy theology. This conclusion is proved thus: For by such exorcisms creatures be charged to be of higher virtue than their own kind, and we see no thing of change in no such creature that is so charmed but by false belief, the which is the principal of the Devil's craft. The corollary of this, that is the book that charmeth holy water spread in Holy Church were all true, us thinks verily that holy water used in holy church should be the best medicine to all manner of sickness. *Cuius contrarium experimur.*

THE SIXTH CONCLUSION: CLERICS IN SECULAR OFFICES

The Sixth Conclusion that maintaineth much pride is: that a king and a bishop all in one person, a prelate and a justice in temporal cause, a curate and an officer in worldly service, make every realm out of good rule. This conclusion is openly showed, for temporality and spirituality be two parts of Holy Church and therefore he that hath taken him to the one should not meddle him with the other, quia nemo potest duobus dominis servire. Us thinketh that hermaphrodite or ambidexter were a good name to such men of double estate. The corollary is that for we, procurators of God, for this cause pursue to this Parliament that all manner of curates, both high and low, be fully excused of temporal office and occupy them with their cure and naught else.

THE SEVENTH CONCLUSION: PRAYERS FOR THE DEAD

The Seventh Conclusion that we mightily affirm is: that special prayers for dead men's souls made in our church, preferring one by name more than another, this is the false ground of alms deeds, on the which all alms houses in England be wickedly grounded. This conclusion is proven by two skills. One is for prayer meritorious and of value should be a work proceeding from high charity, and perfect charity accepts no persons, *quia diliges proximum tuum, etc.* Wherefore us thinks that the gifts of temporal goods to priests and to alms houses is the principal cause of special prayers, the which is not far from simony. Another skill for special prayer made for men damned to everlasting pain is to God greatly displeasing, and though it be doubt, it is lightly to true Christian people that the founders of the alms houses for their venomous dotacion be for the most part passed the broad way. The corollary is the prayer of value s[ringing out of perfect charity should embrace in general all those that God would have saved and leave their merchandise now used for special prayers made to mendicants and possessioners and other souls' priests, the which be a people of great charge to all the realm maintained in idleness, for it was proved in a book that the king heard that an hundred of alms houses sufficed to the realm and thereof should fall the greatest increase possible to temporal part.

THE EIGHTH CONCLUSION: PILGRIMAGES

The Eighth Conclusion needful to tell the people beguiled is the pilgrimage, prayers, and offerings made to blind roods and deaf images of tree and stone be near kin to idolatry and far from alms deeds. And though this forbidden imagery be a book of errors to the lewd people, yet the image used of Trinity is most abominable. This conclusion God openly showeth, commanding to do almsdeeds to men that be needy. for they be the image of God in a more likeness than the stock of the stone, for God sayeth not *Faciamus lignum ad ymaginem et similitudinem nostram aut lapidem,* but *faciamus hominem etc.* For the high worship that clerks call *latria* longeth to the godhead alone and the lower worship that is called *dulia* longeth to man and to angel and to lower creatures. The corollary is that the service of the Rood, done twice every year in our church, is fulfilled of idolatry, for if the Rood tree, nails, and the spear, and the crown of God should be so holy worshipped, then were Judas' lips, whoso might them get, a wonder great relic. But we pray thee, pilgrim, us to tell when thou first offerest to saints' bones enshrined in any place, whether relieves thou the saint that is in bliss or the alms house that is so well endowed. For men be canonized, God knows how, and for to speak more in plain, true Christian men suppose that the points of that noble man that men call Saint Thomas, were no cause of martyrdom.

THE NINTH CONCLUSION: CONFESSION

The Ninth Conclusion that holdeth the people low is, that the articles of confession that is said necessary to the salvation of man, with a feigned power of absolution enhanceth priests' pride, and giveth them opportunity of calling other than we will not say. For lords and ladies be arrested that for fear of their confessors, that they dare not say a truth, and in time of confession is the best time of wooing and of privy continuance of deadly sin. They say that they be commissaries of God to deem of every sin, to foul and cleanse whomso they like. They say that they have the keys of heaven and of hell, they may curse and bless, bind and unbind at their own will, in so much that for a bushel of wheat or twelve pence by year they will sell the bliss of heaven by charter of clause of warranty, ensealed with the common seal. This conclusion is seen in use that it needeth none other proof. Correlarium: The Pope of Rome that feigneth him high treasurer of holy church, having the worthy jewel of Christ's passion in his keeping, with the deserts of all hallows of heaven, by which he giveth the pardon *a pena et a culpa*. He is a treasurer most banished out of charity, since he may deliver the prisoners that be in pain at his own will, and make himself so that he shall never come there, Here may every true Christian well see that there is much privy falseness hid in our church.

THE TENTH CONCLUSION: WAR, BATTLE, AND CRUSADES

The Tenth Conclusion is that manslaughter by battle or law of righteousness for temporal cause or spiritual without special revelation is express contrary to the New Testament, the which is a law of grace and full of mercy. This conclusion is openly proved by example of Christ's preaching here on earth. the which most taught to love and to have mercy on his enemies. and not for to slay them. The reason is of this, that for the more party, there men fight, after the first stroke charity is broken; and who so dyeth out of charity goth the high way to hell. And over this, we know well that no clerk can find by scripture or by reason lawful punishment of death for one sin and not for another. But the law of mercy, that is the New Testament, forbade all manslaughter: *in euangelio dictum est antiquis. Non occides.* The corollary is: it is an holy robbing of poor people when lords purchase indulgences *a pena et a culpa* to them that helpeth with his host. and gathereth to slay the Christian men in far lands for good temporal, as we have seen. And knights, that run to heathenness to get them a name in slaying of men, get much maugré of the King of Peace; for the meekness and sufferance our belief was multiplied, and fighters and manslayers Jesus Christ hateth and menaceth. *Qui gladio percutit, gladio peribit.*

THE ELEVENTH CONCLUSION: FEMALE VOWS OF CONTINENCE AND ABORTION

The Eleventh Conclusion is shameful for to speak: that a vow of continence made in our church of women, the which be fickle and imperfect in kind, is cause of bringing in of most horrible sin possible to mankind. For though slaying of children ere they be christened, abortion, and destroying of kind by medicine be full sinful, yet knowing with themselves [i.e., *having intercourse with*] or [*either*] unreasonable beast or creature that beareth no life passeth in worthiness to be punished in pains of hell. The corollary is that widows and which as have taken the mantle and the ring, deliciously fed, we would they were wedded for we cannot excuse them from privy sins.

THE TWELFTH CONCLUSION: ARTS AND CRAFTS

The Twelfth Conclusion is that the multitude of crafts not needful used in our church nourisheth much sin in waste, curiosity, and disguising. This showeth experience, and reason proveth, for nature with a few crafts sufficeth to need of man. The corollary is, since Saint Paul sayeth, we having our bodily food and clothing, we should hold ourselves satisfied, us thinketh that goldsmiths and armourers and all manner crafts not needful to men, after [*according to*] the Apostle, should be destroyed for the increase of virtue. For though to these crafts named were much more needful in the Old Law, the New Testament hath voided these and many others.

This is our embassy that Christ has commanded us to pursue, at this time most acceptable for many causes. And though these matters be here shortly knit they be in another book longly declared, and may another more, all in our language, the which we would were communed to all true Christian men. We pray God of his endless goodness reform our church. all out of joint, to the perfections of the first beginning. Amen.

Translated from "The Twelve Conclusions of the Lollards", *English Historical Review*, 22 (1907), 292-304 [Widener Br 5.1].

Shortly after the posting of "The Twelve Conclusions..." the Church and Crown moved to wipe out the Lollard movement. In 1401 the English Parliament passed a law supporting the burning heretics. In that same year William Sawtrey became the first Lollard martyr. From that point on, many Lollards were burned, and they were often burned with their copies of the Wycliffe Bible around their necks. I should also note that in 1410 about 200 copies of Wycliffe's writings were burned in Oxford. There were other public burnings of Wycliffe Bibles and books as well.

There were so many Lollards that were executed in one place in England that it is called the Lollards pit. If they died in London they were often kept in the Lollards Tower at Lambeth Palace and then taken out and burned at Smithfield.

In the early days of the Reformation, people celebrated St. Bartholomew's Day in a very strange way at Smithfield. People came from all over England for a week of celebration. They camped out and pitched in tents all over the area. It was a time of celebration. There was a festive spirit. But, a part of the entertainment was the public burning of those who dared to preach the Bible, possess the Bible, or read the Bible in their own language.

Perhaps the most famous of the Lollard martyrs was **Sir John Oldcastle**, also known as Lord Cobham. He was barbarously put to death at Christmas time in 1417 for his faith in the Word of God and his rejection of Rome's authority. Specifically, he had paid to have scribes copy many copies of the Wycliffe Bible and then distributed them among people. When he was brought to the place of execution, he refused to recant his faith but instead urged the people "to obey God's commands written down in the Bible, and always shun such teachings as they saw to be contrary to the life and example of Christ." (*History of the Christian Church* Vol. II; by Henry C. Shelton – 1895; Reprinted 1994 by Hendrickson Publishers; p.426). Sir John was then hung in chains and burned alive, suspended over the fire. In fact, one of

William Shakespeare's greatest comic characters, Sir John Flagstaff, was based on Sir John Oldcastle.

I agree wholeheartedly with Luke Walmsley who concluded, John "Wyclif was the Daniel of his era—he dared to be singular, and to offend even to exasperate a power the most dreadful and overwhelming and implacable that then existed. He stood almost alone on the earth; unimpressed by example, and unawed by the execrations of adoring millions, he indignantly refused to fall down before the idol. He appears to have been a man at once amiable and ardent, bold and cautious—a lover of civil and sacred freedom, yet one who rebuked every species of licentiousness with the freedom and severity of an apostle." (*Fighters & Martyrs for the Freedom of Faith* by Luke S. Walmsley; p.36).

WYCLIFFE'S DEATH & POSTSCRIPT

Despite blatantly contradicting the doctrines of the church and criticizing the corruption of the clergy, John Wycliffe was never excommunicated in his lifetime nor did he leave the Roman Catholic Church that he pastored at Lutterworth. As he advanced in age, he enlisted three men to give him a hand. John Horn served as the assistant pastor at the Lutterworth parish and John Purvey became his personal secretary, diligent co-worker and personal confidential friend. After the death of Wycliffe, Purvey did a complete revision of the Wycliffe Bible in 1388. Dr. Nicolas Hereford stood by Wycliffe until his death.

"Toward the close of 1382, Wycliffe was visited by a stroke of paralysis, which disabled him from continuing those public labors in which he had hitherto engaged." (*The Life and Times of John Wycliffe;* p.93). Perhaps it was because he had suffered this stroke that Ecclesiastical officials did not go after him. But I rather think it was God's hand of protection because over the next two years, before he passed into the presence of the Lord, he wrote a systematic statement of his views, called *Trialogus,* and had it published in manuscript books and distributed.

Two years later, "on December 28, 1384, while he was hearing mass in his parish church at Lutterworth, at the very moment of the elevation of the host, he had a second paralytic seizure of great violence, and immediately fell to the ground." (Ibid.) From that moment on he could not speak. He was placed in his chair (which still sits in the church to this day) and carried out the door and taken to his parsonage where he died at home in bed on New Years Eve, 1384 A.D. "Thus was removed from the Church on earth one of the boldest witnesses of the truth. It was a glorious conclusion to a noble life. 'None of its years, scarcely any of its days, were passed unprofitably on the bed of sickness. The moment his great work was finished, that moment the voice spake to him, which said, Come up hither!'"

LUTTERWORTH CHURCH.

THE SCENE OF WYCLIFFE'S MINISTRATIONS, 1374-1384.

He was buried in the Lutterworth church-yard soon after. But that is not the end of the story. The English Catholic Church wanted to stamp out the influence Wycliffe had even after his death. You can see the animosity by reading what Archbishop Arundel wrote to the Pope in 1411: "This pestilent and wretched John Wyclif, of cursed memory, that sone of the old serpent... endeavored by doctrine of Holy Church, devising – to fill up the measure of his malice – the expedient of a new translation of the Scriptures into the mother tongue." (*The Wycliffite Versions – The Cambridge History of the Bible;* by Henry Hargreaves; Cambridge University Press – 1969).

Thirty years after Wycliffe's death the Roman Church finally took official action at the Council of Constance in 1415. These are the alleged "errors" of which he was convicted.

THE "ERRORS" OF JOHN WYCLIFFE AS PROCLAIMED BY THE COUNCIL OF CONSTANCE 1414-1418, SESSION VIII, MAY 4, 1415.

[Condemned in Council and by the Bulls "Inter Cunctas" and "In eminentis" Feb. 22, 1418.]

1. In the sacrament of the altar the material substance of bread and likewise the material substance of the wine remain.
2. In the same sacrament the accident of the bread do not remain without a subject.
3. In the same sacrament Christ is not identically and really with His own bodily presence.
4. If a bishop or priest is living in mortal sin, he does not ordain, not consecrate, nor perform, nor baptize.
5. It is not established in the Gospel that Christ arranged the Mass.
6. God ought to obey the devil.
7. If man is duly contrite, every exterior confession on his part is superfluous and useless.
8. If the pope is foreknown and evil, and consequently a member of the devil, he does not have power over the faithful given to him by anyone, unless perchance by Caesar.
9. After Urban VI no one should be received as pope, unless he live according to the customs of the Greeks under their laws.
10. It is contrary to Sacred Scripture that ecclesiastical men have possessions.
11. No prelate should excommunicate anyone, unless first he knows that he has been excommunicated by God; and he who so excommunicates becomes, as a result of this, a heretic or excommunicated.
12. A prelate excommunicating a cleric who has appealed to the king, or to a council of the kingdom, by that very act is a traitor of the king and the kingdom.
13. Those who cease to preach or to hear the word of God because of the excommunication of men, are themselves excommunicated, and in the judgment of God they will be considered traitors of Christ.

261

14. It is permissible for any deacon or priest to preach the word of God without the authority of the Apostolic See or a Catholic bishop.
15. No one is a civil master, no one a prelate, no one a bishop, as long as he is in mortal sin.
16. Temporal rulers can at their will take away temporal goods from the church, when those who have possessions habitually offend, that is, offend by habit, not only by an act.
17. People can at their will correct masters who offend.
18. The tithes are pure alms and parishioners can take these away at will because of the sins of their prelates.
19. Special prayers applied to one person by prelates or religious are not of more benefit to that person than general (prayers), all other things being equal.
20. One bringing alms to the Brothers is excommunicated by that very thing.
21. If anyone enters any private religious community of any kind, of those having possessions or the mendicants [beggars / Friars], he is rendered unfit and unsuited for the observance of the laws of God.
22. Saints, instituting private religious communities, have sinned by instituting them.
23. Religious living in private religious communities are not of the Christian religion.
24. Brothers are bound to acquire their food by the labor of hands and not by begging.
25. All are simoniacs who oblige themselves to pray for others who assist them in temporal matters.
26. The prayer for the foreknown is of avail to no one.
27. All things happen from absolute necessity.
28. The confirmation of youths, ordination of clerics, and consecration of places are reserved to the pope and bishops on account of their desire for temporal gain and honor.
29. Universities, studies, colleges, graduations, and offices of instruction in the same have been introduced by a vain paganism; they are of as much value to the Church as the devil.
30. The excommunication of the pope or of any prelate whatsoever is not to be feared, because it is the censure of the Antichrist.
31. Those who found cloisters sin and those who enter (them) are diabolical men.
32. To enrich the clergy is contrary to the rule of Christ.

33. Sylvester, the Pope, and Constantine, the Emperor, erred in enriching the Church.
34. All of the order of mendicants [beggars / Friars] are heretics, and those who give alms to them are excommunicated.
35. Those entering religion or any order, by that very fact are unsuited to observe divine precepts, and consequently to enter the kingdom of heaven, unless they apostatize from them.
36. The pope with all his clergy who have possessions are heretics, because they have possessions; and all in agreement with these, namely all secular masters and other laity.
37. The Roman Church is the synagogue of Satan, and the pope is not the next and immediate vicar of Christ and His apostles.
38. The decretal letters are apocryphal and they seduce from the faith of Christ, and the clergy who study them are foolish.
39. The emperor and secular masters have been seduced by the devil to enrich the Church with temporal goods.
40. The election of the pope by cardinals was introduced by the devil.
41. It is not necessary for salvation to believe that the Roman Church is supreme among other churches.
42. It is foolish to believe in the indulgences of the pope and bishops.
43. Oaths are illicit which are made to corroborate human contracts and civil commerce.
44. Augustine, Benedict, and Bernard have been damned, unless they repented about this, that they had possessions and instituted and entered religious communities; and thus from the pope to the last religious, all are heretics.
45. All religious communities without distinction have been introduced by the devil.

(Source: The Sources of Catholic Dogma, translated by Roy J. Deferrari, from the Thirtieth Edition of Henry Denzinger's *Enchiridion Symbolorum*, copyright 1957 by B. Herder Book Co., published by Marian House, Powers Lake N.D. 58773, Library of Congress Catalog Card Number 57-5963, pages 208-211.)

THE DESECRATION OF WYCLIFFE'S GRAVE

They burned John Hus, Wycliffe's disciple, at the stake and condemned John Wycliffe on the above 45 errors and many others for a total of 260 different counts. They ordered that his bones be exhumed from the consecrated ground at Lutterworth and burned. Their orders were not carried out for another 13 years. Hence 44 years after John Wycliffe's death, his bones were exhumed and burned along with all the Bibles and books they could find authored by him. His ashes were thrown into the river Swift. The Church of Rome thought this would stamp out his influence and stand as a warning to any future would-be "heretics."

THE WORLD-WIDE INFLUENCE OF WYCLIFFE

In conclusion, I would like to share several paragraphs from a set of books that I finally obtained after years of searching. The author is Thomas Fuller. Usually, other authors cite just a small portion of his quote. I desire that you see it in its context.

"Hitherto the corpse of John Wickliffe had quietly slept in his grave, about one-and-forty years after his death, till his body was reduced to bones, and his bones almost to dust. For though the earth in the chancel of Lutterworth in Leicestershire, where he was interred, had not so quick a digestion with the earth of Aceldama, to consume flesh in twenty-four hours, yet such the appetite thereof, and all other English graves, to leave small reversions of a body after so many years.

"But now, such the spleen of the council of Constance, as they not only cursed his memory, as dying an obstinate heretic, but ordered his bones (with this charitable caution, "if it may be discerned from the bodies of other faithful people") to be taken out of the ground, and thrown far off from any Christian burial.

"In obedience hereunto, Richard Fleming, bishop of Lincoln, diocesan of Lutterworth, sent his officers (vultures with a quick sight scent at a dead carcase!) to ungrave him accordingly. To Lutterworth they come,—Sumner, Commissary, Official, Chancellor, Proctors, Doctors, and the servants (so that the remnant of the body would not hold out a bone, amongst so many hands) take what was left out of the grave, and <u>burnt them to ashes, and cast them into Swift, a neighbouring brook running hard by. Thus this brook hath conveyed his ashes into Avon, Avon into Severn, Severn into the narrow seas, they into the main ocean. And thus the ashes of Wickliffe are the emblem of his doctrine, which now is dispersed all the world over</u>." *(Fullers Church History of Britain* by Thomas Fuller; 3rd Edition of 1842; Vol. 1; p. 493).

John Wycliffe's English Bible and other works lighted a fire that spread the Word of God and biblical doctrine throughout Europe and ultimately to the United States. In truth, Dr. John Wycliffe was the Morning Star of the Reformation. The Roman Catholic Church has never been the same since, particularly in England, because of his influence. The Wycliffe English Bible, handscribed, and the messages of the Lollard preachers loosed the bands that held tightly so many to popish dogma. The truth of the Word of God set the captives free.

CHAPTER #12

THREE KEY EVENTS THAT BROUGHT AN END TO THE DARK AGES AND THE PRINTING OF THE ENGLISH BIBLE

There were three key events that brought about the end of the Dark Ages and laid the foundation for the printing and distribution of the English Bible.

1. **The Development of the moveable type printing press by Gutenberg**

2. **The Fall of Constantinople to the Turks which resulted in the introduction of the Greek language and Greek New Testament into Western Europe**

3. **The Greek New Testament was translated into the languages of the common man**
   (*The Legacy of our English Bible;* John Wesley Sawyer; self-published 1990; p.3)
   We will examine each one more closely.

THE DEVELOPMENT OF THE MOVEABLE TYPE PRINTING PRESS BY GUTENBERG

Johann Gensfleisch zum Gutenberg (meaning - John Gooseflesh of the Good Mountain) was born between 1394-1399 in Mainz, Germany. He had an older brother Friele, named after his father, and an older sister Else, named after her mother.

His father, Friele Gensfleisch zur Luden zum Gutenberg, was a scribe, whose job it was to copy long, intricate manuscripts for the clergy, nobility and lawyers. Young Hans, (Hans, Henne or Henchin were local nick names for Johann) would spend hours watching his father work. The story is told that one day while his father busied himself copying a manuscript, young Johann carved the first letter of his nickname into a block of wood. As he went to show it to his father, he dropped it into a pot of blue die being used by his father. He carefully retrieved it and set it on a piece of paper only to discover that it left the imprint of an "H" on the paper. Though I cannot solidly verify that this story is historically accurate, if it is, it could have been this incident that put Johann's mind in motion concerning making books in a different way than inscribing them.

I do know this. Gutenberg had a heart for God and a desire to get His teaching to the people. My friend Dr. Jewell Smith provided me with the text of a letter Gutenberg wrote showing that he had a vision for the printing press –

"God suffers because of the great multitudes whom His Sacred Word cannot reach. Religious truth is captive in a small number of manuscript books which guard the treasures. Let us break the seal which holds the holy things; give wings to the truth that by means no longer written at great expense by the hand that wearies itself, but multiplied by an unwearied machine it may fly to every soul born into the world."

As he moved into adulthood we know that he was familiar with the goldsmith's craft and records show that he was also knowledgeable in the art of gem cutting. Yet he was experimenting with printing as well. By the time he was 28 years old, Johann had already sunk large portions of his personal finances into printing experiments. At this point he encountered a great deal of resistance from the scribes' guilds. They feared that if Gutenberg were successful, their jobs would be in jeopardy. Rumors began to circulate that Johann was an alchemist working of devilish things in his shop. He experimented another five years until he was at the end of his financial rope. In 1449 he borrowed money from Mainz lawyer, Johann Fust, to keep going. At that point he began printing leaflets, pamphlets and indulgence cards to repay his debt. I should point out that the development of type that could be assembled, disassembled and reassembled for a new printing job was his "claim to fame." The printing going on before this time consisted of using the wood block method, which carved the entire message into a single wood block which was then inked and pressed onto the paper. He adapted a press to use his moveable type. This proved to revolutionize the world and Time Magazine named him the Man of the Millennium because of that development.

1455 A.D. – GUTENBERG BIBLE

The Gutenberg Bible is also called the 42-line Bible because there are 42 lines per page. It is called the Mazarine Bible because the first copy that attracted attention was discovered about 1760 among the books of the French statesman, Cardinal Jules Mazarin.

Gutenberg wanted to print a book, but not just any book. He wanted to print the Latin Bible. In 1452 he borrowed more money to buy 100,000 sheets of paper and 8,000 calfskins needed to print the 180 (some say 158 and others, 188) Bibles. Of that number about 30 were printed on the vellum. These expensive and beautiful Bibles were sold at the 1455 Frankfurt Book fair and cost the equivalent of three years' pay for the average clerk.

Shortly after the book fair he lost the business completely. He died in 1468 living on a small stipend given him by the Catholic Church. Little did he know that just 50 years later, 20 million books would have been printed on presses and type of his design. Only 80 years later, presses based on his design were printing multiplied thousands of copies of Luther and Tyndale Bibles that would fuel the Reformation's fires and help bring an end to the Dark Ages.

THE FALL OF CONSTANTINOPLE

The second key event that brought an end to the Dark Ages was the fall of Constantinople to the Turks in 1454 A.D. This resulted in the introduction of the Greek language and Greek New Testament into Western Europe. I am reminded of **Romans 8:28** which says, *"And we know that all things work together for good to them that love God, to them who are the called according to his purpose."*

In 1454 Mohammed II captured Constantinople. The result was that many Greek scholars had to flee to Europe with their sacred codices and precious scrolls which included writings of the early church fathers and the Scriptures in the original languages. Many of these Eastern scholars took positions in the great European universities, and the result was a renaissance of ancient learning, including the teaching of the Greek language. At the same time, there was the invention of the printing press, which would multiply the availability of books. The Ottoman Empire continued to expand under the brutal tyrant Suleiman the Magnificence. But God indeed did use this seeming  tragedy for good. He raised Erasmus, who would publish a Greek New Testament and make a new Latin translation correcting the grievous errors in the Latin Vulgate. One of the most important errors in the Latin Vulgate was the use of the word "**pentence**" instead of the proper word "**repentance**." The Greek text cleared this up. As you can imagine Rome was not happy. They had amassed great wealth from the sale of indulgences. Further, they had developed a church authorized theology of salvation by works and rejected Bible-based salvation by God's grace, through faith in Christ.

ERASMUS DESIDERIUS ROTERDAMUS – 1466? - 1536

The date of Erasmus' birth is in question. It was probably 1469 or 1466 or 1467. He was the second illegitimate son of Dutch Catholic priest, Roger Gerard or Gerritt and Margaret, a physician's daughter. His older brother's name was Pieter. Tragically, fornication among priests was common. "His baptismal name, Erasmus, was taken from one of the fourteen auxiliary saints who were popular in the fifteenth century; he added 'Roterodamus' for his birth place, Roterdam; 'Desiderius,' which appeared later, was a literary decoration." (*Erasmus: His Life, Works and Influence* by Cornelius Augustihn; University of Toronto Press – 1995; p.21).

Upon the death of his parents, he and his brother were forced to enter the monastery. Erasmus chose "the Augustinian canons regular at Steyn, near Gouda, where he seems to have remained about seven years (1485-92)." (*Britannica Online* – Erasmus; www.britannica.com).

In 1492, at about the age of 23, he was ordained to the priesthood. "He was happy to escape the monastery by accepting a post as Latin secretary to the influential Henry of Bergen, bishop of Cambrai. But, Erasmus was not suited to a courtier's life, nor did things improve much when the bishop was induced to send him to the University of Paris to study theology (1495). He disliked the quasi-monastic regimen of the Collège de Montaigu, where he lodged initially, and pictured himself to a friend as sitting 'with wrinkled brow and glazed eye' through Scotist lectures." (Ibid.) It is not possible to understand what motivated Erasmus to publish the Greek New Testaments without saying something about the influence of two key men. The first one is John Colet.

THE INFLUENCE OF JOHN COLET

John Colet was born in 1466 or 1467. He was the son of a prosperous merchant who had been Lord Mayor of London. He regularly associated with and influenced such people as Sir Thomas More, Erasmus, and Thomas Linacre, prototype of the scholar-physicians of the Renaissance. Colet was appointed dean of St. Paul's Cathedral in 1504 and founded St. Paul's School in 1509. But I am getting ahead of myself.

In 1499 a pupil, William Blount, Lord Mountjoy, invited Erasmus to come to England. It was there that Erasmus met John Colet, who awakened Erasmus' ambition to be a "primitive theologian," not one who would expound Scripture in the argumentative manner of the scholastics but in the manner of Jerome and the other church fathers, who lived in an age when men still understood and practiced the classical art of rhetoric.

Without a doubt, John Colet had a major influence on Erasmus. Colet had studied mathematics and philosophy at Oxford and then traveled and studied for three years in France and Italy. In Italy he studied New Testament Greek. In addition, "the influence of Savonarola had placed a seal on Colet's life and lit a fire in his soul. Savonarola was the great preacher who called Italian culture back to Christianity. Colet was an enthusiastic student of the Greek New Testament and made a history-altering decision to preach and teach [the New Testament] when he returned to England." (*The Forbidden Book;* Lollard House; p.16). He returned to England about 1496 and was ordained sometime before 1499. He lectured at Oxford University.

Now, here's why Colet is so important in the history of the printing of the English Bible. In 1496 Colet lectured on the Pauline Epistles. He would read them in Greek and then expound the text in terms of its plain meaning as seen in its historical context. His lectures were packed to standing room only. This was a major departure from the argumentative, obscure, mystical, symbolic way the Scriptures were handled in medieval scholasticism. Since the time of Augustine it had been accepted that you treated the Latin Scripture allegorically. "On top of the first meaning, the literal, were piled the **allegorical** (animals, for example, suggesting virtues); the **tropological** or moral, involving tropes (figures) of morality and the **anagogical**, (from the Greek word meaning "to rise"), that is 'elevatory' especially to future glory. The most famous example of this old school biblical exegesis is the word 'Jerusalem,' which literally means "the city of the Jews'; **allegorically**, 'the city of Christ,'; **tropologically**, 'the human soul' and **anagogically**, 'the heavenly city.'" (Ibid. p.18).

This type of biblical teaching was confusing to the common people and, in fact, often obscured and even perverted the meaning of the Scripture being taught. Colet refused to follow this errant pattern.

"He was intent on letting Paul speak for himself. Paul the apostle was a real person to Colet, and his lectures made Paul real for his audience." (Ibid. p.16). He simply taught the Pauline Epistles in plain understandable English.

That's not all. He urged Erasmus to learn Greek and study the early church fathers and do the same thing. Further, the impassioned Colet urged Erasmus to lecture on the Old Testament at Oxford, just like he was lecturing on the Pauline Epistles. But, Erasmus was not ready. He returned to the Continent with a Latin copy of St. Paul's Epistles and the conviction that "ancient theology" required mastery of Greek. In fact, Erasmus owed much of his insight into biblical exegesis to John Colet. Colet died on Sept. 16, 1519 in Sheen, Surrey, England.

Erasmus took John Colet's advice. "On a visit to Artois, France in 1501, Erasmus met the fiery preacher Jean Voirier, who, though a Franciscan, told him that 'monasticism was a life more of fatuous (foolish) men than of religious men.' Admirers recounted how Voirier's disciples faced death serenely, trusting in God, without the solemn reassurance of the last rites. Voirier lent Erasmus a copy of works by Origen, the early Greek Christian writer. By 1502 Erasmus had settled in the university town of Louvain (Brabant) and was reading Origen and St. Paul in Greek. The fruit of his labours was *Enchiridion militis Christiani* (1503/04; *Handbook of a Christian Knight*). In this work Erasmus urged readers to 'inject into the vitals' the teachings of Christ by studying and meditating on the Scriptures, using the spiritual interpretation favoured by the 'ancients' to make the text pertinent to moral concerns. The *Enchiridion* was a manifesto of lay piety in its assertion that 'monasticism is not piety.'" (*Britannica Online* – Erasmus; www.britannica.com).

While Erasmus was rummaging around at Park Abbey near Louvain, France, he came across a manuscript of Valla's *Adnotationes* on the Greek New Testament. This is a **key** document that needs to be noted. Here's why. "Laurentius Valla (1405-57) was a famous scholar of the Italian renaissance. Valla emphasized the importance of language. According to him, the decline of civilization in the dark ages was due to the decay of the Greek and Latin languages. Hence it was only through the study of classical literature that the glories of ancient Greece and Rome could be recaptured. Valla's *Adnotatione* was a treatise on the Latin Vulgate [the Roman Catholic Bible], comparing it with certain Greek N.T. manuscripts, which he had in his possession. Erasmus, who from his youth had been an admirer of Valla, found a manuscript of Valla's treatise in 1504, published in 1505, with a dedication to John Colet. In *Adnotatione*, <u>Valla favored the Greek New Testament text over the Vulgate</u>. The Latin text often differed from the Greek, he reported. Also there were omissions and additions in the Latin translation, and the Greek wording was generally better than that of the Latin." (*Way of Life Encyclopedia* by David Cloud; p.151).

THE INFLUENCE OF JOHANNES OECOLAMPADIUS

Another man that greatly influenced Erasmus was Johannes Oecolampadius. He was born in 1482 Johannes Hussgen. "He later changed his name to its humanist form: Oecolampadius, meaning "house light." It is a Latin play on words for his German name, which sounds much like "haus-schein." He was truly one of the bright lights of the Reformation and gave his life to the study of God's Word, Biblical languages, and the Church Fathers. Oecolampadius completed his studies at the University of Heidelberg in 1499. His love of learning caused him to enroll as an older student at the University in Tubingen where he matriculated in 1513. There <u>he mastered Greek, Hebrew, and Latin</u>." (*Western Reformed Seminary Journal* – August 1996; www.wrs.edu/journals/jour896/oecolampadius.html).

In 1515 he met and worked with Erasmus, who was very impressed with his linguistic skills. <u>Oecolampadius became a very valuable resource and aid to Erasmus</u>, and was very instrumental in the publication of Erasmus' Greek New Testament. This connection with Erasmus likely stimulated his interest in the writings of the Greek Fathers, and he began to translate many of their writings. Oecolampadius became a pastor at Augsburg in 1518, where he was influenced by the teachings of Martin Luther. In turn, as *"Iron sharpeneth iron; so a man sharpeneth the countenance of his friend."* **Proverbs 27:17**, so Oecolampadius persuaded Erasmus of the biblical nature of much of Luther's doctrinal perspective. While Erasmus disagreed with Luther on the freedom of the will and the Lord's table, "there can be no doubt that Erasmus was in sympathy with the main points in the Lutheran criticism of the Church." (*Internet Encyclopedia of Philosophy – Erasmus*).

In 1523 Oecolampadius lectured on Isaiah at the university in Basel. Because they were given in German, these lectures proved to be very popular with the citizens of Basel, his audience being often as large as 400. These lectures became the basis for his commentary on Isaiah published in 1525, a commentary praised by both Luther and Calvin. This was the beginning of his involvement with the Reformation. His influence at this time is shown in Erasmus' declaration, "Oecolampadius is reigning here."

In 1525 Oecolampadius took on Luther's rival, John Eck. Unfortunately the dispute was held in Baden, a Catholic stronghold. It was essentially for this reason that he lost the debate. But he emerged much the wiser for the experience. In 1528 the Reformers set up the Bern Colloquy. Here the Reformers gathered to deliver sermons on such theses as: **"The Holy Christian Church, whose only head is Christ, is born of the Word of God, remains in the same, and does not listen to the voice of strangers."**

"These meetings were a great success, and the participants from Basel went home discouraged, not because of the good doctrinal preaching they had heard, but because they felt that their city lagged so far behind Zurich and Bern in the application of these Biblical principles. Perhaps in response to this sentiment, the Basel preachers got together and developed their own liturgy. Basel was still very much in the control of a Catholic core in its inner Council. The preaching of Oecolampadius became much bolder at this time and he was frequently called to appear before the Council to account for statements made in his sermons. His appearances were respectful but firm. He lectured on Haggai, Zechariah, Malachi, Daniel, Jeremiah, Ezekiel, Lamentations, Job, Hebrews, the Gospel of John, Hosea, Amos, Obadiah, Jonah, Genesis, and Matthew." (Ibid.).

Oecolampadius' health began to suffer, and it is perhaps on this account that he decided to marry. He had been living with his parents, but his mother had recently passed away, so that he was left to care for his father. By this time Oecolampadius was in his forties, no doubt quite set in his ways. Erasmus commented that his assistant had taken a beautiful wife to mortify the flesh and that it was time to stop talking about the Lutheran tragedy, for it was much more a comedy, which always ended in a wedding! So, Johannes Oecolampadius married Wibrandis Rosenblatt, the widow of Reformer Ludwig Keller. She was 26, and was to be in turn the wife of Oecolampadius, of his friend Capito, and of his friend Bucer, leading one author to suggest that "her offspring represent a history of the Reformation in several volumes." Oecolampadius dearly loved his three children, whom he named Eusebius (godly), Irene (peace), and Aletheia (truth). Truly, John Oecolampadius was a great help to and influence on Erasmus. On November 23, 1531, in the presence of this wife and children John Oecolampadius went home to be with the Lord.

1516 – ERASMUS GREEK NEW TESTAMENT

"When Erasmus came to Basel in July 1515, to begin his work, he found five Greek N.T. manuscripts ready for his use. These are now designated by the following numbers: **1** (an 11th-century manuscript of the Gospels, Acts, and Epistles), **2** (a 15th-century manuscript of the Gospels), **2ap** (a 12th-14th-century manuscript of Acts and the Epistles), **4ap** (a 15th-century manuscript of Revelation). Of these manuscripts Erasmus used 1 and 4ap only occasionally. In the Gospels, Acts, and Epistles his main reliance was on 2 and 2ap." (*Way of Life Encyclopedia of the Bible* – Electronic Edition; Erasmus Article).

"Although he had only five late maniscules, he had already translated a Latin New Testament and in preparation for this labor he had collected and gathered variant readings from many Greek manuscripts. He wondered all over Europe to libraries, and to anyone from whom he could gather readings from manuscripts." (*The King James Defended* by Edward Hills; Christian Research Press; p.198). Erasmus organized his findings and made notes for himself concerning different readings. These travels brought him into contact with several hundred manuscripts and Erasmus divided them into two camps, i.e., those he considered **spurious** and those he deemed **trustworthy**. (*An Inquiry into the Integrity of the Greek Vulgate or Received Text of the New Testament* by Frederick Nolan; p.413). I should also note "Erasmus had access to Codex Vaticanus but rejected its readings that were at variance with the Byzantine text. He also had access to D, Codex Bezae and also rejected it." (*Myths About The King James Bible: Reformation Editors Lacked Sufficient Manuscript Evidence* by David Cloud; p.9).

"Between the years 1516 and 1535 Erasmus published five editions of the Greek N.T. In the first edition (1516) the text was preceded by a dedication to Pope Leo X, an exhortation to the reader, a discussion of the method used, and a defense of this method. Then came the Greek N.T. text accompanied by Erasmus' own Latin translation, and then this was followed by Erasmus' notes, giving his comments on the text." (*Way of Life Encyclopedia of the Bible* – Electronic Edition; Erasmus Article).

In the preface, "Erasmus makes it clear that his desire is to see the Bible available to everyone. He says, "**Would that these were translated into each and every language.... Would that the farmer might sing snatches of Scripture at his plough, that the weaver might hum phrases of Scripture to the tune of his shuttle.**" (*Christian History* Magazine; Issue 43 Vol. XIII, No.3; p.20).

"In 1514 Martin Dorp of the University of Louvain wrote to Erasmus asking him not to publish his forthcoming Greek N.T. Dorp argued that if the Vulgate contained falsifications of the original Scriptures and errors, the [Roman Catholic] Church would have been wrong for many centuries, which was impossible. The references of most [Catholic] Church Councils to the Vulgate, Dorp insisted, proved that the Church considered this Latin version to be the official Bible and not the Greek N.T., which, he maintained, had been corrupted by the heretical Greek [Orthodox] Church." (Ibid.).

After Erasmus' Greek N.T. had been published in 1516, Stunica, a noted Spanish scholar, accused it of being an open condemnation of the Latin Vulgate, the version of the Church. About the same time Peter Sutor, once of the Sorbonne and later a Carthusian monk, declared that "If in one point the Vulgate were in error, the entire authority of Holy Scripture would collapse."(Ibid.).

"The 3rd edition (1522) is chiefly remarkable for the inclusion of 1 John 5:7, which had been omitted in the previous editions. The 4th edition (1527) contained the Greek text, the Latin Vulgate, and Erasmus' Latin translation in three parallel columns. The 5th edition (1535) omitted the Vulgate, thus resuming the practice of printing the Greek text and the version of Erasmus side by side." (*Way of Life Encyclopedia of the Bible* – Electronic Edition; Erasmus Article).

Because Erasmus was the first to publish a Greek New Testament, this gave rise to the saying, "Erasmus laid the egg that Luther hatched." In fact, **Tyndale hatched the "English egg"** of Erasmus with greater results than Luther. "The English would believe and practice it, an empire would be built, the Word would be spread to the ends of the earth and English would become an international language." (*The Legacy of our English Bible;* John Wesley Sawyer; self-published 1990; p.4)

In the later years of his life he made a multitude of enemies, though he did retain some faithful friends. He would not join the Protestants but neither would he attack them. In his final years Erasmus busied himself with solitude and study. Erasmus died in Basel on July 12, 1536 at the age of 67, in the midst of his Protestant friends, without a relationship of any sort with the Roman Catholic Church.

REVIEW

Let us take a moment to **review** before we move on. You will recall that Wycliffe's Bible made a dramatic impact upon the people. Historians write that at the end of the fourteenth century every other man in the street was a Lollard. This can be accounted for

because of the efforts of Wycliffe's so called "poor priests,"
"Gospellers," or "Evangelical Men." These pilgrim preachers
traveled across the land stopping by barn or hall or village green and
preached and read the Bible in the speech of the common people.
Church authorities were outraged by such practices! They urged the
Crown and Parliament to enact laws to stop such practices and for
the first time in the history of England "the civil sword was used to
smite down conscience in religion. The 15th century opened its age
of blood by the burning of William Sawtree (February, 1401), priest
and Wyclifite – the first name in the Book of English Martyrdom.
Lollardry is crushed and as a visible force or organization now
passes out of history." (*Fighters & Martyrs for the Freedom of Faith* by Luke
S. Walmsley; p.69).

One historian observes, "the Church of Rome had sent more
innocent blood than any other institution that has ever existed
among mankind." In fact, with the crushing of Wycliffe's Lollard
preachers in England, "outwardly there now sets in a long darkness
in Britain. But, behind barred shutter and hidden in superstitious
books the Light of the Word of God, in the language of the people
flickers." (Ibid.) The primary example comes to us from the
Gutenberg of England, printer William Caxton.

THE FIRST PRINTED BIBLE PORTIONS IN ENGLISH

"The first printed English book in which any portion of the Scriptures appeared was the *Golden Legend,* translated by William Caxton from French and Latin originals, and issued by the father of English printing (William Caxton). It was the largest book printed by Caxton, and even he found it no easy task to accomplish. The first English edition appeared in 1483." (*The Printed English Bible 1525-1885* by Richard Lovett; The Religious Tract Society of London; p.12). This work was originally written in Latin by Roman Catholic prelate Jacobus de Voragine (1230-1298). The work is made up of a large number of legends and superstitions of "saints," martyrs, bishops and monks. *Golden Legend* was first printed in Latin in 1470. And for the next six decades no book was reprinted more often than *Golden Legend* than the Bible.

Caxton knew of the great need and benefit an English Bible would have on his countrymen, but printing the Bible in English was a capital crime. He was a shrewd, far-seeing man but not a martyr. So he came up with a "middle course. He printed this collection of monkish legends as a book not obnoxious to the ecclesiastical authorities, and he inserted into it a very larger number of Bible stories and Bible words than any other edition of the *Golden Legend* contains. In this way the English reader was enabled to gather the outlines of the Gospel history and also of Old Testament story from Adam to Job. The special insertions made by Caxon practically covered the whole of the Old Testament narrative...As the only book in which for about twenty-five years Englishmen had access in a printed form to any part of God's Word, this sumptuous volume deserves to be held in reverence." (Ibid.).

Here is a famous example of the biblical insertions of William Caxton, the Gutenberg of England, in the 1483 *Golden Legend.*
"And when his oldest bother heard him speak to the people, he was wroth with him, and said, Wherefore art thou come hither and hast left the few sheep in the desert? I know well thy pride, thou art come for to see the battle. And David said, What have I done? Is it not as the people have said? I dare fight well with this giant, and declined from his brother to other of the people. And all this was shewed to Saul, and David was bought to him, and said to Saul, I thy servant shall fight against this giant, if thou wilt. And Saul said to him, Thou mayest not withstand this Philistine, nor fight against him, for thou art but a child; this giant hath been a fighter from his childhood. David said to Saul, I thy servant kept my father's sheep, and there came a lion and a bear, and took away a wether from the middle of my flock, and I pursued after, and took it again from their mouths, and they arose and whould have devoured me, and I caught them by the jaws and slew them. I thy servant slew the lion and the bear, therefore the Philistine uncircumcised shall be one of them. I shall now go and deliver Israel from this opprobrium and shame. How is this Philistine uncircumcised so hardly to curse the host of the living God? And yet said David, The Lord that kept me from the might of the lion and from the strength of the bear, He shall well deliver me from the power of this Philistine. Saul then said to David, Go, and the Lord be with thee."

Look in your Bible and read the account in 1 Samuel 17:28-37. You will discover that Caxton did a pretty good job relating the story.

Now we come to the **third and final key** that brought an end to the Dark Ages and prepared the way for the printing of the English Bible and that was...

CHAPTER #13

THE ENGLISH BIBLE AND THEIR TRANSLATORS

A new day had dawned with the development of the moveable type printing press and the fall of Constantinople, which precipitated the new learning by the revival of the Greek culture and language.

WILLIAM TYNDALE (BORN ABOUT 1492 – MARTYRED OCTOBER 6, 1536)

William Tyndale was the first man to translate the Erasmus Greek New Testament into English. He gave us the first printed English New Testament.

📖 FIRST EDITION TYNDALE NEW TESTAMENT – 1526
📖 SECOND REVISED & CORRECTED TYNDALE NEW TESTAMENT EDITION – 1534

In every book that I have read about William Tyndale, the authors rely heavily upon *Acts and Monuments* by John Foxe (Fox), commonly called *Fox's Book of Martyrs*, for their information. Now, when I say *Fox's Book of Martyrs* some think I am referring to what is available in the bookstores today. I am not. What is in the stores today has been severely edited and scarcely resembles the genuine original. The 9th edition of *Fox's Book of Martyrs* was published in 1683-84 and is the last ancient edition. It was published in three massive folio volumes and contains nearly 3,000 pages of type about the size that I am using. Most all of the primary information about Tyndale comes from John Fox. The abridged information I am sharing below comes primarily from John Fox's work.

William Tyndale, (also spelled Tindale & Tyndall), sometimes referred to himself as William Hychyns or Hutchins. Some sources say he was born as early as 1477. Others place his birth as late as 1505. Most place his birth around 1492 in the Gloucestershire area of England, possibly at Slymbridge. I have read several books that claim that he was born in North Nibley to Richard and possibly

Tebota Tyndale and he had a brother named Thomas. Professor David Daniell points out that <u>this is not possible</u> because this particular William Tyndale married Alice Hunt for one thing, and secondly, this William Tyndale "was still alive in the 1540's" (*William Tyndale: A Biography* by David Daniell; Yale University Press; 1994; p.10). William Tyndale the translator was burned at the stake in 1536.

The reason I believe <u>William Tyndale the translator</u> was born at Slymbridge is because "three miles north of Sinchcombe, beside the Severn (river), is the village of Slimbridge. In a house a mile and a half south-west of Slimbridge, known as Hurst Farm, lived an able and successful man named <u>Edward Tyndale</u>, who, according to a separate strand of information, was brother to <u>William the translator</u>. There exists two letters dated 1533 from the Bishop of London, John Stokesley, probably sent to Henry VIII's secretary, Thomas Cromwell, asking (with a sweetener of cash accompanying the second letter) that a certain Gloucestershire farm be given to an old servant of his, and not to the rival claimant, who 'hath an kinsman called Edward Tyndale the arch-heretic.'" (Ibid.)

Little is known of William Tyndale's childhood, except that he grew up in a very beautiful area of England. The main occupation of those living in Gloucestershire was agriculture. But, its close proximity to Bristol, the second largest sea port in England, after London, enabled the people of the area to be acquainted with the events going on in other parts of the world. The arrival of each ship brought news from different parts of the world.

We do not really know much about Tyndale's early life either. In about 1512 he entered Oxford. By 1515 he had earned his M.A. He then transferred to Cambridge University for a time. It is at Cambridge that he likely picked up his Protestant convictions because the teachings of Luther were prevalent at Cambridge in the early 1520's. John Foxe simply says, "This goodman, William Tyndale, the faithful minister and constant martyr of Christ, was born upon the boarders of Wales, and brought up even of a child in the University of Oxford, being always of most upright manners and pure life...**he increased** as well in the knowledge of tongues (languages), and other liberal arts, as especially **in the knowledge of the Scriptures, whereunto his mind was singularly addicted**."

Tyndale was a brilliant student. He had mastered seven languages – Hebrew, Greek, Latin, Italian, Spanish, French and English. It was said that he spoke each language so fluently that a person was unable to tell that it was not his mother tongue. In addition, he had a working know-ledge of German, which allowed him to translate and interpret the writings of Martin Luther.

In 1521 he left the university and entered into the employ of Sir John and Lady Anne Walsh at Little Sodbury Manor. Sir John hired Tyndale to tutor his two children shortly after he left Cambridge. Tyndale was a part time preacher. John Walsh gave Tyndale a small room in the loft. I have been up in that room. That room has a small window from which he could see the fields and plowboy plowing those fields. It was here that Tyndale began to feel compelled to translate the Bible into the English language because he knew that without it the plowboy and all common people had no hope of salvation without it. (Tyndale's loft room).

Tyndale's desire to translate the Bible into English became public one evening in the Great Hall at Little Sodbury Manor. Sir John and Lady Anne regularly entertained abbots, archdeacons, doctors and other area church officials. On this particular evening Tyndale became embroiled in a controversy over the ignorance of the clergy when it came to the Bible. The great doctor would point to some teaching of the pope and then Tyndale would answer by quoting what the Bible had to say on the matter. Time and time again the doctor would bring up some church dogma only to be corrected, and rightly so, by Tyndale quoting the Bible. Finally the doctor could stand no more. He raised his voice angrily and said, **"We were better to be without Gods laws than the popes."**

To that Tyndale responded, **"I defy the pope and all his laws. If God spare my life, ere many years pass, I will cause a boy that driveth the plow shall know more of the Scripture than thou dost."**

My wife Linda stands in The Great Hall where the Exchange Took Place

Tyndale had studied Erasmus' Greek New Testament. Perhaps he was echoing the famous inscription in that Erasmus had written in the preface of his Greek New Testament of 1516 –

"I would to God that the plowman would sing a text of the Scripture at his plow and that the weaver would hum them to the tune of his shuttle."

Soon after this encounter Tyndale felt compelled to leave Little Sodbury Manor. He went to London desiring to get ecclesiastical approval to translate the Bible from Greek into English from the Bishop of London, Cuthbert Tunstall. It soon became evident that permission would not be forthcoming. But what Tyndale did get was backing from Humphrey Manmoth and other merchants to start his translation work. In 1524 Tyndale sailed for Germany, never to see England again.

In Hamburg he worked on the New Testament, which was ready to be printed the next year. He found a printer in Cologne. As the pages of Matthew began to come off the press Tyndale was warned that a raid had been planned by Johann Dobneck (alias Cochlaeus). Dobneck was a leading opponent of the Reformation. Tyndale fled out the back door <u>with the pages that had been printed</u>, just as the authorities were coming in the front door. These Gospels of Matthew were bound and smuggled into England and distributed. Today, only one original 1525 Gospel portion is known to exist. It is called the Cologne Fragment. I had the opportunity to inspect that volume when there was a special display at the Library of Congress in Washington D.C. I found that the fragment ends in the middle of the verse in Matthew 22:12. It reads, "and sayed unto hym: frende howe caymrth thou in hydder and..."

Tyndale moved to Worms to continue his printing. It was a more reformed-minded city. It is evident to me that he consulted with Martin Luther during his stay. The reason I say this is because it is obvious that Tyndale used Luther's *Introduction to the Book of Romans*, as a basis for his *Prologue to Romans* and then added additional material. Luther's prologue, translated into English contains a little more than 6,400 words. Tyndale's prologue contains about 11,000 words. While a careful reading makes it obvious that Luther's prologue was the basis of Tyndale's prologue, it is clear that Tyndale deleted, changed and amplified the prologue another 4,600 words. Note: Luther had published his German September New Testament in 1522 translated from Erasmus' Greek New Testament.

In 1526 he printed 3,000 (some say 6,000) of these complete New Testaments. And yet, only two complete Bibles survived and one partial copy owned by St. Paul's. The second complete copy was just discovered in November of 1996 in Stuttgart, Germany. One reason so few survived was because Bishop Tunstall made arrangements to buy all of them he could get his hands on. He paid top dollar. In 1526 he preached against the translation and had great numbers of them ceremoniously burned at St. Paul's Cross. This stunned Tyndale greatly but the money he received enabled him to survive and produce the 1534 revision.

Tyndale moved to Antwerp, Belgium around 1527. Thomas Poyntz, the brother of Lady Ann Walsh of Little Sodbury Manor, befriended him and gave him a place to stay. There he translated the Pentateuch. He decided to sail to Hamburg to find a printer for this work but "along the coast of Holland a storm grounded the ship and it was wrecked. William survived, but lost all his work...his translations, his Hebrew Bible and dictionary and all his notebooks."(*The Tyndale Society of Oxford, Geneva and San Diego*; Audio-visual presentation on The Life and Work of William Tyndale; p.5).

cxiv.

The Gospell off
¶ Sancte Jhon.
¶ The fyrst Chapter.

IN the begynnynge was that worde / ād that worde was with god: and god was thatt worde. The same was in the begynnynge wyth god. All thyngf were made by itt / and with out it / was made noo thige / that made was. In it was lyfe / And lyfe was the light of mē / And the light shyneth i darcknes / ād darcknes cōprehēded it not. There was a mā sent from god / whose name was Jhon. The same cā as a witnes / to beare witnes of the light / that all men through hi myght beleve. He was nott that light: but to beare witnes of the light. That was a true light / which lighteneth all men that come ito the worlde. He was in the worlde / ād the worlde by hi was made: and the worlde knewe hym not. He cā ito his awne / ād his received hi not. vnto as meny as received hi / gave he power to be the sōnes of god: i that they beleved ō his name: which were borne not of bloude noz of the will of the flesshe / noz yet of the will of men: but of god. And that worde was made flesshe / and dwelt amonge vs / and we sawe the glory off yt / as the glory off the only begotten sonne off the father /

Page from 1526 Tyndale New Testament – John 1

Tyndale returned to Antwerp and began all over again. In 1530 he published the Pentateuch. In 1531 he published Jonah in pamphlet form. Between 1530 and 1535 he translated Joshua to 2 Chronicles, but they were not published until after his death. Finally, in 1534 Tyndale published his revised edition and they were smuggled into England. <u>Later on in this book you will be able to see how Romans 1 to 3 was translated in the Tyndale, Geneva and King James Bible.</u>

By 1535 orders had been given to hunt down Tyndale and stop him. Several Englishmen were hot on his trail. It was the underhanded Henry Phillips who found Tyndale and set the trap. On about May 21, 1535 two soldiers seized Tyndale as he left the home of Thomas Poyntz, Tyndale's friend. He was imprisoned in the dungeon of the Castle of Vilvoorde, which was located six miles north of Belgium. There he was kept for 18 months until everything was set for his trial. During his dungeon imprisonment he was able to lead the jailor and his family to the Lord. Despite the deplorable conditions in the dungeon, he desired to continue his translation work. With that thought in mind, I am including the letter he wrote.

A LETTER FROM PRISON, IN TYNDALE'S OWN HAND

The only known writing in Tyndale's hand still extant, this correspondence came from Tyndale sometime in the winter of 1535, as he was imprisoned in Vilvoorde Castle. It was addressed to the governor of the castle, that very Marquis of Bergen to whom Lord Chancellor Thomas Cromwell had already appealed on Tyndale's behalf. It appears here in Tyndale's hand, along with a printed transcription of Tyndale's Latin and an English translation of that Latin. Note Tyndale's respectful tone and concern for the governor's spiritual well-being, and the centrality of Tyndale's request for his Bible-translating books. (*Christian History: William Tyndale, Issue 16;* 1997 – Electronic Edition).

THE LATIN TRANSCRIBED

Credo non latere te, vir praestantissime, quid de me statutum sit. Quam ob rem, tuam dominationem rogatum habeo, idque per Dominum Jesum, ut si mihi per hiemem hic manendum sit, solicites apud dominum commissarium, si forte dignari veldt, de rebus meis quas habet, mittere calidiorem birettum; frigus enim patior in capite nimium, oppressus perpetuo catarro qui sub testitudine nonnihil augetur.

Calidiorem quoque tunicam, nam, haec quam habeo admodum tenuis est. Item pannum ad caligas reficiendas. Diplois detrita est; camiseae detritae sunt etiam. Camiseam laneam habet, si mittere velit. Habeo quoque apud eum caligas ex crassiori panno ad superius induendum; nocturna biretta calidiora habet etiam: utque vesper; lucernam habere liceat; tediosum quidem est per tenebras solitarie sedere.

Maxime autem omnium tuam clementiam rogo atque obsecro ut ex animo agere velit apud dominum commissarium quatenus dignari velit mihi concedere Bibliam Hebraicam, Grammaticam Hebraicam, et Vocabularium Hebraicum, ut eo studio tempus conteram. Sic tibi obtingat quod maxime optas modo cum animae tuae salute fiat: Verum si aliud consilium de me ceptum [sic] est, ante hiemem perficiendum, patiens ero, Dei expectans voluntatem, ad gloriam gratiae Domini mei Jesu Christi, Cujus Spiritus tuum semper regat pectus. Amen.
W. Tindalus

THE ENGLISH TRANSLATION

I believe, right worshipful, that you are not ignorant of what has been determined concerning me [by the Council of Brabant]; therefore I entreat your Lordship, and that by the Lord Jesus, that if I am to remain here [in Vilvoorde] during the winter, you will request the Procurer to be kind enough to send me from my goods, which he has in his possession, a warmer cap, for I suffer extremely from cold in the head, being afflicted with a perpetual catarrh, which is considerably increased in the cell.

A warmer coat also, for that which I have is very thin; also a piece of cloth to patch my leggings: my overcoat has been worn out; my shirts are also worn out. He has a woolen shirt of mine, if he will be kind enough to send it. I have also with him leggings of thicker cloth for the putting on above; he also has warmer caps for wearing at night. I wish also his permission to have a candle in the evening, for it is wearisome to sit alone in the dark.

But above all, I entreat and beseech your clemency to be urgent with the Procurer that he may kindly permit me to have my Hebrew Bible, Hebrew Grammar, and Hebrew Dictionary, that I may spend my time with that study. And in return, may you obtain your dearest wish, provided always it be consistent with the salvation of your soul. But if any other resolutions have been come to concerning me, before the conclusion of the winter, I shall be patient, abiding the will of God to the glory of the grace of my Lord Jesus Christ, whose spirit, I pray, may ever direct your heart. Amen. W. Tyndale

Finally, a long list of charges was drawn up against him. Here are just a few of the "heresies" he was charged with.

- **He maintained that faith alone justifies.**
- **He maintained that to believe in the forgiveness of sins, and to embrace the mercy offered in the gospel, was enough for salvation.**
- **He denied that there is any purgatory.**
- **He affirmed that neither the Virgin nor the Saints pray for us in their own person.**
- **He asserted that neither the Virgin nor the Saints should be invoked by us.**

William Tyndale was condemned as an heretic early in August, 1536. A few days later, with great pageantry and pomp he was cast out of the Church, defrocked from the priesthood and turned over to the state for punishment. For some strange reason he was returned to Vilvoorde Castle for another two months. Finally, early on the morning of **October 6, 1536** Tyndale was led to the stake. His feet were bound tightly to the stake. He was chained at the waist. A noose of hemp was threaded through the stake and placed abound Tyndale's neck. The crowd grew silent. Then, with a loud voice Tyndale prayed, "**Lord, open the king of England's eyes**." The executioner then snapped down on the noose and strangled him and then he was burned to ashes. It should be noted that God did answer Tyndale's prayer for within a year afterwards; a Bible was placed in every parish church by the King's command.

Though the translator was dead, the word of God was loosed! Many of the Tyndale Bibles got to England. But, the law still had not changed. It was illegal to possess, read or preach from any Bible in the language of the people. Dr. Jewell Smith gives this account of what happened to these men. Pastors William Woosley and Robert Pigot believed that it was more important to obey God rather than men and so they regularly did street preaching from the Tyndale Bible. They knew that *"faith cometh by hearing, and hearing by the word of God."* (**Romans 10:17**). One day as they were reading and preaching from the Tyndale Bible to the people gathered on the street, they were arrested and brought into court. Before the sentence was pronounced the judge asked Pastor Wolsey his belief concerning the Bible. If the pastors would have confirmed their allegiance to the Latin Vulgate of the Catholic Church and renounced their preaching of the Tyndale Bible as being heretical they could have been spared. But, they would not. Instead Pastor Wolsey said –

"I take the eternal God to my record that I do err no point or part of God's Word, The Holy Bible, but hold and believe the same to be the most firm sound doctrine in all points most worthy of my salvation and for all other Christians, to the end of the world."

The angry judge said, "William Wolsey and Robert Pigot, I sentence you to be burned at the stake with a slow burning." As soon as these two men heard their sentence read they knelt in prayer, in court, and prayed for the judge who had just condemned them to death. They prayed for the people in court. They prayed and asked the Lord to give them dying grace. When they were finished praying they got up off their knees and the historian tells us that they sang the Psalms and rejoiced, walking to the stake as joyfully as if they were going to a wedding instead of going to their deaths. They were chained to the stake by the waist and the fires were set. The green material burned slowly and almost went out. One of the religious leaders said, "Bring those Tyndale Bibles we confiscated." Two servants brought a sheet filled with Tyndale Bibles and they began to tear them up and throw them on the fire. Pastor Wolsey said, "Give me one of them." And while the fire burned their feet and their legs, Pastor Wolsey turned to the Gospel of John and read it to the people while Pastor Pigot prayed. The Holy Spirit moved in a mighty way. Many of the people came under a holy conviction and cried out, "Lord help these men." At least <u>one third of the people in the crowd</u> that had gathered to see the execution <u>came to know Christ as their Savior</u> according to one historian.

When the fire got so high that he could no longer read, he clutched the Bible to his breast while the fire did its work. Both pastors soon dropped their heads in physical death but they lifted them in Heaven unto eternal life in the presence of the Lord Jesus the next moment! Jesus says, *"...be thou faithful unto death, and I will give thee a crown of life."* **Revelation 2:10**

These two men had the attitude of the Apostle Paul – *According to my earnest expectation and my hope, that in nothing I shall be ashamed, but that with all boldness, as always, so now also Christ shall be magnified in my body, whether it be by life, or by death. 21 For to me to live is Christ, and to die is gain.* **Philippians 1:20-21**. Or as it read in their Tyndale Bibles – *" as I heartily look for and hope, that in nothing I shall be ashamed, but that with all confidence, as always in times past, even so now Christ shall be magnified in my body, whether it be through life, or else death. For Christ is to me life, and death is to me advantage."* (Tyndale 1526)

GEORGE JOYE'S UNAUTHORIZED MODIFICATION OF TYNDALE'S NEW TESTAMENT

"It is true that George Joye, in August, 1534, published an edition of the New Testament, which he claimed to have diligently corrected. He did it, he assertes, because Tindale was idle. Speaking of the interval, 1525-1534, (It was in 1534 that Tyndale published his revised edition), he says, 'All this while Tindale slept, for nothing came from him, as far as I could perceive.'" (*The Printed English Bible* by Rev. Richard Lovett; Religious Tract Society, 1894; p.49).

Joye could not have been more inaccurate in making this wild statement about Tyndale being asleep. During those nine years you will remember he was a hunted man, moving from place to place. And, despite those terrible circumstances he wrote, – *The Parable of the Wicked Mammon, Obedience of a Christian Man, The Practice of Prelates, the Answer to Sir Thomas More* and also translated into English the Pentateuch, and revised his New Testament, which came out in November of 1534. That's a fair amount of work in anyone's book.

It should come as no surprise to find out that Joye's New Testament was merely a reprint of Tyndale's, altered slightly, and where it is altered it is almost "invariably for the worse." In fact, "William Tyndale had to rebuke George Joye for secretly and without authorization publishing a corrected version of Tyndale's work which omitted the word *resurrection*. The preface of Tyndale's New Testament of 1534 describes the problem and Tyndale's response." (*The Testimony Founded For Ever* by James H. Sightler, 1999; M.D.; p.84).

Here is what Tyndale wrote –

"For throughout Matthew, Mark, and Luke perpetually: and oft in the Acts, and sometime in John and also in Hebrews, where he findeth this word Resurrection, he changeth it into the life after this life, or very life, and such like, as one that abhorred the name of the resurrection...Moreover ye shall understand that George Joye hath had of a long time marvellous imaginations about this word resurrection, that it should be taken for the state of the souls after their departing from their bodies, and hath also (though he hath been reasoned with thereof and desired to cease) yet sown his doctrine by secret letters on that side of the sea, and caused great division among the brethren.. .Thereto I have been since informed that no small number through his curiosity, utterly deny the resurrection of the flesh and body, affirming that the soul when she is departed, is the spiritual body of the resurrection, and other resurrection shall there none be... Wherefore concerning the resurrection I protest before God and our Saviour Jesus Christ, and before the universal congregation that believeth in Him, that I believe according to the open and manifest scriptures and catholic faith, that Christ is risen again in the flesh which He received of His mother the blessed virgin Mary, and body wherein He died. And that we shall both good and bad rise both flesh and body, and appear together before the judgment seat of Christ, to receive every man according to his deeds. And that the bodies of all that believe and continue in the true faith of Christ, shall be endued with like immortality and glory as is the body of Christ."

To my knowledge there is only one copy of George Joye's work known to exist. It is in the British Museum. His New Testament had scarce influence on the course of English Bible Translation.

MYLES COVERDALE – 1488-1569

📖 *1535 – COVERDALE BIBLE: THE FIRST COMPLETE PRINTED ENGLISH BIBLE*
📖 *1537 – COVERDALE REVISED & CORRECTED EDITION*

MILES COVERDALE.

Myles (Miles) Coverdale was born in Yorkshire, England in 1487 or 1488. He was educated at Cambridge. Coverdale was ordained (1514) and entered the house of Augustinian friars at Cambridge. In 1527 he writes a letter to a friend telling how the love of Bible study has possessed his soul. He writes – "Now I begin to taste of the Holy Scripture; now, honour be to God! I am set to the sweet smell of holy letters, with the godly savor of holy and ancient doctors..."

The study of the Bible obviously changes him. From this point on there is a major shift in his beliefs. Coverdale developed an appreciation of Martin Luther and his teachings and becomes an advocate of church reform. The record shows that he was forced (1528) to reside abroad for his preaching against confession to the priest and images. There he met William Tyndale and worked with him on his translation efforts, primarily as a proofreader.

But Coverdale was not idle! When Tyndale was imprisoned, Coverdale felt compelled to get the entire Word of God in English to the people. And he succeeded. At almost the same time that the flames were consuming William Tyndale for the heresy of translating the Bible into English, Myles Coverdale was publishing the first complete English Bible (1535). But, he was neither a Hebrew nor Greek scholar like Tyndale and he knew his limitations, and admitted them! Yet the demand and need for the Bible was great so he was willing to assume both the task and the risk. Here is what he says in his own words...

"Considering how excellent knowledge and learning an interpreter of Scripture ought to have in the tongues, and pondering also mine own insufficiency therein, and how weak I am to perform the office of a translator, I was the more loath to meddle with this work. Notwithstanding, when I considered how great pity it was we should want for so long, *and call to my remembrance the adversity of them which were not only of ripe knowledge, but would also with all their hearts have performed that they began, it they had not had impediment...* I was fain to take it in hand. And to help me therein, I have had sundry translations, not only in Latin, but also of the Dutch (i.e. German) interpreters, whom, because of their singular gifts and special diligence in the Bible, I have been the more glad to follow for the most part, according as I was required."

He went forward with his task to completion and made this comment in the dedication to Henry VIII in his 1535 Bible - "I have with a clear conscience purely and faithfully translated this out of five sundry interpreters, having only the manifest truth of the Scriptures before mine eyes."

"Scholars who have been at the pains of collating this Bible with the Latin and German versions to which Coverdale would have access, are generally agreed in specifying his *"five* sundry interpreters" to have been as follows:

1. The Swiss-German (or Zurich) Bible, by Zwingli and Leo Juda, which was completed in 1529, and which is characterised rather by smoothness, grace, and rhythmic flow of phrase, than by any very rigorous fidelity to the original.
2. Luther's German Bible.
3. The Vulgate.
4. The Latin Bible of 1528 by Pagninus, a Dominican monk, a pupil of Savonarola, and a teacher of Oriental literature at Rome under Leo X.
5. Either Tyndale's translation, or else some additional Latin, or perhaps German, version." (*The Evolution of The Bible* by W. H. Hoare; p. 125).

Coverdale's translation efforts were not finished. Henry VIII's Secretary of State, Thomas Cromwell, asked Coverdale to prepare a new translation since Henry would never sanction Tyndale's New Testament. Coverdale had proven that he was a careful editor and compiler and had a natural ability to select and use whatever materials he had available to him in his own Bible. Yet he knew that improvements were needed, so he accepted the task. The result **was the Great Bible** or **Chained Bible** (1539). He also edited the revision called **Cranmer's Bible** (1540). By decree, Cranmer's revision of the Great Bible was put in all the English churches so it could be available to the people. I should also note that Coverdale **contributed to the Geneva Bible** (1560).

With the passage of the anti-reformation Six Articles, Coverdale fled to the continent again, returning in 1547 after the death of Henry VIII. He enjoyed high favor under Edward VI, serving as bishop of Exeter from 1551 to 1553. On Mary's (Bloody Mary) accession he lost his pastorate and was arrested and put in prison with many of the other leading English reformers. His letters indicate that they expected to be burned at the stake for their faith. He wrote –

"You shall see in us that we preached no lies, nor tales of tubs, but even the true word of God, for which we, by God's grace, and help of your prayers, will willingly and joyfully give our blood to be shed for confirmation of the same."

The reference to "*tales of tubs*" refers to the fabulous tale of Saint Nicholas (i.e. Nicholas of Myra) who is alleged to have brought back to life two boys who had been murdered and butchered and hidden in a pickle tub of brine.

In another letter he exhorts the professors of the gospel to be steadfast in their course. He exhorted them –

"Like God's children let us go on forward apace; the wind is on our back. Hoist up the sails, lift up your hearts and hands unto God in prayer; and keep your anchor of faith to cast in time on the rock of God's Word, and on his mercy in Christ...."

The "powers that be" fully intended that Coverdale should suffer martyrdom, but he had become related, by marriage, to the Chaplin of the King of Denmark, so the King of Denmark intervened on his behalf. It took twelve months to secure his release. Bloody Mary tried to evade complying with the Danish King's request by alleging that Coverdale was in prison for a debt due to her by reason of his bishopric. But that ruse did not work because the King said he would gladly pay any outstanding monies owed to her by Coverdale. Queen Mary finally released Coverdale on the condition that he leave England. He first went to Denmark, but because he did not know the language and therefore was unable to preach the Word, he left and went to Geneva, where he ministered, preaching and teaching. It was not long before he connected with the several other fellow exiles and joined them in preparing the Geneva translation of the English Bible released in 1560.

He returned after Elizabeth's succession, and became widely known for his eloquent sermons and addresses. He was rector of St. Magnus, London Bridge, from 1563 to 1566, but resigned when Archbishop Parker sought to enforce the Act of Uniformity, which Coverdale objected to. He went home to be with the Lord in **February of 1568**.

Below is the text from the Elizabeth's 1559 Act of Uniformity. This particular Act is distinguished among the several Uniformity Acts by the stringency of its penalties. It was passed in April of 1559.

> "Where at the death of our late sovereign lord King Edward VI there remained one uniform order of common service and prayer, and of the administration of sacraments, rites, and ceremonies in the Church of England, which was set forth in one book, intituled: The Book of Common Prayer, and Administration of Sacraments, and other rites and ceremonies in the Church of England; authorized by Act of Parliament holden in the fifth and sixth years of our said late sovereign lord King Edward VI, intituled: An Act for the uniformity of common prayer, and administration of the sacraments; the which was repealed and taken away by Act of Parliament in the first year of the reign of our late sovereign lady Queen Mary, to the great decay of the due honour of God, and discomfort to the professors of the truth of Christ's religion:

"Be it therefore enacted by the authority of this present Parliament, that the said statute of repeal, and everything therein contained, only concerning the said book, and the service, administration of sacraments, rites, and ceremonies contained or appointed in or by the said book, shall be void and of none effect, from and after the feast of the Nativity of St. John Baptist next coming; and that the said book, with the order of service, and of the administration of sacraments, rites, and ceremonies, with the alterations and additions therein added and appointed by this statute, shall stand and be, from and after the said feast of the Nativity of St. John Baptist, in full force and effect, according to the tenor and effect of this statute; anything in the aforesaid statute of repeal to the contrary notwithstanding.

"And further be it enacted by the queen's highness, with the assent of the Lords (sic) and Commons in this present Parliament assembled, and by authority of the same, that all and singular ministers in any cathedral or parish church, or other place within this realm of England, Wales, and the marches of the same, or other the queen's dominions, shall from and after the feast of the Nativity of St. John Baptist next coming be bounden to say and use the Matins, Evensong, celebration of the Lord's Supper and administration of each of the sacraments, and all their common and open prayer, in such order and form as is mentioned in the said book, so authorized by Parliament in the said fifth and sixth years of the reign of King Edward VI, with one alteration or addition of certain lessons to be used on every Sunday in the year, and the form of the Litany altered and corrected, and two sentences only added in the delivery of the sacrament to the communicants, and none other or otherwise.

"And that if any manner of parson, vicar, or other whatsoever minister, that ought or should sing or say common prayer mentioned in the said book, or minister the sacraments, from and after the feast of the nativity of St. John Baptist next coming, refuse to use the said common prayers, or to minister the sacraments in such cathedral or parish church, or other places as he should use to minister the same, in such order and form as they be mentioned and set forth in the said book, or shall wilfully or obstinately standing in the same, use any other rite, ceremony, order, form, or manner of celebrating of the Lord's Supper, openly or privily, or Matins, Evensong, administration of the sacraments, or other open prayers, than is mentioned and set forth in the said book (open prayer in and throughout this Act, is meant that prayer which is for other to come unto, or hear, either in common churches or private chapels or oratories, commonly called the service of the Church), or shall preach, declare, or speak anything in the derogation or depraving of the said book, or anything therein contained, or of any part thereof, and shall be thereof lawfully convicted, according to the laws of this realm, by verdict of twelve men, or by his own confession, or by the notorious evidence of the fact, shall lose and forfeit to the queen's highness, her heirs and successors, for his first offence, the profit of all his spiritual benefices or promotions coming or arising in one whole year next after his conviction; and also that the person so convicted shall for the same offence suffer imprisonment by the space of six months, without bail or mainprize.

"And if any such person once convicted of any offence concerning the premises, shall after his first conviction eftsoons offend, and be thereof, in form aforesaid, lawfully convicted, that then the same person shall for his second offence suffer imprisonment by the space of one whole year, and also shall therefore be deprived, ipso facto, of all his spiritual promotions; and that it shall be lawful to all patrons or donors of all and singular the same spiritual promotions, or of any of them, to present or collate to the same, as though the person and persons so offending were dead.

"And that if any such person or persons, after he shall be twice convicted in form aforesaid, shall offend against any of the premises the third time, and shall be thereof, in form aforesaid, lawfully convicted, that then the person so offending and convicted the third time, shall be deprived, ipso facto, of all his spiritual promotions, and also shall suffer imprisonment during his life.

"And if the person that shall offend, and be convicted in form aforesaid, concerning any of the premises, shall not be beneficed, nor have any spiritual promotion, that then the same person so offending and convicted shall for the first offence suffer imprisonment during one whole year next after his said conviction, without bail or mainprize. And if any such person, not having any spiritual promotion, after his first conviction shall eftsoons offend in anything concerning the premises, and shall be, in form aforesaid, thereof lawfully convicted, that then the same person shall for his second offence suffer imprisonment during his life.

"And it is ordained and enacted by the authority aforesaid, that if any person or persons whatsoever, after the said feast of the Nativity of St. John Baptist next coming, shall in any interludes, plays, songs, rhymes, or by other open words, declare or speak anything in the derogation, depraving, or despising of the same book, or of anything therein contained, or any part thereof, or shall, by open fact, deed, or by open threatenings, compel or cause, or otherwise procure or maintain, any parson, vicar, or other minister in any cathedral or parish church, or in chapel, or in any other place, to sing or say any common or open prayer, or to minister any sacrament otherwise, or in any other manner and form, than is mentioned in the said book; or that by any of the said means shall unlawfully interrupt or let any parson, vicar, or other minister in any cathedral or parish church, chapel, or any other place, to sing or say common and open prayer, or to minister the sacraments or any of them, in such manner and form as is mentioned in the said book; that then every such person, being thereof lawfully convicted in form abovesaid, shall forfeit to the queen our sovereign lady, her heirs and successors, for the first offence a hundred marks.

"And if any person or persons, being once convicted of any such offence, eftsoons offend against any of the last recited offences, and shall, in form aforesaid, be thereof lawfully convicted, that then the same person so offending and convicted shall, for the second offence, forfeit to the queen our sovereign lady, her heirs and successors, four hundred marks.

"And if any person, after he, in form aforesaid, shall have been twice convicted of any offence concerning any of the last recited offences, shall offend the third time, and be thereof, in form abovesaid, lawfully convicted, that then every person so offending and convicted shall for his third offence forfeit to our sovereign lady the queen all his goods and chattels, and shall suffer imprisonment during his life.

"And if any person or persons, that for his first offence concerning the premises shall be convicted, in form aforesaid, do not pay the sum to be paid by virtue of his conviction, in such manner and form as the same ought to be paid, within six weeks next after his conviction; that then every person so convicted, and so not paying the same, shall for the same first offence, instead of the said sum, suffer imprisonment by the space of six months, without bail or mainprize. And if any person or persons, that for his second offence concerning the premises shall be convicted in form aforesaid, do not pay the said sum to be paid by virtue of his conviction and this statute, in such manner and form as the same ought to be paid, within six weeks next after his said second conviction; that then every person so convicted, and not so paying the same, shall, for the same second offence, in the stead of the said sum, suffer imprisonment during twelve months, without bail or mainprize.

"And that from and after the said feast of the Nativity of St. John Baptist next coming, all and every person and persons inhabiting within this realm, or any other the queen's majesty's dominions, shall diligently and faithfully, having no lawful or reasonable excuse to be absent, endeavour themselves to resort to their parish church or chapel accustomed, or upon reasonable let thereof, to some usual place where common prayer and such service of God shall be used in such time of let, upon every Sunday and other days ordained and used to be kept as holy days, and then and there to abide orderly and soberly during the time of the common prayer, preachings, or other service of God there to be used and ministered; upon pain of punishment by the censures of the Church, and also upon pain that every person so offending shall forfeit for every such offence twelve pence, to be levied by the churchwardens of the parish where such offence shall be done, to the use of the poor of the same parish, of the goods, lands, and tenements of such offender, by way of distress.

"And for due execution hereof, the queen's most excellent majesty, the Lords temporal (sic), and all the Commons, in this present Parliament assembled, do in God's name earnestly require and charge all the archbishops, bishops, and other ordinaries, that they shall endeavour themselves to the uttermost of their knowledges, that the due and true execution hereof may be had throughout their dioceses and charges, as they will answer before God, for such evils and plagues wherewith Almighty God may justly punish His people for neglecting this good and wholesome law.

"And for their authority in this behalf, be it further enacted by the authority aforesaid, that all and singular the same archbishops, bishops, and all other their officers exercising ecclesiastical jurisdiction, as well in place exempt as not exempt, within their dioceses, shall have full power and authority by this Act to reform, correct, and punish by censures of the Church, all and singular persons which shall offend within any their jurisdictions or dioceses, after the said feast of the Nativity of St. John Baptist next coming, against this Act and statute; any other law, statute, privilege, liberty, or provision heretofore made, had, or suffered to the contrary notwithstanding.

"And it is ordained and enacted by the authority aforesaid, that all and every justices of oyer and terminer, or justices of assize, shall have full power and authority in every of their open and general sessions, to inquire, hear, and determine all and all manner of offences that shall be committed or done contrary to any article contained in this present Act, within the limits of the commission to them directed, and to make process for the execution of the same, as they may do against any person being indicted before them of trespass, or lawfully convicted thereof.

"Provided always, and be it enacted by the authority aforesaid, that all and every archbishop and bishop shall or may, at all time and times, at his liberty and pleasure, join and associate himself, by virtue of this Act, to the said justices of oyer and terminer, or to the said justices of assize, at every of the said open and general sessions to be holden in any place within his diocese, for and to the inquiry, hearing, and determining of the offences aforesaid.

"Provided also, and be it enacted by the authority aforesaid, that the books concerning the said services shall, at the cost and charges of the parishioners of every parish and cathedral church, be attained and gotten before the said feast of the Nativity of St. John Baptist next following; and that all such parishes and cathedral churches, or other places where the said books shall be attained and gotten before the said feast of the Nativity of St. John Baptist, shall, within three weeks next after the said books so attained and gotten, use the said service, and put the same in use according to this Act.

"And be it further enacted by the authority aforesaid, that no person or persons shall be at any time hereafter impeached or otherwise molested of or for any the offences above mentioned, hereafter to be committed or done contrary to this Act, unless he or they so offending be thereof indicted at the next general sessions to be holden before any such justices of oyer and terminer or justices of assize, next after any offence committed or done contrary to the tenor of this Act.

"Provided always, and be it ordained and enacted by the authority aforesaid, that all and singular lords of the Parliament, for the third offence above mentioned, shall be tried by their peers.

"Provided also, and be it ordained and enacted by the authority aforesaid, that the mayor of London, and all other mayors, bailiffs, and other head officers of all and singular cities, boroughs, and towns corporate within this realm, Wales, and the marches of the same, to the which justices of assize do not commonly repair, shall have full power and authority by virtue of this Act to inquire, hear, and determine the offences abovesaid, and every of them, yearly within fifteen days after the feasts of Easter and St. Michael the Archangel, in like manner and form as justices of assize and oyer and terminer may do.

"Provided always, and be it ordained and enacted by the authority aforesaid, that all and singular archbishops and bishops, and every their chancellors, commissaries, archdeacons, and other ordinaries, having any peculiar ecclesiastical jurisdiction. shall have full power and authority by virtue of this Act, as well to inquire in their visitation, synods, and elsewhere within their jurisdiction at any other time and place, to take occasions (sic) and informations of all and every the things above mentioned, done, committed, or perpetrated within the limits of their jurisdictions and authority, and to punish the same by admonition, excommunication, sequestration, or deprivation, and other censures and processes, in like form as heretofore has been used in like cases by the queen's ecclesiastical laws.

"Provided always, and be it enacted, that whatsoever person offending in the premises shall, for the offence, first receive punishment of the ordinary, having a testimonial thereof under the said ordinary's seal, shall not for the same offence eftsoons be convicted before the justices: and likewise receiving, for the said offence, first punishment by the justices, he shall not for the same offence eftsoons receive punishment of the ordinary; anything contained in this Act to the contrary notwithstanding.

"Provided always, and be it enacted, that such ornaments of the church, and of the ministers thereof, shall be retained and be in use, as was in the Church of England, by authority of Parliament, in the second year of the reign of King Edward VI, until other order shall be therein taken by the authority of the queen's majesty, with the advice of her commissioners appointed and authorized, under the great seal of England, for causes ecclesiastical, or of the metropolitan of this realm.

"And also, that if there shall happen any contempt or irreverence to be used in the ceremonies or rites of the Church, by the misusing of the orders appointed in this book, the queen's majesty may, by the like advice of the said commissioners or metropolitan, ordain and publish such further ceremonies or rites, as may be most for the advancement of God's glory, the edifying of His Church, and the due reverence of Christ's holy mysteries and sacraments.

"And be it further enacted by the authority aforesaid, that all laws, statutes, and ordinances, wherein or whereby any other service, administration of sacraments or common prayer, is limited, established, or set forth to be used within this realm, or any other the queen's dominions or countries, shall from henceforth be utterly void and of none effect. (*Documents Illustrative of English Church History – Elizabeth's Act of Uniformity* (1559), 1 Elizabeth, Cap. 2; Gee, Henry, and William John Hardy, ed., published by Macmillan, 1896; pp. 458-67).

Coverdale had come to believe that it was the Bible, particularly the New Testament that was to guide the faith and practice of the Church, not the Book of Common Prayer.

As I conclude this section, I would like to point out just a few of the passages from Coverdale's Bible that were assimilated into the King James Bible –

"Seek the Lord while he may be found, call upon him while he is nigh." **Isaiah 55:6**

"My flesh and my heart faileth, but God is the strength of my heart and my portion for ever." **Psalm 73:26**

"Thou, Lord, in the beginning hast laid the foundations of the earth, and the heavens are the works of thy hands. They shall perish but thou shalt endure; they all shall wax old, as doth a garment, and as a vesture shalt thou change them, and they shall be changed. But thou art the same, and thy years shall not fail." **Hebrews 1:10-12**

Finally, I have included **Psalm 23 – Coverdale Translation**

"The Lorde is my shepherde, I can wante nothing. He fedeth me in the grene pasture, and leadeth me to a fresh water. He quickeneth my soule and bringeth me forth in the way of righteousness for his names sake. Though I should walke now in the valley of the shadowe of death, yet I feare no evell, for thou art with me: thy staffe and thy shepehoke comforte me. Thou preparest a table before me against mine enemies: thou anoyntest my head with oyle, and fyllest my cuppe full. Oh let thy lovying kindness and mercy folowe me all the dayes off my life, that I maye dwell in the house of the Lorde for ever."

JOHN ROGERS BORN IN 1500 – MARTYRED FEBRUARY 4, 1555

📖 1537 FIRST EDITION OF MATTHEWS BIBLE

Who was Thomas Matthew? Historians disagree on the answer. Some say it was an alias of William Tyndale. Most believe it was the alias of John Rogers. A few believe it was a real person who assisted John Rogers in the preparation of this Bible. But, historians do agree that it was John Rogers who was the editor of this Bible published in 1537.

John Rogers was born about 1500 and martyred in 1555. He received his B.A. degree at Cambridge in 1525. From there he entered the priesthood and went to Christ Church, then called Cardinal College in Oxford, England. About 1534 he became chaplain to the Merchant

Adventurers at Antwerp. There he met William Tyndale and Myles Coverdale. These two men witnessed to him and as a result he came to a saving knowledge of Jesus Christ. John Foxe writes of his conversion – **"In conferring with them the Scriptures, he came to great knowledge in the Gospel of God, insomuch that he cast off the heavy yoke of popery, perceiving it to be impure and filthy idolatry...."**

In May of 1535 Tyndale was arrested and imprisoned, but he continued to work on his translation of the Old Testament. On October 6th, 1536 he was tied to a stake in Vilvorde, prayed "Lord, Open the King's eyes," and was strangled and burned to ashes. But, Tyndale had given his disciple, John Rogers, his unpublished manuscripts from Johsua through Chronicles. Tyndale had published the Pentateuch in 1530 and Jonah in 1531. Rogers busied himself preparing to publish all of Tyndale's Bible translation work. The **"Matthews" Bible was better than Coverdale's version because it had been carefully translated from the original Hebrew and Greek**. What was missing (Ezra through Malachi) he filled in with Coverdale's translation. The only translation that Rogers actually did was the prayer of Manasses in the Apocrypha, which he translated from the 1535 Olivetan Bible.

The editorial and collation work were at last completed and it was sent to the printer, probably in Antwerp. The printed pages were then sent to England under the name of the "Matthew's Bible," no doubt because Tyndale Bibles were illegal in England. The London printers Grafton and Whitechurch were to complete the Bible and sell it.

The Bible included a flattering dedication to the King and was signed, **"Your Grace's faithful and true subject, Thomas Matthew."** They passed along a proof copy to Archbishop Thomas Cranmer. On August 4, 1537 the archbishop sent a letter to King Henry VIII's Secretary of State saying –

"You shall receive...a Bible in English, both of a new translation and of a new print, dedicated unto the King's Majesty...which in my opinion is very well done, and therefore I pray your lordship to read the same. And as for the translation, so far as I have read thereof, I like it better than any other translation herefore made; yet not doubting that there may and will be found some fault therein, as you know no man ever did or can do so well, but it may be from time to time amended. And for as much as the book is dedicated to the King's Grace, and also great pains and labour taken in setting forth of the same, I pray you, my lord, that you will exhibit the book unto the King's Highness, and that you will obtain of his Grace, if you can, a license that the same may be sold and read of every person, without danger of any Act, or proclamation, or ordinance heretofore granted to the contrary, until such time that we, the bishops, shall set forth a better translation, which I think will not be until a day after doomsday."

Thomas Cromwell did take it to the King and amazingly the King licensed the Matthew's Bible. We know this because on August 13th Cranmer receives a letter from Cromwell saying that "he hath not only exhibited the Bible to the King's Majesty, but also obtained of his grace that the same shall be allowed by his authority to be bought and read within this realm." This is ironic. Why? Because Tyndale's huge initials **WT** and even his name are found throughout in the prefaces and notes in it. Obviously neither the King nor

Cromwell examined the book that closely, though I believe the Archbishop knew full well its contents.

There are two editions of the Matthew's Bible that have a strange nickname. The 1549 & 1551 editions are called **the Wife Beaters Bible** because of a note on 1 Peter 3, which probably originated with Erasmus. The note reads...

"He dwelleth wyth his wife according to knowledge, that taketh her as a necessarye healper, and not as a bonde seruaunte or bonde slaue. And yf she be not obedient and healpfull vnto hym endeueureth to beate the feare of God into her heade, that therby she maye be compelled to learne her dutie, and to do it. But chiefely he muste beware that he halte not in anye parte of his dutie to her ward. For his evill example, shall destroye more than al the instructions he can geve, shall edifie."

As strange as it may seem, this was an era when the corporeal punishment of an errant wife was perfectly legal. The "rule of thumb" was law. Some have claimed that this phrase has its origins in a British common law rule which, allowed husbands to beat their wives with a stick no thicker than their thumb.

Blackstone, in his enormously influential *Commentaries on the Laws of England* (1765), writes that "The husband also (by the old law) might give his wife moderate correction. For, as he is to answer for her misbehaviour, the law thought it reasonable to intrust him with this power of restraining her, by domestic chastisement, in the same moderation that a man is allowed to correct his servants or children; for whom the master or parent is also liable in some cases to answer. But this power of correction was confined within reasonable bounds; and the husband was prohibited to use any violence to his wife, aliter quam ad virum, ex causa regiminis et castigationis uxoris suae, licited et rationabiliter pertinet [other than what is reasonably necessary to the discipline and correction of the wife]. The civil law gave the husband the same, or a larger, authority over his wife; allowing him, for some misdemeanors, flagellis et fustibus acriter verbare uxorem [to wound his wife severely with whips and fists]; for others, only modicam castigationem adhibere [to apply modest corrective punishment]."
(Taken from information at:

http://www.urbanlegends.com/language/etymology/ruleofthumb. html).

In light of the times, <u>it would be wrong to conclude that John Rogers was a woman hater and poor testimony</u>. Some scholars believe the note did not even originate with Rogers but with Erasmus. No one knows for sure. We do know that Rogers had a dedicated wife and eleven children. However, it is true that John Rogers was a strong, uncompromising, preacher. He rose through the ranks in King Edward's reign until he was appointed as "divine lecturer" at St. Paul's Church in London. When Bloody Mary came to the throne, he preached a strong message at St. Paul's Cross telling the people to follow the Bible doctrines taught in King Edward's time and warning them against "pestilent Popery, idolatry and superstition." The queen had him arrested and brought to trial. His popish judges urged him to revoke his stand on the Bible in English and his preaching against Catholic dogma. He responded **"That which I have preached I will seal with my blood!"** On January 28th and 29th he came before the ecclesiastical court and was sentenced to be burned at Smithfield for heretically denying the Christian character of the Church of Rome and denying the real presence of Christ in the Sacraments. On **February 4th, 1555** he was led out of prison to Smithfield. On the way his wife and ten of their eleven children (he had married back in 1537) met him. The French Ambassador writes of his amazement at seeing the support given to John Rogers by the people and his own family. He wrote, **"even his children assisted at it, comforting him in such a manner that it seemed as if he had been led to a wedding."** He was tied to the stake and the fires were lit and as they engulfed him the historian says, "he washed his hands in the flames, as though it had been in cold water."

John Rogers was the first martyr of Bloody Mary's reign, and his friend, John Bradford, wrote that **"he broke the ice valiantly."**

"The permanent interest of the 'Matthew' Bible lies in the fact that it forms the real basis of all later revisions, and that through the line of the Great Bible, and of the Bishops' Bible, our Authorised Version is descended from it as from a direct ancestor." (*The Evolution of The English Bible* by W. H. Hoare; p. 129).

I will conclude this section on John Rogers and his Matthews Bible by including **Psalm 23** from the Matthews Bible.

> The Lord is my Shepherd, I can want nothing. He feedeth me in a green pasture, and leadeth me to a fresh water. He quickeneth my soul, and bringeth me forth in the eay of righteousness for his name sake. Though I should walk now in the valley of the shadow of death, yet I fear no evil, for thou art with me: thy staff and thy sheephook comfort me. Thou prepareth a table before me against my enemies: Thou anointest my head with oil, and fillest my cup full, Oh let thy loving kindness and mercy follow me all the days of my life, that I may dwell in the house of the Lord forever.

📖 1539 - TAVERNER'S BIBLE

It did not take long for the true history of Matthew's Bible to become known, and the King's advisers realized the very unpleasant fact, that in procuring for it a royal license they had fooled the King. They realized this could cause their heads to be separated from their bodies! After all, King Henry the VIII, upon the advice of these same spiritual leaders had ordered Tyndale's translations to be burned, supposedly because the translation was replete with error. Further, the King had employed an agent to search for Tyndale and apprehend him as a promoter of heresies and sedition. Yet the King had been persuaded, unknowingly, to grant a license for the circulation of what was essentially Tyndale's translation. This was extremely awkward for Henry's advisers. When Cromwell and Cranmer discovered the real import of their act, they set to work as quickly and as quietly as possible to minimize the effects of the license.

Neither the Bible of Coverdale nor the Bible of Rogers (Matthews Bible) was altogether satisfactory. The inaccuracy of Coverdale's version caused it to lose ground. Remember, it was not a translation from the Greek. The boldness of Matthew's notes was unpalatable to the powers that be. Therefore, the ecclesiastical powers that be thought it was necessary to revise all the existing translations. Richard Taverner, an excellent Greek scholar, was persuaded by Thomas Cromwell to undertake the work.

Taverner "was born at Brisley, Norfolk, about 1505, and after some time spent at Benet College (Corpus Christi), Cambridge, entered the Cardinal College, Oxford, under the patronage of Cromwell. He took the degree of B.A. there in 1529. For reading Tyndale's New Testament he and some others were imprisoned in the college cellar, and it is said that he owed his speedy release to his musical skill. In 1534 he went to court, became attached to the service of (Thomas) Cromwell, and through his recommendation was appointed in 1537, a clerk of the signet." (*English Versions of The Bible* by Rev. J. I. Mombert, D.D.; Bagster & Sons, 1883; p.194-195).

Translating the Bible is a monumental and time-consuming task. Taverner was under such pressure and given such little time to complete the project that what he did was little more than to correct the English of Matthew's Bible by the Vulgate, and to delete many of its notes. "The influence of the Vulgate is very pronounced in his rendering of the Old Testament. And in the New Testament his changes, though sometimes from a desire to adhere closely to the original, are obscure, and through haste he has left uncorrected errors which could not have escaped him, if he had paid greater attention to his work." (Ibid. p.198-190).

He explains in his dedication how absurd it was for anyone to suppose that any single man could make a faultless translation of the Bible in a year's time.

This Bible, published in London in 1539, was allowed to be publicly read in the churches. The truth of the matter is that this translation had very little influence on subsequent versions.

📖 1539 – FIRST EDITION GREAT BIBLE

📖 1540 – CRANMER EDITION APPOINTED TO BE READ IN THE CHURCHES
(Also known as Cranmer's, Cromwell's, Whitchurch's or the Chained Bible)

Two English Bibles, Coverdale's and Matthews, were now being sold by the authorization of the King. There had been no further decrees. However, Coverdale's Bible was inaccurate in places and was not translated from the originals. Further, it was feared that the

Matthew's Bible, which could be called the joint Tyndale-Coverdale Bible, might cause trouble for its promoters, if the shrewd Bishop Gardiner and his friends should succeed in unmasking it for what it was. Thomas Cromwell did not want to put his eggs, as it were, all in the Taverner basket. He saw these deficiencies in Coverdale's first work and the dangers associated with the Matthews Bible. Therefore, he again

THOMAS CROMWELL.

appealed to Myles Coverdale to prepare another Bible. He instructed that it must contain no notes. The outcome was called "The Great Bible" because of its large dimensions. It was the largest English Bible ever published to that time. Though the pages with margins were larger, "its actual dimensions of engraved space are 13 ½ X 9 inches." (*English Versions of The Bible* by J. I. Mombert; 1883; p.204). Indeed it was a large folio, in black letter, without notes, and without any dedication. Its title-page reads as follows:

"The Byble in Englyshe, that is to saye the content of all the holy scripture, bothe of the old and newe testament, truly translated after the veryte of the Hebrue and Greke texts by the dylygent studye of dyuerse excellent learned men, expert in the forsayde tongues. Prynted by Rychard Grafton & Edward Whitchurch. *Cum prilegio ad imprimendum solum*, 1539."

It at once took rank as the "authorized version" of its time. In order that the "Great Bible" might achieve the objective for which its publication was designed, that of superseding all former licensed versions, a royal order was issued, "that every clergyman in England should provide on this side of the feast next coming 'one boke of the whole Bible of the largest volume in Englysshe, and have the same sett up in summe convenient place within the churche that he has cure of, whereat his parishioners may most commodiously resort to the same and rede yt.'" Guppy goes on to say, "This order was not universally respected by the clergy; but it was partially obeyed, and in a large number of churches Bibles were set up for free and public reading." (*A Brief Sketch of The History of the Transmission of the Bible Down to the Revised English Version of 1881-1885* by Henry Guppy; 1936; p.49).

Coverdale had used the Matthews Bible as the basis for the Great Bible. He revised it to bring it into conformity with the Hebrew and Latin text of the Complutensian Polyglot. "In respect of the Old Testament the Great Bible is practically Roger's compilation *(i.e.,* "Matthew's" Bible) corrected by aid of the Latin translation of Sebastian Munster, which had come out while Coverdale's Bible of 1535 was in the Press, and which was far more literal and trustworthy than the Zurich version. In respect of the New Testament it is Tyndale's version revised by reference to the Latin of Erasmus, and by aid of the Vulgate. <u>It is owing</u>, we may observe, <u>to the Vulgate that the Great Bible made a very considerable number of slight additions to the text</u>, and **for that reason was never popular with the reformers**. It is worth remarking that in this Bible one serious mistranslation is introduced which Tyndale had avoided and which was left undisturbed till 1881, viz., the rendering *"fold"* in lieu of *"flock"* in John 10:16." (*The Evolution of The English Bible* by H. W. Hoare; p. 133).

England was not yet equipped to print such beautiful and extensive work as was desired. Therefore, permission from the French King (Francis) was secured for the printing to be done in Paris, by the famous printer Regnault. Coverdale and Grafton went over to supervise the work. However, the inquisition was on and it was feared that the work might be stopped. Bishop Bonner was Ambassador at Paris and as such, might travel without having his baggage inspected. Thus the finished sheets of the printing went to Cromwell via Bonner. Shortly after, an order for confiscation came from the Inquisitor-General, and the printer was arrested. There was a delay in the execution and *"four great dry vats"* of printed matter were sold as waste paper instead of being burned. Cromwell, by shrewd management, bought from Regnault the type, presses and other outfit, and transferred them, along with the printer, to England. The First Edition of this wonderful specimen of the art of printing was ready for distribution in 1539.

The Great Bible is often spoken of as "Cranmer's Bible," but this title is a misnomer. The promoter of the revision was Cromwell; the editor was Coverdale; the printers were Regnault, the famous French typo-graphist, and Grafton. Thomas Cranmer had little or nothing to do with the 1539 edition! The misnomer has very naturally grown out of the fact that the Primate, Thomas Cranmer, composed an elaborate preface, in excellent English of the Tudor type, which was printed in 1540 as an introduction to the <u>second edition</u>, and which was reproduced in all the five later editions.

Finally, it has been called the "Chained Bible" because it was chained to the reading podium to insure that it would not be removed from its appointed location.

As is my pattern, whenever possible, included is...

PSALM 23 – THE GREAT BIBLE

> The Lord is my shepherde, therefore I can want nothing. He shall fede me in a grene pasture & leade me for the beside the waters of comforte. He shall converte my soule & bring me forth in the pathes of righteousness for hys names sake. Yee though I walke thorow ye walley of the shadow of death, I will fear no evell, for thou art with me, thy rodde & thy staffe comforte me. Thou shalt prepare a table before me against them that trouble me, thou hast anointed my head with oyle, & my cuppe shall be full. But (thy) lovynge kindness & mercy shall followe me all the dayes of my lyfe, I will dwell in the house of the Lord for ever.

ROBERT ESTIENNE OR STEPHANUS 1503-1559

Robert Estienne (French), also known as Stephanus (Latin), is responsible for the verse divisions we have in our English Bibles today. He printed the Erasmus Greek New Testament with some modifications. He printed four editions in 1546, 1549, 1550 and 1551. His printing of these Greek New Testaments aroused the opposition of the Roman Catholic Church to such an extent that he was forced to leave Paris and flee to Lyons in 1550. He put his family in the carriage but he rode on horseback. To occupy his time he took out one of the small 1549 New Testaments he printed and marked the place where the verse divisions were to be made and numbered them accordingly. The first Bible to be printed in the modern chapter-verse format was Stephanus' Latin Bible of 1555. The first English Bible to incorporate these verse divisions was The Geneva New Testament of 1557. Though it is true that a Latin Bible was printed in 1538 with different verse divisions, it is the Stephanus system that we use in our New Testaments to this day. Regarding the Old Testament verse divisions, Stephanus followed those made by a French Hebrew scholar Vatablus in the 1530's. The 1st edition of the Geneva Bible, 1560, was the first printed English Bible to include verse divisions both in the Old and New Testaments. Finally, an English churchman named Stephen Langton in the 1200's made the chapter divisions that were used. However, others claim the chapter divisions were the work of Hugo de Sancto Caro (Cardinal Hugo) in 1250 A.D.

STORMY YEARS OF UNREST AND UNCERTAINTY

MARY TUDOR – BLOODY MARY

The last years of Henry VIII's reign were stormy ones. The wholesale confiscation of ecclesiastical properties, destruction of images, shrines and other symbols, the plundering of monasteries, monks and abbots, the wrecking of buildings connected with worship, caused a Roman Catholic reaction and rebellion throughout the kingdom. Cromwell's work was done and he was beheaded by the will of the reactionists. By 1543 all Tyndale Bibles were prohibited and all notes and controversial matter in the Matthew's Bible were ordered effaced. The reading of the Bibles was confined to the upper classes. There was an extensive burning of English Bibles.

In 1547 Henry died and the son of Henry VIII and Jane Seymour, Edward VI, was the next King. He was ten years old when he came to the throne. During his reign the English Prayer Book was adopted. However, his reign was short lived. The young king died July 6th, 1551 when he was just 15 years old. He passed the crown to his 16-year-old cousin, Lady Jane Grey, because his half-sister Mary was unalterably Catholic. Lady Jane was reluctant to accept the crown. But on Monday, July 10th, 1553 Jane Grey was crowned Queen. She was a scholarly and devoted Christian young lady and no match for Henry VIII's daughter. On July 19th, 1553 Mary I (Mary Tudor also known as "Bloody" Mary) took the throne by force and Queen Jane was deposed after only nine days. Mary Tudor was determined to restore Roman Catholicism to the realm and root out and crush anyone who opposed her, including her Protestant cousin, Jane Grey.

Queen Mary I offered to spare Jane if she would recant. She sent a priest to examine her to find out what she believed.

John Fecknam pressed Jane on <u>her belief concerning transubstantiation</u>. She replied – "I think that at the supper I neither receive flesh nor blood, but bread and wine; which bread when it is broken, and the wine when it is drunken, put me in remembrance how that for my sins the body of Christ was broken, and his blood shed on the cross. ...I ground my faith upon God's word, and not upon the church... The faith of the church must be tried by God's word, and not God's word by the church; neither yet my faith." (Taken from: *Foxe's Book of Martyrs*; 1684).

Fecknam asked <u>what is necessary for a man to become a Christian</u>. Jane responds, "That he should believe in God the Father, the Son, and the Holy Ghost, three persons and one God."

Fecknam asks if there is anything else necessary. (He claimed that works are necessary for salvation). Jane responds – "I deny that, and <u>I affirm that faith only saveth</u>: but it is meet (right) for a Christian, in token that he followeth his master Christ, to do good works; yet may we not say that they profit to our salvation. For when we have done all, yet we be unprofitable servants, and <u>faith only in Christ's blood saveth us</u>."

Jane refused to recant her biblical beliefs and was sent to the block on February 8th 1554 and beheaded. This was the beginning of Mary's bloody reign.

One of Queen Mary's first steps back to Romanism was to re-introduce "**The Six Articles**." The House of Commons passed them on April 2, 1554.

- In the sacrament of the altar after the consecration there remaineth no substance of bread and wine, but under these forms, the natural body and blood of Christ are present.
- Communion in both kinds is not necessary to salvation to all persons by the law of God; both the flesh and blood of Christ are in the bread and wine.
- Priests may not marry by the law of God.
- The vow of chastity ought to be observed by the law of God.
- The use of private masses is to continue, as men receive great benefit by them.
- Auricular confession is expedient and necessary.

📖 *THE GENEVA BIBLE – 1560*

The Geneva Bible was one of the results of the persecution under "Bloody Mary." Mary reigned England from 1553 to 1558. During that time the circulation of the Bible in the vulgar tongue was suppressed. "The public reading of Scripture was prohibited by a proclamation dated 18th August, 1553; by another proclamation in June, 1555, the importation of such books as the works of Tindale, Coverdale, and Cranmer was prohibited, and in 1558 the delivery of wicked and seditious writings of the reformers was required under penalty of death. A relentless persecution was also directed against all who endeavoured to promote the reformers' opinions, with the result that nearly three hundred persons were burned at the stake, and far more were imprisoned or otherwise punished." (*A Brief Sketch of The History of The Transmission of The Bible… by Henry Guppy; p.50*).

It is estimated that as many as 800 reformers sought shelter on the Continent. "Geneva became the favorite place of resort of the refugees, for the reason that Protestantism was there supreme. The ruling spirit of the city was John Calvin, and the man at his right hand was Theodore Beza. This attracted so many Englishmen that they formed by themselves a considerable congregation. In 1556-57 they had **John Knox** for their pastor. He was succeeded in 1557 by another distinguished exile, William Whittingham, who married a sister of Calvin's wife." (Ibid.) (A drawing of Knox to the right).

There had been no translations for 20 years, so William Whittingham was a scholarly man and devoted himself to the work of perfecting the English version of the Scriptures. The first installment of his labors was a revised translation of the New Testament, "with most profitable annotations of all hard places," which was published in Geneva by Conrad Badius in 1557. To this translation was prefixed an epistle by Calvin, which helped to introduce the book to the favorable notice of Protestants and the Bible-reading section of the English people. This Epistle declared that "Christ is the End of the Law."

There was also a preface "To the Reader Mercy and peace through Christ our Saviour." It reads...

"In the Church of Christ there are three kinds of men: some are <u>malicious despisers of the Word</u> and graces of God, who turn all things into poison, and a further hardening of their hearts: others <u>do not openly resist and contemn (condemn) the Gospel, because they are struck as it were in a trance with the majesty thereof</u>, yet either they quarrel and cavil, or else deride and mock at whatsoever is done for the advancement of the same. The <u>third sort are simple lambs</u> which partly are already in the fold of Christ, and so willingly hear their Shepherd's voice, and partly wandering astray by ignorance tarry the time till the Shepherd find them and bring them unto His flock. To this kind of people in this translation I chiefly had respect, as moved unto zeal, counselled by the godly, and drawn by occasion, both of the place where God hath appointed us to dwell, and also for the store of heavenly learning and judgment which so aboundeth in this city of Geneva, that justly it may be called the patron and mirrour of true religion and godliness."

Immediately after the issue of Whittingham's Testament the Genevan exiles entered upon a revision of the whole Bible. English exiled reformers, assisted by Beza and Calvin did the translating. It is impossible to say how many had a hand in it. Coverdale was residing at Geneva for a time and may have assisted, whilst a similar claim may be advanced in favour of John Knox, but it is generally admitted that the chief credit of the work belongs to William Whittingham, who was assisted by Thomas Sampson and Anthony Gilby. It took two years and more for these worthy men to complete their task, and in 1560 they gave to the world the fruit of their labors in the book, which is now known as the "Geneva Bible." The revision was made from a careful collation of Hebrew and Greek originals, with the use of Latin versions, especially Beza's, and the standard French and German versions. It was dedicated to Queen Elizabeth "in bold and simple language, without flattery or reserve."

The Geneva Version quickly became very popular in England. Here is why. It was backed by the great reformers Knox, Calvin, Beza, and others. It was a very handy size. But, the primary reason it was so popular with the people was because it was the first "study Bible" filled with copious notes by the Reformers. The Geneva Bible was popularly called, the *"Breeches Bible"* because **Genesis 3:7** reads, "Then the eyes of them bothe were opened, & they knewe that they were naked, and they sewed fig tree leaves together, and made them selves <u>breeches</u>.

It was issued as late as 1644 and had at least 160 editions. But, its influence did not end there. Numerous editions of the King James Bible carried the Geneva Bible notes.

PSALM 23 – GENEVA BIBLE

1 The Lord is my Shepherd, I shall not want.
2 He maketh me to rest in grene pasture, and leadeth me by the stil waters.
3 He restoreth my soule, and leadeth me in the paths of righteousness for his Names sake.
4 Yea, thogh I shulde walke through the valley of the shadow of death, I wil feare no evil: for thou art with me: thy rod and thy staffe, they comfort me.
5 Thou doest prepare a table before me in the sight of mine adversaries: thou doest anoint my head with oyle, and my cup runneth over.
6 Douteles kindness, and mercie shal follow me all the dayes of my life, and I shal remain a long season in the house of the Lord.

📖 *1568 – FIRST EDITION OF THE BISHOPS BIBLE*

The widespread popularity of the Geneva Bible was undermining the authority of the Great Bible, and also the power of the Bishops. Puritanism, influenced by the reformers on the European Continent was springing up; non-conformity was in the air. Archbishop Parker and the bishops felt that something should be done in Bible translations. In 1564 a revision committee containing eight or nine bishops was formed.

The plan was to follow the Great Bible, except where it varied from the Hebrew and Greek and to attend to the Latin versions of Munster (often inaccurate) and Pagmnus, as well as to avoid bitter notes. There were also numerous tables, calendars, maps and other helps.

The Bishops Bible was not popular. Elizabeth took no public notice of it, nor did she ever give it her formal sanction and authority. The translation was stiff, formal and difficult. It was unpopular with the people and could not displace the Geneva Bible.

The whole work is described as **"the most unsatisfactory and useless of all the old translations."** One of the examples was the awkward translation of **Ecclesiastes 11:1** "Lay thy bread vpon wette faces, and so shalt thou finde it after many dayes." The Geneva Bible had previously translated the passage – "Cast thy bread vpon the waters: for after many daies thou shalt finde it."

For forty years it was held in esteem by the clergy and twenty editions were issued, the last being in 1606. But the most popular version with the people was the Geneva Bible.

PSALM 23 – BISHOPS BIBLE

1 The Lorde is my Shephearde: therefore can I lacke nothing.
2 He shal feede me in a greene pasture: and leade me foorth besyde the waters of comort.
3 He shal convert my soule: and bring me foorth in the pathes of ryghteousnesse, for his names sake.
4 Yea though I walke through the valley of the shadowe of death, I wyll feare no evyl: for thou art with me, thy rodde and staffe comfort me.
5 Thou shalt prepare a table before me, agaynst them that trouble me: thou hast annoynted my head with oyle, and my cup shalt be full.
6 But thy lovyin kyndnesse and mercy shalt folowe me al the dayes of my life: and I wyl dwell in the house of the Lord for ever.

CATHOLIC RHEIMS NEW TESTAMENT – 1582
DOUAY OLD TESTAMENT – 1609

The Church of Rome had always bitterly opposed any attempt to circulate the Bible in the language of the people. They did not even want the people to read the Scriptures. Even when they made their own translation, it was allowed but sparingly.

In spite of the denunciations uttered by the Roman Catholic priests against, what they called, the incorrect and untruthful translations which were in circulation, the Bible continued to be read by increasing numbers of people. "The attempts to suppress it created a prejudice against the Roman Catholic Church; and, as time wore on, it was felt by many Catholics that something more must be done than the mere denunciation of the corrupt translations in the direction of providing a new version which the Roman Church could warrant to be authentic and genuine." (*A Brief Sketch of The History of The Transmission of The Bible...* by Henry Guppy; p.54).

Guppy goes on to say that during the reign of Queen Elizabeth there ceased to be a Roman hierarchy in England. The faithful Catholics were scattered abroad, but to their honor be it said, many of them, true to their principles and professions, did in their exile what the Protestant refugees had done before at Geneva. They set themselves the task of translating the Bible, and in 1582 they issued from the press of John Fogny at Rheims an English translation of the New Testament. The Old Testament was not issued, from lack of means, until 1609-10, when they were able to complete their labours at Douai. From these circumstances arose the designation "Douay Bible," by which the Roman Catholic version has since been known.

According to the preface, the source from which this version was derived was "the authentical Latin, . . . diligently conferred vvith the Greeke and other editions in diuers languages." The objects for which it was published were "the discouerie of the Corrvptions of diuers late translations, and for cleering the Controversies in religion, of these daies."

The work on this Romish translation was carried out by a number of Catholic scholars, under the direction of Gregory Martin, a man who was reputed to be the best Hebrew and Greek scholar of his college, William Allen, who was afterwards made Cardinal, and Richard Bristow.

Public attention was soon directed to this Rheims Version. There were a number of flaws in the translation, none the least being it was a translation from the Latin Vulgate and not the Hebrew and Greek. One of the most obvious corruptions to me is in "The Lord's Prayer" in Matthew 6:11 which reads – "Give us to day **our supersubstantial** bread. None of the previous English versions say anything like "supersubstantial." **Tyndale** translated it, "Geve us this daye oure <u>dayly</u> breede." **Coverdale** says "our "dayly bred." **Matthew** says, our "dayly bread." The **Great Bible** says, our "dayly bred." The **Geneva** Bible says, our "dayly bread." It is obvious that the Catholics corrupted the translation in an effort to support their spurious doctrine of transubstantiation.

There is another ominous error as well. Instead of using the word **"repent"** they translate the word do or have **"penance."** Two illustrations are easily seen in **Luke 13:3, 5**. Tyndale translated it, "I tell you naye. But excepte ye repent, ye all shall lyke wyse perisshe." But the Rheims version says, "No, I say to you but unless you **have penance**, you shal al likevvise perish."

The Catholic Bible is clearly a tainted translation, but succeeded somewhat in keeping Reformation Bibles out of the hands of Catholics in later years.

📖 1611 – THE KING JAMES BIBLE (ALSO KNOWN AS THE AUTHORIZED VERSION)

PUBLISHED CONTINUOUSLY FOR 400 YEARS

The year 2011 was the 400th Anniversary of the King James Bible. According to Vanderbilt University Press, the King James Bible is <u>the best-selling book of all times.</u> (*Translating for King James* by Allen Ward; Vanderbilt Press, 1969; back cover – by way of *Majestic Legacy* compiled by Dr. Phil Stringer; published by The Bible Nation Society, 2011; p. 7). "More than five billion copies of the King James Bible have been sold over the last 399 years." (*Majestic Legacy* compiled by Dr. Phil Stringer; published by The Bible Nation Society, 2011; p. 7).

"The King James Version is <u>the crown jewel of English literature</u>." (*A Visual History of the English Bible;* Donald L. Brake; Baker Books 2008; p. 224) "The King James Bible is <u>the most frequently quoted document in existence</u>." (*History Channel Magazine* – An advertisement by Thomas Nelson Publishers for *KJV400 Celebration*). In fact, the King James Bible is "the most influential book in the history of English civilization." (*Compton's Encyclopedia;* 1995 Edition, by way of Phil Stringer's book).

HOW THE KING JAMES BIBLE CAME TO BE

Mary Queen of Scots (Mary I of Scotland or Mary Stuart), not to be confused with Henry VIII's daughter, Mary I or "Bloody Mary" of England, and her second husband, was queen regent of Scotland from December 14, 1542 to July 24, 1567 and queen consort of France from July 10, 1559 to December 15, 1560. Mary was the only surviving legitimate child of King James V of Scotland. She was 6 days old when her father died and she was crowned nine months later.

James Stuart (1566-1625) was born to Mary Stuart of Scotland and her second husband, Henry Stuart, Lord Darnley at Edinburgh Castle. He was baptized Catholic because of his mother's faith. It was a turbulent time in Scotland, the Presbyterians prevailing over Catholics for religious domination. He ascended the throne of Scotland in July 1567, at age 13 months, when his Roman Catholic mother, Mary Queen of Scots (1542-1587), was forced to abdicate. His mother, Mary, left the kingdom on May 16, 1568, and never saw her son again.

The reason Mary was forced to abdicate was James's father, Henry Stuart, was murdered in mysterious circumstances shortly after James was born. He was assassinated and it was rumored that Mary had a part in the crime. There had developed a rift between Mary and Henry that became public knowledge. For help, Mary turned to a Scottish nobleman, a very powerful man, the Earl of Bothwell. He engaged the help of other Scottish noblemen to do whatever they could to help the queen in her dilemma. This led to a failed explosion plot and to the strangulation death of Henry Lord Darnley. A few months later, Mary and the Earl married. This incensed the populace who suspected Lord Bothwell's participation in the murder of their King. Her outraged subjects turned against her.

In July of 1567, at the age of 13 months, James ascended to the throne as King James the VI of Scotland. Though baptized Catholic, he was brought up under the influence of reformed Scottish Protestants. His tutor was the historian and poet George Buchanan who was a positive influence on him. James proved to be a capable scholar.

A succession of regents ruled Scotland until 1576, when James became nominal ruler, although he did not actually take control until 1581. He proved to be an astute ruler who effectively controlled the various religious and political factions in Scotland.

In 1586, James and Elizabeth I became allies under the Treaty of Berwick. When his mother, Mary Stuart, was executed by Elizabeth the following year, James did not protest too loudly because he hoped to be named as Elizabeth's successor.

Some wonder why Mary was executed. Here is why. Mary fled to England when she abdicated, seeking the protection of her first cousin once removed, Queen Elizabeth I of England. She hoped to inherit her kingdom. Mary had previously claimed Elizabeth's throne as her own and was considered the legitimate sovereign of England by many English Catholics, including participants in the Rising of the North in 1569; the unsuccessful attempt by the Catholic nobles of Northern England to depose Elizabeth and make Mary Stuart, Queen. Perceiving her as a threat, Elizabeth had her arrested. After 19 years in custody in a number of castles and manor houses in England, the 44-year-old former queen was tried for treason on charges that she was involved in three plots to assassinate Elizabeth and found guilty. She was beheaded at Fortheringhay Castle in 1587. Interestingly enough, in 1612 James moved his mother's body to Westminster Abbey, constructing for her a magnificent tomb that rivaled that of Elizabeth.

In 1589, James married Anne of Denmark. They had eight children, of whom only three lived beyond infancy: Henry, Prince of Wales (1594-1612), Elizabeth Stuart (1596-1662), and Charles, who became king upon James' death (1600-1649).

In March 1603, Elizabeth died and James VI of Scotland became King James I of England and Ireland in a remarkably smooth transition of power. After 1603 he only visited Scotland once, in 1617.

James was known as the most educated sovereign in Europe. While he had some good qualities, he was not very popular. Catholics hatched a plot to kill him and others on November 5, 1605, in the *Gunpowder Plot*. Guy Fawkes was caught in the act of attempting to carry out the deed.

THE DIVISION IN THE CHURCH OF ENGLAND

When James came to the throne all was not well in the Church of England. There were three Protestant versions of the English Bible in circulation:

- **The Great Bible of 1539 still was used in the Church of England in its Psalm readings.**
- **The Geneva Bible of 1560 was loved by the people because of the verse divisions and the commentary.**
- **The Bishops' Bible of 1568 was the official Bible of the Church but the translation was stiff, formal and difficult. It has been described as *"the most unsatisfactory and useless of all the old translations."***

Likewise, the Church of England was very divided. There were 3 factions. The **Romanists** wanted to return to the Roman Catholic Church. The Low Church or **Puritan** party wanted to "purify" the church of Catholicism and maintain an evangelical stance in the church. The Anglo-Catholics or **High** party was the ritualistic group who wanted an independent English church but keep many of the Roman Catholic rituals, doctrines and traditions. King James did not agree with any of these groups.

The Puritan party complained of certain grievances they had with church officials. James had been proclaimed King on the 24th of March in 1603. It was not until May 7th that he entered London to take possession of the throne. "Between these two dates, and while he was the guest of the Cromwell's of Hinchinbrook, near Huntingdon, he was approached by certain of the puritan clergy who presented him with what is known as the **Millenary Petition**." (*The Authorized Version of 1611* formerly found at www.bible4u.com). It was claimed by the circulators of the petition that 1,000 Puritan ministers had hand-signed the petition.

The Puritans objected to the priests making the sign of the cross during Baptism; the use of the ring for marriage which had no biblical basis; the rite of confirmation; Ministers' wearing of surplices (robes). They viewed them as too Catholic, unessential and extra-biblical, if not completely unbiblical.

This is the petition that the new King was presented with:

THE MILLENARY PETITION, 1603
(*The Church History of Britain* by Thomas Fuller; Volume 3, pp.193-195)

The humble Petition of the Ministers of the Church of England desiring reformation of certain ceremonies and abuses of the Church

To the most Christian and Excellent Prince, our gracious and dread Sovereign James, by the grace of God, etc. We, the ministers of the Church of England that desire reformation, wish a long, prosperous, and happy reign over us in this life, and in the next everlasting salvation.

Most gracious and dread Sovereign seeing it hath pleased the Divine Majesty, to the great comfort of all good Christians, to advance your Highness, according to your just title, to the peaceable government of this Church and commonwealth of England; we, the ministers of the Gospel in this land, neither as factious men affecting a popular parity in the Church, nor as schismatics aiming at the dissolution of the state ecclesiastical, but as the faithful servants of Christ and loyal subjects to your Majesty, desiring and longing for the redress of divers abuses of the Church, could do no less, in our obedience to God, service to your Majesty, love to his Church, than acquaint your princely Majesty with our particular griefs. For as your princely pen writeth, 'The King, as a good physician, must first know what peccant humours his patient naturally is most subject unto before he can begin his cure.' And although divers of us that sue for reformation have formerly, in respect of the times, subscribed to the Book, some upon protestation, some upon exposition given them, some with condition, rather than the Church should have been deprived of their labour and ministry; yet now we, to the number of more than a thousand, of your Majesty's subjects and ministers, all groaning as under a common burden of human rites and ceremonies, do with one joint consent humble ourselves at your Majesty's feet to be eased and relieved in this behalf. Our humble suit then unto your Majesty is, that of these offences following, some may be removed, some amended, some qualified:

In the Church Service. That the cross in baptism, interrogatories ministered to infants, confirmation, is superfluous, may be taken away: baptism not to be ministered by women, and so explained: the cap and surplice not urged: that examination may go before the communion: that it be ministered with a sermon: that divers terms of priests and absolution, and some other used, with the ring in marriage, and other such like in the Book, may be corrected: the lonesomeness of service abridged: church songs and music moderated to better edification: that the Lord's Day be not profaned, the rest upon holy-days not so strictly urged: that there may be an uniformity of doctrine prescribed: no Popish opinion to be any more taught or defended: no ministers charged to teach their people to bow at the name of Jesus: that the canonical Scriptures only be read in the church.

Concerning Church Ministers. That none hereafter be admitted into the ministry but able and sufficient men, and those to preach diligently, and especially upon the Lord's Day: that such as be already entered and cannot preach, may either be removed and some charitable course taken with them for their relief or else to be forced, according to the value of their livings, to maintain preachers: that non-residency be not permitted: that King Edward's statute for the lawfulness of ministers' marriage be revived: that ministers be not urged to subscribe but, according to the law, to the Articles of Religion and the King's Supremacy only.

For Church Livings and Maintenance. That bishops leave their commendams, some holding prebends, some parsonages, some vicarages with their bishoprics: that double-beneficed men be not suffered to hold, some two, some three benefices with cure, and some two, three, or four dignities besides: that impropriations annexed to bishoprics and colleges be demised only to the preachers incumbents, for the old rent: that the impropriations of laymen's fees may be charged with a sixth or seventh part of the worth to the maintenance of the preaching minister.

For Church Discipline. That the discipline and excommunication may be administered according to Christ's own institution; or, at the least, that enormities may be redressed: as namely, that excommunication come not forth under the name of lay persons, chancellors, officials, etc.; that men be not excommunicated for trifles and twelvepenny matters; that none be excommunicated without consent of his pastor; that the officers be not suffered to extort unreasonable fees; that none having jurisdiction or registers' places put out the same to farm; that divers Popish canons (as for restraint of marriage at certain times) be reversed; that the lonesomeness of suits in ecclesiastical courts, which hang sometimes two, three, four, five, six, or seven years, may be restrained; that the oath ex officio, whereby men are forced to accuse themselves, be more sparingly used; that licences for marriage without banns asked be more cautiously granted.

These, with such other abuses yet remaining and practiced in the Church of England, we are able to shew not to be agreeable to the Scriptures, if it shall please your Highness farther to hear us, or more at large by writing to be informed, or by conference among the learned to be resolved. And yet we doubt not but that without any farther process, your Majesty, of whose Christian judgment we have received so good a taste already, is able of yourself to judge of the equity of this cause. God we trust hath appointed your Highness our physician to heal these diseases.

And we say with Mordecai to Esther, 'Who knoweth whether you are come to the kingdom for such a time?' Thus your majesty shall do that which we are persuaded shall be acceptable to God, honourable to your Majesty in all succeeding ages, profitable to his Church which shall be thereby increased; comfortable to your ministers which shall be no more suspended, silenced, disgraced, imprisoned for men's traditions; and prejudicial to none but to those that seek their own quiet, credit, and profit in the world. Thus with all dutiful submission referring ourselves to your Majesty's pleasure for your gracious answer as God shall direct you, we most humbly recommend your Highness to the Divine Majesty, whom we beseech for Christ's sake to dispose your royal heart to do herein what shall be to his glory, the good of his Church, and your endless comfort.

[from:]

Your Majesty's most humble subjects the ministers of the Gospel, that desire not a disorderly innovation but a due and godly reformation.

King James I desired to bring unity within the Anglican Church; therefore he called a conference to be held at Hampton Court Palace on January 16th, 1604, at which representatives of both parties were to have an opportunity of stating their views to His Majesty.

"The Hampton Court was built by Cardinal Woolsley in 1515 and it pictures the excesses of the age in which it was built. It took 2500 workmen to build its 1000 rooms." (Comment by Dr. Ken Connolly in his video – *The Story of The English Bible*). It took 500 servants or paid employees to keep it. "It happens to have 250 tons of lead pipe that brings special water into it because they would not use the water which came from the River Thames." (Ibid.) <u>Hampton Court</u> aptly illustrates the decadence of the prelates of the church. Remember, the man that built it was the ecclesiastical head of the Church in England in his day.

I find it ironic that on Monday, January 6, 1604 James I called about 50 prelates (high ranking church officials) of the church together in an effort to try to straighten out some problems the two factions were having. On the second day of the proceedings, the Puritan President of Corpus Christi College in Oxford, Dr. John Rainolds **"moved His Majesty that there might be a new translation of the Bible, because those which were allowed in the reign of Henry VIII, and Edward VI were corrupt and not answerable to the truth of the original.**"

The King, sympathetic to the idea, exerted his royal influence to advance the project. King James said he *"wished that some special pains should be taken in that behalf for one uniform translation (professing that he could never yet see a Bible well translated in English, but the worse of all his Majesty through the Geneva to be), and this to be done by the best learned in both Universities; after them to be reviewed by the bishops and the chief learned of the Church; from them to be presented to the Privy Council; and lastly, to be ratified by his royal authority...He gave this caveat (upon a word cast out by my Lord of London) that no marginal notes should be added, having found in them, which are annexed to the Geneva translation, some notes very partial, untrue, seditious, and savouring too much of dangerous and traitorous conceits."* (The Printed English Bible by Richard Lovett; pp.134-135).

THE TRANSLATION

The next step was the actual selection of the men who were to do the translation work. In July of 1604, King James wrote to Bishop Bancroft that he had "appointed certain learned men, to the number of four and fifty, for the translating of the Bible." These men were the best biblical scholars and linguists of their day. In the preface to their completed work it is further stated, **"there were many chosen, that were greater in other men's eyes than in their own, and that sought the truth rather than their own praise. Again, they came or were thought to come to the work, learned, not to learn."** Other men were sought out, according to James, **"so that our said intended translation may have the help and furtherance of all our principal learned men within this our kingdom."**

Although fifty-four men were nominated, only forty-seven were known to have taken part in the work of translation. Historians indicate that a number of these changes were due to death. It should also be noted, as the 11th Edition of Encyclopedia Britannica says, "It is observable also that they [the translators] were chosen without reference to party, at least as many of the Puritan clergy as of the opposite party being placed on the committees." (Encyclopedia Britannica – 11th Edition of 1911; Volume III; p.902). Bishop Lancelot Andrews, who besides having an intimate knowledge of Chaldee, Hebrew, Greek, and Syriac, was familiar with 10 other languages, chaired the translation work. The translating team was divided into 6 divisions; **two at Westminster**, **two at Cambridge**, and **two at Oxford**.

The translation work did not get underway until 1607. When it did, ten at **Westminster** were assigned Genesis through 2 Kings; the second team of 7 had Romans through Jude.

At **Cambridge**, eight worked on <u>1 Chronicles through Ecclesiastes</u>, while seven others handled <u>the Apocrypha</u>.

Oxford employed seven to translate <u>Isaiah through Malachi</u>; eight occupied themselves with the Gospels, Acts, and Revelation.

As each group completed their particular assigned part, it was then subjected to the other 5 sets of men so that each part of the Bible came from all the learned men. When they had completed their work, a final committee of six members at London carefully reviewed it.

These **fifteen general rules** were advanced for the guidance of the translators:

- The ordinary Bible read in the Church, commonly called the Bishops Bible, to be followed, and as little altered as the Truth of the original will permit.
- The names of the Prophets, and the Holy Writers, with the other Names of the Text, to be retained, as nigh as may be, accordingly as they were vulgarly used.
- The Old Ecclesiastical Words to be kept, viz. the Word Church not to be translated Congregation, etc.
- When a Word hath divers Significations, that to be kept which hath been most commonly used by the most of the Ancient Fathers, being agreeable to the Propriety of the Place, and the Analogy of the Faith.
- The Division of the Chapters to be altered, either not at all, or as little as may be, if Necessity so require.
- No Marginal Notes at all to be affixed, but only for the explanation of the Hebrew or Greek Words, which cannot without some circumlocution, so briefly and fitly be expressed in the Text.
- Such Quotations of Places to be marginally set down as shall serve for the fit Reference of one Scripture to another.
- Every particular Man of each Company, to take the same Chapter or Chapters, and having translated or amended them severally by himself, where he thinketh good, all to meet together, confer what they have done, and agree for their Parts what shall stand.

- As any one Company hath dispatched any one Book in this Manner they shall send it to the rest, to be considered of seriously and judiciously, for His Majesty is very careful in this Point.
- If any Company, upon the Review of the Book so sent, doubt or differ upon any Place, to send them Word thereof; note the Place, and withal send the Reasons, to which if they consent not, the Difference to be compounded at the general Meeting, which is to be of the chief Persons of each Company, at the end of the Work.
- When any Place of special Obscurity is doubted of, Letters to be directed by Authority, to send to any Learned Man in the Land, for his Judgment of such a Place.
- Letters to be sent from every Bishop to the rest of his Clergy, admonishing them of this Translation in hand; and to move and charge as many skilful in the Tongues; and having taken pains in that kind, to send his particular Observations to the Company, either at Westminster, Cambridge, or Oxford.
- The Directors in each Company, to be the Deans of Westminster, and Chester for that Place; and the King's Professors in the Hebrew or Greek in either University.
- These translations to be used when they agree better with the Text than the Bishops' Bible: Tyndale's, Matthew's, Coverdale's, Whitchurch's, Geneva.
- Besides the said Directors before mentioned, three or four of the most Ancient and Grave Divines, in either of the Universities, not employed in Translating, to be assigned by the vice-Chancellor, upon Conference with the rest of the Heads, to be Overseers of the Translations as well Hebrew as Greek, for the better observation of the 4th Rule above specified.

Another important issue I want to address is...

THE USE OF ITALICS IN THE KING JAMES BIBLE

Why did the King James Bible translators use *italics* in the King James Bible? Was it because God miraculously gave the translators additional inspiration the same way He did as recorded in 2 Peter 1:21, "holy men of God spake as they were moved by the Holy Ghost"? Or was it, as some have assumed, that these words were

338

printed in this fashion for emphasis? The answer to both of these questions is, NO.

In fact, the words in *italics* in the King James Bible are words that were added by the translators to help the reader. This is usually necessary when translating from one language to another because a word in one language may not have a corollary word in English and idiomatic expressions often do not easily move from one language to another. Hence, the words in italics are words which do not have any equivalence in the Hebrew, Aramaic or Greek text. By adding these words, the translators' goal was to make the meaning of the sentence clearer and produce a more readable translation that read smoothly, yet was true to the original. However, to make sure that the reader understood that these words were not in the manuscripts, they set them in italics.

PROCEDURES AND RULES THAT GUIDED THE MAKING OF THE KJB

I have Gordon Campbell's book entitled, *Bible: The Story of the King James Version*, published by Oxford University Press. Published in 2010, it is a history of the King James Bible. Campbell states that KJB translator Samuel Ward reported to the 1618 Synod of Dort the procedures or rules that guided the making of the KJB. He noted that some of those rules were supplementary rules that added information not found in the fifteen rules given the KJB translators. Campbell asserted that this information reported by Samuel Ward has "the inestimable advantage of reflecting what actually happened rather than what was supposed to happen." (p. 41).

Here is the rule the KJB translators used themselves as presented by Samuel Ward that relates to the use of italics:

"Words that it was anywhere necessary to insert into the text to complete the meaning were to be distinguished by another type, small roman..." (p. 42).

So you are not confused, I remind you that the 1611 Bible was in fancy 𝕭𝖑𝖆𝖈𝖐 𝕷𝖊𝖙𝖙𝖊𝖗 type. The added words were in smaller Roman type and not *italics*. In later editions that were set in Roman type, *italic* type was used. This is what we see in our King James Bibles today.

F. H. A. Scrivener wrote: "The end proposed by the use of italics is thus explained in the Geneva edition of 1578. 'Where as the necessity of the sentence required anything to be added (for such is the grace and propriety of the Hebrew and Greek tongues, that it cannot but either by circumlocution, or by adding the verb, or some word, be understood of them that are not well-practised therein), we have put it in the text with another kind of letter.' If this be the rule which the translators of our present version proposed to themselves (and we have every reason for believing that it was), it follows that such a rule should be carried out uniformly, and on all occasions" (*Supplement to the Authorized English Version of the New Testament, Vol. I*, pp. 60-61).

Scrivener also quoted in a note, a similar comment from the 1557 Whittingham's New Testament.

Thus, the early English translators themselves stated one of the rules or principles that they used for "italics" [or putting some words in a different kind of letter or type], and the above evidence shows that principle was also affirmed and advocated by the KJB translators.

THE WORDS IN ITALICS ARE THERE FOR A PURPOSE

While there are many illustrations to show how helpful the italics are, I will show you just one. We see that David killed Goliath in 1 Samuel 17:49 *"And David put his hand in his bag, and took thence a stone, and slang it, and smote the Philistine in his forehead, that the stone sunk into his forehead; and he fell upon his face to the earth."* That is confirmed in 1 Samuel 21:9 *"And the priest said, The sword of Goliath the Philistine, whom thou slewest in the valley of Elah, behold, it is here wrapped in a cloth behind the ephod: if thou wilt take that, take it: for there is no other save that here. And David said, There is none like that; give it me."* Watch carefully the importance of the italics in II Samuel 21:19, *"And there was again a battle in Gob with the Philistines, where Elhanan the son of Jaareoregim, a Bethlehemite, slew* **the brother of** *Goliath the*

Gittite, the staff of whose spear was like a weaver's beam." But, omitting the italicized words from II Samuel 21:19 as the ESV, NASB, NIV, The Message, etc. read, it would lead you to believe Elhanan was the one who slew Goliath. Look carefully at II Samuel 21:19 from the New American Standard, "And there was war with the Philistines again at Gob, and Elhanan the son of Jaare-oregim the Bethlehemite killed Goliath the Gittite, the shaft of whose spear was like a weaver's beam." However, we know that is not a true statement by reading 1 Chronicles 20:5 *"And there was war again with the Philistines; and Elhanan the son of Jair slew Lahmi the brother of Goliath the Gittite, whose spear staff was like a weaver's beam."*

MY CONCLUSION REGARDING ITALICS IN THE KING JAMES BIBLE

Clearly, the words in italics were not miraculously given to the translators by God as additional inspiration the same way He did as recorded in 2 Peter 1:21, *"holy men of God spake as they were moved by the Holy Ghost."* Neither are the italics there to add emphasis. The words in italics in the King James Bible are words that were added by the translators to help the reader better understand the intent of the passage translated from the original languages.

WHY THE THEE'S, THOU'S, YE'S AND YOU'S?

In the King James Bible, *Thee's, Thou's, Ye's* and *You's* ARE A BIG HELP IN UNDERSTANDING THE BIBLE! *Thee* and *thou, you* and *ye* are more than style in the KJB; they identify singular and plural. *Thee, thou* and *thine* are always singular. *Ye, you* and *your* are always plural. In modern English, *you* and *your* are interchangeably singular or plural. An example of the need for this accuracy is found in John 3:7: "Marvel not that I said unto <u>thee</u> (Nicodemus), <u>ye</u> (everybody) must be born again..

THE TWO IMPRESSIONS OF THE FIRST EDITION

Translating the King James Bible was no small task! "The execution of the work occupied about three years, and both the length of time employed and the elaborate mode of procedure adopted indicate the pains that were taken to make the translation worthy of its high design. In 1611 the new version was given forth to the public. <u>There seem to have been two impressions of this first edition</u>, probably due to the impossibility of one printing office being able to supply in the time allotted the number of copies required, about 20,000." (*A Brief Sketch of The History of the Transmission of the Bible Down to the Revised English Version of 1881-1885* by Henry Guppy; 1936).

Before I move on, I want to clarify Guppy's statement; *there seem to have been two impressions of this first edition.* Here is what he is referring to. There is the so called "**she**" Bible and the "**he**" Bible. The "**he**" Bible is the rarer of the two. The way to distinguish between the two is by turning to **Ruth 3:15** and if it reads – "Also he said, Bring the veil that *thou hast* upon thee, and hold it. And when she held it, he measured six *measures* of barley, and laid *it* on her: and **she** went into the city," it is a "**she**" Bible. If, on the other hand, the last part of the verse reads – "he measured six *measures* of barley, and laid *it* on her: and **he** went into the city," it is a "**he**" Bible. All of the King James Bibles of our time, with the exception of the 1611 Thomas Nelson reprint, are "**she**" Bibles. The context calls for "she" and in 1613 all King James Bibles thereafter said "she" went into the city.

I want to note that in England particularly, the King James Bible is commonly referred to as the "**Authorized Version**." But strangely it was never formally authorized. To date, no evidence has been produced "to show that the version was ever publicly sanctioned by Convocation, or by Parliament, or by the Privy Council, or by the King. It was not even entered at Stationers' Hall, with the result that it is now impossible to say at what period of the year 1611 the book was actually published. (Ibid.).

No other translation past or present has been so meticulously done and carefully reviewed. The superintending hand of God was apparent. As one author put it, "the result was an edition of the Word of God unrivaled for its simplicity, for its force, and for its vigor of language. It was, and is to this day, a compendium of literary excellencies, and much better, has proved itself to be a faithful and accurate translation of the very Word of God."

We can readily discern from the instructions given to the translators that our King James Bible was "Newly translated out of the original tongues and with the former translations diligently compared and revised." It was, "Printed by His Majesty's special command, and appointed to be read in the churches." For the record, I am including "**The Epistle Dedicatory**" and "**The Translators to The Reader**" from the King James Version in the Appendices.

Finally, after a plethora of English Bible translations...Tyndale, Coverdale, Matthews, Great, Geneva, and Bishops, the King James Bible came on the scene! **ALL TRANSLATION WORK CEASED FOR ALMOST 300 YEARS! It is to this day the premier of all English translations, being a most scholarly, accurate, and faithfully executed witness of the very mind of God**. This Bible has been continuously published since 1611.

THE BEGINNING OF THE ATTACKS ON THE KING JAMES BIBLE

THE "REVISED" VERSION OF 1881 & 1885

In February, 1870 both houses of the Convocation of Canterbury unanimously passed a resolution to appoint a committee of scholars to begin the task of a new translation. <u>It was designed to be a revision of the Authorized Version</u>, but that is not what the outcome was. Briefly, here is what happened. The Principle and Rule that was to guide the Committee of Convocation (25th May, 1870) was; "To INTRODUCE AS FEW ALTERATIONS AS POSSIBLE INTO THE TEXT OF THE AUTHORIZED VERSION, CONSISTENTLY WITH FAITHFULNESS."

The instructions could not be more forceful. They were instructed to correct "plain and clear errors." "Necessary emendations" (restoration of original readings) were to be made. But, in the words of the Southern Convocation, "We do not contemplate any new Translation, or any alteration of the language, *except where*, in the judgment of the most competent Scholars, *such change is necessary*." The watchword, therefore, given to the company of Revisionists was, "*necessity*." *Necessity* was to determine whether they were to depart from the language of the Authorized Version, or not; for <u>the alterations were to be *as few as possible*</u>.

But **that is not what happened**! The committee did NOT follow their instructions. In fact they introduced **TWO** new translations.

First, they constructed a completely new Greek Text instead of staying with the Traditional Text, also called the Textus Receptus. The Greek text used as a basis for the so-called "revision" was one developed by B.F. Westcott (1825-1901) and F.J.A. Hort (1828-1892). Westcott and Hort used as their textual basis the corrupt Greek text of Johann Jakob Griesbach (1745-1812), the Unitarian Greek New Testament that followed Griesbach, Sinaiticus and Vaticanus. A copy of their work having been secretly given to every member of the New Testament company of revisionists to guide them in their labors, *under pledge that they should neither show nor communicate its contents to anyone else.*

Here is why that is a problem. The Westcott-Hort Greek Text has omissions in 200 places when compared to the Traditional Text. But that is not the only problem; there are about 8,000 changes in foot-notes and translations when you compare the Westcott-Hort Greek Text with the Traditional Text.

There is no doubt that the revision committee cast aside the Traditional Text (Textus Receptus) and in its place inserted the corrupted text of Westcott-Hort.

Secondly, they made an entirely new translation of the New Testament instead of revising the King James Version as they were instructed, and that translation was based on the corrupt Westcott-Hort text instead of the Traditional Text.

Books have been written on this subject. The great tragedy is that virtually every English Bible translation from 1881 forward has followed the corrupt Westcott-Hort text family instead of the Textus Receptus.

I am committed to the King James Bible. I believe God has preserved his Words, by accurate translation, in the King James Bible. It has been a blessing to millions of the saints of God. It is a part of our national inheritance, which we have received, unimpaired from our fathers, and we are compelled to hand down, unimpaired to our children. It is the grand bulwark of Protestantism and Bible Believing Christianity; the safeguard of the Gospel, and the treasure of the Church. We would be traitors, in every sense of the word, if we consented to give it up to be ransacked by the sacrilegious hands of the skeptic scholars, infidel preachers, deceitful   papists, current day higher critics, gainsaying fundamentalists, and the whole tribe of enemies of GOD and godliness.

CHAPTER #14

UNDERSTANDING THE BATTLE OVER BIBLE VERSIONS

THE PURPOSE

My purpose is to point out some of the basics relating to the battle raging over the different Bible versions so that the average Christian in the pew can understand what is going on and why they should use the King James Bible.

INTRODUCTORY THOUGHTS

The Bible is the foundation of literally everything in New Testament Christianity! Therefore it is imperative that you have an uncorrupted Bible. If something does not have a biblical base, it should be rejected. We read in **1 Thessalonians 5:21** *"Prove all things; hold fast that which is good."* The English word ***prove*** is a translation of the Greek word δοκιμαζετε – dokimazete (*dok-im-ad'zate*). The word carries the idea of ***proving a thing whether it is worthy or not***. So, the question is, how are we to go about ***proving*** something? I believe **Isaiah 8:20** gives us insight into the answer to this question – *"To the law and to the testimony: if they speak not according to this word, it is because there is no light in them."* In other words, **examine everything by the words of the Bible** and if it does not line up, reject it!

Friends, the Bible, **our King James Bible, is the "GOLD STANDARD" for EVERY THING in the Christian life!** 2 **Timothy 3:16-17** says *"All scripture is given by inspiration of God, and is profitable for doctrine, for reproof, for correction, for instruction in righteousness: 17 That the man of God may be perfect, thoroughly furnished unto all good works."*

As I have often said – **The Bible tells us what's right, what's not right, how to get right and how to stay right.**

Since THE BIBLE IS SO IMPORTANT, it should come as no surprise that the true Words of God, as found in our King James Bible, are under attack by our adversary, the Devil, who has transformed himself into an angel of light and his ministers into ministers of righteousness (**2 Corinthians 11:14-15**).

UNDERSTANDING THE BATTLE TERMINOLOGY

In order to understand the Battle over Bible versions, you first need to understand some of ***the battle vocabulary***. Both sides in the Bible version battle toss around these unfamiliar words, and if you do not really understand the *vocabulary,* it is hard to understand exactly what the issues are.

Let's look at and define some of the key words.

Autographs – An autograph is the original texts (of the Bible) that were written either by the hand of the author or by a scribe under the supervision of the author. For centuries there have been NO Hebrew or Aramaic ***autographs*** of any Old Testament book or passage. There were none in Jesus' day. Nor are there any Greek ***autographs*** of any New Testament Book or portion thereof. No one has ever seen one, since probably about 150 A.D.

Apographs – A handwritten copy of the original. There are thousands of ***apographs*** still extant today.

Manuscripts – All Bibles were hand copied; written by scribes onto parchment, vellum, papyrus or paper prior to the printing of the Gutenberg Bible (also called the 42 line Bible & Mazarin Bible) which was printed on a printing press using moveable type in 1454-1455.

THERE ARE FOUR KINDS OF GREEK MANUSCRIPTS

There are **four kinds of Greek manuscripts** that we have in our possession today:
1) **papyri**, 2) **uncials**, 3) **cursives**, and 4) **lectionaries**.

"The Greek manuscripts of the New Testament, so far as known, were written on papyrus, parchment, or paper. The ***autographs,*** both of the historical and epistolary writers, are supposed to have been written on papyrus. The great uncials copies and the most valued of the minuscules and lectionaries were written on parchment, while paper was employed largely in the making of the later lectionaries and the printed texts of the New Testament." (*Praxis In Manuscripts of the Greek New Testament* by Rev. Charles F. Sitterly; 1898; p.15).

NEW TESTAMENT PAPYRI MANUSCRIPTS
For a listing see - www.kchanson.com/papyri.html#NTP

Papyrus is a brittle kind of paper made out of the papyrus plant, which grows in Egypt. To my knowledge there are about <u>123 papyrus fragment manuscripts of the New Testament</u>. See - http://en.wikipedia.org/wiki/List_of_New_Testament_papyri.

Most of those surviving early texts only have a few verses on them. The most ancient example is the John Ryland papyrus fragment p52 (**p** stands for papyrus) which includes portions of **John 18:31-33 & 37-38**. It is housed in John Ryland University Library in Manchester, England. The fragment is believed to have been written sometime around 150 A.D.

There are **6 papyri** that I am aware of, which record large portions of the New Testament. P45, dated around 200 A.D., contains portions of all **four Gospels and Acts**. P46, from the second century, has almost all of **Paul's epistles and Hebrews**. P47, also from the second-century, contains **Revelation 9-17**. These are from what is called the Beatty Papyri housed in Dublin Castle in Dublin, Ireland. Then there are three lengthy papyri from the Bodmer Papyri. P66 is a second century papyrus that contains almost all of **John**. P72, a third or fourth century papyrus, contains all of **1 and 2 Peter and Jude**. Finally, P75, dated between 175-200 A.D., contains most of **Luke through John 15**.

THE UNCIALS OR MAJUSCULE MANUSCRIPTS
See list at – www.en.wikipedia.org/wiki/List_of_New_Testament_uncials

Uncial comes from the Latin word **uncialis**, which means inch-high. It is used to delineate a type of Greek and Latin writing which features capital letters. There are few, if any, divisions between words in uncial manuscripts and no punctuation to speak of. The word majuscule, meaning large or capital letter, is a synonym for uncial. There are about **290 uncial manuscripts** of all text types. **Three of the most famous uncial** New Testament manuscripts are the *Sinaiticus* (also called by the first letter of the Hebrew alphabet a – Aleph) believed to have been written about 350 A.D. Then there is *Vaticanus* (also called "**B**"), believed to have been written about 350 A.D. Then there is **Codex Alexandrinus**, (identified as "**A**"), written about 450 A.D.

Speakers on the Bible versions' issue will often refer to the manuscripts using the uncial letter designations, instead of their longer names.

CURSIVE OR MINUSCULE MANUSCRIPTS

Cursive or minuscule manuscripts are Greek manuscripts written in lower case letters, more like handwriting. The letters flow together, much like writing of today. There are spaces between words and some degree of punctuation. At last count there are 2,764 cursive Greek manuscripts.
See list at www.biblebelievers.net/BibleVersions/kjcforv5.htm#XXIV

LECTIONARY MANUSCRIPTS

The word *lection* comes from a Latin root word meaning "**to read**." Lectionaries are portions of Scriptures in Greek (or Latin) Bibles that were read in the church services during the year. There are at least 2,882 known lectionaries in existence. See www.csntm.org/Manuscripts.aspx

When you add up all the figures, **there are about 6059** Greek manuscripts in existence today for the New Testament. Another source says, "The New Testament has been preserved in more manuscripts than any other ancient work, having over 5,400 (now more than 6,000) complete or fragmented Greek manuscripts, 10,000 Latin manuscripts and 9,300 manuscripts in various other ancient languages including Syriac, Slavic, Gothic, Ethiopic, Coptic and Armenian. The dates of these manuscripts range from the 2nd century up to the invention of the printing press in the 15th century." See - en.wikipedia.org/wiki/Biblical_manuscript.

What you need to know about these 6,000 plus manuscripts and portions is that there are only about 45 to 50 Greek manuscripts that support the type of Greek text that underlies the modern versions of the Bible, but there are 5,000 plus that support the Textus Receptus type text that underlies our King James Bible. Figure it out. Figure it out! About 99% of all the manuscript evidence supports the text type from which the King James Bible is translated.

OTHER WORDS AND PHRASES THAT RELATE TO THE BIBLE VERSION BATTLE

INSPIRATION

The word *inspiration* is derived from the Greek word ψεοπνευστοσ-theopneutos (**2 Timothy 3:16**), which literally means "**God breathed**" or more accurately, "**breathed into by God.**" Charles Ryrie writes that inspiration is – "God's superintending of human authors so that, using their own individual personalities, they composed and recorded without error in the words of the original autographs His revelation to man."

Dr. Thomas Strouse puts it this way – "Inspiration is the process whereby the Holy Spirit led the writers of Scripture to record accurately His very words; the product of the process was an inspired original." (Dr. Thomas Strouse, Dean Emmanuel Baptist Theological Seminary; *The Translation Model Predicated by Scripture* – by way of *The Attack On The Canon of Scripture* by Dr. H. D. Williams; p. 13).

There is an important fact you must know when it comes to biblical inspiration. It was the WORDS that were inspired, not the men! God worked through the men by His Holy Spirit with the result of the WORDS being inspired. That is what **2 Peter 1:20-21** is saying, *"Knowing this first, that no prophecy of the scripture is of any private interpretation. 21 For the prophecy came not in old time by the will of man: but holy men of God spake as they were moved by the Holy Ghost."*

Let me explain what is being said in **verse 21**. The idea is that Scripture neither proceeds from the prophet's own knowledge, thoughts, ideas or inventions, nor was it rooted in the calculation or conjecture of the one to whom it was revealed. As one commentator put it, "**this means that the origin of the Scripture was not of anyone's private or personal ideas**."

VERBAL-PLENARY INSPIRATION

I believe the Bible teaches **verbal-plenary inspiration**.

PLENARY INSPIRATION

Let me first explain the term "*plenary*" as it relates to inspiration. It simply means "**full, complete, entire**." The Bible is equally inspired from Genesis to Revelation. Generally, the term is employed to emphasize that all of the respective components of the Scriptures were given by God. This means that the Bible's historical depictions are true, that incidental scientific references are factual as well, and, in a word, that all biblical documents are completely accurate. **Psalms 119:160** is an example of a passage that teaches *plenary inspiration* – "Thy word *is* true *from* the beginning: and every one of thy righteous judgments *endureth* for ever."

VERBAL INSPIRATION (THE BIBLICAL VIEW OF INSPIRATION)

What does **Verbal Inspiration** mean? This means that the words are divinely inspired and that **every word of the Bible**, as it was originally written, is from God.

The theological explanation of inspiration says that the Holy Spirit guided chosen servants of God in the choice of the very words they used. They retained the proper use of their powers and faculties, yet were guided or assisted to use such language as would convey the mind of the Spirit in its full and unimpaired integrity. Again, this verbal inspiration was of the original autographs alone.

A. A. Hodge put it this way, "It is meant that the divine influence, of whatever kind it may have been, which accompanied the sacred writers in what they wrote, extends to their expression of their thoughts in language, as well as to the thoughts themselves. The effect being that in the original autograph copies the language expresses the thought God intended to convey with infallible accuracy, so that the words as well as the thoughts are God's revelation to us."

Does the Bible teach the concept of **verbal inspiration**? YES! We already looked at **2 Peter 1:20-21.** Another key passage that I mentioned earlier is **2 Timothy 3:16-17** *"All scripture is given by inspiration of God, and is profitable for doctrine, for reproof, for correction, for instruction in righteousness: 17 That the man of God may be perfect, thoroughly furnished unto all good works."*

In fact, the Bible contains hundreds of passages in which the authors claim divine inspiration for their message. Also, there are direct accounts of written revelation. One illustration is Moses receiving the Ten Commandments! The phrase, *"the word of the LORD came..."* occurs 92 times in the King James Bible and another 19 times we read the phrase, *"the words of the Lord."* The phrase, *"thus saith the Lord..."* occurs 415 times as well. In the Bible we have the Word and the Words of God.

Paul makes a most striking contrast between man's word on the one hand, and God's Word on the other in **1 Thessalonians 2:13** *"For this cause also thank we God without ceasing, because, when ye received the word of God which ye heard of us, ye received it not as the word of men, but as it is in truth, the word of God, which effectually worketh also in you that believe."*

So, as we have in our church doctrinal statement – "The process of God's breathing out His Words occurred only once when He breathed out or 'inspired' the Hebrew, Aramaic and Greek texts. Though the process of inspiration has never been repeated, the product of inspiration, that is, the Hebrew, Aramaic, and Greek Words, have been preserved by God in the Words of the Masoretic Hebrew and Textus Receptus Greek that underlie the King James Bible."

THOUGHT-CONCEPT INSPIRATION (THE COUNTERFEIT VIEW OF INSPIRATION)

Doesn't everyone believe in verbal-plenary inspiration? NO! An increasing number of churches, Bible Colleges and seminaries teach that God gave the thoughts BUT NOT THE SPECIFIC WORDS OF

SCRIPTURE! Dr. Thomas Strouse explains the **thought-concept** theory this way, "They believe God inspired His divine concepts and then preserved these concepts in the extant Manuscripts (MSS)." He goes on to say, "Since the concepts are inspired and preserved, the exact words representing these concepts may not be available and may vary." He further notes that the textual critics suggest that, "through the science of textual criticism, man can restore the approximate wording of the original text." (*The Biblical Defense For The Verbal, Plenary Preservation of God's Word* by Dr. T. M. Strouse; www.graceway.com/articles/articles_007.htm)

In fact, *textual criticism* is **not a science at all**! It is the contrived invention of unsaved men!

One commentator gives an illustration of how **thought-concept** inspiration works. "When Paul wrote **1 Corinthians 13** the only thing God gave was some general thoughts on the subject of love. The words of the text we owe to Paul." (*Is the Bible Reliable? Our God-Breathed Bible;* John MacArthur; Tape GC 1343).

That's wrong. In **1 Corinthians 2:13,** Paul shows unmistakably that divine inspiration pertains also to the **words** and not merely to the thought, saying, *"Which things also we speak, not in the words which man's wisdom teacheth, but which the Holy Ghost teacheth."*

Nearly all the "New Versions" come from the thought-conceptual view of inspiration. They deny God inspired His Words. The main point that needs to be made clear is that there is NO PLACE in the Bible that teaches mere thought-concept inspiration. It is a humanly devised invention that is engineered by the Devil!

PROVIDENTIAL PRESERVATION

I hold to the position of Dr. Edward F. Hills (1912-1981) who stated that the Scriptures have been preserved by God in His providence so that the Church would always have the Words as a light to her feet and a lamp to her path. (*The Providential Preservation of The Greek Text of The New Testament;* Fourth edition 1983; by Rev. W. MacLean, M.A.).

This is NOT a unique position! In 1649 the Protestant Reformers in their Westminster Confession of Faith stated – "The Old Testament in Hebrew (which was the native language of the people of God of old), and the New Testament in Greek (which at the time of the writing of it was most generally known to the nations), being immediately inspired by God, and <u>by His singular care and providence kept pure in all ages</u>, are therefore authentic; so as in all controversies of religion the Church is finally to appeal unto them."

Many people are saying today that God abandoned His Hebrew, Aramaic and Greek Words rather than preserving them. The great defender of the Traditional Text and our King James Bible, Dean John Burgon disagreed. He wrote in his work, *The Traditional Text*, – "There exists no reason for supposing that the Divine Agent, who in the first instance thus gave to mankind the Scriptures of Truth, straightway abdicated His office; took no further care of His work; abandoned those precious writings to their fate."

One preacher put it very well in an evening sermon I heard – **"God gave us His original Words by verbal-plenary inspiration. God preserved those Words by verbal-plenary preservation. Almighty God promised and performed both events."** What he said is true! The Bible teaches not only the verbal-plenary inspiration of the original autographs, but also the verbal-plenary preservation of those autographs. The verbal-plenary inspiration for the original autographs of the Bible would be absolutely useless without the providential, verbal-plenary preservation of those Words! Why? Because nobody for 1,800 years or more has ever seen any portion of any book from the original books (autographs) of the Bible. If no one has ever seen the originals, how could they ever know or live by the Words of God? In fact, **the Lord Jesus Christ taught the preservation of the Scriptures**.

Matthew 4:4 says, *"But he answered and said, It is written, Man shall not live by bread alone, but by every word that proceedeth out of the mouth of God."* The phrase **"every word"** in the Greek is *panti rhmati* which means **each and every word**. Christ here is quoting the last portion of **Deuteronomy 8:3**. He clearly believed it had been preserved because if we are to live by "every word that proceedeth out of the mouth of God" we must know what those words are.

I remind you that there were NO original Old Testament autographs in Christ's day, yet He believed the Words of God had been preserved because He authoritatively quoted them.

Our Lord affirms biblical preservation in **Matthew 5:18** when he said, *"For verily I say unto you, Till heaven and earth pass, one jot or one tittle shall in no wise pass from the law, till all be fulfilled."*

Then there are His words recorded in **Luke 16:17** *"And it is easier for heaven and earth to pass, than one tittle of the law to fail."* Here He affirms that the Scriptures are more stable than Heaven and Earth!

Our Lord affirms the preservation of His words in all three Gospels – **Matthew 24:35** *"Heaven and earth shall pass away, but my words shall not pass away."* (See also Mark 13:31 & Luke 21:33).

There is one final passage I want to point out – **Matthew 5:18** *"For verily I say unto you, Till heaven and earth pass, one jot or one tittle shall in no wise pass from the law, till all be fulfilled."* Jesus is reinforcing the accuracy of the Scriptures down to the smallest detail and the slightest punctuation mark - because they are the VERY WORDS OF GOD.

Perhaps the strongest verses affirming the providential preservation of the Bible are **Psalms 12:6-7** *"The words of the LORD are pure words: as silver tried in a furnace of earth, purified seven times. 7 Thou shalt keep them, O LORD, thou shalt preserve them from this generation for ever."*

I will conclude with this statement – "The providential preservation of the Scriptures is also a necessary consequence of their divine inspiration. The God who inspired the Scriptures and gave them to His people to be an authoritative guide and consolation cannot allow this perfect and final revelation of His will to perish. Because God has inspired the Scriptures, He has also preserved them by His providence." (*The King James Version Defended* by Edward F. Hills).

FORMAL EQUIVALENCY OR LITERAL TRANSLA-TION

William Tyndale gave us the first printed English New Testament in 1526. He had a holy fear of God and reverence for His Word. In October of 1536 he was martyred for his faith and for printing a Bible in English for the people to read. Regarding his translation of the New Testament he wrote – "I call God to record against the day we shall appear before our Lord Jesus, to give a reckoning of our doings, that I never altered one syllable of God's Word against my conscience, nor would [I so alter it] this day, if all that is in the earth, whether it be pleasure, honor, or riches, might be given me." Tyndale gave us a formal equivalent translation of the New Testament from the Traditional Text or Textus Receptus.

<u>Why was William Tyndale so cautious in his Bible translating</u>? Look at these verses –

Deuteronomy 4:1-2 *"Now therefore hearken, O Israel, unto the statutes and unto the judgments, which I teach you, for to do them, that ye may live, and go in and possess the land which the LORD God of your fathers giveth you. 2 <u>Ye shall not add unto the word</u> which I command you, <u>neither shall ye diminish ought from it</u>, that ye may keep the commandments of the LORD your God which I command you."*

Proverbs 30:5-6 *"Every word of God is pure: he is a shield unto them that put their trust in him. 6 <u>Add thou not unto his words</u>, lest he reprove thee, and thou be found a liar."*

Revelation 22:18-19 *"For I testify unto every man that heareth the words of the prophecy of this book, If any man shall <u>add unto these things</u>, God shall add unto him the plagues that are written in this book: 19 And if any man shall <u>take away from the words</u> of the book of this prophecy, God shall take away his part out of the book of life, and out of the holy city, and from the things which are written in this book."*

Now to the definition of **Formal Equivalency**: It refers to the method of translating by finding reasonably equivalent words and phrases while following the **forms** of the source language as closely as possible. It is often referred to as **"literal translation."** It is a literal translation, (formal equivalent translation), when, as closely as possible, the Bible is translated *word-for-word*. If the original has a noun, then a noun is used in the translation.

A formal equivalent translation of the Bible is the best method that can be used in translating from the Hebrew, Aramaic and Greek underlying texts. But the underlying text that you translate from must be the Hebrew Masoretic text of the Old Testament and the Textus Receptus in the New Testament.

Let me explain why I say that it is the BEST way of translating the Bible. The Psalmist declared *"Forever, O Lord, thy word is settled in heaven."* **Psalm 119:89**. You might say, the MASTER COPY of the Word of God is in Heaven. Our Lord Jesus Christ declared, *"Heaven and earth shall pass away, but my words shall not pass away."* **Matthew 24:35**. Again He said, *"For verily I say unto you, Till heaven and earth pass, one jot or one tittle shall in no wise pass from the law, till all be fulfilled."* **Matthew 5:18**.

What is a **jot**? The word **"jot"** is the translation of the Hebrew word **"Yodh."**
This is a Hebrew Yodh ׳ , which is the 10th letter of the Hebrew alphabet. It is also the smallest letter of the Hebrew alphabet.

What is a **tittle**? Dr. Thomas Strouse believes that tittle literally means a dot. He says, "Tittle is the specifically accurate English word for a dot, coming through the German from the Hebrew for dot or teat." (Taken from an article, Luke 16:17—One Tittle by Dr. Thomas Strouse, http://www.deanburgonsociety.org/Preservation/tittle.htm).

Why am I explaining this to you? Simply this: Since our Lord Jesus was concerned about the smallest pen stroke of the smallest letter in the Hebrew text, it should also be important to us that we use a Bible translation that is based on **formal equivalency**, using the BEST TEXT GROUP (which is the Received Text). **Our King James Bible is the best formal equivalent translation of the right text group**. There is none better.

A formal equivalent translation lets the reader interpret for himself. And that is exactly what believers are to do. **2 Timothy 2:15** *"Study* *to show thyself approved unto God, a workman that needeth not to be ashamed, rightly dividing the word of truth."*

DYNAMIC EQUIVALENCE OR FUNCTIONAL EQUIVALENCE

This attitude of fear and trembling toward God's holy Word does not exist among most all of the present-day Bible translators. They are not afraid of <u>adding to</u>, <u>subtracting from</u> and <u>changing</u> the eternal Word of God.

Dynamic Equivalence, also called **Functional Equivalence**, is a translation method in which the translator attempts to reflect the thought of the writer in the source language rather than the words and forms. It is not so concerned about the grammatical *form* of the original language as it is with getting across the *thoughts*. DYNAMIC EQUIVALENCE AIMS TO TRANSLATE THOUGHTS RATHER THAN WORDS. However, the BIG problem is, a dynamic equivalence translation is more interpretive. And because it is more interpretive, the translators do not always know whether their interpretation is right. In essence, when dynamic equivalency is used, the translators put their own spin on the Bible!

Here are some actual illustrations where this type of translation has been used. From the KJB, look at **Isaiah 1:18**, *"Come now, and let us reason together, saith the LORD: though your sins be as scarlet, they shall be <u>as white as snow</u>; though they be red like crimson, they shall be as wool."* David Cloud relates this in reference to this passage – "An example of adapting the Bible's language to today's cultural situations (using dynamic equivalency) was related to me by the head of the Bible Society in Nepal. He told of one of the projects of the United Bible Societies, which was done in a part of the world in which the <u>people had not seen snow</u>. The translators, therefore, decided to translate **Isaiah 1:18**—"...though your sins be as scarlet, they shall be <u>white as the inside of a coconut</u>...."

Cloud goes on – "Consider some other examples of the way these versions change the Word of God to conform with culture. The following illustrations were given to us by Ross Hodsdon of Bibles International, formerly with Wycliffe:

In a translation for Eskimos in Alaska, 'lamb' was replaced with 'seal pup.'

In a translation in the Makusi language of Brazil, 'son of man' was replaced with 'older brother.'

In another Wycliffe translation 'fig tree' was replaced with 'banana tree.'"

That is NOT what God said! That is tampering with the Words of God! THAT IS WRONG. When one departs from the principle of a literal translation, the mind of the translator and the culture and understanding of the people become the authority rather than God's actual Words.

The same thing is happening in the modern versions today, because they are using the dynamic equivalent translation model. They are translating thoughts and not the Words of God.

PARAPHRASE

A **paraphrase** is a very, very loose translation of the Bible. In a paraphrase, the translator is neither concerned about translating the exact words, nor even the exact meaning of the original text. In fact, a paraphrase is a retelling of something in your own words. A paraphrase of the Bible is different from a translation. It is like a condensed commentary where the one that is doing the paraphrasing does no translating, but retells what is in the Bible in his own words, paying little or no attention to the exact words of the Bible. In reality, a paraphrase is not a Bible at all. It is the author's explanation of the Bible in his own words. Some popular Paraphrase Bibles are – The Living Bible; The New Living Bible, Good News for Modern Man; The Good News Bible, The Message; The Amplified Bible; The Clear Word Bible, etc. *NOTE*: **A paraphrase Bible is not really a Bible at all**.

I affirm once again: the King James Bible is the best Bible in the English language.

HIGHER CRITICISM

The phrase, **Higher Criticism**, was coined in 1778 by Johann Gottfried Eichhorn who lived from 1752 to 1827. It originally referred to the work of liberal German Biblical scholars, under the leadership of Ferdinand Christian Baur of the Tübingen School, of the University of Tübingen, located in the city of that name in Germany. The phrase "**higher criticism**" became popular in Europe (and England) from the mid-18th century.

So what is "Higher Criticism"? Higher criticism treats the Bible as a text created by human beings at a particular historical time and for various human motives. "They based their interpretations on a presupposition that the Bible is not divinely inspired and that a conglomerate of unknown authors and editors assembled and modified the Bible as they desired."
(www.foundationsforfreedom.net/Topics/Bible/Bible_Reliability.html).

Higher critics question the historical reliability of the Bible, biblical Creation, a real Adam and Eve, Noah, the Ark and the global flood, the miracles recorded in the Bible, the virgin birth of Christ, the literal, physical, bodily resurrection of Christ and more.

Let me give you an illustration. In the 1771 first edition of the Encyclopedia Britannica the editors treated the account of Noah and the Ark as essentially factual, and even offered some scientific calculations demonstrating that the animals could fit on the Ark. Why? Because they considered the Bible to be the Word of God. All that changed by the 8th edition (1852) of the Encyclopedia Britannica. The facts of Noah and the Ark were questioned. Why? It is because the editorial staff had been infected by **higher criticism,** and had adopted the position of the "learned" biblical scholars who did not believe in the inspiration of the Bible.

Now, I will share some illustrations relating specifically to the Bible. "**Higher criticism** has questioned the authenticity of history as the Bible presents it. Higher critics would deny the historicity of Israel's Exodus out of Egypt. With such presumptions, they strongly suggest that the Book of Exodus was just a story written later on to provide the people of Israel a national identity."
(www.foundationsforfreedom.net/Topics/Bible/Bible_Reliability.html).

Another illustration relates to the assertion of **higher critics** who claimed that Isaiah 53 was inserted into the Old Testament book of Isaiah after the time of Jesus. However, with the discovery of the Dead Sea Scrolls, particularly the scroll of Isaiah, which was dated to 335-324 B.C., **it proves that Isaiah 53 was NOT an insertion!**

Previous to the discovery of the Dead Sea Scroll of Isaiah, the oldest scroll of the Old Testament dated to about 900 A.D. Obviously, with the discovery of this older scroll, Isaiah 53 could no longer be said to have been inserted after Jesus' time. The higher critics were shown to be liars!

However, **higher criticism** certainly has done great damage to belief in the Bible because the result of their calling into question the events of the Bible was that the average person who heard these theories postulated by so-called "**Bible scholars,**" stated as facts, was that many of them became disillusioned with the Bible. Christian friends, this higher critical view of the Bible is still alive and well today. You see it being promoted on TV, in modern publication and on the Internet.

Bible believers reject the **higher critical** approach to the Bible! We believe the Bible IS the inspired, inerrant, infallible Word of God. We believe such verses as – **Psalm 119:160** *"Thy word is true from the beginning: and every one of thy righteous judgments endureth for ever."* We believe **2 Timothy 3:16** which says, *"All scripture is given by inspiration of God, and is profitable for doctrine, for reproof, for correction, for instruction in righteousness."*

TEXTUAL CRITICISM

Textual criticism is a humanly contrived method that so-called "Bible scholars" use to discover what the original manuscripts of the Bible most likely said. The object of textual criticism is to restore, as nearly as possible, the original text of a work, the autograph of which has been lost. That is why they have produced numerous editions of the **critical text** of the **Greek New Testament**. They are seeking to restore it but still have not accomplished the job.

The 24th edition of Nestle-Aland Greek New Testament says in the front –

Novum Testamentum Graece seeks to provide the reader with the critical appreciation of the whole textual tradition... It should naturally be understood that <u>this text is a working text</u> (in the sense of the century-long Nestle tradition); <u>it is not to be considered as definitive</u>, but as <u>a stimulus to further efforts towards redefining and verifying the text of the New Testament</u>.

So, how do the editors of these critical Greek New Testaments determine how they make the changes as they go about restoring the New Testament? I think you will be shocked! For the answer we need to look at the 27th edition of the *Novum Testamentum Graece* edited by Kurt Aland and Barbara Aland (27th edition, Stuttgart, 1993). It was agreed upon by the committee as the "best" reading and it has nothing to do with the "original" text. When they disagreed on the best reading to print, <u>they voted</u>. Who voted? Barbara Aland, Kurt Aland, Johannes Karavidopoulos, Cardinal Carlo M. Martini, and Bruce Metzger.

Now, the reason I am explaining this rather technical information is because it is ***the critical text of the New Testament from which nearly all the modern versions of the Bible are translated***. And let me tell you this. If the text the modern Bible translators use for their bibles "**is not to be considered as definitive**" <u>then certainly their translation cannot be considered definitive</u>.

This bogus assertion, that the original readings of the Bible, particularly the New Testament, have been altered or lost and need to be restored, is a major battlefront in the war over Bible versions. **I reject this critical view of the Bible** based on the promises that God has given us in the Bible. **God has preserved His Word and Words**. Those words are in the Hebrew Masoretic text of the Old Testament and the Greek Textus Receptus of our New Testament. As I said previously, I align myself with Dean John William Burgon who said, "If you and I believe that the original writings of the Scriptures were verbally inspired by God, then of necessity they must have been providentially preserved through the ages."

Though I have rehearsed many of these verses earlier in this book, I will do it again so that you will believe God that He has preserved His Words, and we can read those preserved words in our King James Bible.

- **Psalms 12:6-7** *"The words of the LORD are pure words: as silver tried in a furnace of earth, purified seven times. 7 Thou shalt keep them, O LORD, thou shalt preserve them from this generation for ever."*
- **Psalms 33:11** *"The counsel of the LORD standeth for ever, the thoughts of his heart to all generations."*
- **Psalms 100:5** *"For the LORD is good; his mercy is everlasting; and his truth endureth to all generations."*
- **Psalms 111:7-8** *"The works of his hands are verity and judgment; all his commandments are sure. 8 They stand fast for ever and ever, and are done in truth and uprightness."*
- **Psalms 117:2** *"For his merciful kindness is great toward us: and the truth of the LORD endureth for ever. Praise ye the LORD."*
- **Psalms 119:152** *"Concerning thy testimonies, I have known of old that thou hast founded them for ever."*
- **Psalms 119:160** *"Thy word is true from the beginning: and every one of thy righteous judgments endureth for ever."*
- **Isaiah 40:8** *"The grass withereth, the flower fadeth: but the word of our God shall stand for ever."*
- **Isaiah 59:21** *"As for me, this is my covenant with them, saith the LORD; My spirit that is upon thee, and my words which I have put in thy mouth, shall not depart out of thy mouth, nor out of the mouth of thy seed, nor out of the mouth of thy seed's seed, saith the LORD, from henceforth and for ever."*
- **Matthew 24:35** *"Heaven and earth shall pass away, but my words shall not pass away."*
- **John 10:35** *"...the scripture cannot be broken."*
- **1 Peter 1:23-25** *"Being born again, not of corruptible seed, but of incorruptible, by the word of God, which liveth and abideth for ever. 24 For all flesh is as grass, and all the glory of man as the flower of grass. The grass withereth, and the flower thereof falleth away: 25 But the word of the Lord endureth for ever. And this is the word which by the gospel is preached unto you."*

THE CORRUPTION OF THE NEW TESTAMENT TEXT

Before we forge ahead, I want to review several important terms – *Higher criticism* is a philosophy that rejects the inspiration of the Bible and treats the Bible as a text created by different people. *Textual criticism* is the theory that the <u>text of the true words of the New Testament had been lost</u> by the end of the 3rd century and it may or may not be recoverable. They believe that the New Testament remained in a corrupted state for more than 1500 years and that only in the late 19th century, through *textual criticism*, was the process of reconstructing the true text of the New Testament even started. This reconstructed Greek New Testament is called the *Critical Text,* because it was reconstructed using the humanly contrived principles of *textual criticism*. This ever-evolving *Critical Text* is based on early corrupted manuscripts. *Critical scholars* do not believe that the New Testament has been completely reconstructed, but is only in the process of being reconstructed. Therefore, no one knows for sure what it really says, because it is ever changing. There are 27 editions of the Nestle-Aland Greek Critical Text New Testament; each edition changes words in numerous places.

However, there is a **BIG PROBLEM** with the theory of *textual criticism*. **It is a man-made lie!** The same God who inspired the Bible has also preserved the Bible. Let me share with you <u>two additional verses</u> that teach Bible preservation...

- **Isaiah 40:8** *"The grass withereth, the flower fadeth: but <u>the word of our God shall stand for ever</u>."*

- **Isaiah 59:21** *"As for me, this is my covenant with them, saith the LORD; My spirit that is upon thee, and my words which I have put in thy mouth, shall not depart out of thy mouth, nor out of the mouth of thy seed, nor out of the mouth of thy seed's seed, saith the LORD, from henceforth and for ever."*

When we read the phrase *"shall not depart out of thy mouth..."* that means **God's Words will continue** so you can quote it yourself, for your children, for your grandchildren and succeeding generations forever!

What I am saying is this. There is a **preserved line** of Hebrew, Aramaic and Greek texts: the ones that underlie our King James Bible. But there is a **corrupted line of texts** also. This corrupt text line is the one from which nearly ALL of the New Translations come.

THE EARLY CORRUPTION OF THE NEW TESTAMENT

While I have shared some of this material earlier in the book, I want to go over it again, since it is so important. Purposeful efforts to alter and corrupt the New Testament began almost immediately after the Gospels and epistles (letters) were written. This is affirmed by Paul in **2 Corinthians 2:17** – *"For we are not as many, which corrupt the word of God: but as of sincerity, but as of God, in the sight of God speak we in Christ."* The word, **corrupt,** is a translation of the Greek word καπηλευοντεϖ – kapaleuontes (kap-ale-loo-entace) which means a **huckster**. A **huckster** is a shrewd, aggressive salesman who is less than honest. One scholar said this about the word – The Greek word was used to describe shady "wine-dealers *playing tricks with their wines*; mixing the new, harsh wines, so as to make them pass for old. They not only sold their wares in the market, but had *wine-shops* all over the town..." where they peddled their corrupt wine claiming it was genuine. They made a bundle of money by their deception.

So, how is this word **[huckster]** used in reference to the Word of God? Gnostic hucksters, and other enemies of Christianity, took the pure Words of God and, like the shady wine dealers, mixed in their own philosophies, opinions and ideas, and then peddled it as the real thing.

Let me illustrate just how Gnostics corrupted the Alexandrian line of New Testament texts. Consider Marcion. He was **born** between 85 to 110 A.D. No one knows for sure. He founded his own Gnostic-oriented heretical sect in about 144 A.D. He taught that the God of the Old Testament could not have been the Father of Jesus Christ, because Christ speaks of His Father as a God of love, but the God of the Jews was a God of wrath. Marcion taught that Jehovah, the God of the Old Testament, created the world, but that all created flesh was evil. Further, he taught that the soul/spirit of man was created by a greater god, one who was above Jehovah. This greater god created the spiritual realm and was the true Father of Jesus Christ. To release man's soul from his flesh, this greater god sent Christ. Christ appeared, in the form of a thirty-year-old man, in a spiritual body that appeared to be physical but was not a physical body. **Salvation,** he taught, **was gained by renouncing Jehovah and all things physical**. Marcion rejected the Hebrew Scriptures, and the quotations of those Hebrew Scriptures in the New Testament. **The followers of Marcion issued their own New Testament composed of Luke and Paul's letters revised to their liking**. His followers made their revisions to support and reflect their doctrines. Ultimately, these Marcionian revisions reflected their private interpretations, and what is worse, *these perversions have survived in some of the ancient Greek New Testament manuscripts* and account for the differences between the eclectic Critical Greek text and the Textus Receptus.

An early preacher, Irenaeus (c. 115-202 A.D.) points out that *"Marcion cut up that Gospel According to Luke"* (Irenaeus' *Against Heresies*, p. 382). This would account for the large number of changes found in varying manuscripts of Luke and the large number of verses that are left out. It is, for example, understandable why the phrase, *"And when he had thus spoken, he shewed them his hands and his feet."* **(Luke 24:40)** was omitted by Marcion, since he did not believe in the physical resurrection of Jesus but only in a spiritual resurrection. In fact, the apparatus of the United Bible Society's Critical Greek New Testament text points out **that this verse is omitted by both Marcion and Codex D** (United Bible Society, 2nd ed., p. 317). This verse is omitted from the text of the NEB, RSV and the early editions of the NASV. NASV editors have changed more recent editions to show the verse in brackets - [ ], stating "many mss. do not contain this verse." Thus we see that Codex D and the NASB, NEB and RSV reflect some of the tampering done by Marcion and his followers.

1 Timothy 3:16 is another example of a Gnostic corruption that has made it into many of the modern versions. The verse reads – *"And without controversy great is the mystery of godliness: God was manifest in the flesh, justified in the Spirit, seen of angels, preached unto the Gentiles, believed on in the world, received up into glory."*

The Jehovah's Witnesses have adopted a number of the Gnostic heresies. One example is that Jesus is a created god, NOT God manifest in the flesh. In the Watchtower's *New World Translation* **they change** "God was manifest in the flesh," as it says in **1 Timothy 3:16, to** "He was made manifest in flesh." In the Textus Receptus Greek, which underlies our King James Bible, it reads ψεοϖ *(theos)* (God) <2316> εφανερωψη *(Ephanerothe)* (was manifested/revealed) <5319> (5681) εν (in) <1722> σαρκι *(sarki)* (the flesh) <4561>.

BUT, the Greek text which underlies the Jehovah's Witness NWT followed the corrupted texts, so it reflects their Gnostic heresy about Christ. However, the JW Bible is not the only bible that follows this corruption – SO DO THE NIV, NASB, NRSV, ESV, and perhaps others. They say "*He*" instead of "God," thus following the Gnostic corruption which has made its way into the corrupt Alexandrian text line of texts. That is why so many new versions have missing verses or different readings, because they have been translated from a text line that the Gnostics altered.

The same is true of **John 1:18.** In the **King James Bible** it says – *"No man hath seen God at any time; the only begotten Son, which is in the bosom of the Father, he hath declared him."* However, the Jehovah's Witness NWT reads, "the only-begotten **god**" (Gk. *monogenes theos*). Again, this is because the Greek text of the NWT reads differently from the Textus Receptus Greek text from which the King James Bible was translated – The TR Greek says (Gk. *monogenes heios*) – "**only begotten Son**" The NWT uses a Greek text that was influenced by Gnosticism.

1881 Westcott & Hort followed the Gnostic corruption – θεον ουδεις εωρακεν πωποτε μονογενης θεος (*monogenes [only-begotten] theos [god]*) ο ων εις τον κολπον του πατρος εκεινος εξηγησατο.

1894 Scrivener, which underlies our KJV has it right - θεον ουδεις εωρακεν πωποτε ο μονογενης υιος (*monogenes [only-begotten] heios [son]*) ο ων εις τον κολπον του πατρος εκεινος εξηγησατο

Again, in both of these examples, the NASV, NIV, ESV and others agree with the NWT because, they are both based on the same corrupt Greek text. It is clear that Gnostic false doctrines have influenced the various Western/Alexandrian manuscripts, and as a result of the modern translations using Greek texts based on corrupt Western manuscripts, Gnosticism influences translations today.

Back to the point I was making – We know that *false gospels* and *false letters* were written and circulated while the apostles were still alive. We find evidence of this in **2 Thessalonians 2:2** – *"That ye be not soon shaken in mind, or be troubled, neither by spirit, nor by word, nor by letter as from us, as that the day of Christ is at hand."*

It is obvious that someone had written a letter and was circulating it, claiming that it was from the Apostle Paul and other disciples. **Paul says the letter is spurious, a fake, and a fraud**.

Now consider **2 Peter 2:1-3** – *"But there were false prophets also among the people, even as there shall be false teachers among you, who privily shall bring in damnable heresies, even denying the Lord that bought them, and bring upon themselves swift destruction. 2 And many shall follow their pernicious ways; by reason of whom the way of truth shall be evil spoken of. 3 And through covetousness shall they with feigned words make merchandise of you: whose judgment now of a long time lingereth not, and their damnation slumbereth not."*

These false prophets and teachers are said to *"privily...bring in damnable heresies."* That is, they secretly introduced spurious (unauthentic, counterfeit or bogus) teachings that were "damnable heresies" or perversion of the truth. They sought to peddle these heresies among believers. These "damnable heresies" were purposefully written into many New Testament manuscripts and circulated. The modern Bible versions of today are translated from the ancient manuscript group corrupted early on, beginning in the days of the apostles.

WHY YOU SHOULD NOT USE THE MODERN BIBLE VERSIONS

Codex Vaticanus is one of those corrupt manuscripts that the modern Bible versions are based on. An example of that corruption can be seen on this leaf in what would be **Hebrews 1:3.** A marginal note reveals that a corrector had erased and substituted a word in what would be verse 3 (there are no verse divisions in ancient Bibles. Those do not appear until 1560 in the Geneva Bible). A second corrector reinserted the original word with this marginal comment: "**Fool and knave, leave the old reading and do not change it**."

Vaticanus is a very heavily corrected and corrupted text!

I believe that we should NOT use Bible versions that are based on corrupt manuscripts! We have been warned! **Matthew 7:15-20** says, *"Beware of false prophets, which come to you in sheep's clothing, but inwardly they are ravening wolves. (16) Ye shall know them by their fruits. Do men gather grapes of thorns, or figs of thistles? (17) Even so every good tree bringeth forth good fruit; but a corrupt tree bringeth forth evil fruit. (18) A good tree cannot bring forth evil fruit, neither can a corrupt tree bring forth good fruit. (19) Every tree that bringeth not forth good fruit is hewn down, and cast into the fire. (20) Wherefore by their fruits ye shall know them."*

Luke 6:44-49 *"For every tree is known by his own fruit. For of thorns men do not gather figs, nor of a bramble bush gather they grapes. 45 A good man out of the good treasure of his heart bringeth forth that which is good; and an evil man out of the evil treasure of his heart bringeth forth that which is evil: for of the abundance of the heart his mouth speaketh. 46 And why call ye me, Lord, Lord, and do not the things which I say? 47 Whosoever cometh to me, and heareth my sayings, and doeth them, I will show you to whom he is like: 48 He is like a man which built an house, and digged deep, and laid the foundation on a rock: and when the flood arose, the stream beat vehemently upon that house, and could not shake it: for it was founded upon a rock. 49 But he that heareth, and doeth not, is like a man that without a foundation built an house upon the earth; against which the stream did beat vehemently, and immediately it fell; and the ruin of that house was great."*

My premise is a simple one: I will demonstrate to you that the **Modern Bible Versions** are the evil fruit from a corrupt tree, planted by **Wolves in Sheep's clothing**, whose plan was and is to confuse the sheep and ultimately destroy their faith in the Word(s) of God, thus getting them to build their lives on the unsure shifting sands of human reason *instead of* building their lives on the **SURE FOUNDATION OF GOD'S WORD, the King James Bible, which is accurately translated from the texts that God has preserved. Why is that important?**

For genuine believers, the Bible is the foundation of literally every **doctrine, belief** and **practice** in New Testament Christianity! If a belief, principle or practice does not have a biblical base it should be rejected. We read in **1 Thessalonians 5:21**

"Prove all things; hold fast that which is good." The English word **prove** is a translation of the Greek word dokimazete – δοκιμαζετε (*dok-im-ad'zate*). The word carries the idea of **proving a thing whether it is worthy or not**. So, the question is, how are we to go about **proving** something? I believe **Isaiah 8:20** gives us insight into the answer to this question – *"To the law and to the testimony: if they speak not according to this word, it is because there is no light in them."* In other words, **examine everything by the words of the Bible** and if it does not line up, reject it!

It should be obvious to you that I believe in the Verbal Plenary Inspiration for the 66 books of the Bible and I also believe in the Verbal Plenary preservation of those same 66 books! I believe that the process of God breathing out His Words occurred only once when He breathed out or 'inspired' the Hebrew, Aramaic and Greek texts. Though the process of inspiration has never been repeated, the product of inspiration, that is, the Hebrew, Aramaic, and Greek Words, have been preserved by God in the Words of the Masoretic Hebrew and Textus Receptus (traditional) Greek that underlie the King James Bible.

I assert that we DO have the words of God today and that our King James Bible is the best translation of those preserved words. There has been none better, there is none better, there will be none better in the future.

Now here is the problem. **If** the Bible was not inspired, then it CANNOT be used as a reliable standard! **If** the Bible was inspired and the readings lost, then it CANNOT be used as a reliable standard! And lastly, **if** the Bible texts are not preserved, then it CANNOT be used as a reliable standard!

That is the belief and teaching of those who laid the foundation of the modern Bible versions. They do not believe God has preserved His Words and therefore the Bible is **NOT** a reliable standard! They adopted the *higher critical* view of the Bible. But that is **NOT** what I believe!

SO WHAT IS "HIGHER CRITICISM?"

As I explained previously, **higher criticism treats the Bible as a text created by human beings** at a particular historical time and <u>for various human motives</u>. "They based their interpretations on a presupposition that the Bible is not divinely inspired and that a conglomerate of unknown authors and editors assembled and modified the Bible as they desired."
(www.foundationsforfreedom.net/Topics/Bible/Bible_Reliability.html).

BRIEF OVERVIEW OF THE MOTLEY CREW BEHIND THE MODERN BIBLE VERSIONS

There are many men who undermined the authority of the Scriptures by denying its divine inspiration and preservation and promoting what we call textual criticism.

If you were to take the time to look into those who have laid the foundation for the modern Bible versions, you would understand the title of this section. You would find a group of doubters, deceivers, skeptics, occultists, heretics, unbelievers and more. I do not have the time in this series to thoroughly expose the beliefs, teaching and practices of these men; however, I will name some of the key players in this *motley crew* and make brief comments about their beliefs.

RICHARD SIMON

Richard Simon (1638-1712) is often called *the Father of Biblical Criticism.*
(www.1902encyclopedia.com/S/SIM/richard-simon.html). He was a French Roman Catholic who held apostate and heretical views that undermined the authority and preservation of the Word(s) of God. For instance, he believed there were men before Adam. He rejected the Bible as the sole authority for faith and practice and held that Catholic tradition was of equal authority with the Bible. However, his revolutionary apostasy was his contention "that **no original text of the Bible exists**, that the texts one possesses have developed and have been altered through the ages, and that it is therefore necessary to apply the method of critical evaluation to biblical materials to establish the most accurate human form of the

revelation. This method involves philology (study of texts and trying to reconstruct them), textual study, historical researches, and comparative studies." (www.bookrags.com/research/simon-richard-16381712-eoph) This is a key building block undermining the preservation of the Word and Words of God. He published numerous books supporting his apostate teachings including *his 1689 Critical History of the Text of the New Testament* that advances the idea that the Scripture has not been carefully preserved and therefore the Bible cannot be entirely authoritative. Previous to that volume, he published one called *Critical History of the Old Testament* where he denied Moses was the author of the Pentateuch. Further, he stated that the Old Testament is a mixture of truth and myth. In 1702 he published a four volume New Testament based on the Latin Vulgate, but it included variant readings from the Greek and critical remarks.

JOHANN SALOMO SEMLER (1725-1791) is sometimes called the *Father of German Rationalism.* **Rationalism** is basically the theory that human reason is the best guide for belief and actions. It is the theory that the exercise of reason, rather than experience, authority, or spiritual revelation, provides the primary basis for knowledge and truth. "He rejected the deity of Jesus Christ and believed that revelation must be judged by human reason. The sophisticated mind should have no obligation to believe what is 'unreasonable' in the Bible." (http://history-perspective.com/critical_theories.html).

The common thread is that Semler was strongly influenced by Richard Simon, and particularly his 1689 book, *Critical History*. More important to the focus of this message, Semler is *The Father of the Recension Theory*. This theory claims that the Received text is an editorial recension created centuries after the apostles. Additionally, the textual readings favoring theological orthodoxy should be suspect. Why? Because he denied biblical preservation and falsely believed the orthodox readings were created by textual editors during the early centuries. Because of this view, he taught other manuscripts, particularly the older ones, which shortens the passage or leaves it out, should be followed.

I should also point out that Semler began grouping manuscripts into three families: Alexandrian (Egyptian), Western and Asiatic (Byzantine). He believed the Alexandrian was superior to the Byzantine.

As an aside, Semler became a believer in alchemy, whereby ordinary metals are converted into gold. Tragically, what he managed to do was convert the Gold of the Word of God into dirt of doubt.

JOHANN JAKOB GRIESBACH

JOHANN JAKOB GRIESBACH (1745-1812). He adopted Selmer's recension theory that claimed that the Received Text was an editorial revision created centuries after the apostles. This myth, as you well know, was later popularized by Westcott and Hort.

J. J. Griesbach was <u>one of the earliest fathers of modern textual criticism</u>. Marvin R. Vincet says in his book *A History of the Textual Criticism of the New Testament*, published in 1899, "With Griesbach, really critical texts may be said to have begun."

The late Bruce Metzger said, "Griesbach laid the foundations for all subsequent work on the Greek text of the New Testament." He further asserted, "the importance of Griesbach for New Testament textual criticism can scarcely be overestimated." (Metzger, *The Text of the New Testament*) He rejected the deity of Jesus Christ and the supernatural infallibility of Holy Scripture. **Griesbach was the <u>first to declare Mark 16:9-20 spurious</u>**. He omitted it from the 1796 edition of his critical Greek New Testament.

I own a copy of his 1809 American critical edition of his Greek New Testament. It was published by Harvard College. They published this edition because it was "a most powerful weapon to be used against the supporters of verbal inspiration." (Theodore Letis, *The Ecclesiastical Text*) This was done around the same time that Harvard College gave way to Unitarianism.

Here is the point: The enemies of the inspiration of the Bible clearly understood that, in general, modern textual criticism, and specifically Griesbach's critical New Testament, weakened the key doctrines of the Christian faith (such as inspiration, preservation, etc.) and undermines the authority of the Bible.

KARL LACHMANN

KARL LACHMANN (1793-1851) was not even a Bible scholar but a professor of Classical and German Philology at Berlin. He has been described as a German rationalist [human reason is the sole source and final test of all truth]. Lachmann's theory and belief was that all of the extant New Testament manuscripts were corrupt and that it is not possible to dogmatically reconstruct the apostolic text. His goal was to secure the text that was in widest use in the 4th Century, the time of Jerome, and he referenced the Alexandrian manuscripts and the writings of Origin and others. Lachmann did not study the New Testament as the supernaturally-inspired and divinely-preserved Word of God, but as a mere book. He was a profane man who treated the Bible like any other book and his textual research was a mere scholarly venture. He began to apply the same rules that he had used in editing texts of the Greek classics to the N.T. Greek text because he presupposed it was hopelessly corrupted. His theory undermined the doctrine of divine preservation by claiming that the apostolic text cannot possibly be known for certain and the best that could be done was to rediscover the 4th century text.

BROOKE FOSS WESTCOTT AND JOHN ANTHONY HORT

Brooke Foss Westcott (January 12, 1825 – July 27, 1901) (pictured at the left) and **John Anthony Hort** (1828-1892) (pictured right). They are the **Fathers of the Modern Bible Versions**. They got many of their ideas from Griesbach and Lachmann. Westcott and Hort built their own critical Greek New Testament text based primarily on two conflicting Greek uncial MSS – Codex Vaticanus and Codex Sinaiticus. These perverted MSS do not even agree among themselves. In the Gospels alone they differ in over 3,000 places. The ironic thing is that Westcott and Hort knew this when they created their text! Virtually all the modern versions are based on Westcott and Hort's critical Greek New Testament. In the introduction to the 24th edition of Nestle's Greek New Testament, editors Erwin Nestle and Kurt Aland make the following admission: "Thus **THE TEXT, BUILT UPON THE WORK OF THE 19TH CENTURY, HAS REMAINED AS A WHOLE UNCHANGED,** particularly since the research of recent years has not yet led to the establishment of a generally acknowledged N.T. text" (Erwin Nestle and Kurt Aland, *Novum Testamentum Graece*, 24th edition, 1960, p. 62).

EUGENE NIDA

EUGENE NIDA was born in Oklahoma in 1914. He has the dubious distinction of being the father of the **heretical dynamic equivalency theory** of Bible translation that is used in almost all of the modern Bible versions. He believes the record of Jacob wrestling with the Angel was not a literal event. He denies the substitutionary blood atonement of Christ (Nida, *Theory and Practice*, 1969, p.

53). He denies that Christ died to satisfy God's justice. He believes the blood of the cross was merely symbolic of Christ's death and is never used in the Bible "in the sense of propitiation." He retired from being the Executive Secretary for Translations for the American Bible Society in 1980. Today he lives in Brussels, Belgium.

KURT ALAND

KURT ALAND (March 28, 1915-April 13, 1994) of the Nestle-Aland Greek New Testament fame, denied the verbal inspiration of the Bible and wanted to see all denominations united into one "body" by the acceptance of a new ecumenical canon of Scripture which would take into account the Catholic apocryphal books (*The Problem of the New Testament Canon*, pp. 6,7,30-33).

BRUCE MANNING METZGER

Bruce M. Metzger

BRUCE MANNING METZGER (February 9, 1914 – February 13, 2007). He edited and provided commentary for many Bible translations and wrote dozens of books. He was one of the editors of the United Bible Societies' standard Greek New Testament, **the starting point for nearly all translations of the New Testament in recent decades**. In 1952, he became a contributor to the Revised Standard Version (RSV) of the Bible, and became general editor of the *Reader's Digest Bible* (a condensed version of the RSV) in 1982. From 1977 to 1990, he also chaired the Committee on Translators for the New Revised Standard Version (NRSV) of the Bible, which included the Apocrypha.

WHAT METZGER BELIEVED

Metzger believed the Old Testament was a "**matrix** (compilation) **of myth, legend, and history.**" (Note: **Jesus affirmed the Old Testament's authenticity Luke 24:44-45**)

Metzger did not believe that Moses wrote the Pentateuch but that "the Pentateuch took shape over a long period of time." (Note:

Jesus affirmed that Moses wrote it – John 7:19; Matthew 8:4; John 5:46).

Metzger did not believe in the biblical worldwide flood. (Note: **Jesus affirmed the global flood – Matthew 24:37-39)**

Metzger believed the book of Job is a folktale.

Metzger believed Isaiah was written by Isaiah plus two or three unknown men who wrote centuries later. (Note: **Jesus affirmed that Isaiah wrote the book that carries his name – Luke 3:4).**

Metzger believed that Jonah was a "didactic narrative [story intended to teach a lesson] which has taken older material from the realm of **popular legend** and put it to a new, more consequential use." (Note: **Jesus affirmed that Jonah was real – Matthew 12:39-41).**

Metzger believed that Paul did not write the Pastoral Epistles [1 & 2 Timothy and Titus]. **1 Timothy 1:1** says he did. **2 Timothy 1:1** says he did. **Titus 1:1** says he did!

What puzzles me is that Metzger is adored by modern day Bible scholars, theologians, preachers, students and even many fundamental Baptists. I concur with Dr. Jeffrey Khoo who said – **"True and faithful Biblicists ought to be warned that Metzger's scholarship is not one to be desired nor admired."** Christian friend, "Metzger's philosophy and methodology will only lead to chronic uncertainty and perpetual unbelief of the total inspiration and perfect preservation of the Holy Scriptures." **James 3:11-12** *"Doth a fountain send forth at the same place sweet water and bitter? (12) Can the fig tree, my brethren, bear olive berries? either a vine, figs? so can no fountain both yield salt water and fresh."*

CONCLUSION

These men were all apostates! There is not a believer in the bunch. These are indeed a motley crew, each contributing a wide variety of apostate and heretical ideas that undermine the Word(s) of God. These are the men behind the modern versions!

THINGS THAT ARE DIFFERENT ARE NOT THE SAME!

I believe that if I showed you an apple and an orange and asked you, "are these the same or different," you would say "they are different." While they certainly are both in the fruit family, they are different!

If I held up an axe and a chain saw and asked you if they were different or the same, I believe you would say, "they are different." While they are both used to cut wood, they are different.

If I held up a United States One Dollar Bill and United States One Hundred Dollar Bill and asked you if they were different or the same, you would surely say, "they are different." While they are both legal tender for all debts public and private, I believe everyone would rather have a $100 bill than a $1 bill.

Yet, when it comes to the differences in Bible versions, we are being told that there are not that many differences, and that even the differences there are, really do not affect any major doctrines. Therefore it really does not matter! **I DISAGREE!** Why? Because, **THINGS THAT ARE DIFFERENT ARE NOT THE SAME!**

As I have been pointing out in this series, there are two VERY DIFFERENT Greek text streams from which the New Testament has been translated. The Tyndale, Matthews, Great, Geneva and King James New Testaments have all been translated from the Eastern, Antiochian, Traditional, Received or Textus Receptus text group (all names for the same text group). There are more than 5,000 Greek manuscripts and portions in this group. On the other hand, the Modern Bible Versions are translated from the Western, Alexandrian or Minority text group (all names for the same text group). There are about 45 manuscripts or portions in this group.

DR. JACK MOORMAN OF LONDON, ENGLAND, WHO I PERSONALLY KNOW AND HAVE ATTENDED HIS CHURCH, HAS PUBLISHED A BOOK THAT **LISTS THE 8,000 DIFFERENCES BETWEEN THE NEW TESTAMENT**

GREEK WORDS OF THE TEXTUS RECEPTUS UNDERLYING THE KING JAMES NEW TESTAMENT AND THE WORDS OF NESTLES-ALAND'S 26TH & 27TH GREEK NEW TESTAMENT WHICH UNDERLIES THE MODERN BIBLE VERSIONS.

Christian friends, **THINGS THAT ARE DIFFERENT ARE NOT THE SAME!** 8,000 differences should prove that point! In the chart below, I want to point out the **17 verses** that are completely missing from many of the Modern Bible Versions.

17 Verses Completely Missing From the Modern Bible Versions

King James Bible Compared to the New International Version & the English Standard Version

Major Verse Discrepancies between KJV, NIV & ESV

Verses Completely Omitted From Two of the Most Popular Modern Versions

King James Version	New International Version	English Standard Version
Matthew 17:21	**Entire Verse Omitted**	**Entire Verse Omitted**
Matthew 18:11	**Entire Verse Omitted**	**Entire Verse Omitted**
Matthew 23:14	**Entire Verse Omitted**	**Entire Verse Omitted**
Mark 7:16	**Entire Verse Omitted**	**Entire Verse Omitted**
Mark 9:44	**Entire Verse Omitted**	**Entire Verse Omitted**
Mark 9:46	**Entire Verse Omitted**	**Entire Verse Omitted**

Mark 11:26	Entire Verse Omitted	Entire Verse Omitted
Mark 15:28	Entire Verse Omitted	Entire Verse Omitted
Luke 17:36	Entire Verse Omitted	Entire Verse Omitted
Luke 23:17	Entire Verse Omitted	Entire Verse Omitted
John 5:4	Entire Verse Omitted	Entire Verse Omitted
Acts 8:37	Entire Verse Omitted	Entire Verse Omitted
Acts 15:34	Entire Verse Omitted	Entire Verse Omitted
Acts 24:7	Entire Verse Omitted	Entire Verse Omitted
Acts 28:29	Entire Verse Omitted	Entire Verse Omitted
Romans 16:24	Entire Verse Omitted	Entire Verse Omitted
1 John 5:7 (KJV) For there are three that bear record in heaven, the Father, the Word, and the Holy Ghost: and these three are one. 8 And there are three that bear witness in earth, the Spirit, and the water, and the blood: and these three agree in one.	**1 John 5: 7 (NIV)** For there are three that testify: [omit – **in heaven, the Father, the Word, and the Holy Ghost: and these three are one.**] 8 the Spirit, the water and the blood; and the three are in agreement.	**1 John 5:7 (ESV)** For there are three that testify: [omit – **in heaven, the Father, the Word, and the Holy Ghost: and these three are one.**] 8 the Spirit and the water and the blood; and these three agree.

JOHANNINE COMMA

I John 5:7-8 is called the ***Johannine comma***. It lends strong support to the Triune nature of God! Bruce Metzger, one of ***The Motley Crew*** behind the modern Bible versions, wrote in his 1992 book *The Test of the New Testament: Its Transmission, Corruption, and Restoration* on page 62 that the "the first Greek manuscript discovered which contained the passage relating to the *Three Heavenly Witnesses* of **I John 5:7-8** was a New Testament from the late 15th or early 16th century." That is just NOT TRUE! There is an abundance of other ancient manuscript evidence in support of the passage. As Edward Hills says, "The first undisputed citations of the *Johannine comma* occur in the writing of two 4th-century Spanish bishops... In the 5th century the *Johannine comma* was quoted by several orthodox African writers to defend the doctrine of the Trinity against the gainsaying of the Vandals, who...were fanatically attached to the Arian heresy." Evidence for the early existence of the *Johannine comma* is found in the Latin versions and in the writings of the Latin Church Fathers." Among these is Cyprian (c. 250) and Cassiodorus (480–570), as well as an Old Latin manuscript of the 5th or 6th century, and in the *Speculum*, a treatise which contains an Old Latin text.

I stand aligned with those who believe that it is very probable Origen (c. 185-254 A.D.), the great corrupter of the Bible, is responsible for removing **1 John 5:7**. Without **1 John 5:7** <u>the Greek syntax of verses 6-8</u> makes no sense.

Now we move on to the issue of **Mark 1:2-3**. This passage in Mark is an important one because it demonstrates that the underlying text of the King James Bible is the one God has preserved. The KJV correctly says, "it is written by the prophets!" The passage quotes two prophets, Malachi and Isaiah.

Mark 1:2-3 (KJV)	Mark 1:2-3 (NIV)	**Mark 1:2-3 (ESV)**
As it is written in the <u>prophets</u>, Behold, I send my messenger before thy face, which shall prepare thy way before thee.	It is written in <u>Isaiah</u> the prophet: "I will send my messenger ahead of you, who will prepare your way, a voice of one	As it is written in <u>Isaiah</u> the prophet "Behold, I send my messenger before your face, who will prepare your way

The voice of one crying in the wilderness, Prepare ye the way of the Lord, make his paths straight.	calling in the desert, 'Prepare the way for the Lord, make straight paths for him.'	the voice of one crying in the wilderness: 'Prepare the way of the Lord, make his paths straight,'"

Malachi 3:1 (KJV) *Behold, I will send my messenger, and he shall prepare the way before me: and the LORD, whom ye seek, shall suddenly come to his temple, even the messenger of the covenant, whom ye delight in: behold, he shall come, saith the LORD of hosts.*

Isaiah 40:3 (KJV) *The voice of him that crieth in the wilderness, Prepare ye the way of the LORD, make straight in the desert a highway for our God.*

The King James Bible correctly states, it is written by the ***prophets*** **NOT** just by Isaiah the prophet.

There are thousands of other missing phrases, and words in the NIV and ESV. I want to give you some more examples. The NIV and ESV claim that **John 7:53-8:11** are missing in "the earliest and most reliable manuscripts." It is the account of the woman taken in adultery. However, they do not tell you that this passage is designated as the *Pericope De Adultera,* referring to the woman caught in the act of adultery, and is included in numerous uncials such as D05, G, H, K, M, U, and G. Among the minuscule or cursive manuscripts it is in 28, 700, 892, 1009, 1010, 1071, 1079, 1195, 1216, 1344, 1365, 1546, 1646, 2148, and 2174. Most Greek manuscripts contain this passage. It also is in early translations such as the Bohairic Coptic Version, the Syriac Palestinian Version and the Ethiopic Version, all of which date from the second to the sixth centuries. It is clearly the reading of the majority of the Old Latin manuscripts and Jerome's Latin Vulgate. The passage has patristic support: Didascalia (third century), Ambrosiaster (fourth century), Ambrose (fourth century), the Apostolic Constitutions (which are the largest liturgical collections of writings from Antioch Syria in about 380 AD), Jerome (420 AD), and Augustine (430 AD). [Dr. Thomas Holland's *Crowned With Glory*].

Two final illustrations of the thousands to choose from...

Matthew 5:44 (KJV) But I say unto you, Love your enemies, bless them that curse you, <u>do good to them that hate you, and pray for them which despitefully use you, and persecute you;</u>	Matthew 5:44 (NIV) But I tell you: Love your enemies and pray for those who persecute you, [More than half the verse is omitted]	Matthew 5:44 (ESV) – But I say to you, Love your enemies and pray for those who persecute you, [More than half the verse is omitted]
Mark 6:11 (KJV) – And whosoever shall not receive you, nor hear you, when ye depart thence, shake off the dust under your feet for a testimony against them. Verily I say unto you, It shall be more tolerable for Sodom and Gomorrha in the day of judgment, than for that city.	Mark 6:11 (NIV) And if any place will not welcome you or listen to you, shake the dust off your feet when you leave, as a testimony against them." [A third of the verse is missing]	Mark 6:11 (ESV)– And if any place will not receive you and they will not listen to you, when you leave, shake off the dust that is on your feet as a testimony against them. [The last third of the verse is missing]

Christian friends, I have shared this to make it clear that **Things That Are Different Are Not The Same!** Remember, there are 8,000 (perhaps more) differences between the underlying Greek text of the King James Bible and the Modern Versions. I close with **Deuteronomy 4:2** *"Ye shall not add unto the word which I command you, neither shall ye diminish ought from it, that ye may keep the commandments of the LORD your God which I command you."*

CONTRASTING VIEWS OF THE SCRIPTURES: THE VIEW OF THE CRITICS & THE VIEW OF CHRIST

Matthew 7:17-20 *"Even so <u>every good tree bringeth forth good fruit</u>; but a <u>corrupt tree bringeth forth evil fruit</u>. 18 <u>A good tree cannot bring forth evil fruit</u>, neither can <u>a corrupt tree bring forth</u>*

good fruit. 19 Every tree that bringeth not forth good fruit is hewn down, and cast into the fire. 20 Wherefore <u>by their fruits ye shall know them</u>."

I have pointed out how the New Testament autographs came under attack almost before the ink was dry. There were those in the times of the apostles who corrupted the Word of God (**2 Corinthians 2:17**). Further, false Gospels and false letters were circulated, which claimed they were authentic (**2 Thessalonians 2:2**). In **2 Corinthians 4:1-2** the Apostle Paul wrote – *"Therefore seeing we have this ministry, as we have received mercy, we faint not; 2 But have renounced the hidden things of dishonesty, not walking in craftiness, nor <u>handling the word of God deceitfully</u>; but by manifestation of the truth commending ourselves to every man's conscience in the sight of God."* In this verse Paul writes that he and his companions are not like others that were **"handling the word of God deceitfully."** The phrase means, <u>they had not corrupted God's Words with error</u>! We know that there were false teachers and preachers who were introducing "damnable heresies" in their teachings and then amended the Gospels and letters to support their teachings and circulated those corrupted writings. In the days of the apostles, and shortly afterwards, numerous false teachings and heresies were being advocated, among them Nicolaitianism, Gnosticism, Arianism, Donatism, Pelagianism, Neo-Platonism and others.

Jude wrote to the believers of his day (65-67 A.D.) that they need to *"earnestly contend for the faith once delivered to the saints"* because deceitful, ungodly men were changing the nature of the New Testament teaching on grace and salvation! (**Jude 1:3-4**). These false doctrines influenced the transmission of Scripture and account for some of the differences in the line of manuscripts.

CONTRASTING VIEWS OF THE SCRIPTURES

How do the beliefs of Jesus Christ compare to the beliefs of those who produced the **critical text**, which underlies almost all of the modern versions of the Bible?

In any study of the Bible versions' controversy, there are two names that you will come across regularly – **Westcott and Hort**. Many consider them the **fathers of modern textual criticism**. So, let's begin by telling you something about them and their beliefs.

Brooke Foss Westcott (1825-1901) and Fenton John Anthony Hort (1828-1892) produced a Greek New Testament in 1881 based on Codex Vaticanus from the Vatican and the findings of Constantine Tischendorf, Codex Sinaiticus. I visited St. Catherine's Monastery in 2008. St. Catherine's Monastery is historically significant in the textual controversy because it is there that Tischendorf discovered leaves of Codex Sinaiticus in a trash can, ready to be burned.

The **critical Greek New Testament** produced by Westcott and Hort was the basis for the Revised Version (RV), also called the English Revised Version (ERV). The New Testament came out in 1881. The American Standard Version (ASV) was the American edition of this work. Further, Westcott and Hort developed a theory of textual criticism which underlies their Greek New Testament and several other Greek New Testaments (such as the Nestle's text and the United Bible Society's text). Greek New Testaments such as these produced the modern English translations of the Bible we have today. So it is important for us to know what Westcott and Hort believed because they have so greatly influenced modern textual criticism and the modern versions of the Bible.

BELIEFS OF WESTCOTT & HORT

Hort clearly <u>believed in the new theory of evolution</u>. He wrote to the Rev. John Ellerton, April 3, 1860: "But the book which has most engaged me is Darwin. Whatever may be thought of it, it is a book that one is proud to be contemporary with. . . . My feeling is strong that the theory is unanswerable. If so, it opens up a new period." (Hort, *Life of Hort*, I:416).

Westcott did <u>not believe in the literal interpretation of the creation account of Genesis</u>. Westcott wrote to the Archbishop of Canterbury on Old Testament criticism, March 4, 1890: "No one now, I suppose, holds that the first three chapters of Genesis, for example, give a literal history—I could never understand how anyone reading them with open eyes could think they did." (Westcott, *Life of Westcott*, II:69).

Westcott wrote concerning the Scriptures – "I reject the word infallibility of Holy Scriptures over-whelmingly." (Westcott, *The Life and Letters of Brooke Foss Westcott*, Vol. I, p.207).

Dr. Wilbur Pickering writes that, **Hort** <u>did not hold to a high view of inspiration.</u> (*The Identity of the New Testament Text*, p.212).

Westcott believed in Salvation by Baptism! He wrote in a letter – **"by baptism he may if he will, truly live forever.** I do not say that Baptism is absolutely necessary, though from the word of the Scriptures I can see no exception, but I do not think we have a right to exclaim against the idea of the commencement of a spiritual life, **conditionally from Baptism**, any more than we have to deny the commencement of a moral life from birth." (www.workmenforchrist.org/Bible/History/Westcott.html).

Westcott did not believe in a literal Heaven or a literal Hell. He believed Heaven was a state of mind and said so – "heaven is a state and not a place." *and* "(Hell is) not the place of punishment of the guilty, (it is) the common abode of departed spirits."

Westcott did not believe in the miracles recorded in the Bible. He said, "I never read an account of a miracle but I seem instinctively to feel its improbability, and discover somewhat of evidence in the account of it."

Hort said – "The fact is, I do not see how God's justice can be satisfied without every man's suffering in his own person the full penalty for his sins."

Hort believed in the meritorious works of the sacraments. He wrote, "we dare not forsake the Sacraments, or God will forsake us." He further said, "I wish we were more agreed on the doctrinal part; but you know I am a staunch sacerdotalist, and there is not much profit in arguing about first principles."

A whole book could be written (and has been for that matter) on the unbiblical and heretical views of Westcott & Hort. What I want to point out is this. Our Lord says – *"A good tree cannot bring forth evil fruit, <u>neither can a corrupt tree bring forth good fruit.</u> Wherefore by their fruits ye shall know them."* **Matthew 7:18, 20.**

It is clear to me that a corrupt tree cannot produce good fruit! Since the modern versions have at their primary root the critical text produced by Westcott & Hort, it follows that these Bibles will be corrupt also!

I suggest you follow Jesus Christ and His views of the Scripture.

HOW DID JESUS VIEW THE SCRIPTURES?

Jesus never involved Himself in higher or lower criticism nor attempted to recover the original autographs. He never corrected or criticized Scripture, even though He did not possess the original autographs. Rather He said, *"Sanctify them through thy truth: thy word is truth."* **John 17:17**

Jesus accepted the Old Testament Jewish canon, but rejected the Apocrypha (**Luke 24:44**)

Jesus taught that every word of Scripture proceeded from God (**Matthew 4:4**)

Jesus taught the doctrine of the preservation of Scripture (**Matthew 5:17-18; 24:35; Luke 6:17**)

Jesus taught that the Old Testament Scriptures pointed to Him (**Luke 24:27, 44**)

Jesus taught that man will be judged by God's Word (**John 12:47-48**)

Jesus taught the absolute authority of Scripture (**John 10:34-36**)

Jesus pre-authenticated the New Testament writings as Scripture (**John 14:26; 16:12-13**)

Jesus believed in the Genesis account of creation (**Matthew 19:4-6; Mark 10:6-8**)

Jesus believed in the Mosaic authorship of the Pentateuch (**Matthew 8:4; John 5:46; 7:19**)

Jesus believed in the historicity and universality of the Noahic Flood (**Matthew 24:37-39**)

Jesus believed in the historicity of Abraham (**John 8:56**)

Jesus believed in the historicity of Sodom and Gomorrah (**Matthew 10:15; 11:23-24**)
Jesus believed Lot's wife was turned into a pillar of salt (**Luke 17:32**)

Jesus believed God gave manna from heaven to Israel (**John 6:31, 49, 58**)

Jesus believed in the Davidic authorship of the Psalms (**Matthew 22:43**)

Jesus believed in the historicity of Jonah and the whale (**Matthew 12:39-41**)

Jesus believed in the Danielic authorship of Daniel (**Matthew 24:15**)

Jesus believed in the unity of the book of Isaiah (**Matthew 13:14-15; Mark 7:6; John 12:38-41**)

Jesus believed the Jews had a history of rejecting God's Word (**Luke 11:47-51**) [this section adapted from an article by John A. Kohler, III]

Westcott, Hort, Nestle, Aland, Metzger and other modern critics reject the position our Lord held on the Scriptures. I urge you to reject the fruit of these critics, the Modern Bible Versions produced from their works, and **take the position of the Lord Jesus Christ**. If you will do that, that will narrow your choices down to the New Testament of Tyndale, the Geneva Bible or the King James Bible. *The CREAM OF THE CROP IS OUR KING JAMES BIBLE!* That is why we use it. That is why you should use it as well.

CHAPTER #15

THE KING JAMES ONLY
BAPTIST CIVIL WAR
OVER INSPIRATION

by Dr. Phil Stringer

Actually, I don't like the term "King James Only." It is a name given to us by our critics. I want everyone, in every language, to have the pure Word of God in their own tongue. But in this case, I use the term so that it is clear who I am talking about.

A civil war rages among independent Baptists about the "inspiration" of translations. I am not talking about the debate over which text of Scripture to use. Prominent preachers who preach the King James Bible and who defend it against its critics, are vigorously debating one another over the use of the term "inspiration" in describing the King James Bible. Sometimes the conflict is much hotter than a "vigorous debate." Good men, with deep loyalties to the King James Bible, are at odds with one another. Key terms are defined many different ways, motives are called into question and the doctrinal soundness of men is questioned.

Over the last few weeks I have been in many verbal conversations and email discussions over this issue.

I have been asked how these discussions are going. I have answered that I feel like a man trying to stand on an ice flow, in an ocean full of sharks while juggling baby elephants. A debate over the nature of the Bible generates deep emotions.

Good men are trying to defend the King James Bible the best way that they know how. They are tired of the evangelical and fundamentalist critics of the King James Bible. They are tired of self-absorbed, pseudo-scholars. They are tired of people with slender language skills mocking the scholars who were used of God to translate the King James Bible. I completely agree!

Let me be crystal clear! I believe that the King James Bible is God's Word kept intact in English. There is not one word in the King James Bible that I would change. I would not change an italicized word.

I believe that the American republic was created by the influence of the King James Bible. I believe that the modern missions movement was created by the preaching of the King James Bible. I believe that both the fundamentalist movement and the independent Baptist movement were the product of the King James Bible.

I am not one of those preachers who believes that it is Christian liberty to attack the King James Bible but divisive to answer those attacks.

I believe that the evangelical and fundamentalist critics of the King James Bible should be answered. When I heard Elmer Fernandez say that the translators of the King James Bible were evil and wicked men, I knew that he had to be opposed. When I read Calvin George's desperate attempts to belittle the King James Bible (in order to defend the Critical Text readings of the Reina Valera 1960), I understand that he has to be answered.

When I realize that the method of Bible teaching practiced by the professors of Bob Jones University and Detroit Baptist Theological Seminary is to go verse by verse and say "a better translation would be...," I understand that they are pseudo-scholars. The least of the Kings James translators was a greater scholar than any of them.

When I read that the translations sponsored by Charles Keen won't be King James equivalent (his term), I understand what he is up to and that he must be answered by those loyal to the Received Text.

When I see the long-ago disproven criticisms of the King James Bible on the various Trinitarian Bible Society websites—I realize that those loyal to the King James Bible must answer the Trinitarian Bible Society's foolish attacks on the King James Bible.

I believe that the King James Bible is pure, perfect and inerrant!

However, I do not believe that the King James Bible is "inspired." That is not because I believe that there is any weakness or any inferiority in the King James Bible. There is nothing about the King James Bible that needs to be corrected or improved.

The Bible tells us what "inspiration" is! It defines itself. Many of my brethren use the term "inspiration" as a synonym for inerrant. But it means much more than that! Many of my brethren use the secular definition of the term "inspiration"—"to motivate or cause by supernatural influence" (Webster's Illustrated Contemporary Dictionary). But this definition falls far short of what the Bible says about its own "inspiration."

Many of our most famous doctrinal books offer a weak definition of "inspiration."

One prominent advocate of the King James Bible defines "inspiration" this way. "By inspiration we mean the supernatural control by God over the production of the Old Testament and New Testaments." Another King James advocate defines "inspiration" as "divine influence." These men would consider themselves as great advocates of the King James Bible and would describe most other teachers as weak or modernist.

Yet their doctrine of "inspiration" is very weak. It was invented by modernists and spread by neo-evangelicals. Inspiration is much more than what they say it is.

If "inspiration" is really "divine influence" then many sermons, songs and books are "inspired." However, "Biblical inspiration" is much more than that.

"Inspiration" took place when God took control of a person and spoke His words through them or caused them to write down His words. "Inspiration" took place when God dictated His words to a person or even through an animal (Balaam's donkey).

You can't defend the King James Bible by weakening the doctrine of "inspiration." In their zeal to advance the King James Bible, some men have adopted a liberal position about "inspiration."

Many of the brethren are quick to quote II Timothy 3:16—"All Scripture is given by "inspiration" of God." This is, of course, true. God gave His words to men through the Greek, Aramaic and Hebrew languages. This verse means exactly what it says—and nothing more.

However, the verse does not say that the words that God gave are preserved, transmitted or translated by "inspiration." The verse means everything that it says but we have no right to add anything to it.

No matter how pure and proper our motives are—we do not help the cause of the King James Bible by defining incorrectly a Biblical term or by inventing a new Biblical doctrine. Actually we help the critics of that King James Bible by using an argument that they can easily refute.

Virtually everyone in our movement, including me, has used the term "inspiration" carelessly at one time or another. It is time to start being careful.

Recently, I was communicating by email with the head of a translation project in a foreign country. He assured me that his translation was "inspired." I told him that I didn't think so.

He was just finishing ten years of his translation effort. Men who were "moved by the Holy Spirit" (II Peter 1:21) of God wrote down the Words as God gave them. They didn't need ten years. Can you imagine John spending ten years figuring out what to write down in the book of Revelation?

The translator had a team of sixteen national helpers—men who are "inspired" don't need a "team" of helpers. Can you imagine a team of sixteen helpers helping King Saul figure out what to say when the Holy Spirit took him over?

This gentleman is getting ready to release his second edition. Men who are "inspired" of God don't need a second edition. Can you imagine Balaam's donkey issuing a second edition of his words to Balaam?

The response of this translator was to call me a modernist!

The Words of God have been settled forever in heaven. God gave some of them to Moses to record on earth. He gave some to Jeremiah, some to Paul, some to Peter and so on. They recorded the exact words that God gave them. God finished delivering His words to men as John finished the Book of Revelation. That is how "inspiration" works!

The translators of the King James Bible did not need to be "inspired." They already had God's "inspired" Words in front of them. They simply needed to faithfully and accurately translate the Words that had already been given by "inspiration." Translators today do not need to be "inspired." They already have God's "inspired" words available. They simply need to translate them correctly.

John Selden described the method of the King James translators. "The translation in King James time took an excellent way. That part of the Bible was given to him who was most excellent in such a tongue (as the Apocrypha to Andrew Downes) and then they met together and one read that translation the rest holding in their hands some Bible either of the learned tongues or French, Italian, Spanish, etc. If they found any fault they spoke, if not, they read on."

This was not the method of King Saul, Malachi, Isaiah, Matthew or Balaam's donkey when they were being "inspired" of the Lord. It is an example of men being used of God to preserve and transmit His Word.

I know that many men use the word "inspired" to describe the King James Bible because they want to defend it against its many attackers. But the King James Bible doesn't need that kind of help from us. It stands up to its attackers just fine. They always fade away and the King James Bible goes on. It doesn't need us to invent a new definition of "inspiration" or to weaken the doctrine of divine "inspiration" the way that the secular writers do.

There seem to be three prominent positions among those who use the term "inspired" to describe the King James Bible.

Some teach that God repeated the miracle of "inspiration" in 1611. They believe that the English language is the only language that currently has an "inspired Bible." Their concept of missions is to preach and teach from the English Bible to the whole world. This destroys most mission works.

This is an easy doctrine to maintain, if you are only concerned for white, Anglo-Saxon people.

Of course, there is not the slightest hint of any such doctrine anywhere in the King James Bible.

The second group teaches the miracle of "inspiration" took place in 1611 in English and continues to take place in other languages today. They teach that you can recognize an "inspired" Bible if it is used by large "soul-winning" churches.

For those brethren, soul-winning is not based upon doctrine, doctrine is based upon soul-winning. Since most of the Bibles in use around the world are Critical Text Versions and contradict the King James Bible, they assume that God gave one set of words in English and differing words in other languages. Their doctrine of "inspiration" justifies liberal translations.

They usually teach that only a Bible produced by a modern miracle of "inspiration" can be used to lead someone to Christ. Consequently, they would put their stamp of approval on hundreds of modernist translations.

But you can't protect the King James Bible by undermining the basis for Scriptural revelation.

Interestingly enough, both groups spend a lot of time attacking fundamental Baptists who explain "inspiration" in any way different than themselves. But you can't imagine them refuting modernists or liberal Bible societies. Their venom is reserved for the English speaking brethren who use the same Bible that they do.

There is a third group that teaches what they call "derivative inspiration." They are often very good brethren, devoted to the

Bible. They understand that the miracle of "inspiration" only took place with the original earthly Scriptural penmen.

They teach that the Bible today has all the authority, influence, Holy Spirit power and purity of the original "inspired" Words of God. That is exactly what the Bible teaches about itself.

Faithful copies of the Words given by "inspiration" have all the authority and Holy Spirit power of the originals. Faithful copies of Scripture are Scripture.

Faithful translations of the Words given by "inspiration" have all the authority and Holy Spirit power of the originals. Faithful translations of Scripture are Scripture.

However, the Bible calls this preservation not "derivative inspiration" (try finding that term in the King James Bible).

At least the teachers of "derivative inspiration" describe the original act of inspiration correctly, they describe the current state of the Bible correctly and it is possible for them to translate the Bible into other languages correctly. They are good brethren and I do not want to be separated from them.

However, their terminology is not Scriptural. Their teaching is easily confused with the other more dangerous teachings about "inspiration."

You do not defend the Kings James Bible by weakening the Bible's teaching about preservation. One Bible teacher called preserved words "cold, dead museum words." What an insult to a sovereign God!

Nothing could be a stronger statement about words than to say these words are "God's preserved words." God's preservation maintains all the authority and Holy Spirit power that God originally placed on and in His words.

The doctrine of preservation is not a weak doctrine. It is a doctrine filled with Holy Spirit power. It does not need to be upgraded, improved or strengthened. It is the power of God in practice.

I am for everyone that preaches, practices and defends the words of the King James Bible. If my brethren do not use the exact terminology that I think reflects the teaching of Scripture, I will be a little disappointed in them, but I will not reject them. I do not expect perfection from men. I wish to be the friend of all those that honor the words of the King James Bible.

However, I do believe that this discussion has important consequences.

Using a Biblical term in a non-Biblical way opens a new avenue of attack for the enemies of the King James Bible. There is no reason to make it easier for them to make their unholy attacks.

Secondly, this debate is creating unfortunate confusion about the matter of Bible translations. Around the world dozens of projects are taking place. Believers are concerned about getting a faithful translation of the Bible in their national language. There is a revival of understanding the issue of the Received Text.

However, too many men are producing a first edition of a translation, calling it "inspired" and stopping right there. A proper translation requires a rigorous purification process (such as the one that took place with the King James Bible). A weak or secular definition of "inspiration" is hindering the most important work of Bible translation.

Thirdly, this debate causes people to miss the genuinely important debate going on about Scripture today. Some men who are loud advocates of the "inspiration" of the King James Bible are also strong proponents of a Critical Text Bible for the Spanish people and for other language groups.

It may be expedient politics to advocate a Received Text Bible for the English speaking world and a Critical Text Bible for the Spanish speaking world, but it is horrible doctrine. Why would a "King James man" want the Hispanic world to use a Bible that conflicts with the King James Bible in hundreds of places and thousands of words?

This is hypocritical and it has a great price attached to it. If you promote the Critical Text in any language you can no longer consistently oppose Critical Text Bibles in English. Sooner or later your hypocrisy will catch up to you. There is simply no doctrinal or textual foundation to prevent such a change. No matter how loudly a man or a ministry proclaims their loyalty to the King James Bible today, if they advocate the Critical Text in other languages they will probably be using a Critical Text Bible in English in a few years.

No one can consistently claim to be a "King James preacher" and support the Reina Valera 1960 or the TBS Spanish Bible. No one can consistently claim to be a "King James preacher" and support the French Louis Segond Version (either the Bible Society version or the TBS version). The same is true for the Chinese Common Union Version (CUV) and a host of other foreign translations.

Some of the people influenced by Dr. Ruckman have called me a modernist and a Bible corrector (even though they can't identify one word of the King James Bible that I would change). Most recently, some have called me "a King James Bible hater." Other men influenced by Dr. Ruckman have been much kinder to me.

I have been called a Ruckmanite by advocates of the Critical Text. However I have never been influenced by the writings or teachings of Dr. Ruckman (in the interest of full disclosure I met him once when I was fifteen).

Some Hispanic preachers refer to me by their pet nickname, "The Antichrist." I am sure that they mean that in Christian love. However I am grateful to have many Hispanic preacher friends who love me in spite of my faults and limitations.

I am used to being called names. Somehow, I doubt that this article will end that experience. If you preach, practice and defend the words of the King James Bible, I am for you!

I hope that we will all preach, practice and defend those blessed words wisely.

One missionary wrote, "As I understand the Scriptures, 'inspiration' is the process by which God directed and controlled the recording of His exact words for mankind. But after those words were recorded, God ceased to 'inspire.' The process was completed and the message was recorded. God, from that point on, perfectly preserved exactly what He gave so that we would have every word exactly as He gave it. This is called preservation. So if you were to ask me if I believed the Bible is inspired, I would answer by saying, 'Yes, however, to be more theologically accurate, it *was inspired* and is *now preserved.*"

Amen and Amen!

Actually, it seems that much of the "civil war" today is not really about doctrine at all. It seems to be about who is going to "speak for fundamental Baptists." Again, let me be crystal clear. I am an independent Baptist. I do not recognize a pope, bishop, church councils or a Baptist Sanhedrin. I don't believe in model churches or that anyone pastors to pastors. I have no headquarters! I have a Bible and that is my sole authority.

Finally, let me appeal for grace for and from all of us. The founders of fundamentalism, for all their wonderful accomplishments, were not clear or consistent on their definition of "inspiration" or their identification of the Biblical text. We are paying for that confusion now!

Most of the leaders of the independent Baptist movement can be quoted several different ways on both the definition of "inspiration" and on textual issues.

Vigorous debate is appropriate and even beneficial. A "civil war" is not. Let us all find some grace in our hearts for those who love the Bible and strive to reach the souls of men!

Verbal, plenary "inspiration," verbal, plenary preservation, verbal, plenary translation: any other doctrine of Scripture is just not enough.

CHAPTER #16

WHY YOU SHOULD USE THE KING JAMES BIBLE

"The King James Bible is the best version available in the English language today. It is built on the solid rock foundation of faith instead of the shifting sands of doubt that the modern versions are built on."

INTRODUCTION

The battle over Bible versions rages on as you have read in previous chapters. However, I have settled that issue in my mind, based on the facts, many years ago. But, I know there are many people in the pews of our churches who still struggle with the Bible Version issue. I regularly get phone calls from people who have heard that I stand for the Received Text and the King James Bible. They ask me, "Why do you advocate the use of the King James Bible?" and/or "Isn't this version or that version a good version?" While you will be rereading some of the things I have stated in previous chapters, it is NOT "vain repetition." This chapter is designed to persuade the believer who is wavering to use a Bible built on the foundation of faith!

In a clear, concise and uncomplicated way, I want to explain to the Christian struggling with the **version issue**, why I came to the conclusion that **the King James Bible is the best version available in the English language today**. God has preserved His Words for us, by accurate translation of the underlying Hebrew Masoretic and Textus Receptus.

As you are reading this report, there are high stakes races on, in the publishing world, to come out with, so called, "newer and better" versions of the English Bible. And, <u>what is their motive</u>? There are countless versions of the English Bible on store shelves today. In my local "Christian" bookstore I believe there were about 24 different English Versions available.

Is there some noble spiritual objective behind all these modern versions like there was with William Tyndale, Myles Coverdale,

John Rogers, and those behind the Geneva and King James Bible? I think not! The truth be known, **I fear that the publishers are rooting for revenue in the religious pigpen**.

Now, for a moment, let's cut the publishers some slack. Let's assume, for the sake of argument, that they have noble motives. Will noble motives make their translations come out better? The answer is **NO**! Here's why. They are **building on the wrong foundation**, right from the start! There are basically only two foundations that Bible translations have been and are being built upon. It is either the **foundation of faith** or **the foundation of doubt**.

THE FOUNDATION OF FAITH

Let's begin with **the foundation of faith**. The key issue is this: I believe that **God inspired the original writings of the Bible**, which are called the **autographa**. There are many verses that teach this. Here are two key verses that I want you to see...

2 Peter 1:20-21 *"Knowing this first, that no prophecy of the scripture is of any private interpretation* (that is, they did not originate with man). *21 For the prophecy came not in old time by the will of man: but holy men of God spake as they were moved by the Holy Ghost."*

2 Timothy 3:16 *"All scripture is given by inspiration of God, and is profitable for doctrine, for reproof, for correction, for instruction in righteousness:"*

But, there is also the matter of **verbal preservation of the apographa** (copies of the originals). I believe that God has preserved His Words in the copies of those original writings in the Hebrew Masoretic Text of the Old Testament and the Traditional Text (Textus Receptus) of the New Testament.

I have **FAITH** that the God who inspired the original autographs can and did preserve the apographs so that we can say, "Thus saith the Lord; This IS the Word of God" when we hold up our King James Bibles.

Nineteenth century believing Bible scholar par excellence, John Burgon wrote: **"If you and I believe that the original writings of the Scriptures were verbally inspired by God, then of necessity they must have been providentially preserved through the ages."**

The **Westminster Confession of Faith** published in the 1600's says, "The Old Testament in Hebrew, and the New Testament in Greek, <u>being immediately inspired by God</u> and <u>by His singular care and providence kept pure in all ages</u>, are therefore authentic, so as in all controversies of religion the Church is finally to appeal unto them."

My point in quoting this document is simply this; **Bible believing Christians in the past, for the most part, believed in the inspiration and providential preservation of the Word of God**. It is only in the last quarter of the 19th century and 20th century that born again Christians have believed anything else!

In fact, the Bible teaches **providential preservation**! The Lord Jesus Christ taught providential preservation. In **Matthew 4:4** we read, *"But he answered and said, It is written, Man shall not live by bread alone, <u>but by every word that proceedeth out of the mouth of God.</u>"* Did you know that no original manuscripts existed in Christ's day? Yet, Christ confidently quoted a portion of **Deuteronomy 8:3** as the authoritative Word of God, and it was a copy of the original without a doubt.

There are many **<u>Scriptures that indicate God has providentially preserved His Word</u>**. Here are just a few.

Psalms 12:6-7 *"The words of the LORD are pure words: as silver tried in a furnace of earth, purified seven times. 7 Thou shalt keep them, O LORD, thou shalt preserve them from this generation for ever."*

Psalms 33:11 *"The counsel of the LORD standeth for ever, the thoughts of his heart to all generations."*

Psalms 100:5 *"For the LORD is good; his mercy is everlasting; and his truth endureth to all generations."*

Matthew 24:35 *"Heaven and earth shall pass away, but my words shall not pass away."*

Luke 16:17 *"And it is easier for heaven and earth to pass, than one tittle of the law to fail."*

1 Peter 1:23, 25 *"Being born again, not of corruptible seed, but of incorruptible, by the word of God, which liveth and abideth for ever. But the word of the Lord endureth for ever. And this is the word which by the gospel is preached unto you."*

I believe God. What He promised, He is able to perform (**Romans 4:21**). He has promised to preserve His Word(s), and I believe Him. I have the faith that He has done it. Therefore, I have chosen to use the King James Bible, because it is built on the Traditional Text, which is laid on the foundation of faith.

• *THE FOUNDATION OF DOUBT*

What about all of the modern versions of the Bible? What foundation are they built upon? Princeton Theological Seminary textual critic, Dr. Bruce Metzger, who is behind the Greek text used in translating the modern versions of the Bible, writing to Dr. Kurt D. DiVietro, testified that the text they founded their work on was that of Westcott and Hort. He wrote, "**We took as our base at the beginning the text of Westcott and Hort and introduced changes as seemed necessary on the basis of MSS evidence**."

Modern versions are erected on the <u>faulty foundation of doubt</u>! Here's why I say that. Westcott and Hort **speculated**, with no evidence to support their idea, that <u>the "pure" text of the New Testament had been lost</u>. They said that the Antiochian text (also called the Traditional Text, Textus Receptus, etc.), the text type behind the King James New Testament, was an artificial and arbitrarily invented text, fabricated between 250 A.D. and 350 A.D. In fact, Westcott and Hort asserted that it remained lost until the 19th century when Vaticanus was rediscovered in 1845 in the Vatican library, where it had lain since 1481, and Sinaiticus was discovered in a wastebasket in St. Catherine's Monastery in 1844.

Figure it out. If you believe their conjured theory, that means people were without the Word of God for 1500 years! Therefore, the question must be, **were Westcott and Hort correct?** Had the Word of God been lost for 1500 years?

Dr. F. H. A Scrivener wrote:

"Dr. Hort's System is entirely destitute of historical foundation....We are compelled to repeat as emphatically as ever our strong conviction that the hypothesis to whose proof he has devoted so many laborious years, is destitute not only of historical foundation, but of all probability..." (*Dr. F. H. A. Scrivener's Plain Introduction*, 1883, pp. 537, 542).

Further, he stated;

"There is little hope for the stability of their imposing structure (speaking of Westcott & Hort), **if its foundations have been laid on the sandy ground of ingenious conjecture**. And, since barely the smallest vestige of historical evidence has ever been alleged in support of the views of these accomplished editors, their teaching must either be received as intuitively true, or dismissed from our consideration as precarious and even visionary." (*Dr. F. H. A. Scrivener's Plain Introduction*, 1883, p. 531).

In summary, I have chosen to use the English Bible that is built on **the solid foundation of faith**, believing that God has preserved His Words in the Masoretic Hebrew text and the Textus Receptus Greek text, and that the King James Bible "preserves" in the English language, by accurate translation, that preserved Hebrew Masoretic and Textus Receptus Greek texts.

By the same token, I must say that if you hold to a modern version of the Bible, you have chosen *the sandy ground of ingenious conjecture*. The <u>critical scholars behind the modern versions do not believe that God preserved His Words as He said He did</u>. In fact, **they are not sure where His Words are**. They are frantically revising, adding, deleting, modifying, and changing God's Words as is right in their own eyes.

Will you choose the <u>solid foundation of faith</u> or the <u>sandy foundation of doubt</u>?

Once the foundation is laid, the building begins! Those who are building on the **foundation of doubt** have a **low regard for the Scriptures** while those who are building on the **foundation of faith** have a **high regard for the Scriptures.**

• *A LOW REGARD FOR THE SCRIPTURES*

Would you trust a preacher or a Bible scholar who said **the Bible was just a book like any other book**? I hope that not a single person listening to or reading this would trust him. Yet, millions of Christians, who use the modern versions of the Bible, essentially trust the judgment of those who treat the Bible as just another book. Here's proof...

Dr. Edward Hills wrote, "Westcott (pictured above) and Hort followed an essentially naturalistic Method. Indeed <u>they prided themselves on **treating the text of the New Testament as they would that of any other book,** making little or nothing of inspiration and providence</u>." (Edward F. Hills, *The King James Version Defended*, pp. 65, 66).

In other words, they treated the Bible just like they would the works of Plato, Shakespeare, C. S. Lewis, J. K. Rowling or any other fallible book. In fact, <u>neither believed in the infallibility of the Bible</u>.

Brooke Foss Westcott stated emphatically, "<u>No one</u> now, I suppose, <u>holds that the first three chapters of Genesis</u>, for example, <u>give a</u>

literal history - I could never understand how anyone reading them with open eyes could think they did."

Further he wrote, "I never read of the account of a miracle but I seem instinctively to feel its improbability, and discover some want of evidence in the account of it." (*Life and Letters of Brooke Foss Westcott;* page 216). Again Westcott said, "**I reject the word infallibility of Holy Scriptures overwhelmingly.**" (*The Life and Letters of Brooke Foss Westcott,* p.207).

Concerning Fenton John Anthony Hort, (pictured at right) Dr. Wilbur Pickering writes, "**Hort did not hold to a high view of inspiration.**" (*The Identity of the New Testament Text,* p.212).

Some might protest that the low regard of the Scriptures held by Westcott and Hort has nothing to do with the modern versions of today. They are wrong.

First, the new Bible versions are built on the Greek New Testament compiled by them.

Secondly, current day New Version Potentate Princeton Theological Seminary Professor Bruce Metzger has a low regard for the Scriptures as well. He doubts Moses alone authored the Pentateuch. As Co-editor of the *New Oxford Annotated Bible RSV* he wrote or approved of notes asserting that the Pentateuch is "a matrix of myth, legend, and history" that "took shape over a long period of time" and is "not to be read as history." Job is called an "ancient folktale." And the book of Isaiah was written by at least three men. Jonah is called "popular legend." Then add to that, Metzger claims that the Gospels are composed of material gathered from oral tradition. The problem is, he completely ignores the inspiration of the Holy Spirit and the testimony of the Bible itself!

Exodus 24:4 *"And <u>Moses wrote all the words of the LORD</u>, and rose up early in the morning, and builded an altar under the hill, and twelve pillars, according to the twelve tribes of Israel."*

John 7:19 Jesus said, *"Did not Moses give you the law, and yet none of you keepeth the law? Why go ye about to kill me?"*

Matthew 12:40 Jesus said, *"For as Jonas was three days and three nights in the whale's belly; so shall the Son of man be three days and three nights in the heart of the earth."*

Let me ask you a question. **How can you trust a Bible that has been tampered with by men who neither respect it nor hold it in any higher regard than they would the works of Shakespeare?** The answer is clear; **you cannot**.

• *A HIGH REGARD FOR THE BIBLE*

I have a high regard for the Scriptures. I believe it stands forever. **Isaiah 40:8** *"The grass withereth, the flower fadeth: but <u>the word of our God shall stand for ever</u>."*

I believe that through the Word of God people are born again. **John 20:31** *"But these are written, that ye might believe that Jesus is the Christ, the Son of God; and that believing ye might have life through his name."* **Romans 10:17** *"So then faith cometh by hearing, and hearing by the word of God."* **1 Peter 1:23** *"Being born again, not of corruptible seed, but of incorruptible, by the word of God, which liveth and abideth for ever."*

<u>I will not align myself with those who profane the Scriptures</u>. **The King James Bible is founded upon Traditional Text types collated by men who had a high regard for the Bible**. Consider for instance, the often-maligned **Desiderius Erasmus**. He wrote the following in the Preface to his Greek New Testament, which clearly shows he reverenced and loved the Holy Scriptures...

"These holy pages will summon up the living image of His mind. They will give you Christ Himself, talking, healing, dying, rising, the whole Christ in a word; they will give Him to you in an intimacy so close that He would be less visible to you if He stood before your eyes." *(An Introduction to the Textual Criticism of the New Testament;* Robertson; p. 54).

Erasmus also wrote this:

"Therefore if you will dedicate yourself wholly to the study of the Scriptures, if you will meditate on the law of the Lord day and night, you will not be afraid of the terror of the night or of the day, but you will be fortified and trained against every onslaught of the enemy." *(Advocates of Reform: From Wyclif to Erasmus;* Matthew Spinka; p. 304: by way of Sorenson; *Touch Not The Unclean Thing).*

Further he proclaimed,

"Christ Jesus...is the true light, alone shattering the night of earthly folly, the Splendor of paternal glory, who as he was made redemption and justification for us reborn in him, so also was made Wisdom (as Paul testifies): 'We preach Christ crucified, to the Jews a stumbling block, and to the Gentiles foolishness; but to them that are called, both Jew and Greeks, Christ is the power of God and the wisdom of God.'" *(Advocates of Reform: From Wyclif to Erasmus;* Matthew Spinka; p. 309: by way of Sorenson; *Touch Not The Unclean Thing).*

There are others to consider, such as Theodore Beza. Does anyone doubt the fact that <u>Theodore Beza</u> had a high regard for the Bible? The reason I bring this up is that the <u>King James translators are said to have worked primarily from his 5th edition of the Received Text.</u> If you do have any doubts about where Beza stood, I challenge you to read his book, *The Christian Faith.* He says this: **"On the subject of the Word of God, the canonical books of the Old** and New Testament...proceed from the mouth of God Himself."

I use the King James Bible because it is built upon texts that were collated by people who had a high regard for the Word(s) of God. Further, it is the most meticulous English translation ever produced.

Next, let's consider the manuscripts that were used; what the modern versions are built on...

A FEW CORRUPT MANUSCRIPTS

For a more complete treatment of this issue, log on to www.logosresourcepages.org/uncials.htm and read my article "**The Great? Uncials.**"

As you will recall, I shared with you a quote by Bruce Metzger. He tells how they developed their Greek text for the modern versions. He said, "**We took as our base at the beginning the text of Westcott and Hort and introduced changes as seemed necessary on the basis of MSS evidence.**"

So, what manuscripts did Westcott and Hort use to get their Greek New Testament? They used primarily two old 4th century manuscripts for their work. Hort's partiality for Codex Vaticanus (B) was practically absolute. Intuitively, (without evidence) he believed it to be a near perfect representation of the Greek New Testament. Whenever pages were missing in Vaticanus he would use Codex Sinaiticus (ALEPH) to fill in the gap. While most modern version "scholars" claim that "**the oldest is the best**," (and they have these two manuscripts in mind), this certainly is NOT true with these two manuscripts.

For example, we read this about **Codex Vaticanus (B) – "The entire manuscript has had the text mutilated, every letter has been run over with a pen, making exact identification of many of the characters impossible.**" More specifically, the manuscript is faded in places; scholars think it was overwritten letter by letter in the 10th or 11th century, with accents and breathing marks added along with corrections from the 8th, 10th and 15th centuries. Those who study manuscripts say, **All this activity makes precise paleographic analysis impossible**. <u>Missing portions were supplied in the 15th century</u> by copying other Greek manuscripts. How can you call this manuscript "the oldest and the best?"

Back on page 368, you will see an example of the problems that come into play when there are multiple corrections within a manuscript. The page is from 4th century Codex Vaticanus. Here we see Hebrews 1 of Codex Vaticanus. Though hard to see in this size, notice <u>the marginal note between the first and second column</u>. A corrector of the text had erased a word in verse 3 and substituted another word in its place. A second corrector came along, erased the correction, reinserted the original word, and wrote a note in the margin to castigate the first corrector. The note reads, **"Fool and knave, leave the old reading, don't change it!"**

What about **Codex Sinaiticus (ALEPH)?** This is a Greek manuscript of the Old and New Testaments, found on Mount Sinai, in St. Catherine's Monastery, which was a Greek Orthodox Monastery, by Constantin Tischendorf. He was visiting there in 1844, under the patronage of Frederick Augustus, King of Saxony, when he discovered 34 leaves <u>in a rubbish basket</u>. He was permitted to take them, but did not get the remainder of the manuscript until 1859. Constantin Von Tischendorf identified the handwriting of <u>four different scribes in the writing of that text</u>. But that is not the end of the scribal problems! The <u>early corrections</u> of the manuscript are made <u>from Origen's corrupt source</u>. **As many as ten scribes tampered with the codex**. Tischendorf said he "counted 14,800 alterations and corrections in Sinaiticus." Alterations, and more alterations, and more alterations were made, and in fact, most of them are believed to be made in the 6th and 7th centuries. So much for the oldest!

"On nearly every page of the manuscript there are corrections and revisions, done by 10 different people." He goes on to say, **"...the New Testament...is extremely unreliable...on many occasions 10, 20, 30, 40, words are dropped...letters, words even whole sentences are frequently written twice over, or begun and immediately canceled. That gross blunder, whereby a clause is omitted because it happens to end in the same word as the clause preceding, occurs no less than 115 times in the New Testament.**"

Here are several examples of *di homoeotéleuton omissions*. The word *di homoeotéleuton is* Greek for "because of a similar ending." Here are some examples of the sloppy work of the scribes.

Note: In the following passages the italicized, bold words are <u>omitted</u> in Sinaiticus...

1 Cor. 13:1-2. Though I speak with the tongues of men and of angels, and have not charity, *I am become as sounding brass, or a tinkling cymbal. 2 And though I have the gift of prophecy, and understand all mysteries, and all knowledge; and though I have all faith, so that I could remove mountains, and have not charity,* I am nothing.

Here the scribe had copied the verse up to the end of the *first* "and have not charity," but when he looked up to his example again to continue copying, his eye fell upon the *second* occurrence of the phrase, from which he continued, omitting all of those words between the two occurrences of the phrase.

Now a more complicated example:

1 Cor. 15:25-27. For he must reign, till he hath put all enemies under his feet. 26 The last enemy that shall be destroyed is death. *27 For he hath put all things under his feet*.

Here it is not immediately clear what has happened. But when it is known that in some early manuscripts the order of clauses is as shown below, once again we see that the scribe's eye has jumped from the first occurrence of a phrase to the second occurrence:

For he must reign, till he hath put all enemies under his feet. ***For he hath put all things under his feet***. The last enemy that shall be destroyed is death.

And in the very next verse another such omission:

1 Cor. 15:27-28. But when he saith all things are put under him, it is manifest that he is excepted, which did subject unto him all things. ***28 And when there shall be subjected unto him all things,*** then shall the Son also himself be subject unto him that put all things under him, that God may be all in all.

These *di homoeotéleuton* omissions number about 300 in the New Testament of Codex Sinaiticus. They are not taken seriously as various readings by the editors of critical editions and in fact are not even mentioned in the notes of the critical editions of currently used translations. (Information - http://www.bible-researcher.com/faulty.html).

While these manuscripts may be (or may not be) old, <u>it is obvious that they are corrupt</u>. **It is these corrupt manuscripts that form the basis to the modern Bible versions**.

However, that is NOT the case with our King James Version of the Bible. It is based on...

MASSIVE MANUSCRIPT EVIDENCE

While it is true that there are about 45 to 50 Greek manuscripts that support the Westcott/Hort Greek text that underlies the modern versions of the Bible, you must realize that there are more than 5000 that support the Textus Receptus type text that underlies our King James Bible. Figure it out. 99% of all the manuscript evidence supports the text type that the King James Bible is translated from. Further, this text type is overwhelmingly supported by the early church fathers.

Christian friends, there is no doubt in my mind that underlying the King James New Testament is a superior Greek text!

While there are many more things that could be said, this will be my final point relating to the method of translation.

FORMAL EQUIVALENCY – A SUPERIOR METHOD OF TRANSLATION

The King James Bible translators used a superior method in translating called **formal equivalency.** Formal Equivalence, sometimes called <u>Verbal Equivalence</u> is a method of translation, which takes the Greek, and Hebrew words and <u>renders them as closely as possible into English</u>. This is the method used by the King James translators and is certainly a superior method, seeing that our Lord is concerned about every word, even the jots and tittles (**Matthew 5:18; 24:35**).

DYNAMIC EQUIVALENCY & PARAPHRASING – AN INFERIOR METHOD OF TRANSLATING

The modern versions of the Bible use **dynamic equivalency**, also called **concept inspiration** in their translations. Dynamic Equivalence is not following a word for word translation but changing, adding, or subtracting from the original to make it flow as the translator sees fit. We are warned against this in the Bible (**Deuteronomy 4:2; Proverbs 30:5-6; Revelation 22:19**). The New International Version is this type of a version.

Then, there is one further step that is even worse and that is **paraphrasing**. Paraphrasing is simply taking what the text says and rewriting it to what you think it says. It is more like a condensed commentary than a Bible. The most popular paraphrase is the *Living Bible*. It is really not a translation at all!

I use the King James Bible because it certainly is superior in its translation.

SUMMARY

- **The King James Bible is built on the <u>foundation of faith</u> by men who had a <u>high regard</u> for the Bible, using massive manuscript evidence to support their work. They meticulously translated the Greek and Hebrew words, rendering them as closely as possible into English.**

414

- **The Modern versions are built on a <u>foundation of doubt</u> by men who have a <u>low regard</u> for the Bible. A few corrupt manuscripts were used to support their work. For the most part, they loosely translated the concepts of the Greek and Hebrew and some versions are even sloppier, not translating at all but paraphrasing.**

I have to wonder, if you are not using the King James Bible, why not?

CHAPTER #17

THE MATERIALS INCLUDED BY THE TRANSLATORS IN THE 1611 KING JAMES BIBLE

Note from the author: Me thinks that the claims of "Double Inspiration," "Advanced Inspiration," etc. could be cleared up if those making and believing those claims would read what the translators had to say. Since this information is NOT included in most of today's King James Bible, I thought is expedient to include it in the final chapter of this book without comment.

(EPISTLE DEDICATORY TO THE AUTHORIZED KING JAMES VERSION)

TO THE MOST HIGH AND MIGHTY PRINCE

JAMES,

BY THE GRACE OF GOD

KING OF GREAT BRITAIN, FRANCE, AND IRELAND, DEFENDER OF THE FAITH,

The Translators of the Bible wish Grace, Mercy and Peace, through JESUS CHRIST, our Lord.

GREAT and manifold were the blessings, most dread Sovereign, which Almighty God, the Father of all mercies, bestowed upon us the people of England, when first he sent Your Majesty's Royal Person to rule and reign over us. For whereas it was the expectation of many, who wished not well unto our Sion, that upon the setting of that bright Occidental Star, Queen Elizabeth of most happy memory, some thick and palpable clouds of darkness would so have overshadowed this Land, that men should have been in doubt which way they were to walk; and that it should hardly be known, who was to direct the unsettled State; the appearance of your Majesty, as the Sun in his strength, instantly dispelled those supposed and surmised mists, and gave unto all that were well affected exceeding cause of comfort; especially when we beheld the Government established in Your Highness, and Your hopeful Seed, by an undoubted Title, and this also accompanied with peace and tranquillity at home and abroad.

But among all our joys, there was no one that more filled our hearts, than the blessed continuance of the preaching of God's sacred Word among us; which is that inestimable treasure, which excelleth all the riches of the earth; because the fruit thereof extendeth itself, not only to the time spent in this transitory world, but directeth and disposeth men unto that eternal happiness which is above in heaven.

Then not to suffer this to fall to the ground, but rather to take it up, and to continue it in that state, wherein the famous Predecessor of Your Highness did leave it: nay, to go forward with the confidence and resolution of a Man in maintaining the truth of Christ, and propagating it far and near, is that which hath so bound and firmly knit the hearts of all Your Majesty's loyal and religious people unto You, that Your very name is precious among them: their eye doth behold You with comfort, and they bless You in their hearts, as that sanctified Person who, under God, is the immediate Author of their true happiness. And this their contentment doth not diminish or decay, but every day increaseth and taketh strength, when they observe, that the zeal of Your Majesty toward the house of God doth not slack or go backward, but is more and more kindled, manifesting itself abroad in the farthest parts of Christendom, by writing in defence of the Truth, (which hath given such a blow unto that man of sin, as will not be healed,) and every day at home, by religious and learned discourse, by frequenting the house of God, by hearing the Word preached, by cherishing the Teachers thereof, by caring for the Church, as a most tender and loving nursing Father.

There are infinite arguments of this right christian and religious affection in Your Majesty; but none is more forcible to declare it to others than the vehement and perpetuated desire of accomplishing and publishing of this work, which now with all humility we present unto Your Majesty. For when Your Highness had once out of deep judgment apprehended how convenient it was, that out of the Original Sacred Tongues, together with comparing of the labours, both in our own, and other foreign Languages, of many worthy men who went before us, there should be one more exact Translation of the holy Scriptures into the English Tongue; Your Majesty did never desist to urge and to excite those to whom it was commended, that the work might be hastened, and that the business might be expedited in so decent a manner, as a matter of such importance might justly require.

And now at last, by the mercy of God, and the continuance of our labours, it being brought unto such a conclusion, as that we have great hopes that the Church of England shall reap good fruit thereby; we hold it our duty to offer it to Your Majesty, not only as to our King and Sovereign, but as to the principal Mover and Author of the work: humbly craving of Your most Sacred Majesty, that since things of this quality have ever been subject to the censures of illmeaning and discontented persons, it may receive approbation and patronage from so learned and judicious a Prince as Your Highness is, whose allowance and acceptance of our labours shall more honour and encourage us, than all the calumniations and hard interpretations of other men shall dismay us. So that if, on the one side, we shall be traduced by Popish Persons at home or abroad, who therefore will malign us, because we are poor instruments to make God's holy Truth to be yet more and more known unto the people, whom they desire still to keep in ignorance and darkness; or if, on the other side, we shall be maligned by self-conceited Brethren, who run their own ways, and give liking unto nothing, but what is framed by themselves, and hammered on their anvil; we may rest secure, supported within by truth and innocency of a good conscience, having walked the ways of simplicity and integrity, as before the Lord; and sustained without by the powerful protection of Your Majesty's grace and favour, which will ever give countenance to honest and christian endeavours against bitter censures and uncharitable imputations.

> The Lord of heaven and earth bless Your Majesty with many and happy days, that, as his heavenly hand hath enriched Your Highness with many singular and extraordinary graces, so You may be the wonder of the world in this latter age for happiness

and true felicity, to the honour of that great GOD, and the good of his Church, through Jesus Christ our Lord and only Saviour.

THE TRANSLATORS TO THE READER
PREFACE TO THE KING JAMES VERSION 1611
THE BEST THINGS HAVE BEEN CULMINATED

Zeal to promote the common good, whether it be by devising anything ourselves, or revising that which hath been laboured by others, deserveth certainly much respect and esteem, but yet findeth but cold entertainment in the world. It is welcomed with suspicion instead of love, and with emulation instead of thanks: and if there be any hole left for cavil to enter, (and cavil, if it do not find a hole, will make one) it is sure to be misconstrued, and in danger to be condemned. This will easily be granted by as many as know story, or have any experience. For, was there ever any-projected, that savoured any way of newness or renewing, but the same endured many a storm of gainsaying, or opposition? A man would think that Civility, wholesome Laws, learning and eloquence, Synods, and Church-maintenance, (that we speak of no more things of this kind) should be as safe as a Sanctuary, and out of shot, as they say, that no man would lift up the heel, no, nor dog move his tongue against the motioners of them. For by the first, we are distinguished from brute beasts lead with sensuality; By the second, we are bridled and restrained from outrageous behaviour, and from doing of injuries, whether by fraud or by violence; By the third, we are enabled to inform and reform others, by the light and feeling that we have attained unto ourselves; Briefly, by the fourth being brought together to a parley face to face, we sooner compose our differences than by writings which are endless; And lastly, that the Church be sufficiently provided for, is so agreeable to good reason and conscience, that those mothers are holden to be less cruel, that kill their children as soon as they are born, than those nursing fathers and mothers (wheresoever they be) that withdraw from them who hang upon their breasts (and upon whose breasts again themselves do hang to receive the Spiritual and sincere milk of the word) livelihood and support fit for their estates. Thus it is apparent, that these things which we speak of, are of most necessary use, and therefore, that none, either without absurdity can speak against them, or without note of wickedness can spurn against them.

Yet for all that, the learned know that certain worthy men [Anacharsis with others] have been brought to untimely death for none other fault, but for seeking to reduce their Countrymen to god order and discipline; and that in some Commonwealths [e.g. Locri] it was made a capital crime, once to motion the making of a new Law for the abrogating of an old, though the same were most pernicious; And that certain [Cato the elder], which would be counted pillars of the State, and patterns of Virtue and Prudence, could not be brought for a long time to give way to good Letters and refined speech, but bare themselves as averse from them, as from rocks or boxes of poison; And fourthly, that he was no babe, but a great clerk [Gregory the Divine], that gave forth (and in writing to remain to posterity) in passion peradventure, but yet he gave forth, that he had not seen any profit to come by any Synod, or meeting of the Clergy, but rather the contrary; And lastly, against Church-maintenance and allowance, in such sort, as the Ambassadors and messengers of the great King of Kings should be furnished, it is not unknown what a fiction or fable (so it is esteemed, and for no better by the reporter himself [Nauclerus], though superstitious) was devised; Namely, that at such a time as the professors and teachers of Christianity in the Church of Rome, then a true Church, were liberally endowed, a voice forsooth was heard from heaven, saying: Now is poison poured down into the Church, etc. Thus not only as oft as we speak, as one saith, but also as oft as we do anything of note or consequence, we subject ourselves to everyone's censure, and happy is he that is least tossed upon tongues; for utterly to escape the snatch of them it is impossible. If any man conceit, that this is the lot and portion of the meaner sort only, and that Princes are privileged by their high estate, he is deceived. "As the sword devoureth as well one as the other," as it is in Samuel [2 Sam 11:25], nay as the great Commander charged his soldiers in a certain battle, to strike at no part of the enemy, but at the face; And as the King of Syria commanded his chief Captains to "fight neither with small nor great, save only against the King of Israel:" [1 Kings 22:31] so it is too true, that Envy striketh most spitefully at the fairest, and at the chiefest. David was a worthy Prince, and no man to be compared to him for his first deeds, and yet for as worthy as act as ever he did (even for bringing back the Ark of God in solemnity) he was scorned and scoffed at by his own wife [2 Sam 6:16]. Solomon was greater than David, though not in virtue, yet in power: and by his power and wisdom he built a Temple to the Lord, such a one as was the glory of the land of Israel, and the wonder of the whole world. But was that his magnificence liked of by all? We doubt it. Otherwise, why do they lay it in his son's dish, and call unto him for easing the burden, "Make", say they, "the grievous servitude of thy father, and his sore yoke, lighter?" [1 Kings 12:4] Belike he had charged them with some levies, and troubled them with some carriages; Hereupon they raise up a tragedy, and wish in their heart the Temple had never been built. So hard a thing it is to please all, even when we please God best, and do seek to approve ourselves to every ones conscience.

If we will descend to later times, we shall find many the like examples of such kind, or rather unkind acceptance. The first Roman Emperor [C. Caesar. Plutarch] did never do a more pleasing deed to the learned, nor more profitable to posterity, for conserving the record of times in true supputation; than when he corrected the Calendar, and ordered the year according to the course of the Sun; and yet this was imputed to him for novelty, and arrogance, and procured to him great obloguy. So the first Christened Emperor [Constantine] (at the leastwise that openly professed the faith himself, and allowed others to do the like) for strengthening the Empire at his great charges, and providing for the Church, as he did, got for his labour the name Pupillus, as who would say, a wasteful Prince, that had need of a Guardian or overseer [Aurel. Victor]. So the best Christened Emperor [Theodosius], for the love that he bare unto peace, thereby to enrich both himself and his subjects, and because he did not see war but find it, was judged to be no man at arms [Zosimus], (though indeed he excelled in feats of chivalry, and showed so much when he was provoked) and condemned for giving himself to his ease, and to his pleasure. To be short, the most learned Emperor of former times [Justinian], (at the least, the greatest politician) what thanks had he for cutting off the superfluities of the laws, and digesting them into some order and method? This, that he had been blotted by some to be an Epitomist, that is, one that extinguishes worthy whole volumes, to bring his abridgments into request. This is the measure that hath been rendered to excellent Princes in former times, even, Cum bene facerent, male audire, For their good deeds to be evil spoken of. Neither is there any likelihood, that envy and malignity died, and were buried with the ancient. No, no, the reproof of Moses taketh hold of most ages; "You are risen up in your fathers' stead, and increase of sinful men." [Num 32:14] "What is that that hath been done? that which shall be done; and there is no new thing under the Sun," saith the wiseman: [Ecc 1:9] and S. Stephen, "As your fathers did, so do you." [Acts 7:51]

HIS MAJESTY'S CONSTANCY, NOTWITHSTANDING CULMINATION, FOR THE SURVEY OF THE ENGLISH TRANSLATIONS

This, and more to this purpose, His Majesty that now reigneth (and long, and long may he reign, and his offspring forever, "Himself and children, and children's always) knew full well, according to the singular wisdom given unto him by God, and the rare learning and experience that he hath attained unto; namely that whosoever attempteth anything for the public (especially if it pertain to Religion, and to the opening and clearing of the word of God) the same setteth himself upon a stage to be gloated upon by every evil eye, yea, he casteth himself headlong upon pikes, to be gored by every sharp tongue. For he that medleth with men's Religion in any part, medleth with their custom, nay, with their freehold; and though they find no content in that which they have, yet they cannot abide to hear of altering. Notwithstanding his Royal heart was not daunted or discouraged for this that colour, but stood resolute, "as a statue immovable, and an anvil not easy to be beaten into plates," as one [Suidas] saith; he knew who had chosen him to be a Soldier, or rather a Captain, and being assured that the course which he intended made for the glory of God, and the building up of his Church, he would not suffer it to be broken off for whatsoever speeches or practices. It doth certainly belong unto Kings, yea, it doth specially belong unto them, to have care of Religion, yea, it doth specially belong unto them, to have care of Religion, yea, to know it aright, yea, to profess it zealously, yea to promote it to the uttermost of their power. This is their glory before all nations which mean well, and this will bring unto them a far most excellent weight of glory in the day of the Lord Jesus. For the Scripture saith not in vain, "Them that honor me, I will honor," [1 Sam 2:30] neither was it a vain word that Eusebius delivered long ago, that piety towards God was the weapon and the only weapon, that both preserved Constantine's person, and avenged him of his enemies [Eusebius lib 10 cap 8].

THE PRAISE OF THE HOLY SCRIPTURES

But now what piety without truth? what truth (what saving truth) without the word of God? What word of God (whereof we may be sure) without the Scripture? The Scriptures we are commanded to search. John 5:39. Isa 8:20. They are commended that searched and studied them. Acts 17:11 and 8:28,29. They are reproved that were unskilful in them, or slow to believe them. Matt 22:29. Luke 24:25. They can make us wise unto salvation. 2 Tim 3:15. If we be ignorant, they will instruct us; if out of the way, they will bring us home; if out of order, they will reform us; if in heaviness, comfort us; if dull, quicken us; if cold, inflame us. Tolle, lege; Tolle, lege,

Take up and read, take up and read the Scriptures [S. August. confess. lib 8 cap 12], (for unto them was the direction) it was said unto S. Augustine by a supernatural voice. "Whatsoever is in the Scriptures, believe me," saith the same S. Augustine, "is high and divine; there is verily truth, and a doctrine most fit for the refreshing of men's minds, and truly so tempered, that everyone may draw from thence that which is sufficient for him, if he come to draw with a devout and pious mind, as true Religion requireth." [S. August. de utilit. credendi cap. 6] Thus S. Augustine. and S. Jerome: "Ama scripturas, et amabit te sapientia etc." [S. Jerome. ad Demetriad] Love the Scriptures, and wisdom will love thee. And S. Cyril against Julian; "Even boys that are bred up in the Scriptures, become most religious, etc." [S. Cyril. 7 contra Iulianum] But what mention we three or four uses of the Scripture, whereas whatsoever is to be believed or practiced, or hoped for, is contained in them? or three or four sentences of the Fathers, since whosoever is worthy the name of a Father, from Christ's time downward, hath likewise written not only of the riches, but also of the perfection of the Scripture? "I adore the fulness of the Scripture," saith Tertullian against Hermogenes. [Tertul. advers. Hermo.] And again, to Apelles an heretic of the like stamp, he saith; "I do not admit that which thou bringest in (or concludest) of thine own (head or store, de tuo) without Scripture." [Tertul. de carne Christi.] So Saint Justin Martyr before him; "We must know by all means," saith he, "that it is not lawful (or possible) to learn (anything) of God or of right piety, save only out of the Prophets, who teach us by divine inspiration." So Saint Basil after Tertullian, "It is a manifest falling way from the Faith, and a fault of presumption, either to reject any of those things that are written, or to bring in (upon the head of them) any of those things that are not written. We omit to cite to the same effect, S. Cyril B. of Jerusalem in his 4::Cataches., Saint Jerome against Helvidius, Saint Augustine in his 3::book against the letters of Petilian, and in very many other places of his works. Also we forebear to descend to later Fathers, because we will not weary the reader. The Scriptures then being acknowledged to be so full and so perfect, how can we excuse ourselves of negligence, if we do not study them, of curiosity, if we be not content with them? Men talk much of [an olive bow wrapped about with wood, whereupon did hang figs, and bread, honey in a pot, and oil], how many sweet and goodly things it had hanging on it; of the Philosopher's stone, that it turned copper into gold; of Cornu-copia, that it had all things necessary for food in it, of Panaces the herb, that it was good for diseases, of Catholicon the drug, that it is instead of all purges; of Vulcan's armor, that it was an armor of proof against all thrusts, and all blows, etc. Well, that which they falsely or vainly attributed to these things for bodily god, we may justly and with full measure ascribe unto the Scripture, for spiritual. It is not only an armor, but also a whole armory of weapons, both offensive and defensive; whereby we may save ourselves and put the enemy to flight. It is not an herb, but a tree, or rather a whole paradise of trees of life, which bring forth fruit every month, and the fruit thereof is for meat, and the leaves for medicine. It is not a pot of Manna, or a cruse of oil, which were for memory only, or for a meal's meat or two, but as it were a shower of heavenly bread sufficient for a whole host, be it never so great; and as it were a whole cellar full of oil vessels; whereby all our necessities may be provided for, and our debts discharged. In a word, it is a Panary of wholesome food, against fenowed traditions; a Physician's shop (Saint Basil called it) [S. Basil in Psal. primum.] of preservatives against poisoned heresies; a Pandect of profitable laws, against rebellious spirits; a treasury of most costly jewels, against beggarly rudiments; finally a fountain of most pure water springing up unto everlasting life. And what marvel? The original thereof being from heaven, not from earth; the author being God, not man; the inditer, the holy spirit, not the wit of the Apostles or Prophets; the Penmen such as were sanctified from the womb, and endued with a principal portion of God's spirit; the matter, verity, piety, purity, uprightness; the form, God's word, God's testimony, God's oracles, the word of truth, the word of salvation, etc.; the effects, light of understanding, stableness of persuasion, repentance from dead works, newness of life, holiness, peace, joy in the holy Ghost; lastly, the end and reward of the study thereof, fellowship with the Saints, participation of the heavenly nature, fruition of an inheritance immortal, undefiled, and that never shall fade away: Happy is the man that delighted in the Scripture, and thrice happy that meditateth in it day and night.

TRANSLATION NECESSARY

But how shall men meditate in that, which they cannot understand? How shall they understand that which is kept close in an unknown tongue? as it is written, "Except I know the power of the voice, I shall be tohim that speaketh, a Barbarian, and he that speaketh, shall be a Barbarian to me." [1 Cor 14] The Apostle excepteth no tongue; not Hebrew the ancientest, not Greek the most copious, not Latin the finest. Nature taught a natural man to confess, that all of us in those tongues which we do not understand, are plainly deaf; we may turn the deaf ear unto them. The Scythian counted the Athenian, whom he did not understand, barbarous; [Clem. Alex. 1 Strom.] so the Roman did the Syrian, and the Jew (even S. Jerome himself called the Hebrew tongue barbarous, belike because it was strange to so many) [S. Jerome. Damaso.] so the Emperor of Constantinople [Michael, Theophili fil.] calleth the Latin tongue, barbarous, though Pope Nicolas do storm at it: [2::Tom. Concil. ex edit. Petri Crab] so the Jews long before Christ called all other nations, Lognazim, which islittle better than barbarous. Therefore as one complaineth, that always in the Senate of Rome, there was one or other that called for an interpreter: [Cicero 5::de finibus.] so lest the Church be driven to the like exigent, it is necessary to have translations in a readiness. Translation it is that openeth the window, to let in the light; that breaketh the shell, that we may eat the kernel; that putteth aside the curtain, that we may look into the most Holy place; that removeth the cover of the well, that we may come by the water, even as Jacob rolled away thestone from the mouth of the well, by which means the flocks of Laban were watered [Gen 29:10]. Indeed without translation into the vulgar tongue, the unlearned are but like children at Jacob's well (which is deep) [John 4:11] without a bucket or something to draw with; or as that person mentioned by Isaiah, to whom when a sealed book was delivered, with this motion, "Read this, I pray thee," he was fain to make this answer, "I cannot, for it is sealed." [Isa 29:11]

THE TRANSLATION OF THE OLD TESTAMENT OUT OF THE HEBREW INTO GREEK

While God would be known only in Jacob, and have his Name great in Israel, and in none other place, while the dew lay on Gideon's fleece only, and all the earth besides was dry; then for one and the same people, which spake all of them the language of Canaan, that is, Hebrew, one and the same original in Hebrew was sufficient. [S. August. lib 12 contra Faust c32] But, when the fulness of time drew near, that the Sun of righteousness, the Son of God should come into the world, whom God ordained to be a reconciliation through faith in his blood, not of the Jew only, but also of the Greek, yea, of all them that were scattered abroad; then lo, it pleased the Lord to stir up the spirit of a Greek Prince (Greek for descent and language) even of Ptolemy Philadelph King of Egypt, to procure the translating of the Book of God out of Hebrew into Greek. This is the translation of the Seventy Interpreters, commonly so called, which prepared the way for our Saviour among the Gentiles by written preaching, as Saint John Baptist did among the Jews by vocal. For the Grecians being desirous of learning, were not wont to suffer books of worth to lie moulding in Kings' libraries, but had many of their servants, ready scribes, to copy them out, and so they were dispersed and made common. Again, the Greek tongue was well known and made familiar to most inhabitants in Asia, by reason of the conquest that there the Grecians had made, as also by the Colonies, which thither they had sent. For the same causes also it was well understood in many places of Europe, yea, and of Africa too. Therefore the word of God being set forth in Greek, becometh hereby like a candle set upon a candlestick, which giveth light to all that are in the house, or like a proclamation sounded forth in the market place, which most men presently take knowledge of; and therefore that language was fittest to contain the Scriptures, both for the first Preachers of the Gospel to appeal unto for witness, and for the learners also of those times to make search and trial by. It is certain, that that Translation was not so sound and so perfect, but it needed in many places correction; and who had been so sufficient for this work as the Apostles or Apostolic men? Yet it seemed good to the holy Ghost and to them, to take that which they found, (the same being for the greatest part true and sufficient) rather than making a new, in that new world and green age of the Church, to expose themselves to many exceptions and cavillations, as though they made a Translations to serve their own turn, and therefore bearing a witness to themselves, their witness not to be regarded. This may be supposed to be some cause, why the Translation of the Seventy was allowed to pass for current. Notwithstanding, though it was commended generally, yet it did not fully content the learned, no not of the Jews. For not long after Christ, Aquila fell in hand with a new Translation, and after him Theodotion, and after him Symmachus; yea, there was a fifth and a sixth edition, the Authors whereof were not known. [Epiphan. de mensur. et ponderibus.] These with the Seventy made up the Hexapla and were worthily and to great purpose compiled together by Origen. Howbeit the Edition of the Seventy went away with the credit, and therefore not only was placed in the midst by Origen (for the worth and excellency thereof above the rest, as Epiphanius gathered) but also was used by the Greek fathers for the ground and foundation of their Commentaries. Yea, Epiphanius above named doeth attribute so much unto it, that he holdeth the Authors thereof not only for Interpreters, but also for Prophets in some respect [S. August. 2::de dectrin. Christian c. 15]; and Justinian the Emperor enjoining the Jews his subjects to use especially the Translation of the Seventy, rendreth this reason thereof, because they were as it were enlightened with prophetical grace. Yet for all that, as the Egyptians are said of the Prophet to be men and not God, and their horses flesh and not spirit [Isa 31:3]; so it is evident, (and Saint Jerome affirmeth as much) [S. Jerome. de optimo genere interpret.] that the Seventy were Interpreters, they were not Prophets; they did many things well, as learned men; but yet as men they stumbled and fell, one while through oversight, another while through ignorance, yea, sometimes they may be noted to add to the Original, and sometimes to take from it; which made the Apostles to leave them many times, when they left the Hebrew, and to deliver the sense thereof according to the truth of the word, as the spirit gave them utterance. This may suffice touching the Greek Translations of the Old Testament.

TRANSLATION OUT OF HEBREW AND GREEK INTO LATIN

There were also within a few hundred years after CHRIST, translations many into the Latin tongue: for this tongue also was very fit to convey the Law and the Gospel by, because in those times very many Countries of the West, yea of the South, East and North, spake or understood Latin, being made Provinces to the Romans. But now the Latin Translations were too many to be all good, for they were infinite (Latini Interprets nullo modo numerari possunt, saith S. Augustine.) [S. Augustin. de doctr. Christ. lib 2 cap II]. Again they were not out of the Hebrew fountain (we speak of the Latin Translations of the Old Testament) but out of the Greek stream, therefore the Greek being not altogether clear, the Latin derived from it must needs be muddy. This moved S. Jerome a most learned father, and the best linguist without controversy, of his age, or of any that went before him, to undertake the translating of the Old Testament, out of the very fountain with that evidence of great learning, judgment, industry, and faithfulness, that he had forever bound the Church unto him, in a debt of special remembrance and thankfulness.

THE TRANSLATING OF THE SCRIPTURE INTO THE VULGAR TONGUES

Now through the Church were thus furnished with Greek and Latin Translations, even before the faith of CHRIST was generally embraced in the Empire; (for the learned know that even in S. Jerome's time, the Consul of Rome and his wife were both Ethnics, and about the same time the greatest part of the Senate also) [S. Jerome. Marcell.Zosim] yet for all that the godly-learned were not content to have the Scriptures in the Language which they themselves understood, Greek and Latin, (as the good Lepers were not content to fare well themselves, but acquainted their neighbors with the store that God had sent, that they also might provide for

themselves) [2 Kings 7:9] but also for the behoof andedifying of the
unlearned which hungered and thirsted after righteousness, and had souls
to be saved as well as they, they provided Translations into the vulgar for
their Countrymen, insomuch that most nations under heaven did shortly
after their conversion, hear CHRIST speaking unto them in their mother
tongue, not by the voice of their Minister only, but also by the written word
translated. If any doubt hereof, he may be satisfied by examples enough,
if enough will serve the turn. First S. Jerome saith, Multarum gentium
linguis Scriptura ante translata, docet falsa esse quae addita sunt, etc. i.e.
"The Scripture being translated before in the languages of many Nations,
doth show that those things that were added (by Lucian and Hesychius)
are false." [S. Jerome. praef. in 4::Evangel.] So S. Jerome in that place.
The same Jerome elsewhere affirmeth that he, the time was, had set forth
the translation of the Seventy suae linguae hominibus, i.e., for his
countrymen of Dalmatia [S. Jerome. Sophronio.] Which words not only
Erasmus doth understand to purport, that S. Jerome translated the Scripture
into the Dalmatian tongue, but also Sixtus Senensis [Six. Sen. lib 4], and
Alphonsus a` Castro [Alphon. lb 1 ca 23] (that we speak of no more) men
not to be excepted against by them of Rome, do ingenuously confess as
much. So, S. Chrysostom that lived in S. Jerome's time, giveth evidence
with him: "The doctrine of S. John [saith he] did not in such sort [as the
Philosophers' did] vanish away: but the Syrians, Egyptians, Indians,
Persians, Ethiopians, and infinite other nations being barbarous people
translated it into their [mother] tongue, and have learned to be [true]
Philosophers," he meaneth Christians. [S. Chrysost. in Johan. cap.I.
hom.I.] To this may be added Theodoret, as next unto him, both for
antiquity, and for learning. His words be these, "Every Country that is
under the Sun, is full of these words (of the Apostles and Prophets) and the
Hebrew tongue [he meaneth the Scriptures in the Hebrew tongue] is turned
not only into the Language of the Grecians, but also of the Romans, and
Egyptians, and Persians, and Indians, and Armenians, and Scythians, and
Sauromatians, and briefly into all the Languages that any Nation useth.
[Theodor. 5. Therapeut.] So he. In like manner, Ulfilas is reported by
Paulus Diaconus and Isidor (and before them by Sozomen) to have
translated the Scriptures into the Gothic tongue: [P. Diacon. li. 12.] John
Bishop of Sevil by Vasseus, to have turned them into Arabic, about the
year of our Lord 717; [Vaseus in Chron. Hispan.] Bede by Cistertiensis, to
have turned a great part of them into Saxon: Efnard by Trithemius, to have
abridged the French Psalter, as Beded had done the Hebrew, about the year
800: King Alfred by the said Cistertiensis, to have turned the Psalter into
Saxon: [Polydor. Virg. 5 histor.] Methodius by Aventinus (printed at

Ingolstadt) to have turned the Scriptures into Slavonian: [Aventin. lib. 4.] Valdo, Bishop of Frising by Beatus Rhenanus, to have caused about that time, the Gospels to be translated into Dutch rhythm, yet extant in the Library of Corbinian: [Circa annum 900. B. Rhenan. rerum German. lib 2.] Valdus, by divers to have turned them himself into French, about the year 1160: Charles the Fifth of that name, surnamed the Wise, to have caused them to be turned into French, about 200 years after Valdus his time, of which translation there be many copies yet extant, as witnesseth Beroaldus. Much about that time, even in our King Richard the second's days, John Trevisa translated them into English, and many English Bibles in written hand are yet to be seen with divers, translated as it is very probable, in that age. So the Syrian translation of the New Testament is in most learned men's Libraries, of Widminstadius his setting forth, and the Psalter in Arabic is with many, of Augustinus Nebiensis' setting forth. So Postel affirmeth, that in his travel he saw the Gospels in the Ethiopian tongue; And Ambrose Thesius allegeth the Pslater of the Indians, which he testifieth to have been set forth by Potken in Syrian characters. So that, to have the Scriptures in the mother tongue is not a quaint conceit lately taken up, either by the Lord Cromwell in England, [Thuan.] or by the Lord Radevile in Polony, or by the Lord Ungnadius in the Emperor's dominion, but hath been thought upon, and put in practice of old, even from the first times of the conversion of any Nation; no doubt, because it was esteemed most profitable, to cause faith to grow in men's hearts the sooner, and to make them to be able to say with the words of the Psalms, "As we have heard, so we have seen." [Ps 48:8]

THE UNWILLINGNESS OF OUR CHIEF ADVERSARIES, THAT THE SCRIPTURES SHOULD BE DIVULGED IN THE MOTHER TONGUE, ETC.

Now the Church of Rome would seem at the length to bear a motherly affection towards her children, and to allow them the Scriptures in their mother tongue: but indeed it is a gift, not deserving to be called a gift, an unprofitable gift: [Sophecles] they must first get a licence in writing before they may use them, and to get that, they must approve themselves to their Confessor, that is, to be such as are, if not frozen in the dregs, yet soured with the leaven of their superstition. Howbeit, it seemed too much to Clement the Eighth that there should be any Licence granted to have them in the vulgar tongue, and therefore he overruleth and frustrateth the grant of Pius the Fourth. [See the observation (set forth by Clemen. his authority) upon the 4. rule of Pius the 4. his making in the index, lib. prohib. pag. 15. ver. 5.] So much are they afraid of the light of the Scripture, (Lucifugae Scripturarum, as Tertulian speaketh) that they will not trust the people with it, no not as it is set forth by their own sworn men, no not with the Licence of their own Bishops and Inquisitors. Yea, so unwilling they are to communicate the Scriptures to the people's understanding in any sort, that theyare not ashamed to confess, that we forced them to translate it into English against their wills. This seemeth to argue a bad cause, or a bad conscience, or both. Sure we are, that it is not he that hath good gold, that is afraid to bring it to the touchstone, but he that hath the counterfeit; [Tertul. de resur. carnis.] neither is it the true man that shunneth the light, but the malefactor, lest his deeds should be reproved [John 3:20]: neither is it the plaindealing Merchant that is unwilling to have the weights, or the meteyard brought in place, but he that useth deceit. But we will let them alone for this fault, and return to translation.

THE SPEECHES AND REASONS, BOTH OF OUR BRETHREN, AND OF OUR ADVERSARIES AGAINST THIS WORK

Many men's mouths have been open a good while (and yet are not stopped) with speeches about the Translation so long in hand, or rather perusals of Translations made before: and ask what may be the reason, what the necessity of the employment: Hath the Church been deceived, say they, all this while? Hath her sweet bread been mingled with leaven, here silver with dross, her wine with water, her milk with lime? (Lacte gypsum male miscetur, saith S. Ireney,) [S. Iren. 3. lib. cap. 19.] We hoped that we had been in the right way, that we had the Oracles of God delivered unto us, and that though all the world had cause to be offended and to complain, yet that we had none. Hath the nurse holden out the breast, and nothing but wind in it? Hath the bread been delivered by the fathers of the Church, and the same proved to be lapidosus, as Seneca speaketh? What is it to handle the word of God deceitfully, if this be not? Thus certain brethren. Also the adversaries of Judah and Jerusalem, like Sanballat in Nehemiah, mock, as we hear, both the work and the workmen, saying; "What do these weak Jews, etc. will they make the stones whole again out of the heaps of dust which are burnt? although they build, yet if a fox go up, he shall even break down their stony wall." [Neh 4:3] Was their Translation good before? Why do they now mend it? Was it not good? Why then was it obtruded to the people? Yea, why did the Catholics (meaning Popish Romanists) always go in jeopardy, for refusing to go to hear it? Nay, if it must be translated into English, Catholics are fittest to do it. They have learning, and they know when a thing is well, they can manum de tabula. We will answer them both briefly: and the former, being brethren, thus, with S. Jerome, "Damnamus veteres? Mineme, sed post priorum studia in domo Domini quod possums laboramus." [S. Jerome. Apolog. advers. Ruffin.] That is, "Do we condemn the ancient? In no case: but after the endeavors of them that were before us, we take the best pains we can in the house of God." As if he said, Being provoked by the example of the learned men that lived before my time, I have thought it my duty, to assay whether my talent in the knowledge of the tongues, may be profitable in any measure to God's Church, lest I should seem to laboured in them in vain, and lest I should be thought to glory in men, (although ancient,) above that which was in them. Thus S. Jerome may be thought to speak.

A SATISFACTION TO OUR BRETHREN

And to the same effect say we, that we are so far off from condemning any of their labors that travailed before us in this kind, either in this land or beyond sea, either in King Henry's time, or King Edward's (if there were any translation, or correction of a translation in his time) or Queen Elizabeth's of ever renowned memory, that we acknowledge them to have been raised up of God, for the building and furnishing of his Church, and that they deserve to be had of us and of posterity in everlasting remembrance. The judgment of Aristotle is worthy and well known: "If Timotheus had not been, we had not had much sweet music; but if Phrynis [Timotheus his master] had not been, we had not had Timotheus." Therefore blessed be they, and most honoured be their name, that break the ice, and giveth onset upon that which helpeth forward to the saving of souls. Now what can be more available thereto, than to deliver God's book unto God's people in a tongue which they understand? Since of a hidden treasure, and of a fountain that is sealed, there is no profit, as Ptolemy Philadelph wrote to the Rabbins or masters of the Jews, as witnesseth Epiphanius: [S. Epiphan. loco ante citato.] and as S. Augustine saith; "A man had rather be with his dog than with a stranger (whose tongue is strange unto him)." [S. Augustin. lib. 19. de civil. Dei. c. 7.] Yet for all that, as nothing is begun and perfected at the same time, and the later thoughts are thought to be the wiser: so, if we building upon their foundation that went before us, and being holpen by their labours, do endeavor to make that better which they left so good; no man, we are sure, hath cause to mislike us; they, we persuade ourselves, if they were alive, would thank us. The vintage of Abienzer, that strake the stroke: yet the gleaning of grapes of Ephraim was not to be despised. See Judges 8:2. Joash the king of Israel did not satisfy himself, till he had smitten the ground three times; and yet he offended the Prophet, for giving over then. [2 Kings 13:18-19] Aquila, of whom we spake before, translated the Bible as carefully, and as skilfully as he could; and yet he thought good to go over it again, and then it got the credit with the Jews, to be called accurately done, as Saint Jerome witnesseth. [S. Jerome. in Ezech. cap. 3.] How many books of profane learning have been gone over again and again, by the same translators, by others? Of one and the same book of Aristotle's Ethics, there are extant not so few as six or seven several translations. Now if this cost may be bestowed upon the gourd, which affordeth us a little shade, and which today flourisheth, but tomorrow is cut down; what may we bestow, nay what ought we not to bestow upon the Vine, the fruit whereof maketh glad the conscience of man, and the stem whereof abideth forever? And this is the word of God, which we translate. "What is the chaff to the wheat, saith the Lord?" [Jer 23:28] Tanti vitreum, quanti verum margaritum (saith Tertullian,) [Tertul. ad Martyr.] if a toy of glass be of that reckoning with us, how ought we to value the true pearl? [Jerome. ad Salvin.] Therefore let no man's eye be evil, because his Majesty's is good; neither let any be grieved, that we have a Prince that seeketh the increase of the spiritual wealth of Israel (let Sanballats and Tobiahs do so, which therefore do bear their just reproof) but let us rather bless God from the ground of our heart, for working this religious care in him, to have the translations of the Bible maturely considered of and examined. For by this means it cometh to pass, that whatsoever is sound already (and all is sound for substance, in one or other of our editions, and the worst of ours far better than their authentic vulgar) the same will shine as gold more brightly, being rubbed and polished; also, if anything be halting, or superfluous, or not so agreeable to the original, the same may be corrected, and the truth set in place. And what can the King command to be done, that will bring him more true honour than this? and wherein could they that have been set a work, approve their duty to the King, yea their obedience to God, and love to his Saints more, than by yielding their service, and all that is within them, for the furnishing of the work? But besides all this, they were the principal motives of it, and therefore ought least toquarrel it: for the very Historical truth is, that upon the importunate petitions of the Puritans, at his Majesty's coming to this Crown, the Conference at Hampton Court having been appointed for hearing their complaints: when by force of reason they were put from other grounds, they had recourse at the last, to this shift, that they could not with good conscience subscribe to the Communion book, since it maintained the Bible as it was there translated, which was as they said, a most corrupted translation. And although this was judged to be but a very poor and empty shift; yet even hereupon did his Majesty begin to bethink himself of the good that might ensue by a new translation, and presently after gave order for this Translation which is now presented unto thee. Thus much to satisfy our scrupulous Brethren.

AN ANSWER TO THE IMPUTATIONS OF OUR ADVERSARIES

Now to the latter we answer; that we do not deny, nay we affirm and avow, that the very meanest translation of the Bible in English, set forth by men of our profession, (for we have seen none of theirs of the whole Bible as yet) containeth the word of God, nay, is the word of God. As the King's speech, which he uttereth in Parliament, being translated into French, Dutch, Italian, and Latin, is still the King's speech, though it be not interpreted by every Translator with the like grace, nor peradventure so fitly for phrase, nor so expressly for sense, everywhere. For it is confessed, that things are to take their denomination of the greater part; and a natural man could say, Verum ubi multa nitent in carmine, non ego paucis offendor maculis, etc. [Horace.] A man may be counted a virtuous man, though he have made many slips in his life, (else, there were none virtuous, for in many things we offend all) [James 3:2] also a comely man and lovely, though he have some warts upon his hand, yea, not only freckles upon his face, but also scars. No cause therefore why the word translated should be denied to be the word, or forbidden to be current, notwithstanding that some imperfections and blemishes may be noted in the setting forth of it. For whatever was perfect under the Sun, where Apostles or Apostolic men, that is, men endued with an extraordinary measure of God's spirit, and privileged with the privilege of infallibility, had not their hand? The Romanists therefore in refusing to hear, and daring to burn the Word translated, did no less than despite the spirit of grace, from whom originally it proceeded, and whose sense and meaning, as well as man's weakness would enable, it did express. Judge by an example or two. Plutarch writeth, that after that Rome had been burnt by the Gauls, they fell soon to build it again: but doing it in haste, they did not cast the streets, nor proportion the houses in such comely fashion, as had been most slightly and convenient; [Plutarch in Camillo.] was Catiline therefore an honest man, or a good patriot, that sought to bring it to a combustion? or Nero a good Prince, that did indeed set it on fire? So, by the story of Ezra, and the prophecy of Haggai it may be gathered, that the Temple built by Zerubbabel after the return from Babylon, was by no means to be compared to the former built by Solomon (for they that remembered the former, wept when they considered the latter) [Ezra 3:12] notwithstanding, might this latter either have been abhorred and forsaken by the Jews, or profaned by the Greeks? The like we are to think of Translations. The translation of the Seventy dissenteth from the Original in many places, neither doth it come near it, for perspicuity, gravity, majesty; yet which of the Apostles did condemn it? Condemn it? Nay, they used it, (as it is apparent, and as Saint Jerome and most learned men do confess) which they would not have done, nor by their example of using it, so grace and commend it to the Church, if it had been unworthy of the appellation and name of the word of God. And whereas they urge for their second defence of their vilifying and abusing of the English Bibles, or some pieces thereof, which they meet with, for that heretics (forsooth) were the Authors of the translations, (heretics they call us by the same right that they call themselves Catholics, both being wrong) we marvel what divinity taught them so. We are sure Tertullian was of another mind: Ex personis probamus fidem, an ex fide personas? [Tertul. de praescript. contra haereses.] Do we try men's faith by their persons? we should try their persons by their faith. Also S. Augustine was of another mind: for he lighting upon certain rules made by Tychonius a Donatist, for the better understanding of the word, was not ashamed to make use of them, yea, to insert them into his own book, with giving commendation to them so far forth as they were worthy to be commended, as is to be seen in S. Augustine's third book De doctrina Christiana. [S. August. 3. de doct. Christ. cap. 30.] To be short, Origen, and the whole Church of God for certain hundred years, were of another mind: for they were so far from treading under foot, (much more from burning) the Translation of Aquila a Proselyte, that is, one that had turned Jew; of Symmachus, and Theodotion, both Ebionites, that is, most vile heretics, that they joined together with the Hebrew Original, and the Translation of the Seventy (as hath been before signified out of Epiphanius) and set them forth openly to be considered of and perused by all. But we weary the unlearned, who need not know so much, and trouble the learned, who know it already.

Yet before we end, we must answer a third cavil and objection of theirs against us, for altering and amending our Translations so oft; wherein truly they deal hardly, and strangely with us. For to whomever was it imputed for a fault (by such as were wise) to go over that which he had done, and to amend it where he saw cause? Saint Augustine was not afraid to exhort S. Jerome to a Palinodia or recantation; [S. Aug. Epist. 9.] and doth even glory that he seeth his infirmities. [S. Aug. Epist. 8.] If we be sons of the Truth, we must consider what it speaketh, and trample upon our own credit, yea, and upon other men's too, if either be any way an hindrance to it. This to the cause: then to the persons we say, that of all men they ought to be most silent in this case. For what varieties have they, and what alterations have they made, not only of their Service books, Portesses and Breviaries, but also of their Latin Translation? The Service book supposed to be made by S. Ambrose (Officium Ambrosianum) was a great while in special use and request; but Pope Hadrian calling a Council with the aid of Charles the Emperor, abolished it, yea, burnt it, and commanded the Service book of Saint Gregory universally to be used. [Durand. lib. 5. cap. 2.] Well, Officium Gregorianum gets by this means to be in credit, but doth it continue without change or altering? No, the very Roman Service was of two fashions, the New fashion, and the Old, (the one used in one Church, the other in another) as is to be seen in Pamelius a Romanist, his Preface, before Micrologus. the same Pamelius reporteth out Radulphus de Rivo, that about the year of our Lord, 1277, Pope Nicolas the Third removed out of the Churches of Rome, the more ancient books (of Service) and brought into use the Missals of the Friers Minorites, and commanded them to be observed there; insomuch that about an hundred years after, when the above name Radulphus happened to be at Rome, he found all the books to be new, (of the new stamp). Neither were there this chopping and changing in the more ancient times only, but also of late: Pius Quintus himself confesseth, that every Bishopric almost had a peculiar kind of service, most unlike to that which others had: which moved him to abolish all other Breviaries, though never so ancient, and privileged and published by Bishops in their Dioceses, and to establish and ratify that only which was of his own setting forth, in the year 1568. Now when the father of their Church, who gladly would heal the sore of the daughter of his people softly and slightly, and make the best of it, findeth so great fault with them for their odds and jarring; we hope the children have no great cause to vaunt of their uniformity. But the difference that appeareth between our Translations, and our often correcting of them, is the thing that we are specially charged with; let us see therefore whether they themselves be without fault this way, (if it be to be counted a fault, to correct) and whether they be fit men to throw stones at us: O tandem maior parcas insane minori: they that are less sound themselves, out not to object infirmities to others.

[Horat.] If we should tell them that Valla, Stapulensis, Erasmus, and Vives found fault with their vulgar Translation, and consequently wished the same to be mended, or a new one to be made, they would answer peradventure, that we produced their enemies for witnesses against them; albeit, they were in no other sort enemies, than as S. Paul was to the Galatians, for telling them the truth [Gal 4:16]: and it were to be wished, that they had dared to tell it them plainlier and oftener. But what will they say to this, that Pope Leo the Tenth allowed Erasmus' Translation of the New Testament, so much different from the vulgar, by his Apostolic Letter and Bull; that the same Leo exhorted Pagnine to translate the whole Bible, and bare whatsoever charges was necessary for the work? [Sixtus Senens.] Surely, as the Apostle reasoneth to the Hebrews, that if the former Law and Testament had been sufficient, there had been no need of the latter: [Heb 7:11 and 8:7] so we may say, that if the old vulgar had been at all points allowable, to small purpose had labour and charges been undergone, about framing of a new. If they say, it was one Pope's private opinion, and that he consulted only himself; then we are able to go further with them, and to aver, that more of their chief men of all sorts, even their own Trent champions Paiva and Vega, and their own Inquisitors, Hieronymus ab Oleastro, and their own Bishop Isidorus Clarius, and their own Cardinal Thomas a Vio Caietan, do either make new Translations themselves, or follow new ones of other men's making, or note the vulgar Interpreter for halting; none of them fear to dissent from him, nor yet to except against him. And call they this an uniform tenor of text and judgment about the text, so many of their Worthies disclaiming the now received conceit? Nay, we will yet come nearer the quick: doth not their Paris edition differ from the Lovaine, and Hentenius his from them both, and yet all of them allowed by authority? Nay, doth not Sixtus Quintus confess, that certain Catholics (he meaneth certain of his own side) were in such an humor of translating the Scriptures into Latin, that Satan taking occasion by them, though they thought of no such matter, did strive what he could, out of so uncertain and manifold a variety of Translations, so to mingle all things, that nothing might seem to be left certain and firm in them, etc.? [Sixtus 5. praefat. fixa Bibliis.] Nay, further, did not the same Sixtus ordain by an inviolable decree, and that with the counsel and consent of his Cardinals, that the Latin edition of the old and new Testament, which the Council of Trent would have to be authentic, is the same without controversy which he then set forth, being diligently corrected and printed in the Printing-house of Vatican? Thus Sixtus in his Preface before his Bible. And yet Clement the Eighth his immediate successor, published another edition of the Bible, containing in it infinite differences from that of Sixtus, (and many of them weighty and material) and yet this must be authentic by all means. What is to have the faith of our glorious Lord JESUS CHRIST with Yea or Nay, if this be not? Again, what is sweet harmony and consent, if this be? Therefore, as Demaratus of Corinth advised a great King, before he talked of the dissensions of the Grecians, to compose his domestic broils (for at that time his Queen and his son and heir were at deadly feud with him) so all the while that our adversaries do make so many and so various editions themselves, and do jar so much about the worth and authority of them, they can with no show of equity challenge us for changing and correcting.

THE PURPOSE OF THE TRANSLATORS, WITH THEIR NUMBER, FURNITURE, CARE, ETC.

But it is high time to leave them, and to show in brief what we proposed to ourselves, and what course we held in this our perusal and survey of the Bible. Truly (good Christian Reader) we never thought from the beginning, that we should need to make a new Translation, nor yet to make of a bad one a good one, (for then the imputation of Sixtus had been true in some sort, that our people had been fed with gall of Dragons instead of wine, with whey instead of milk:) but to make a good one better, or out of many good ones, one principal good one, not justly to be excepted against; that hath been our endeavor, that our mark. To that purpose there were many chosen, that were greater in other men's eyes than in their own, and that sought the truth rather than their own praise. Again, they came or were thought to come to the work, not exercendi causa (as one saith) but exercitati, that is, learned, not to learn: For the chief overseer and [NOTE: Greek letters omitted] under his Majesty, to whom not only we, but also our whole Church was much bound, knew by his wisdom, which thing also Nazianzen taught so long ago, that it is a preposterous order to teach first and to learn after, yea that [NOTE: Greek letters omitted] to learn and practice together, is neither commendable for the workman, nor safe for the work. [Idem in Apologet.] Therefore such were thought upon, as could say modestly with Saint Jerome, Et Hebreaeum Sermonem ex parte didicimus, et in Latino pene ab ipsis incunabulis etc. detriti sumus. "Both we have learned the Hebrew tongue in part, and in the Latin we have been exercised almost from our very cradle." S. Jerome maketh no mention of the Greek tongue, wherein yet he did excel, because he translated not the old Testament out of Greek, but out of Hebrew. And in what sort did these assemble? In the trust of their own knowledge, or of their sharpness of wit, or deepness of judgment, as it were in an arm of flesh? At no hand. They trusted in him that hath the key of David, opening and no man shutting; they prayed to the Lord the Father of our Lord, to the effect that S. Augustine did; "O let thy Scriptures be my pure delight, let me not be deceived in them, neither let me deceive by them." [S. Aug. lib. II. Confess. cap. 2.] In this confidence, and with this devotion did they assemble together; not too many, lest one should trouble another; and yet many, lest many things haply might escape them. If you ask what they had before them, truly it was the Hebrew text of the Old Testament, the Greek of the New. These are the two golden pipes, or rather conduits, where-through the olive branches empty themselves into the gold. Saint Augustine calleth them precedent, or original tongues; [S. August. 3. de doctr. c. 3. etc.] Saint Jerome, fountains. [S. Jerome. ad Suniam et Fretel.] The same Saint Jerome affirmeth, [S. Jerome. ad Lucinium, Dist. 9 ut veterum.] and Gratian hath not spared to put it into his Decree, That "as the credit of the old Books" (he meaneth of the Old Testament) "is to be tried by the Hebrew Volumes, so of the New by the Greek tongue," he meaneth by the original Greek. If truth be tried by these tongues, then whence should a Translation be made, but out of them? These tongues therefore, the Scriptures we say in those tongues, we set before us to translate, being the tongues wherein God was pleased to speak to his Church by the Prophets and Apostles. Neither did we run over the work with that posting haste that the Septuagint did, if that be true which is reported of them, that they finished it in 72 days; [Joseph. Antiq. lib. 12.] neither were we barred or hindered from going over it again, having once done it, like S. Jerome, if that be true which himself reporteth, that he could no sooner write anything, but presently it was caught from him, and published, and he could not have leave to mend it: [S. Jerome. ad Pammac. pro libr. advers. Iovinian.] neither, to be short, were we the first that fell in hand with translating the Scripture into English, and consequently destitute of former helps, as it is written of Origen, that he was the first in a manner, that put his hand to write Commentaries upon the Scriptures, [Sophoc. in Elect.] and therefore no marvel, if he overshot himself many times. None of these things: the work hath not been huddled up in 72 days, but hath cost the workmen, as light as it seemeth, the pains of twice seven times seventy two days and more: matters of such weight and consequence are to be speeded with maturity: for in a business of movement a man feareth not the blame of convenient slackness. [S. Chrysost. in II. Thess. cap. 2.] Neither did we think much to consult the Translators or Commentators, Chaldee, Hebrew, Syrian, Greek or Latin, no nor the Spanish, French, Italian, or Dutch; neither did we disdain to revise that which we had done, and to bring back to the anvil that which we had hammered: but having and using as great helps as were needful, and fearing no reproach for slowness, nor coveting praise for expedition, we have at length, through the good hand of the Lord upon us, brought the work to that pass that you see.

REASONS MOVING US TO SET DIVERSITY OF SENSES IN THE MARGIN, WHERE THERE IS GREAT PROBABILITY FOR EACH

Some peradventure would have no variety of senses to be set in the margin, lest the authority of the Scriptures for deciding of controversies by that show of uncertainty, should somewhat be shaken. But we hold their judgment not to be sound in this point. For though, "whatsoever things are necessary are manifest," as S. Chrysostom saith, [S. Chrysost. in II. Thess. cap. 2.] and as S. Augustine, "In those things that are plainly set down in the Scriptures, all such matters are found that concern Faith, Hope, and Charity." [S. Aug. 2. de doctr. Christ. cap. 9.] Yet for all that it cannot be dissembled, that partly to exercise and whet our wits, partly to wean the curious from the loathing of them for their every-where plainness, partly also to stir up our devotion to crave the assistance of God's spirit by prayer, and lastly, that we might be forward to seek aid of our brethren by conference, and never scorn those that be not in all respects so complete as they should be, being to seek in many things ourselves, it hath pleased God in his divine providence, here and there to scatter words and sentences of that difficulty and doubtfulness, not in doctrinal points that concern salvation, (for in such it hath been vouched that the Scriptures are plain) but in matters of less moment, that fearfulness would better beseem us than confidence, and if we will resolve upon modesty with S. Augustine, (though not in this same case altogether, yet upon the same ground) Melius est debitare de occultis, quam litigare de incertis, [S. Aug li. S. de Genes. ad liter. cap. 5.] "it is better to make doubt of those things which are secret, than to strive about those things that are uncertain." There be many words in the Scriptures, which be never found there but once, (having neither brother or neighbor, as the Hebrews speak) so that we cannot be holpen by conference of places. Again, there be many rare names of certain birds, beasts and precious stones, etc. concerning the Hebrews themselves are so divided among themselves for judgment, that they may seem to have defined this or that, rather because they would say something, than because they were sure of that which they said, as S. Jerome somewhere saith of the Septuagint. Now in such a case, doth not a margin do well to admonish the Reader to seek further, and not to conclude or dogmatize upon this or that peremptorily? For as it is a fault of incredulity, to doubt of those things that are evident: so to determine of such things as the Spirit of God hath left (even in the judgment of the judicious) questionable, can be no less than presumption. Therefore as S. Augustine saith, that variety of Translations is profitable for the finding out of the sense of the Scriptures: [S. Aug. 2. de doctr. Christian. cap. 14.] so diversity of signification and sense in the margin, where the text is no so clear, must needs do good, yea, is necessary, as we are persuaded. We know that Sixtus Quintus expressly forbiddeth, that any variety of readings of their vulgar edition, should be put in the margin, [Sixtus 5. praef. Bibliae.] (which though it be not altogether the same thing to that we have in hand, yet it looketh that way) but we think he hath not all of his own side his favorers, for this conceit. They that are wise, had rather have their judgments at liberty in differences of readings, than to be captivated to one, when it may be the other. If they were sure that their high Priest had all laws shut up in his breast, as Paul the Second bragged, [Plat. in Paulo secundo.] and that he were as free from error by special privilege, as the Dictators of Rome were made by law inviolable, it were another matter; then his word were an Oracle, his opinion a decision. But the eyes of the world are now open, God be thanked, and have been a great while, they find that he is subject to the same affections and infirmities that others be, that his skin is penetrable, and therefore so much as he proveth, not as much as he claimeth, they grant and embrace.

REASONS INDUCING US NOT TO STAND CURIOUSLY UPON AN IDENTITY OF PHRASING

Another things we think good to admonish thee of (gentle Reader) that we have not tied ourselves to an uniformity of phrasing, or to an identity of words, as some peradventure would wish that we had done, because they observe, that some learned men somewhere, have been as exact as they could that way. Truly, that we might not vary from the sense of that which we had translated before, if the word signified that same in both places (for there be some words that be not the same sense everywhere) we were especially careful, and made a conscience, according to our duty. But, that we should express the same notion in the same particular word; as for example, if we translate the Hebrew or Greek word once by PURPOSE, never to call it INTENT; if one where JOURNEYING, never TRAVELING; if one where THINK, never SUPPOSE; if one where

PAIN, never ACHE; if one where JOY, never GLADNESS, etc. Thus to mince the matter, we thought to savour more of curiosity than wisdom, and that rather it would breed scorn in the Atheist, than bring profit to the godly Reader. For is the kingdom of God to become words or syllables? why should we be in bondage to them if we may be free, use one precisely when we may use another no less fit, as commodiously? A godly Father in the Primitive time showed himself greatly moved, that one of newfangledness called [NOTE: Greek omitted but was a dispute over the word for "a bed"] [Niceph. Calist. lib.8. cap.42.] though the difference be little or none; and another reporteth that he was much abused for turning "Cucurbita" (to which reading the people had been used) into "Hedera". [S. Jerome in 4. Ionae. See S. Aug: epist. 10.] Now if this happens in better times, and upon so small occasions, we might justly fear hard censure, if generally we should make verbal and unnecessary changings. We might also be charged (by scoffers) with some unequal dealing towards a great number of good English words. For as it is written of a certain great Philosopher, that he should say , that those logs were happy that were made images to be worshipped; for their fellows, as good as they, lay for blocks behind the fire: so if we should say, as it were, unto certain words, Stand up higher, have a place in the Bible always, and to others of like quality, Get ye hence, be banished forever, we might be taxed peradventure with S. James his words, namely, "To be partial in ourselves and judges of evil thoughts." Add hereunto, that niceness in words was always counted the next step to trifling, and so was to be curious about names too: also that we cannot follow a better pattern for elocution than God himself; therefore he using divers words, in his holy writ, and indifferently for one thing in nature: [see Euseb. li. 12. ex Platon.] we, if we will not be superstitious, may use the same liberty in our English versions out of Hebrew and Greek, for that copy or store that he hath given us. Lastly, we have on the one side avoided the scrupulosity of the Puritans, who leave the old Ecclesiastical words, and betake them to other, as when they put WASHING for BAPTISM, and CONGREGATION instead of CHURCH: as also on the other side we have shunned the obscurity of the Papists, in their AZIMES, TUNIKE, RATIONAL, HOLOCAUSTS, PRAEPUCE, PASCHE, and a number of such like, whereof their late Translation is full, and that of purpose to darken the sense, that since they must needs translate the Bible, yet by the language thereof, it may be kept from being understood. But we desire that the Scripture may speak like itself, as in the language of Canaan, that it may be understood even of the very vulgar.

Many other things we might give thee warning of (gentle Reader) if we had not exceeded the measure of a Preface already. It remaineth, that we commend thee to God, and to the Spirit of his grace, which is able to build further than we can ask or think. He removeth the scales from our eyes, the vail from our hearts, opening our wits that we may understand his word, enlarging our hearts, yea correcting our affections, that we may love it to the end. Ye are brought unto fountains of living water which ye digged not; do not cast earth into them with the Philistines, neither prefer broken pits before them with the wicked Jews. [Gen 26:15. Jer 2:13.] Others have laboured, and you may enter into their labours; O receive not so great things in vain, O despise not so great salvation! Be not like swine to tread under foot so precious things, neither yet like dogs to tear and abuse holy things. Say not to our Saviour with the Gergesites, Depart out of our coast [Matt 8:34]; neither yet with Esau sell your birthright for a mess of pottage [Heb 12:16]. If light be come into the world, love not darkness more than light; if food, if clothing be offered, go not naked, starve not yourselves. Remember the advice of Nazianzene, "It is a grievous thing" (or dangerous) "to neglect a great fair, and to seek to make markets afterwards:" also the encouragement of S. Chrysostom, "It is altogether impossible, that he that is sober" (and watchful) "should at any time be neglected:" [S. Chrysost. in epist. ad Rom. cap. 14. oral. 26.] Lastly, the admonition and menacing of S. Augustine, "They that despise God's will inviting them, shall feel God's will taking vengeance of them." [S. August. ad artic. sibi falso object. Artic. 16.] It is a fearful thing to fall into the hands of the living God; [Heb 10:31] but a blessed thing it is, and will bring us to everlasting blessedness in the end, when God speaketh unto us, to hearken; when he setteth his word before us, to read it; when he stretcheth out his hand and calleth, to answer, Here am I, here we are to do thy will, O God. The Lord work a care and conscience in us to know him and serve him, that we may be acknowledged of him at the appearing of our Lord Jesus Christ, to whom with the holy Ghost, be all praise and thanksgiving. Amen.

SOURCES CONSULTED

Abba, Raymond. *The Nature and Authority of the Bible*. James Clark & Co, 1992.

Adair, James R., Jr. "Codex Sinaiticus." *Eerdmans Dictionary of the Bible*.

Aland, Kurt. *The Problem of the New Testament Canon*. A. R. Mowbray & Company, 1962.

Alford's Greek New Testament. Volume 1, Part II. "Publisher's Foreword." Guardian Press.

Alliborne, S. Austin. *The Evidences of the Divine Origin, Preservation, Credibility and Inspiration of the Holy Scriptures*. American Sunday School Union, 1871.

Armitage, Thomas, D.D. *A History of Baptists*. New York: Bryant, Taylor & Company, 1890.

Augustijn, Cornelius. *Erasmus: His Life, Works and Influence*. University of Toronto Press, 1995.

Backhouse, Janet. *The Lindisfarne Gospels*. Phaidon Press, 1986.

Bagster, Samuel. *The English Hexapla*. "An Historical Account of the English Versions of the Scriptures." London: Samuel Bagster and Sons, 1841.

Bates, J. Michael. *A Syllabus On Inspiration, Preservation and the KJV*. Newington, CT: Emmanuel Baptist Church.

Beacham, Roy E., and Kevin T. Bauder, eds. *One Bible Only?* Grand Rapids: Kregel Publications, 2001.

Blackburn, William Maxwell. *History of the Christian Church from its Origin to the Present Time*. Walden and Stowe, 1880.

_____. *Commentaries on the Laws of England*, 1765.

Bosworth, Joseph, and George Waring. *The Gospels Gothic, Anglo-Saxon, Wycliffe and Tyndale Versions*. 4th ed. London: Gibbings and Company, 1907.

Brake, Donald L. *The New Testament In English- Wicliffe Facsimile*. "Introduction." Portland, OR: International Bible Publications, 1986.

_____. *A Visual History of the English Bible*. Baker Books, 2008.

Brougham, Lord, and other distinguished authors. *Old England's Worthies Being Full and Original Biographies*. James Sangster, 1862.

Burgon, Dean John William. *The Last Twelve Verses of the Gospel of Mark*. Collingswood. NJ: Dean Burgon Society Press, 1978.

_____. *The Causes of Corruption of The Traditional Text*. Collingswood, NJ: Dean Burgon Society Press.

Burkitt, F.C. *Texts and Studies*, IV. "The Old Latin and the Itala." Cambridge: 1896.

Burton, Barry. *Let's Weigh the Evidence*. Chino, CA: Chick Publications, 1983.

Cahill, Thomas. *How The Irish Saved Civilization*. Doubleday, 1995.

Callender, J. P. *Illustrations of Popery: The Mystery of Iniquity Unveiled*. New York, 1838.

Christian History Magazine. Issue 60. "Patrick The Saint."

Christian History. Volume II, No 2, Issue 3. Worcester, PA: Christianity History Institute.

_____. Volume II, No.2, Issue 3. Worcester, PA: Christianity History Institute.

Christie-Murray, David. *A History of Heresy*. Oxford University Press, 1976.

Cloud, David W. *Rome and The Bible*. Port Huron, MI: Way of Life Literature.

_____. *John Wycliffe and The First English Bible*. Port Huron, MI: Way of Life Literature.

_____. *Myths About The King James Bible: Reformation Editors Lacked Sufficient Manuscript Evidence*. Port Huron, MI: Way of Life Literature.

_____. *Way of Life Bible Encyclopedia*, Port Huron, MI: Way of Life Literature, 1997.

Cobern, Camden M. *The New Archeological Discoveries and Their Bearing Upon the New Testament*. Funk and Wagnalls, 1922.

Codex Alexandrinus. The Catholic Encyclopedia; Online edition.

Comfort, Philip W. and David P. Barrett. *The Complete Text of the Earliest New Testament Manuscripts*. Baker Books, 1999.

Conant, H. C. *The English Bible – History of the Translation of the Holy Scriptures Into the English Tongue*. 1856.

Condit, Blackford. *The History of the English Bible: Extending from the Early Anglo Saxon Translations to the Present Anglo-American Revision*. New York: A.S. Barnes & Co., 1881.

Connolly, W. Kenneth. *The Indestructible Book*. Grand Rapids, MI: Baker Books, 1996.

Cosin, John. *The Scholastic History of The Canon of The Holy Scripture*. Cambridge University, 1657.

Cronin, H.S. ed., Oxford Journals "The Twelve Conclusions of the Lollards." *English Historical Review*. XXII, 292-304. Oxford University Press, April, 1907 [Widener, Br. 5.1].

Crosby, Thomas. *History of the English Baptists*. Vol. I. London: 1740.

Cyprian, *The Treatises of Cyprian* I.

D'Oyly, Reverend and Reverend Mant. *The Holy Bible - The Authorized Version*. "General Introduction," Oxford: 1817.

Dalmus, Joseph H. Translation from Latin, *The Prosecution of John Wyclyf*. Yale University Press, 1952.

Daniell, David. *William Tyndale: A Biography*. Yale University Press, 1994.

Davidson, Samuel. *The Hebrew Text of the Old Testament*. 2nd ed. S. Bagster and Sons, 1855.

De Hamel, Christopher. *The Book: A History of The Bible*. New York: Phaidon Press Limited. 2001.

Deanesly, Margaret. *The Lollard Bible and Other Medieval Biblical Versions*. Cambridge University Press, 1920.

Deferrari, Roy J. "The Sources of Catholic Dogma," translated from the Thirtieth Edition of Henry Denzinger's *Enchiridion Symbolorum*, copyright 1957 by B. Herder Book Co., Powers Lake, ND: Marian House. Library of Congress Catalog Card Number 57-5963.

Dionysius. *Conciliations* I.

Durant, Will. *The Story Of Civilization*. Vol. III.

Dymok, Roger. *Against the Twelve Heresies.*

Eadie, John. *History of the English Bible.*

Myers, Allen C., John W. Simpson, et al. *Eerdmans Dictionary of the Bible*. Grand Rapids: Wm. Eerdmans Publishing Co., 1996.

Encyclopedia Britannica - 11th Edition, Vol. 3. New York: University Press, 1911.

Encyclopedia Britannica, 11th Edition, Vol. 28. New York: University Press, 1911.

Erasmus, Desiderius. *Enchridion Militis Christiani - Handbook of a Christian Knight*. 1503.

Fisher, George Park. *History of The Christian Church*. Charles Scribner's Sons, 1907.

Fountain, David Guy. *John Wycliffe:The Dawn of The Reformation*. Mayflower Christian Books, 1984.

Foxe, John. *The Ecclesiastical History: Containing The Acts and Monuments of Martyrs: With A general Discourse of these latter Persecutions, horrible Troubles and Tumults, stirred up by Romish Prelates in the Church*. London: Stationers, 1684.

_____. *The Ecclesiastical History: Containing The Acts and Monuments.... 1563,* 1641 and 1684 editions, Volumes 1, 2, 3, 4, Book 7. Ages CD.

Fuller, David Otis. *Which Bible? "Our Authorized Bible Vindicated."* Institute for Biblical Textual Studies, 1975.

Fuller, Thomas. *Fuller's Church History of Britain*. Vol. 1. London: Thomas Tegg, 1842.

Gee, Henry, and William John Hardy, eds. *Documents Illustrative of English Church History – Elizabeth's Act of Uniformity* (1559), 1 Elizabeth, Cap. 2. Macmillan, 1896.

Geisler, Norman L., and William E. Nix, *A General Introduction to the Bible.* Chicago: Moody Press, 1968.

Geisler, Norman, and Peter Bocchino. *Unshakeable Foundations.* Minneapolis, MN: Bethany House Publishers, 2001.

Green, Rev. Samuel G. *A Handbook of Church History.* Fleming H. Revelle.

Green, Sr., Jay. P., Editor. *Unholy Hands on the Bible.* Sovereign Grace Publishers.

Guppy, Henry. *A Brief Sketch of The History of The Transmission of the Bible Down To The Revised English Version of 1881-1895.* Manchester University, 1934 and 1936.

Halley, Henry. *Halley's Bible Handbook.* Regency Reference Library Edition. Zondervan.

Hargreaves, Henry. *The Wycliffite Versions, The Cambridge History of the Bible.* Cambridge University Press, 1969.

Hassell, Cushings Briggs. *History of the Church of God from the Creation to A.D. 1885.* Atlanta: Turner Lassetter, 1955.

Hastings' Dictionary of the Bible (five volumes).

Hastings, James, ed. *A Dictionary of the Bible.* IV.

Hemphill, Samuel. *The Diatessaron of Tatian.*

Heron, James. *The Evolution of Latin Christianity.* London: J. Clark and Co., 1919.

Hills, Edward F. *The King James Version Defended.* Des Moines, IA: Christian Research Press, 1984.

Hippolytus. *Against the Heresies of Noetus I.*

Hoare, W. H. *The Evolution of The Bible.* London: John Murray, 1901.

Hoeller, Stephan A. *Jung and the Lost Gospels.* Wheaton, IL: Quest Books, 2004.

Holland, Dr. Thomas. *Crowned With Glory*. Writers Press Club, 2000.

_____. *Early Heresies* - Online lessons: http://prophets-see-all.tripod.com/46570.htm

Hort, Arthur Fenton. *Life and Letters of Fenton Anthony Hort*. Vol. I, 416. New York: MacMillan and Co., 1896.

Hoskier, Herman C. *Codex B and Its Allies*. Vol. 2. London: Bernard Quaritch, 1914.

How We Got Our Bible: Christian History. Issue 43, 1997. Worcester, PA: Christianity History Institute.

Irenaeus. *Against Heresies* III. Digital Edition.

_____. "Against Heresies," *Early Christian Fathers*. Vol. 1. Translated by Cyril C. Richardson and published by The Westminster Press.

Ironside, H. A. *The Real Saint Patrick*. Corona, NY: FBC Press.

Ivimey, Joseph. *History of the English Baptists*. Vol. 1, 1811.

Jackson, Samuel Mccauley. *The New Schaff-Herzog Religious Encyclopedia*. Volume II. Funk and Wagnalls, 1910.

Jackson, Wayne. *Which Is The Right Version of the Bible*. www.waynejackson.freeserve.co.uk/kjv/v2.htm.

Jones, William. *A History of the Christian Church*. Vol. II. London: 1819.

Jones, Floyd Nolen. *Which Version is The Bible?* Goodyear, AZ: Global Evangelism Ministries.

_____. *The Septuagint: A Critical Analysis*. Global Evangelism Ministries, 1998.

Kennedy, H.A.A. *Hastings' Dictionary of the Bibl*. "Old Latin VSS."

Kenyon, Frederic G. *Our Bible and the Ancient Manuscripts*. Edinburgh: Eyre and Spottiswoode, 1895.

_____. *Handbook to the Textual Criticism of the New Testament*. London: 1901

_____. *Our Bible and The Ancient Manuscripts*. London: Eyre and Spottiswoode, 1898.

Kohler, John A., III. "What Jesus Believed About The Bible." Elkton, MD: Maranatha Baptist Watchman.

Lampe, Craig. *The Forbidden Book*. Lollard House, 1992.

Lampe, G.W.H., ed. *The Cambridge History of The Bible*. Vol. 2. Cambridge University Press.

Lechler, Professor and translated by Peter Lorimer. *John Wiclif and His English Persecutors*. Vol. 1, 1887.

Lewis, John. *The Life of Dr. John Wiclif*. London: Robert Knaplock, 1720.

Liddell, Robert. "The History and Legacy of Foxe's Book of Martyrs." U-TURN, Volume 6, Number 1, Autumn 1998.

Life and Times of John Wycliffe The Morning Star of the Reformation (no author given). The Religious Tract Society, 1884.

Lightner, Robert P. *The Savior and the Scriptures*. 1978.

Loserth, John, editor. *John Wycliffe, Speculum Seculum Dominous, Opera Minora*. London: Wycliffe Society, 1913.

Lovett, Richard. *The Printed English Bible 1525-1885*. The Religious Tract Society of London, 1894.

MacLean, Rev. W. *The Providential Preservation of The Greek Text of The New Testament*. 4th ed., 1983.

Matthew, F. D. *The English Works of Wyclif Hitherto Unprinted*. London: The Early English Tract Society, 1880.

McClure, Alexander. *Translators Revived*. 1858. Republished by Maranatha Publications.

McHugh, Michael J. *Saint Patrick - Pioneer Missionary to Ireland*. Christian Liberty Press.

Mead, G.R.S. *Fragments of a Faith Forgotten*. 3rd ed., 1931.

Mehrning, Jacob. *History of Baptism*.

Metzger, Bruce. *The Text of the New Testament: Its Transmission, Corruption and Restoration*. New York: Oxford University Press, 1992.

Meyer, Marvin. *The Gnostic Discoveries*. San Francisco: Harper Collins, 2005.

_____. "Innocent III." *Microsoft Encarta Digital Multimedia Encyclopedia – Funk & Wagnall's Corporation -* from *Grolier Electronic Publishing, 1992*.

Miller, H. S. *General Biblical Introduction*. Houghton, NY: The Word-bearer Press, 1937.

Milner, Robert. *The History of the Church of Christ*. Vol. III. London: Seeley, Burnside and Seeley, 1819.

Mombert, J. I. *English Versions of The Bible*. Bagster & Sons, 1883.

Moore, T. V. *The Culdee Church*. Presbyterian Committee of Publication, 1868.

Moorman, Jack. *8,000 Differences Between the New Testament Greek Words of the Textus Receptus Underlying the King James New Testament and the Words of Nestles-Aland's 26th & 27th Greek New Testament Which Underlies the Modern Bible Versions*. Collingswood, NJ: Dean Burgon Society Press, 2006.

_____. *Forever Settled*. Collingswood, NJ: Bible for Today, 1999.

Nestle, Erwin, and Kurt Aland. *Novum Testamentum Graece*. 24th ed., 1960.

Nichol, Thomas, Wordsworth and White. *Old Latin Biblical Texts*. 4 volumes.

Nida, Eugene. *Theory and Practice*. American Bible Society, 1969.

Nolan, Frederick. *An Inquiry into the Integrity of the Greek Vulgate or Received Text of the New Testament, in which Greek manuscripts are newly classed, the integrity of the Authorized Text vindicated, and various readings traced to their origin; (1784-1864)*. London: F.C. and J. Rivington, 1815.

Orchard, G. H. *A Concise History of Baptists from the Time of Christ their Founder to the 18th Century*. American Edition- 1885.

Orr, James, ed., *International Standard Bible Encyclopedia*. Vol. 1, the section on the canon. Grand Rapids, MI: Wm. B. Eerdmans Publishing Co., 1947.

Pres. and Ref. Review. April, 1902.

Price, Ira Maurice. *Ancestry of Our English Bible.* Philadelphia: Sunday School Times Co., 1920.

Purves, George T. *Testimony of Justin Martyr to Early Christianity.* Lect V. New York: Anson D. F. Randolph and Company, 1889.

_____. *The Life and Times of John Wycliffe The Morning Star of The Reformation.* Religious Tract Society London, 1884.

Reumann, John H. P. *The Romance of Bible Scripts and Scholars.* Prentice Hall, 1965.

Robertson, A. T. *An Introduction to the Textual Criticism of the New Testament.* Hodder & Stoughton, 1925.

Robinson, Robert. *Ecclesiastical Researches.* Cambridge England: 1792.

Robinson, H. Wheeler. *Ancient and English Versions of the Bible.* Oxford University Press, 1940.

Sawyer, John Wesley. *The Legacy of our English Bible.* self published, 1990.

Schaff, Philip. *History of The Christian Church.* Vol. 3. Eerdmans Publishing, 1910.

Schaff, Philip. *History of the Christian Church.* Volumes III, IV, V, VI. Eerdmans Publishing, 1910.

Scott, Dr. W. Eugene. *Codex Vaticanus.* 1996.

Scrivener, F. H. A. *Plain Introduction to New Testament Criticism.* 3rd ed., quoted in Wilkinson.

Scrivener, F. H. A. *Plain Introduction to Textual Criticism of the New Testament.* New York: George Bell & Sons, 1883.

Shelton, Henry C. *History of the Christian Church.* Vol. II. 1895, Hendrickson Publishers, Reprinted 1994.

Sightler, James H. *The Testimony Founded For Ever.* Sightler Publications, 1999.

Simms, Paris Marion. *The Bible From The Beginning.* The MacMillan Company, 1929.

Sitterly, Charles F. *Praxis In Manuscripts of the Greek New Testament*. 1898.

Smith, William. *Smith's Bible Dictionary*, 1884.

Sorenson, David H. *Touch Not The Unclean Thing*. Duluth, MN: NorthStar Baptist Ministries, 2001.

Spinka, Matthew. *Advocates of Reform: From Wyclif to Erasmus*. From Sorenson, *Touch Not The Unclean Thing*.

Standish, Russell R. and Colin D. *Modern Bible Translations Unmasked*. Rapidan, VA: Hartland Publications, 1993.

Stone, Larry. *The Story of The Bible*. Nashville, TN: Thomas Nelson, 2010.

Strouse, Dr. T. M. *"The Biblical Defense For The Verbal, Plenary Preservation of God's Word."* www.graceway.com/articles/articles_007.htm.

_____. Dean, Emmanuel Baptist Theological Seminary, "The Translation Model Predicated by Scripture," from *The Attack On The Canon of Scripture*, Dr. H. D. Williams.

Sturz, Harry A. *The Byzantine Text-Type and New Testament Textual Criticism."* Nashville, TN: Thomas Nelson,1984.

Swete, Henry Barclay. *Introduction of the Old Testament in Greek*. Cambridge University Press, 1900.

Tertullian. *On Baptism* I.

Tertullian. *On Modesty* I.

_____. *On Prescriptions Against Heresies* 1.

The Encyclopedia Britannica - 11ᵗʰ Edition. Vol. 4, 11, 14. New York: University Press, 1911.

The Holy Bible. "General Introduction to the Bible." The Society for Promoting Christian Knowledge. Oxford, 1817.

The Old Testament Canon. http://www.columbia.edu/cu/augustine/arch/ sbrandt/canon.htm; section 3.2).

Thomas, Joshua. *History of the Welsh Baptists*.

Turner, Sharon. "Bede, lib.1.c.15.," *The History of the Anglo-Saxon: Comprising The History of England*. 4th ed., London: 1823.

Turretin, Francis. *Institutes of Elenctic Theology*. 1696.

Van Braght, Thieleman J. *The Bloody Theater or Martyrs Mirror of the Defenseless Christians*. first English edition 1837 - this addition 1996.

Vaughn, Robert. *Tracts and Treatises of John De Wycliffe D.D.-On Civil Dominion*. Published for the Lollard Society by Blackburn and Pardon, London, 1845.

Vedder, Henry. *Our New Testament*. Philadelphia: The Griffith & Rowland Press, 1908.

Waite, D. A. *Defending The King James Bible*. Collingswood, NJ: Bible For Today Press.

Walmsley, Luke S. *Fighters & Martyrs for the Freedom of Faith*. London: 1912.

Warren, Rev. Roy D. Jr. *Patrick of Ireland: The Untold Story*.

Webster's Illustrated Contemporary Dictionary.

Wells, H. G. *The Outline of History*. New York: P F Collier & Son, 1925.

Westcott, Brooke Foss. *A General View of the History of the English Bible*. MacMillan, 1916.

Westcott, Arthur. *Life and Letters of Brook Foss Westcott*. Vol. I and II. New York: MacMillan and Co., 1903.

Westcott, Brook Foss and Fenton John Anthony Hort. *Introduction to the New Testament in The Original Greek*. Harper & Brothers, 1882.

Whitaker, William. *Disputations on Holy Scripture*. Soli Deo Gloria Publishers, 1588/2000.

Wordsworth, Christopher. *Ecclesiastical Biography or Lives of Eminent Men Connected with the History of Religion in England; from the Commencement of the Reformation to the Revolution*. Vol. 1. London: Francis & John Rivington, 1853.

World Magazine April 29 & May 20, 2006; God's World Publication, Asheville, NC.

Wycliffe, John. *Christian History*. Volume II, No.2, Issue 3. Worcester, PA: Christian History Institute, 1997.

Loserth, John, editor. *John Wycliffe, Speculum Seculum Dominous, Opera Minora*. London: Wycliffe Society, 1913.

Zerbe, Alvin Sylvester. *The Antiquity of Hebrew Writing and Literature*. Central Publishing House of Cleveland Ohio, 1911.

Zion's Fire Magazine, Special Edition. March/April. Winter Garden: FL: Zion's Hope Publisher, 1991.

INTERNET and AUDIO VISUAL LINKS

"Which Is The Right Version of the Bible," www.waynejackson. freeserve.co.uk/kjv/v2.htm.

Britannica Online, "Erasmus," www.britannica.com.

Christian History: William Tyndale, Issue 16; 1997 – Electronic Edition.

Codex Alexandrinus; The Catholic Encyclopedia; On line edition.

Codex Sinaiticus by Navida Shahid; www.beyond-the-illusion.com/files/Religion/Islam/research/codx0894.html.

en.wikipedia.org/wiki/Biblical_manuscrip.

Gregory, Nestle, and Lake. - http://www.bible-researcher.com/oldlatin.html.

http://en.wikipedia.org/wiki/List_of_New_Testament_papyri.

http://history-perspective.com/critical_theories.html.

http://www.urbanlegends.com/language/etymology/ruleofthumb.html.

"Innocent III," *Microsoft Encarta Digital Multimedia Encyclopedia – Funk & Wagnall's Corporation* - from *Grolier Electronic Publishing, 1992.*

Internet Encyclopedia of Philosophy – Erasmus, www.iep.utm.edu.

MacArthur, John. *Is the Bible Reliable? Our God-Breathed Bible-*
Tape GC 1343; Grace To You, Panorama City, CA, October 13, 1974.

The Catholic Encyclopedia online; *Codex Alexandrinus.*

Burton, Edwin *The Catholic Encyclopedia;* "Richard Rolle de Hampole," Online edition.

Athanasius, *The Christian Ethereal Classics Library-* "The Festal Letters of Athanasius," Letter 20; part 3-5;, www.ccel.org/.

The Old Testament Canon;
http://www.columbia.edu/cu/augustine/arch/ sbrandt/canon.htm; section 3.2).

"Outlines on Church History:The Collection of the Old Testament Scriptures" - http:// thechristian.org/churchhistory/ot_history.html.

"The Life and Work of William Tyndale" *The Tyndale Society of Oxford, Geneva and San Diego*; Audio-visual presentation personally viewed.

Vaticanus and Sinaiticus - ww.waynejackson. freeserve. co.uk/kjv /v2.htm.

Western Reformed Seminary Journal – August 1996, www.wrs.edu/journals/jour896/oecolampadius.html.

WIKIPEDIA, the free Online Encyclopedia.

"Old Testament Texts" www.angelfire.com/la2/prophet1/ott.html.

www.biblebelievers.net/BibleVersions/kjcforv5.htm#XXIV.

BookRags, "Simon, Richard (1638-1712)" "www.bookrags.com/research/simon-richard-16381712-eoph.

Christian Classics Ethereal Library - Online, www.ccel.org/.

The Center for the Study of New Testament Manuscripts - www.csntm.org/Manuscripts.aspx.

Biblical Foundations For Freedom - www.foundationsforfreedom.net/Topics/Bible/Bible_Reliabilit y.html.

Catalogue of New Testament Papyri & Codices 2nd to 10th Centuries, www.kchanson.com/papyri.html#NTP.

Midgett, Chris, *Workmen For Christ,* www.workmenforchrist.org/Bible/History/Westcott.html.

INDEX OF WORDS AND PHRASES

(When searching proper names, search the first **and** last names e.g., Bruce Metzger and Metzger)

ABOUT THE AUTHOR

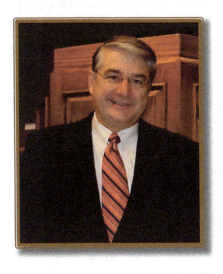

David L. Brown was born in Michigan. He came to know Christ as his Savior as the result of a Sunday school teacher throwing away the liberal curriculum, teaching through the book of Romans, and sharing the Gospel. He has been married to Linda for 45 years. She was a young lady from his home church.

David attended a Michigan University then transferred to a Christian University and Seminary where he completed a Bachelor's Degree in Social Science and Theology. He holds a Master's Degree in Theology, and Ph.D. in History, specializing in the history of the English Bible.

Since December 1979, he has been the Pastor of the First Baptist Church of Oak Creek, Wisconsin (an independent, fundamental, Baptist Church using the King James Bible and conservative music). Previous to that, he pastored an independent Baptist Church in Michigan for five years, was an assistant pastor for 4 years, and served with his wife as short term missionaries in Haiti.

Dr. Brown is the president of the ***King James Bible Research Council*** (www.kjbresearchcouncil.com), an organization dedicated to promoting the King James Bible and its underlying texts and other traditional text translations around the world in a solid and sensible way.

He is also the president of ***Logos Communication Consortium, Inc***. (www.logosresourcepages.org), a research organization that produces a large variety of materials warning Christians of present dangers in our culture.

He is also the vice president of the **Midwest Independent Baptist Pastor's Fellowship**, a fellowship of independent Baptist pastors, missionaries, and evangelists from fourteen upper Midwest states.

Dr. Brown is the Curator of the **Christian Heritage Bible Collection** and regularly takes his rare Bible, manuscript and artifact collection to fundamental Baptist Churches teaching and preaching on the history of our English Bible, showing how God has preserved His Word(s), and why we should use the King James Bible.

He also serves as a consultant for individuals, museums, colleges, universities, and seminaries that desire to acquire or have collections of biblical manuscripts and Bibles. He is an antiquarian book dealer with contacts around the world.

He can be contacted at:
        Dr. David L. Brown
        8044 S. Verdev Dr.
        Oak Creek, WI. 53154
        Phone: 414-768-9754
        Email: PastorDavidLBrown@gmail.com

CPSIA information can be obtained
at www.ICGtesting.com
Printed in the USA
LVHW081959280619
622722LV00002B/8/P

9 780998 777894